Other Edens
The Life and Work
of Brian Coffey

Editors

BENJAMIN KEATINGE
AENGUS WOODS

IRISH ACADEMIC PRESS
DUBLIN • PORTLAND, OR

First published in 2010 by Irish Academic Press

2 Brookside
Dundrum Road
Dublin 14, Ireland

920 NE 58th Avenue, Suite 300
Portland, Oregon,
97213-3786, USA

This edition © 2010 Irish Academic Press
Individual Chapters © Contributors

www.iap.ie

British Library Cataloguing in Publication Data
An entry can be found on request

978 0 7165 2910 1 (cloth)

Library of Congress Cataloging-in-Publication Data
An entry can be found on request

Printed by MPG Books Group, King's Lynn and Bodmin

In memory of
Richard Arthur Davis Keatinge
1947–2008

O other eden
no live eye has seen

(Brian Coffey, 'Mindful of You')

Contents

Illustrations

Front cover: Etching by Brian Coffey (1978). Courtesy of University of Delaware Library, Special Collections.

Back cover: Brian Coffey at his desk, 1971. Courtesy of John Parsons.

1. Engraving by S.W. Hayter for limited edition of *Third Person*. S.W. Hayter, courtesy of DACS, imaging by University of Delaware Library, Special Collections.

2. Four engravings by S.W. Hayter for limited edition of *Death of Hektor*. S.W. Hayter, courtesy of DACS, imaging by University of Delaware Library, Special Collections.

3. Postcard from Samuel Beckett to Brian Coffey, 1978, with a variant of one of Beckett's *mirlitonnades* inscribed. Courtesy of the Estate of Samuel Beckett and the University of Delaware Library, Special Collections.

4. Typewritten letter from Brian Coffey to Thomas MacGreevy (1959) expressing regret over the death of Denis Devlin (TCD MS 8110/43). Courtesy of the Board of Trinity College Dublin.

5. A youthful Brian Coffey, *c*.1935, courtesy of John Coffey.

6. Coffey family photo taken in Muswell Hill, 1956, courtesy of John Coffey.

7. Brian and Bridget Coffey with John F. Deane (Dedalus Press), Ursula Foran and President Mary Robinson, 1991. Photograph by Niamh Foran, courtesy of John F. Deane.

8. Brian Coffey with Michael Smith of New Writers' Press. Courtesy of Michael Smith.

9. George Reavey as a young man, courtesy of the Harry Ransom Humanities Research Center, University of Texas at Austin and the Estate of George Reavey.

10. Thomas MacGreevy at the Ecole Normale, Paris in the 1920s. Courtesy of Margaret Farrington and Robert Ryan and the Thomas MacGreevy Archive, University of Maryland.

11. Brian Coffey from front cover of his *Selected Poems* (New Writers' Press, 1971). Courtesy of John Parsons.

Contributors

John Coffey, eldest son of Brian Coffey, was born in Dublin in 1939. He is a retired teacher of science and educational technology and a former Fellow of the Chartered Institute of Personnel and Development. He lives in Southampton, England, with his wife, Patricia, where he teaches yoga and writes stories for his numerous grandchildren.

Gerald Dawe has published seven collections of poetry, most recently *Points West* (Gallery Press, 2008), as well as volumes of essays, including *The Proper Word: Collected Criticism* (Creighton University Press, 2007), and several anthologies of Irish literary criticism and poetry, including *Earth Voices Whispering: Irish War Poetry, 1940–1945* (Blackstaff Press, 2009). He is Senior Lecturer in English at Trinity College Dublin, Director of the Oscar Wilde Centre for Irish Writing and a Fellow of Trinity College Dublin. He has also held visiting professorships at Boston College and Villanova University, Philadelphia. *The World as Province: Selected Prose 1980–2008* is forthcoming.

Kit Fryatt holds a BA degree from the University of Cambridge and a Ph.D from Trinity College Dublin. She currently lectures in English at the Mater Dei Institute of Eduction, Dublin City University, where she is involved in running the Irish Centre for Poetry Studies and where she co-edits the journal *Post*.

Harry Gilonis is a poet, editor, publisher and critic. His books of poetry include, from Irish imprints, *Reliefs* (hardPressed Poetry), *peuran/pears* (Coracle Press) and *Forty Fungi* (also from Coracle), the latter a collaboration with the visual artist Erica Van Horn. He edited *For the Birds: Proceedings of the First Cork Conference on New and Experimental Irish Poetry* (1997), co-published by hardPressed Poetry in 1998, which contained a long essay by Alex Davis and work by a variety of non-mainstream Irish poets. He has written elsewhere on Coffey's work, and his small press imprint Form Books published Coffey, as well as other significant contemporary Irish poets –

Randolph Healy, David Lloyd, Billy Mills, Eoghan Ó Tuairisc, Maurice Scully, Michael Smith, Geoffrey Squires, Catherine Walsh and Augustus Young. He also co-edited the little magazine *Eonta* which contained both poetry and prose by Brian Coffey, and featured him as a cover artist for its first issue.

Andrew Goodspeed is a lecturer in English literature at the South East European University, Macedonia. He studied Russian at the University of Michigan and English at the University of Oxford and he holds a Ph.D from Trinity College Dublin on the life and work of Oliver St John Gogarty. He has published essays and reviews on Slavic and Irish authors. He currently lives in Skopje, Macedonia.

Wacław Grzybowski teaches American literature at the University of Opole, Poland. He published his doctoral thesis in 2006 with the title *Spirituality and Metaphor: the Poetics and Poetry of Thomas Merton*. He has published articles on the poetry of Thomas Merton, Karol Wojtya (Pope John Paul II) and Emily Dickinson and on the fiction of William Faulkner and Joseph Conrad. He is currently working on a monograph on Thomas MacGreevy.

Maria Johnston holds a Ph.D from Trinity College Dublin, where she teaches American poetry. She is a regular reviewer of contemporary poetry for *Poetry Ireland Review* and *Contemporary Poetry Review*, and is co-editor, with Gerald Dawe, of *High Pop: The Irish Times Column of Stewart Parker* (Lagan Press, 2008). She is currently preparing a monograph on Sylvia Plath and contemporary poetry and is also editing a collection of essays on poetry and politics.

Benjamin Keatinge is Head of English at the South East European University, Macedonia, where he teaches English literature. He holds a doctorate from Trinity College Dublin on Samuel Beckett and he has published essays on Beckett in the *Journal of Modern Literature* and the *Irish University Review*. He has also published reviews on the likes of Harry Clifton and Maurice Scully in *Poetry Ireland Review* and he occasionally writes poetry himself.

J.C.C. Mays retired as Professor of English and American Literature at University College Dublin in 2004. He has published widely on diverse writers and notably has edited the *Collected Poems of Denis Devlin* (Dedalus Press, 1989) and written several pioneering articles on the poetry of Brian Coffey, including the 'Introductory Essay' to the 1975 *Irish University Review Brian Coffey Special Issue*. J.C.C. Mays also wrote the preface to Brian Coffey's *Poems and Versions 1929–1990* (Dedalus Press, 1991) and has published other essays on Coffey in *Krino* and the *Irish University Review*.

Billy Mills is a poet and publisher and founder (with Catherine Walsh) of hardPressed Poetry. His books include *Five Easy Pieces* (Shearsman, 1997), *A Small Book of Songs* (Wild Honey, 1999) and *What is a Mountain?* (hardPressed Poetry, 2000). His collected poems, *Lares/Manes*, was published by Shearsman in 2009.

Sandra Andrea O'Connell received her doctorate from Trinity College Dublin. She is an independent scholar, critic and editor living in Dublin. Her research area is modernism in Irish literature, in particular the Irish-Russian poet, publisher, literary critic and translator George Reavey (1907–76). In 2007 she was director of the George Reavey International Centenary Symposium held at the School of English, TCD, which brought together scholars from Ireland, the UK, US and Russia. She is currently editing a collection of essays on George Reavey, forthcoming from Lilliput Press.

John Parsons was born in 1941 in Northampton. He studied at Horsey School of Art from 1958 to 1961. A painter, printmaker and sculptor, he helped Brian Coffey set up Advent Books as designer/printer and illustrator. He also worked with Asa Benveniste at Trigram Books as designer and printer. His books *Poems 1* and *Songs for the Poodles* have been published by Advent Books and his *A Shadow Across Closed Lids* and *Three Mountains* were published by Labyrinth Books. He has also written two books of haiku, *Choosing the Stone* and *On the Journey Home*, both published by Hub Editions. At present, he publishes haiku regularly in the *British Haiku Society Journal*, *Ko Magazine* (Tokyo) and *Presence*.

Thomas Dillon Redshaw is Professor of English and Director of the Centre for Irish Studies at the University of St Thomas, St Paul, Minnesota. He has edited *Éire-Ireland* and the *New Hibernia Review* and is currently a contributing editor to *An Sionnach*. His publications include an annotated edition of John Montague's *The Rough Field* (1989), *Well Dreams: Essays on John Montague* (2004) and numerous articles on Irish writers in such journals as *Études Irlandaises*, *Canadian Journal of Irish Studies* and *South Carolina Review*. He is currently preparing a checklist of books by John F. Deane and is researching a history of the Dolmen Press.

Michael Smith is a poet, translator and literary critic. Born in Dublin in 1942, he founded New Writers' Press in 1967, which did much to promote the work of Coffey and his contemporaries in Ireland. He was also founder and editor of the influential literary magazine *The Lace Curtain*. A member of the Arts Council from 1984 to 1989, he has translated into English the work of leading Spanish-language poets including Federico García Lorca and Pablo Neruda. His own poetry publications include *The Purpose of the Gift: Selected Poems* (NWP, 2004) and *Maldon & Other Translations* (NWP/Shearsman, 2004).

Geoffrey Squires is a poet and translator. Born in 1942, he studied English at the University of Cambridge and has since travelled widely. His *Untitled and Other Poems 1975–2002* appeared in 2004 (Wild Honey Press), drawing on his five previous collections. More recently, several video poems have been published by Wild Honey Press and Shearsman. He is currently working on translations of the Persian poet Hafez and lives in Hull.

James Matthew Wilson is Assistant Professor of Humanities and Augustinian Traditions at Villanova University. His essays, poems and reviews appear regularly in such journals as *Modern Age*, *Contemporary Poetry Review*, *Christianity and Literature*, *New Hibernia Review* and *Éire-Ireland*. He has published several articles on Thomas MacGreevy, Denis Devlin and Brian Coffey, and wrote his doctoral dissertation on 'Catholic Modernism and the "Irish Avant-Garde"'. He is at work on two critical books, 'T.S. Eliot, Jacques Maritain, and the Return of the Real' as well as 'Catholicism and Modern American Poetry'.

Aengus Woods holds a BA from NUI Maynooth and an MA from University College Dublin in philosophy and is currently completing a Ph.D on Kant, Hegel and Levinas at the New School for Social Research in New York. He has written and published variously on the relationship between philosophy and the arts. An essay on John McGahern was included in the inaugural *John McGahern Yearbook* (NUI Galway, 2008), while 'Painting and Progress: Merleau-Ponty's Open-Ended Aesthetics' is forthcoming from the *Kent State University Graduate Conference Journal*.

Augustus Young is the *nom de plume* of James Hogan. Born in Cork in 1943, he is the author of eight books of poetry, including *Rosemaries* (Advent Press, 1976) and *Days and Nights in Hendon* (Menard Press, 2002) and two books of auto-fiction: *Light Years* (2002) and *Storytime* (2005). His current publications include: *The Secret Gloss: a film play on the life and work of Soren Kierkegaard* (Elliott and Thompson, 2008). *Diversifications: Brecht, Mayakovsky and Me* (Shearsman, 2009) and *The Nicotine Cat and Other People, Chronicles of the Self* (New Island/ Duras Press, 2009). He lives in Port-Vendres, France.

Acknowledgements

This book originated in a symposium held at Trinity College Dublin in October 2005 (Coffey's centenary year) under the heading 'Continuings': A Celebration of the Life and Work of Brian Coffey. We would like to thank the School of English, TCD for helping us to host that event. We would also like to thank all those who participated, including: Augustus Young, Harry Gilonis, Billy Mills, Catherine Walsh, Gerald Dawe, Maria Johnston and John Coffey, many of whom have contributed to this volume. We are particularly grateful to Dr Philip Coleman of the School of English, TCD, who helped us organize the symposium and who has been an invaluable advisor in the preparation of this book. We also gratefully acknowledge the generous financial assistance provided by the Arts Council of Ireland towards the 'Continuings' symposium.

We are also grateful to John Coffey, Brian Coffey's son, who has very been supportive of this project and, in particular, for permission to quote from Brian Coffey's unpublished poems, letters and manuscripts, as well as published works. We also thank Dedalus Press for permission to quote from their volume *Poems and Versions 1929–1990* by Brian Coffey. We have received generous financial assistance from the TCD Association and Trust towards the cost of copyright permissions for this volume and we are very grateful to them for their support. We also gratefully acknowledge permission from the editors of *The Recorder* magazine to reprint J.C.C. Mays' essay, which first appeared in *The Recorder*, 18, 1–2 (Fall 2005). For permission to reproduce archival materials from their collections, we are grateful to the Harry Ransom Humanities Research Center, University of Texas at Austin. We are also grateful to the Special Collections, University of Delaware Library, Newark, Delaware for their kind permission to quote from the Brian Coffey Papers at Delaware. For their assistance while researching the Brian Coffey papers, special thanks to Timothy D. Murray, L. Rebecca Johnson Melvin, Anita Wellner and Shaun D. Mullen. We thank Dedalus Press, Dublin (for Stephen Devlin) for permission to quote from materials by Denis Devlin. We also thank the Estate of George

Reavey for their kind permission to quote from the poems and papers of George Reavey and for permitting us to reproduce a photograph of the youthful Reavey held at the Harry Ransom Humanities Research Center, University of Texas at Austin, to whom we are also grateful.

This volume is generously illustrated. We thank John Coffey, John Parsons, John F. Deane and Michael Smith for their help in gathering a range of photographs of Brian Coffey and his family. For permission to reproduce a letter by Brian Coffey to Thomas MacGreevy held at TCD, we are grateful to the Board of Trinity College Dublin. For permission to reproduce a postcard from Samuel Beckett to Brian Coffey, including a variant of one of Beckett's *mirlitonnades*, we are grateful to the Samuel Beckett Estate and to the Special Collections, University of Delaware Library. For permission to reproduce a photograph of Thomas MacGreevy, we are grateful to Margaret Farrington and Robert Ryan and also to Susan Schreibman of the Thomas MacGreevy Archive, University of Maryland for helping us source it. We thank Michael Smith for his permission to reproduce a photograph of himself and Brian Coffey and we thank John Coffey, John Parsons and John F. Deane for likewise granting permission to reproduce photos in their possession. We are grateful to the Design and Artists Copyright Society (DACS) for permission to reproduce the following drawings by S.W. Hayter: 'Third Person' (© ADAGP, Paris and DACS, London, 2007); 'Head of Zeus' (© ADAGP, Paris and DACS, London, 2007); 'Echoes of War' (© ADAGP, Paris and DACS, London, 2007); 'Death of Hektor' (© ADAGP, Paris and DACS, London, 2007); 'Fall of Troy' (© ADAGP, Paris and DACS, London, 2007).

The editors would like to thank all the contributors to this volume for all their work. We thank particularly Lisa Hyde of Irish Academic Press, who has been very supportive of this project from the outset and who has been an excellent editor throughout. The editors would like to thank the following friends and colleagues for their advice and support during the preparation of this book: Neil Baldwin, David Bird, Daria Brennan, Eamonn Casey, Philip Coleman, John-Paul Colgan, Alexandra Cooney, Simon Critchley, Fionnuala Dillane, Brian Elliott, Harry Gilonis, Andrew Goodspeed, Nicholas Grene, James Hogan, Mark Hutcheson, Maria Johnston, Athene Keatinge, Douglas Keatinge, Rebecca Keatinge, Suzanne Keatinge, Declan Kiely, Belinda McKeon, Henry Nicholls, Sandra O'Connell, Grace O'Regan-Mills, Tadgh O'Sullivan, Anthony Rudolf at Menard Press, Diane Sadler, Christina Sfekas, Gerry Smyth, Caroline Walsh, Nancy Woods and Shane Woods.

Abbreviations

The following abbreviations have been adopted and follow quotations in the text:

ABC   Dónal Moriarty, *The Art of Brian Coffey* (Dublin: University College Dublin Press, 2000)

PV   Brian Coffey, *Poems and Versions 1929–1990* (Dublin: Dedalus Press, 1991)

In the notes and bibliographies:

HRHRC   Harry Ransom Humanities Research Centre, University of Texas at Austin

TCD   Trinity College Dublin

CHAPTER ONE

Introduction

BENJAMIN KEATINGE and AENGUS WOODS

There are perhaps few Irish poets on whom critical opinion is so divided as Brian Coffey. Pioneering scholarship by Stan Smith (whose 1974 essay 'On Other Grounds: The Poetry of Brian Coffey' was the first serious discussion of his verse) and J.C.C. Mays (notably the 1975 *Irish University Review: Brian Coffey Special Issue*, in which *Advent* first appeared) has been followed up in notable contributions by Gerald Dawe (1989), Jack Morgan (1993), Alex Davis (1995) and Dónal Moriarty (2000).[1] Against this, Coffey has received less than his due from the Irish critical establishment, with parsimonious inclusions in major anthologies[2] and negative judgements from the likes of Alan Gillis and Justin Quinn, both of whom underestimate Coffey's distinctive voice in their recent studies of modern Irish poetry.[3]

This new volume of essays on Brian Coffey has its origins in a centenary symposium held in October 2005 at Trinity College Dublin celebrating Coffey's life and work. The symposium, which included both academics and contemporary poets, was held under the heading 'Continuings' taken from Coffey's best-known poem 'Missouri Sequence': 'Beginnings we see, / and continuings, / and endings in due course' (*PV*, p.83). A modest affair, it stood in stark contrast to the expansive celebrations held for both the 2004 anniversary of Bloomsday and the 2006 centenary of Samuel Beckett's birth. As wholly appropriate as such festivities were, in this context the contrast serves to underline the value of admittance into the higher echelons of the Irish literary canon and, less comfortably, the price of its refusal.

Attention to Coffey's work has, of course, been discontinuous, ressembling the 'broken line' of Irish Modernism identified by Alex Davis in his book *A Broken Line: Denis Devlin and Irish Poetic Modernism* (2000). But, as this volume shows, there are continuities too. Indeed, Coffey's persistent voice may have disappeared from view,

from time to time, but it has been consistently reclaimed from
obscurity by such notable critics as Mays, Davis and Dawe. However,
this volume attempts a more extensive reclamation by assessing the
entirety of Coffey's achievement from his early publications in the
1930s to his death in 1995. We will consider ongoing debates about
the 1930s Irish cultural map while resisting the reductive label of
1930s Irish Modernism in an attempt to survey Coffey's entire career.
The focus will necessarily be on Coffey's major achievements: *Third
Person* (1938), 'Missouri Sequence' (1962), *Advent* (1975) and *Death
of Hektor* (1979), while also finding space for a consideration of
Coffey's substantial body of love poetry. We are conscious that this is
not an exhaustive list of Coffey's achievement. Such a comprehensive
approach would also need to include the various 'observations and
experiments' from the 1971 New Writers' Press *Selected Poems* as well
as shorter poems from the late volume *Chanterelles* (1985), in addition
to Coffey's numerous translations and his satirical works: 'LEO'
(1975), *The Big Laugh* (1976) and 'Topos' (1981). It should also be
noted that our efforts come up against the current lack of an
authoritative collected edition of Coffey's poetry, or of his prose and
translations. We have drawn from Coffey's most comprehensive extant
volume, *Poems and Versions 1929–1990* (Dedalus Press, 1991), but
there remain numerous uncollected Coffey poems, which we have
listed in the complete bibliography that concludes this volume. The
bibliography also lists Coffey's equally numerous essays, reviews and
translations, which are currently uncollected. It is regrettable that the
Dedalus Press *Poems and Versions* is no longer in print, and we believe
there is an urgent need for a Coffey collected poems which future
scholars can draw from.

The contributors to this volume seek to re-establish Coffey's
reputation 'on other grounds' to those posited by critics of the 1930s
Irish Modernist paradigm. While the 1930s cannot be ignored, they
are only one chapter in Coffey's evolution as a poet. It is not always
helpful to view Coffey's poetry simply in terms of Irish cultural
problematics. True, Coffey did see himself as an Irish writer and he
sought to retain his sense of Irish identity even during long periods
spent abroad.[4] He regretted being unable to live and work in Ireland
and compensated for this by trying to connect his work with Ireland.[5]
However, when one actually reads his poems, one is immediately
struck by the lack of local reference points and his self-consciously
non-topographical allusiveness (with the significant exception of
'Missouri Sequence'). Notwithstanding Coffey's wish to connect

himself with Ireland, the aesthetics of *Third Person*, *Advent* or *Death of Hektor* owe little to local colour and what local reference points they do contain are more coded and less obvious than is customary in twentieth-century Irish poetry. The image of 1930s Irish Modernist poets as *déraciné* and international thus contains a partial truth in the case of Coffey. But if his poetic inclinations were towards French models and experimental modes, his brand of exile was reluctant and involuntary and these impulses run counter to each other. A wish to live on home ground and deal with the matter of Ireland sits alongside Coffey's wish to absorb and work within an international poetic tradition. It is perhaps most fruitful to explore Coffey's poems on their own terms, as poems, variously written in Paris, Missouri, London with preoccupations which are related to, but extend well beyond, Irish cultural politics.

It is perhaps unfortunate that Coffey has been recruited, notably in Michael Smith's New Writers' Press project, to challenge a particular brand of home-grown and insular Irish poetry exemplified by Patrick Kavanagh. This polemical position, in favour of an expatriate counter-tradition to challenge a notionally homogenous mainstream,[6] has served as a useful critical construct in the past, but it can now be seen to obscure a more complex reality. It is clear that local does not always mean conservative in the realm of literature (Yeats' modernism, Austin Clarke's experimentalism, Flann O'Brien's parody of modernism), while expatriate poets can be mired in local cultural politics (MacGreevy's Catholic nationalism, Coffey's response to Yeats).[7] We can easily see here how experimental margin and conservative mainstream have operated as binary constructs, whereas in fact there are cross-overs and cross-currents between all these writers. Of course, the original polemical stance was taken by Samuel Beckett in his 1934 review of 'Recent Irish Poetry', where he posits 'antiquarians' against 'others', those who have recognized Beckett's alleged 'breakdown of the object' and 'rupture of the lines of communication'.[8] This critical stance uses the binary model as a politicized two-party system that tends to obscure the individuality of the poets it seeks to describe. It is a model which we are only now moving beyond.

These essays seek to evade this polemical background by suggesting other ways of reading Coffey. Maria Johnston analyzes *Third Person* in terms of music and musicality. The attention drawn there to word and syllable as units of sound provide a sensitive example of how to appreciate the formalities of Coffey's composition. In this light we might align him with other significant proponents of poetry as an inherently musical form, Basil Bunting and T.S. Eliot to name but two. Poet and friend of Coffey, Geoffrey Squires also demonstrates just how deceptively intricate Coffey's prosody can be, while making a clear-eyed assertion of the value Coffey might have gained from having a trusted reader of a Poundian sort to comment on his work. Kit Fryatt, in a suggestive alignment of Coffey with the work of Maurice Scully, identifies both formal and thematic 'points of contact' between these two poets while resisting the temptation to see a full-blown counter-tradition in their work. Thomas Dillon Redshaw contextualizes Coffey's work in terms of the *livre d'artiste*, focusing on Coffey's collaboration with visual artists such as Stanley William Hayter and his own publishing ventures in the Advent Press. Such a consideration also multiplies the contexts within which it is possible to appreciate Coffey's efforts, placing him in both the broader context of European artistic modernism and also the small press movement in the UK during the later half of the twentieth century.

A significant feature of Coffey's intellectual background was his training in philosophy – he completed a Ph.D on Thomas Aquinas at the Institut Catholique in Paris in 1947 and was professor of philosophy for a number of years at the University of St Louis, Missouri. This provides the context for James Matthew Wilson's examination of the influence of Jacques Maritain, whose Thomism reverberates through Coffey's work. It also underpins the suggestive analogies drawn by Aengus Woods between Coffey's intersubjective love poems and philosophers such as G.W.F. Hegel and Emmanuel Levinas. Harry Gilonis offers a fascinating 'Aquinas-map' of *Advent* while elucidating Coffey's complex methods of allusion. Meanwhile, Wacław Grzybowski demonstrates that *Death of Hektor* is strongly coloured by Coffey's Catholic faith while Andrew Goodspeed clarifies the lines of connection between antiquity and modernity in that poem.

These authors seek to establish new contexts and new readings of Coffey's poetry. The nexus of relationships between Coffey and his Irish contemporaries (Beckett, Devlin, MacGreevy, Reavey) comes into focus in essays by Sandra O'Connell, Benjamin Keatinge and J.C.C. Mays and many fascinating, unpublished archival materials are cited here which show these relationships in a new light. But it is perhaps worth stating clearly that the notion of a 'group' of 1930s Irish Modernists can be somewhat misleading. Clearly, during the 1930s these writers formed a loose association, sharing a certain outward-looking admiration for French poetry and Continental ideas. This brief period of shared interests and ambitions (manifest, for example, in

George Reavey's Europa Press enterprise) was not sustained. And so, in order to view Coffey's career in its entirety, we must acknowledge 'the variety of impulses and the individuality' of these writers, as J.C.C. Mays suggests in an important recent discussion of Irish experimental poetry.[9] Mays argues that 'none of them, at any time – except perhaps Brian Coffey, retrospectively – thought of themselves as members of a group'.[10] If Coffey expresses regret over the 'accidents that scattered us' in a letter to Thomas MacGreevy in 1959 (reproduced in this volume), his sense of disappointment does not correlate with the perceptions of Beckett, Devlin or Reavey. Certainly, whatever loose affiliation existed in Paris before the war, no sense of common purpose could be sustained after the war, even if Coffey might have wished it.

So, this volume of essays foregrounds, above all, the individuality of a writer like Coffey. Indeed, it is for reasons of our sensitivity to this individuality that we have chosen to intersperse critical essays with a number of more intimate personal reflections by friends and family of the poet. In spite of the risk of introducing a certain unevenness to the volume, we feel these vignettes serve as candid and illuminating windows on Coffey the man. Coffey's close relations with younger writers and artists, as evinced in pieces by Augustus Young, John Parsons and Michael Smith, are a testament to his deep passion and support for creative endeavour. In a similar vein, the poet's son, John Coffey, gives a revealing and intimate portrait of the family man who snatched moments to write while his children, 'play Follow-my-Leader' (*PV*, p.69), 'scrambling' across the house and distracting the poet from his 'never perfect work' (*PV*, p.80). Brian Coffey's hitherto unpublished account of his friendship with Samuel Beckett 'More and/or Less Than Fifty Years Ago' reveals his deep affection for his Irish compatriot and the deep humanity he shares with him. Essays, too, by the likes of Billy Mills and Geoffrey Squires fall into both categories, critical and reflective, and are all the more revealing for that.

Commentators, including J.C.C. Mays and Dónal Moriarty, have written persuasively of the unique timbre of Coffey's verse, its sonic particularity, its range of tones and registers as well as its philosophical scope and thematic diversity. J.C.C. Mays draws our attention to 'the way [Coffey] makes sounds echo in your head' and asks that his voice 'be heard' on its own terms.[11] According to Mays, we hear Coffey's distinctive voice before thematic understanding is reached and thus immediate conceptual clarity is not the point of his poetry. As Beckett wrote of Denis Devlin, he 'does not dabble in the clear and does not make clear'.[12] This is not necessarily a case of choosing between the well-made lyric poem and the less conventional modality Coffey works in. But we do need to acknowledge, and understand, the different type of excellence his work embodies.

Once again, J.C.C. Mays provides a useful vocabulary with which to appreciate Coffey's particularity. Mays draws a disinction between 'reception-oriented and production-oriented' poetry.[13] Reception-oriented poetry enters the literary marketplace with clear expectations of an audience in what Mays calls 'an "I–thou" communication model'.[14] By contrast, production-oriented poetry uses an 'I–it' model whereby the poet has responsibility for the artwork but does not aim at any particular poetry-reading audience.[15] His responsibility ends when the poem is complete and questions of circulation, publication and publicity are less important than with the 'I–thou' model. To use Roland Barthes' distinction, Coffey's poetry is 'writerly' rather than 'readerly' because it does not serve up readily paraphrasable meanings and does not adhere to a 'reception-oriented' aesthetic. Rather, Coffey relies on his own sense of poetic integrity where the poem as writerly artefact holds primacy over its reception by its readers.

But Coffey is far from being a solipsistic poet and questions of reception, reputation and indeed sales were important to him. We need to consider the reasons for Coffey's relative invisibility in the poetic marketplace and also to consider the richly intersubjective and communicative nature of his work. His neglect has specific reasons behind it, reasons which are considered in this volume; but a brief comparison with other Irish writers may serve to illuminate this problem. Beckett and Joyce made their reputations outside of Ireland long before they were reincorporated into a national canon. Likewise, Coffey's friend and contemporary Denis Devlin (whose work Coffey tirelessly advocated) gained a reputation in New York in the 1940s where New Critical luminaries Robert Penn Warren and Allen Tate hailed his 1946 volume *Lough Derg and Other Poems*.[16] Coffey was a poor self-publicist who sometimes passed over opportunities that more worldly poets would have taken.[17] His reputation has suffered because he could not gain an audience in Ireland (where he would have most wished to be recognized), but he did not succeed in establishing himself overseas, which might, in turn, have given him a foothold on the Irish cultural scene. At the same time, Mays conjectures that his particular poetic gift may have flourished best in this comparative obscurity and certainly, Coffey was content, most of the time, to sustain himself on his own sense of writerly values.[18]

If Coffey's poetry still demands to be read, it can also be puzzling, difficult, elliptical as well as liberating. This mixture of reactions is reflected in the diversity of contributors to this volume, who all attest to Coffey's rewarding complexity. In his 'Introductory Essay' to the 1975 *Irish University Review: Brian Coffey Special Issue*, J.C.C. Mays suggests that Coffey's work

> consistently invites rejection at the moment it aims at success ... it is as if, thrown back and brooding on his own resources, the poet has chosen not to speak a language but to provide the materials for the reader to construct one himself.[19]

This comment gives an acute insight into the creative complexity of Coffey's work. Back in 1981, Marjorie Perloff argued for a 'poetics of indeterminacy' to describe the aesthetic practices of poets she identifies within the Pound tradition whose lineage, she suggests, runs back to Rimbaud's *Illuminations*. On this view, the Pound tradition is a line which 'goes from Rimbaud to Stein, Pound and Williams by way of Cubist, Dada, and early Surrealist art, a line that also includes the great French/English verbal compositions of Beckett'.[20] The link with Beckett is suggestive. The famous opening line of *The Unnamable* – 'Where now? Who now? When now?' – is nothing if not indeterminate.[21] This bears comparison with a less-famous opening line in Coffey's *Advent*: 'Who wakes now being here if not one alone' (*PV*, p.111). Questions immediately multiply. Who is the speaker? Is there any unified voice behind the utterance? Where are we? The following lines do little to clarify such questions:

> where where lifts no sail no dew cools
> far stars of their purity presage none
> voiceless unfeatured unrapturing deep
> own the place dice dead naught to please   (*PV*, p.111)

We sense something subterranean, primaeval, the world as void with 'darkness solid' (*PV*, p.111). Like Beckett's closed-space texts, locations are vague, ill-defined and desolate. Perloff argues that Beckett achieves his aporias not through 'the *juxtaposition* of items drawn from disparate contexts' (as would be the case with Rimbaud, Surrealism or Pound's *Cantos*) but through the enigmatic '"fragility" of the words themselves, words whose meanings are constantly eroded and reformulated'.[22] The insistent negations of Coffey's *Third Person* are perhaps akin to this linguistic 'fragility', which is also echoed in the Beckettian uncertainty of the subjective voice as, for example, in these lines from 'Thirst':

He has desired not to desire
he has hoped not to hope
he has no part where he is
he will have no part where she is   (*PV*, p.31)

An ablation of self becomes a negative linguistic mode and images cease
to have a direct referential quality. This makes it difficult to visualize
or conceptualize Coffey's landscape of meaning since images are
negated as they are uttered as, for example, in 'White':

Think no flower no surface
no smile no extreme star
think you can see no soul   (*PV*, p.24)

This linguistic self-cancellation is similar to Beckett's procedure in *The
Unnamable* where the narrative voice asks:

What am I to do, what shall I do, what should I do, in my
situation, how proceed? By aporia pure and simple? Or by
affirmations and negations invalidated as uttered, or sooner or
later?[23]

If Coffey is aware of the 'breakdown of the object', as Beckett claims
in his review of 'Recent Irish Poetry', then his textual indeterminacy is
a response to this 'new thing that has happened', a realization of which
Beckett and Coffey share.[24]

Textual indeterminacy implies that the reader must play an
unusually active role in reckoning with the text. This indeterminacy
may be structural, syntactic, semantic or metrical and it implies that the
reader must actively engage with the poem in order to complete it.
And this is an important aspect of Coffey's writerly aesthetics. His
poetry uses plural signifiers and openness of form to force the reader
to reckon with the poem. It is arguably this, more than anything, which
has earned Coffey's reputation as a 'difficult' poet.

But if, on one level, Coffey witnesses the 'breakdown of the object',
on another, his poetry is very much engaged with intersubjective
processes. This is particularly true of the large body of love poetry
Coffey wrote which matches linguistic openness with what
contemporary theorists called openness to 'the other', the addressee or
dedicatee, and the alterity that s/he represents. This openness towards
the other is a notable feature of *Third Person* and 'Missouri Sequence'
and it is strongly present in such love poems as 'Mindful of You', 'How
Far From Daybreak', 'For What For Whom Unwanted' and 'Fidelities'.

Some lines from 'No Fault' (from the 1985 volume *Chanterelles*) illustrate Coffey's concern with relatedness to others and otherness both as an abstract principle and as a concrete, human reality:

> If in a garden
> she finds him
> when he finds her
> their only greeting
> "You" "You"
>
> First sight a flash
> What each had sought
> each gave
> withholding naught
> naught imposing
> purely open
> in come what might   (*PV*, p.187)

These lines seem to affirm a 'purely open' attitude towards 'the other', or the loved one. Such openness, following the terms used by Emmanuel Levinas (and used persuasively by Aengus Woods in his essay), might be deemed 'ethical' in its receptivity to alterity and its openness to 'other edens' embodied in the beloved. Perhaps we begin to see here an 'ethics of form', such as that suggested by critic and poet Robert Sheppard, in which poetry is (or should be) 'ethical, processual, interhuman, dialogic' rather than 'ontological and fixed'.[25] Many of Coffey's love poems open up meanings through dialogic interaction; words find their meanings in the process of reaching towards another. It is suggestive also that Coffey's writing engages with important ethico-political issues including: war (*Death of Hektor*), environmental despoilation (*Advent*), invasive bureaucracy ('LEO'), the tyranny of the market (*Advent* again). These considerations take us a long way from the Irish cultural debates mentioned above. It is perhaps time to broaden the range of perspectives on Coffey, to suggest 'other Coffeys', and this volume, we hope, will go some way towards acccomplishing this task.

NOTES

1. See Aengus Woods' bibliography in this volume for details of these publications.
2. For example, Coffey is left out entirely from Edna Longley's *The Bloodaxe Book of 20th Century Poetry* (2000), which includes many Irish poets. He is also omitted from *The Penguin Book of Twentieth Century Irish Poetry* edited by Peter Fallon and Derek Mahon (1990) and

the *Penguin Book of Irish Verse* edited by Brendan Kennelly (1981). Patrick Crotty finds room for short extracts from *Death of Hektor* and 'For What for Whom Unwanted' in his *Modern Irish Poetry: An Anthology* (Blackstaff Press, 1995), while J.C.C. Mays notes that the 'scant selection in *The Faber Book of Irish Verse* (edited by John Montague, Faber & Faber, 1974) was included only at the last moment because a group of younger poets threatened to withdraw their contributions if Coffey was not among them' (J.C.C. Mays, 'Introductory Essay', *Irish University Review: Brian Coffey Special Issue*, vol. 5, no. 1 [spring 1975], p.12).

3. Alan Gillis in his *Irish Poetry of the 1930s* (Oxford University Press, 2005) writes trenchantly, if unfairly, that 'Coffey's poems ... tend to reveal the hermetically self-indulgent contortions of a dull imagination' in his negative evaluation of *Third Person* (pp.109–19), while Justin Quinn in his *Modern Irish Poetry 1800–2000* (Cambridge University Press, 2008) is equally dismissive. In a brief assessment (pp.99–100), Quinn questions Coffey's experimentalist credentials, arguing that his work 'is derivative of American Modernist poetry and can only be viewed as experimental if one's horizon is restricted to Ireland' (p.99). Glancing references to Coffey's allegedly 'obscure idiom' and 'bizarre punctuation and spacing of words' (pp.99–100) do little to inspire confidence in Quinn's critical judgements.

4. For much of the 1930s Coffey lived in Paris, he spent the war years in England, then a spell in Missouri, USA followed by long-term residence in London and Southampton, UK.

5. In an interview with Parkman Howe, Coffey says: 'I gradually came to see more and more that a person is at their best if they're on home ground. I have always regretted that I haven't been able to remain in Ireland, because we could have had some fun. But since I haven't been able to end up in Ireland, the other thing I did was simply connect any work I did with Ireland, because that was nearer to the kind of things I felt instinctively.' Parkman Howe, 'Brian Coffey: An Interview', *Éire-Ireland*, vol. 13, no. 1 (spring 1978), p.122.

6. Michael Smith's essay 'Irish Poetry Since Yeats: Notes Towards a Corrected History' sets out the polemical viewpoint of a counter-tradition which Smith's 1960s New Writers' Press initiative endorsed. See Michael Smith, 'Irish Poetry Since Yeats: Notes Towards a Corrected History', *Denver Quarterly*, no. 5 (winter 1971), pp.1–26.

7. In his 'Introductory Essay' to the *Irish University Review: Brian Coffey Special Issue*, J.C.C. Mays notes that 'MacGreevy's version of an Irish tradition is closest to Brian Coffey's' (p.15). Coffey and MacGreevy shared a Catholic outlook and a shared affection for their native soil which found expression in MacGreevy's decision to repatriate himself to Ireland during the war years and in Coffey's attempts to find work and to set up home in Ireland during the 1950s. The Catholic Modernism of MacGreevy has received attention from J.C.C. Mays in his essay 'How is MacGreevy a Modernist?' in *Modernsim and Ireland: The Poetry of the 1930s* edited by Patricia Coughlan and Alex Davis (Cork: Cork University Press, 1995, pp.103–28) and more recently in essays by James Matthew Wilson ('Thomas MacGreevy reads T.S. Eliot and Jack B.Yeats: Making Modernism Catholic', *Yeats Eliot Review*, vol. 23, nos. 3–4 [fall 2006], pp.14–26) and Seán Kennedy ('Beckett Reviewing MacGreevy: A Reconsideration', *Irish University Review*, vol. 35, no. 2 [autumn 2005], pp.273–87). The subject of Coffey's relationship with Yeats is a large one. In an interview with Michael Smith published in the *Lace Curtain*, Mervyn Wall comments: 'I do not think that Devlin and Coffey were influenced by Yeats at all. Their early interest was in the Surrealists, and they had read a great deal of contemporary French. They read and examined Eliot and Pound ... All honoured and respected Yeats, but no one wanted to live in the great man's shadow' ('Michael Smith Asks Mervyn Wall Some Questions About the Thirties', *Lace Curtain*, vol. 4 [summer 1971], p.82). Against this judgement we should consider Coffey's allusions to 'Easter 1916' and 'Among School Children' in *Advent* IV and *Advent* II respectively and the following lines from 'Missouri Sequence': 'Our William Butler Yeats / made island flowers grow / that need as much / the local rain / as wind from overseas' (*PV*, p.72). Clearly, whatever Coffey's objections to Yeats' Anglo-Irish rhetoric, he responded to the older poet's rhythms and language in ways which have still to be fully elucidated. See Moriarty's comments (*The Art of Brian Coffey* [Dublin: University College Dublin Press, 2000], pp.4–5, 94–95) and Coffey's own brief essay on Yeats, 'A Note on Rat Island' (*Irish University Review*, vol. 3, no. 8 [1966], pp.25–28) as well as Jack Morgan's essay 'Yeats and Brian Coffey: Poems for their Daughters' (*Studies: An Irish Quarterly Review*, vol. 88, no. 351 [autumn 1999], pp.270–77).

8. Samuel Beckett, 'Recent Irish Poetry', originally published in *The Bookman* (August 1934) under Beckett's pseudonym Andrew Belis. Reprinted in Michael Smith's *Lace Curtain*, no. 4 (summer 1971), pp.58–63, with Brian Coffey as Assistant Editor. Collected in Samuel

Beckett, *Disjecta: Miscellaneous Writings and a Dramatic Fragment*, ed. Ruby Cohn (London: John Calder, 1983), pp.70–76.

9. J.C.C. Mays, *N11 A Musing* (Clonmel: Coracle Press, 2006), paragraph 6.1.1.
10. As J.C.C. Mays suggests in paragraph 6.1.1 of *N11 A Musing*.
11. Brian Coffey, *Poems and Versions 1929–1990*, intro. J.C.C. Mays (Dublin: Dedalus Press, 1991), p.7.
12. Samuel Beckett, 'Intercessions by Denis Devlin', *Disjecta*, p.94.
13. Mays, *N11*, paragraph 6.2.1.
14. Ibid., paragraph 6.2.2.
15. Ibid.
16. Mays comments: 'one must reckon that Devlin sought assimilation (see the revisions to *Intercessions* and the new style developed in the *Lough Derg* volume). Coffey worked to his own agenda, which sufficed (he had no particular interest in burning bridges though he was stimulated by fresh fields).' Mays, *N11*, paragraph 4.1.4.
17. Mays cites an example of Coffey passing over an opportunity to read in Buffalo, New York alongside W.H. Auden and Stephen Spender. Mays, *N11*, paragraph 7.2.1.
18. Ibid.
19. J.C.C. Mays, 'Introductory Essay', *Irish University Review: Brian Coffey Special Issue*, vol. 5, no. 1 (spring 1975), pp.16–17.
20. Marjorie Perloff, *The Poetics of Indeterminacy: Rimbaud to Cage*, 1981 (Evanston, IL: Northwestern University Press, 1983), p.v.
21. Samuel Beckett, *The Unnamable*, in *Trilogy: Molloy, Malone Dies, The Unnamable* (London: John Calder, 1959), p.293.
22. Perloff, *Indeterminacy*, p.200, her italics.
23. Beckett, *The Unnamable*, p.29.
24. Beckett, *Disjecta*, p.70.
25. Robert Sheppard, *The Poetry of Saying: British Poetry and its Discontents 1950–2000* (Liverpool: Liverpool University Press, 2005), p.13.

CHAPTER TWO

Seeing Brian Coffey: 'word hidden for all'[1]

AUGUSTUS YOUNG

I found this scrap of paper in my Brian file:

> Dr Coffey was a notable scholar and a courteous gentleman who
> looked like a fashionable musician from the Edwardian era. His
> favourite form of transport was a horse drawn cab (he was allergic
> to the internal combustion engine). He wore a high collar and was
> reputed never to have used a fountain pen. But for all his surface
> conservatism he understood the younger generation and was an
> excellent President.

The handwriting is my mother's. She transcribed it from an obituary
of Denis Coffey, the first President of University College Dublin.
When I showed it to Brian, he told me his father had given him a little
Union Jack to greet Edward VII when the Prince of Wales visited
Dublin. A decade later at a college debating society, Dr Coffey talked
the gun out of the hand of a student, no less than Rory O'Connor, who
was executed for burning down the Four Courts during the civil war.
Denis's Kerry roots were adventitious enough to adapt to variable
weather conditions. They transplanted well.

Unlike father, unlike son? Denis, a successful academic politician,
a big fish in a smallish pond, and Brian, a wandering poet 'unknown
in six continents' (his joke). Still they had a lot in common. Scholarship, studied dandyism, distrust of modern transport and gadgets
(Brian preferred to take the bus and used an erratic Erica typewriter,
not even electric), surface conservatism, yes, and a great understanding of youth.

He was a mentor to many young people, and not only to poets and
artists. His ability to listen patiently and offer down-to-earth advice

was exceptional. Only his daughters' boyfriends were slow to take it. The exception was John Parsons, who paid court to his eldest and ended up, when Mary married someone else, as Brian's oldest young-person friend. John wrote songs for a pop group called the Fabulous Poodles and had a genius for making water features. In a way, Brian was protecting his daughters from wanderers like himself.

Brian's patient listening and pertinent response extended to his writing, particularly his translations, which were as important to him as so-called original work (he hated the word 'original'). His chosen poets, always French, were allowed their say and then engaged in a gently persuasive conversation. His work is interactive. I could imagine him in some writers' otherworld talking the gun out of Verlaine's hand, so the poet would weep on Rimbaud's shoulder rather than put a bullet in it. On reflection, he might have held back. While in prison Verlaine wrote *'Le ciel est par dessus le toit'*. *'Qu'as-tu fait, o toi que voila'* (What have you done to yourself?) was a favourite line.

Dr Coffey was ambitious for his brilliant son. I think he had in mind for Brian either the chair of chemistry or philosophy in UCD (at least he gave him a choice!). But for Brian self-determination, rather than the fulfilment of expectations, was his driving force. He saw himself as 'a good bantamweight boxer who wrote poems', and 'a thinker rather than a teacher'. He would have to study abroad and chose voluntary exile in Paris (Jean Perrin in physical chemistry and Jacques Maritain under whom he completed his doctorate; top men both). Though proudly Irish, he was never to return. Questing intellects never settle down.

His friends in Paris were Sam Beckett and Thomas McGreevy. It was almost a literary conspiracy. Somewhere in Beckett's *Murphy* there are buried quotes from Brian Coffey's poetry, and Sam gave Brian the title of his first significant book of poems, *Third Person*. Michael Smith says Tom's 'vice was piosity'. Brian's brand of unsentimental Catholicism would have clashed with that. I fancy Beckett quietly taking notes, dreaming of *Fair to Middling Women* (his most impenetrable book and certainly his most Irish). Their mutual love of light philosophical conversation, and painting, would have kept them talking late into the night, and a shared fear of being sucked into the Joyce family, as one of James' willing slaves, kept them together during the day. Curiously it was Beckett who took the bait, hook and all, in the shape of Lucia, Joyce's troubled daughter, and when he was stabbed by an 'existential vagrant', Brian called on Joyce to tell him, and famously didn't cross the threshold.

The war, and marriage to Bridget Baynes, brought Brian to England.

It was a confusing time and, to make a living, separations were enforced. When his first child, John, was born he was teaching in Sheffield and Bridget lived with relatives near London. It was the closest of marriages, and not just domestically. I like to think Bridget was the 'whom' to whom he addressed his poems.

Coffey is first and foremost a love poet, in the tradition of Dante rather than Robert Graves (whom Brian knew only too well in his Laura Riding phase). Romantic poets woo their 'whoms', while the Dantes 'explain the world' to them and are not expecting an answer back. What Beatrice thought of her poems is less interesting than Bridget. She only knew Dante slightly and was unlikely to have read him. Bridget, though, lived fifty-eight years with her poet. But I doubt she had much time for thinking of herself as a muse, bringing up nine children in a household that moved between continents. As a critic of Brian's poetry, Bridget was a silent partner. But, I imagine, over the years she weighed and considered Brian's weighing and considerings. Two things I know for certain. She found the reference to Darby and Joan in the 'Answering Mindful' vulgar, but the hymn to the universal mother at the end of *Death of Hektor* received the nod.

The years immediately before and after the war were interesting times for Brian. T.S. Eliot published him regularly in *The Criterion*. His Thomism, aligned to modern developments in philosophy, appealed to the Christian poet and literary broker. Brian was to write innumerable essays and reviews in and around philosophy for the *Modern Schoolman*, and by the time he went to St Louis, Missouri, with a growing family, he looked set to have the academic career his father wanted. But Brian did not let it happen. He resigned from the university on 'a matter of principle'. While walking in the New Forest in the mid-1980s I asked him about it, but his explanation seemed so scholastic that I felt it was not the real reason. Now I'd say he was bored with the matter and just trying to make it interesting to himself.

Brian Coffey's return to London in 1952 was another rejection of what seemed inevitable. He wanted to make his own life, not an academic one, settling down to teaching higher maths in schools and adult colleges, and concentrating on his poetry, publishing now and then in the *Irish University Review* and with the Dolmen Press. Fame of any kind did not interest him.

Poetry was his inner life. Even in the years between leaving Paris and returning from America when he wrote little new, it preoccupied him constantly. He never stopped writing it in his head. Creative patience – knowing how to wait for the right moment to commit to paper – is a rare virtue. Brian had it (one of the similarities he shared with his contemporary George Oppen). In 1975 he told me his main concern was 'to produce a body of work and that would take a life-time'. It was just before he started on his major work. (I wonder who told him he had twenty more years to live?)

Michael Smith's *Selected Poems* (published by New Writers' Press in 1971) brought him to the attention of the young. I was amongst the many who sat at his feet in the early 1970s. His sprawling house in Muswell Hill was busy with the comings and goings of a lively and remarkably good-looking family – the daughters all arts, crafts, com-munes, cults and godknowswhat (boyfriends sulking in their wake), the sons making their way in the world, seemingly without effort. Serious people. Only the youngest, the easy-going Dominic, I felt I could talk to, but sadly never did. He was always rushing off on his motorbike (a mode of transport his father mastered as a part-time RAF instructor during the war).

I quickly learned *not* to make myself a son to Brian. He was already well served in that department and seeing that he didn't suffer defer-ence gladly, I pretended to be an equal. At first it was a game, but we be-came friends in time. Working together on Advent Books, a few hand-printed slim volumes, helped. By the 1980s after every time we met we exchanged letters. It must have been every other week from the number I have.

Little escaped his ever-amused interest in the world of others. Sharp intelligence, in itself, does not cut ice. It needs to be put in the flame to incise. Brian's had great warmth and friendship came with fun. If you relaxed enough in his company to enjoy the play of light on hard surfaces, it was easy skating. He could be difficult when put on a high horse by fools who didn't know it. I made that mistake a few times and experienced his hard edge. I had no problem with taking it on the chin because I knew if I got up smiling he would have forgotten my fall. 'Vanity', he said, 'is not even a vice. It's a defect.'

Brian was anything but a 'dried out intellectual'. He could talk of cultivating red onions for his allotment with as keen enthusiasm as of Mallarmé or Heidegger or computerised word counts in literature. Nobody was better to go to a Chinese Circus with or a concert on the South Bank of, say, his beloved Schubert. Bridget often had to nudge him when he nodded off ('I was only closing my eyes to *see* better', a rare Oirish bull from the least Oirish Irishman I think I've known). I avoided conversations on science fiction and his *bête noire*, administrators (for I had become a medical one, a fate shared with his son John and, indeed, his father, who ran the Anatomy Department before he became College President).

Jealous of his privacy, he allowed gossip to slip out from time to time. But never to glorify himself (his enduring friendship with Beckett was a well-kept secret). I put the bits and pieces together in a ballad and read it to him standing on a table for his 80th birthday in the Conway Hall, London. Tony Rudolf, who published his major poems, had rounded up a large gathering of friends and admirers. I was less nervous of the audience than of Brian. But he encouraged me with a wink. I like to think he indulged my breach of his public code because once in the early 1980s I thought I was treating the Coffeys at the BBC's expense to an extravagant dinner at Verseys, including Pouilly-Fuissé, a wine Brian loved and could rarely afford. A bit of swank I paid for. Bridget didn't want anything to do with an expensive dizzy blonde and so I ordered her a dark and handsome Barolo. The BBC refused to foot the bill.

Four things Brian Coffey said ring in my memory. When I complained about my job preventing me from writing, he said 'James, you make time. It's part of the creative process.' Brian knew what he was talking about. A large family to support with multiple jobs and still he managed to put more time and thought into his work than any poet I know.

Secondly, as a silly young man I interrupted him to ask 'what about happiness?' He laughed and said, 'happiness is an *idée d'amateur*'. I was miserable for twenty years until I learned that in French *amateur* means a passionate enthusiast, and not a Sunday thinker. Brian pursued *la chasse du bonheur* all his life. Always with a strong sense of responsibility, of course.

Thirdly, annoyed by someone who claimed not to understand his work, he said to me, 'My intention is not to communicate.' I was too amazed to ask why or bother to write it down then. I only understood what he meant when I encouraged a reluctant Cyril Cusack to read *Death of Hektor* for the BBC ('I haven't a clue what it's about'). I don't think there was a listener left in the dark as to what his great poem meant. Even the reviewers in the *Times*, *Listener* and *Daily Telegraph* were quite clear. J.C.C. Mays in his preface to Brian Coffey's *Poems and Versions, 1929–1990* says, 'the way he makes sounds echo in your head is where his meanings begin'.

I have no patience with people who say Coffey's work is difficult. Listen to the verbal free jazz of *Advent* and you can hear his thought processes humming to themselves, musing on deep questions, but the effect is simple. It is not direct communication but rather communion mediated through the unique sound. Musical thoughts and half-thoughts. Still, the feeling behind them comes through like a bell.

The fourth thing Brian said was 'I translate poetry to understand it better.' Dónal Moriarty's *The Art of Brian Coffey* explicates in detail how Coffey's version of *Coup de dés* (Dice Thrown Never Will Annul Chance) is a colloquy between Coffey and Mallarmé. He is talking directly to the poet through the poem. The reader eavesdrops on this conversation, Brian gently persuading Stéphane to explain himself. He is negotiating his translation and the outcome is a remarkable compromise between two minds at work in different languages. Coffey's version, apart from being probably the most faithful in literality and prosody published in English, is certainly the only one that competes with the original as a poem itself.

In a way, all Coffey's poetry is an attempt at translation. His themes are the great ones that cry out to be explained (it is not enough to state them and colour them in with rhetoric and verbal music). His poetry struggles, often through analogy rather than direct logic, to understand firstly what *is* and what *might be*. That he has found a unique sound to carry his ideas and feelings is the bonus of genius (Brian would have mocked the word, '*gêne* would do for me').

Earlier I said that his poems are addressing Bridget (and that is undoubtedly true for *Advent*, which treats the death of their son Dominic), but before he can do that Brian Coffey must attempt to translate the world for himself, and, when that fails, as fail it must, himself to himself. I don't think he ever freed himself sufficiently to express the *might be*. There are intimations of a paradise in his poetry – rare word scatters that take wing. But the flight is more Icarus than Ascension. Its dying fall is expressed in the last line of *Death of Hektor*, 'word hidden for all' (for me as poignant as Pound's at the end of *The Cantos*, 'I am not a demigod / I cannot make it cohere').

Brian collaborated with Stanley Hayter in an engraved edition of *Death of Hektor*, and subsequently developed his print-making skills to a pitch that made poetry less necessary. He was working on 'The Prayers' in order to conclude *Advent*, but it was never to be completed. Brian in his late artwork seems to me to be rounding off unfinished business. I have seen his 'Finisterre', where the waters meet at the end of the world. Blood-red merging into the heavenly blue. And I possess a small print, 6 inches by 9 (dated 14 August 1986). It is titled 'Erl King'. Black on black. At first you merely see the darkness. Then you notice the scratches on the plate. And a face appears. A man's, contorted. He is naked, hands helplessly before him. What had been in his arms has been snatched away.

In the Schubert song it is the son's voice that reverberates. The Erl King is the whirlwind taunting the father, who is too deaf to hear, blinded by the thought that he has failed somehow to save his son (Goethe's words). In the Coffey etching, the Erl King is represented as the death process, the wearing away of life (an echo of the refrain in 'The Prayers'). The viewer only detects the father emerging out of the darkness and on the edge of the encroaching forest seven letters carved into an oblong slat, E-r-l K-i-n-g. Two words dying into a rotting plank. That's all. The son too has disappeared into the decay. Still, there is enough light in the darkness for a man, laid bare and trembling, to be seen. We have become his son's eyes, his Greek chorus of sight.

I think with his 'Erl King' Brian Coffey completed his body of work.

NOTES

1   This chapter is based on the opening address to the Brian Coffey Symposium, Trinity College Dublin, which took place on 21 October 2005.

CHAPTER THREE

Brian Coffey:
Opposing the Inevitable

GERALD DAWE

It was almost thirty years ago when I started to read the poetry of Brian Coffey after having met him briefly with Lorna Reynolds and heard him lecture on Denis Devlin at the IASIL conference, which was held in University College Galway (as it then was) in 1976. Looking back to the mid-1970s also suggests a useful timeframe within which to encounter the poetry of Brian Coffey. For 1975 saw the publication of three important 'markers' in the slow critical recognition of Coffey's poetic achievement. In that year the special issue of the *Irish University Review* appeared, 'devoted to some of [Coffey's] recent poems, in the year of his seventieth birthday, in the hope that they will be valued at their true worth', to quote from the 'Introductory Essay' by J.C.C. Mays.[1] This essay marked, in itself, an important step forward, gathering sparse bibliographical material together and articulating a clear argument on the value of Coffey's poetry:

> The situation, which has restricted Coffey's reputation, at the same time defines his achievement: his poetry consistently invites rejection at the moment that it aims at success. It is a poetry of *intention* which, from opposing the inevitable, has struck its authentic note.[2]

The introduction also established the unpredictable and disarming energies of Coffey's work in a phrase that has remained with me ever since. 'It is as if', J.C.C. Mays remarked, 'thrown back and brooding on his own resources, the poet has chosen not to speak a language but to provide the materials for the reader to construct one himself'.[3]

This was not the critical language with which I had been accustomed, and it certainly was not the dominant discourse within which

poetry from Ireland had been conventionally read. I found the suggestion of vulnerability, improvisation and freedom, of placing the poem
squarely in the reader's hands to create, both disturbing and liberating.
And still do. Could this really be feasible as a poetic practice?

The third important 'marker' was the inclusion of Stan Smith's 'On
Other Grounds: The Poetry of Brian Coffey', originally published in
Michael Smith's pioneering *Lace Curtain*,[4] in Douglas Dunn's key critical text of the time, *Two Decades of Irish Writing*.[5] While Michael
Smith's 1971 revisionist essay, 'Irish Poetry Since Yeats: Notes Towards
a Corrected History'[6] took a panoramic view, Stan Smith's essay was,
as Mays noted,[7] 'the only serious discussion of Coffey's poetry' to have
appeared by 1975. So that year was something of a watershed. In the
thirty years since the situation is roughly as follows.

Until fairly recently Coffey's critical fate has remained on the margins
of the literary mainstream. Attention has been spasmodic, notwithstanding the invaluable critical work of Augustus Young, Trevor Joyce,
Stan Smith, Parkman Howe and Jack Morgan.[8] Academic dissertations
by Sally Devlin on silence in *Advent* and *Leo* (1991) and Sandra
O'Connell on the *Europa* Poets (1994)[9] showed the dynamic interest of
an independent-minded critical engagement that would flourish with
the publication in 1995 of the indispensable *Modernism and Ireland:
The Poetry of the 1930s*.[10]

The present writer's collection, *Against Piety: Essays in Irish Poetry*[11]
appeared in the same year and included the text of 'An Absence of
Influence', a lecture given in 1989[12] which sought to widen the terms by
which Irish poetry was viewed, both popularly and in terms of current
academic and critical discourse. However, it was Dónal Moriarty's
groundbreaking study, *The Art of Brian Coffey*, that made the crucial step
forward of critical consolidation.[13] A millennial shift, we could say. Yet the
signs of a critical recognition are still far off.

Alan Gillis' recently published *Irish Poetry of the 1930s* raises
the stakes when he gives voice to an overwhelmingly negative view of
Coffey.[14] Here Gillis casts Coffey's *Third Person* (1938) into eternal
damnation in trenchant critical language: 'Coffey's poems ... tend to
reveal the hermetically self-indulgent contortions of a dull imagination
... Rather than fling us into an other world of new possibility, Coffey
mostly bores us with inane preciosity.'[15] According to Gillis, the poems'

> obscurity comes to be salved by a proleptic organicism as a spiri-
> tually binding and redemptive anima is gradually intimated and
> almost manifested through the riddling mantras' semantically

vacant but aurally resonant echoing. The intimation of this redemptive force is slight, however ... Coffey's monotone style fails to generate any voltage ... leads merely to a wistful stoicism ... he ultimately fails to convey that there is anything of consequence at stake ... a merely scholastic disturbance.[16]

But as Coffey would have known, the critical damage has been done by that term 'obscurity'. As Coffey remarked in an essay 'About the Poetry of Denis Devlin', the term obscurity, 'once used about a poet has such a burr-like quality of sticking, with bad effects on his reputation and on his sales, it is necessary to attempt to place such difficulty of meaning as does arise in Devlin's case in the correct perspective of his work as a whole'.[17]

Some may well gasp at the audaciously negative tone of Alan Gillis' judgement, but it marks an honest and open appraisal with which many will undoubtedly disagree. The reality of the matter is that many more will wholeheartedly endorse this view – though one can well imagine the shockwaves if, for example, Louis MacNeice or Patrick Kavanagh were dismissed in similar terms. Unlike his contemporaries, Coffey still produces contention, not consensus. And he does so because his poetry shakes the foundations of what is generally considered to be in Ireland and Britain the harmonics and shape of 'our' poetry.

Against the overwhelmingly negative reading of Alan Gillis, J.C.C. Mays, who, along with Michael Smith, has maintained the imaginative integrity of Coffey's poetic and his legacy, makes a strongly counter-vailing argument in Coffey's favour in *The UCD Aesthetic: celebrating 150 years of UCD writers*. Mays writes:

> *Third Person* ... is the book in which [Coffey] discovered an appropriate style. All poetry separates words from their everyday syntactical moorings so they connect with each other as well as with their referents, and it does this in different ways which produce different kinds of poetry. Thus, aural and visual connections in a Shakespearean sonnet typically actualize a sense of real-life drama while Coffey's neo-Thomist aesthetic takes him in the opposite direction. Interconnections of sound are more widely spaced, overlapped images are less individually realised, syntax is typically paratactic. Sense gathers in a way that allows clear light (*claritas*) to shine through, like blinding sun filtered through bare branches.[18]

Whether we agree with Alan Gillis' view of Coffey's *Third Person* as 'a merely scholastic disturbance' or follow Mays' description, that the poems are 'like blinding sun filtered through bare branches', what is clear is that Coffey's poetic achievement, like his pronouncements on the making of poetry, remains problematic. At long last this has come out in the open. I can only think that this is a good thing because it will, or maybe that is, *should*, make readers of poetry all the more alert to what makes up the 'Irish poetic', a much more complicated picture than the relay race it is more often presented as being. The crucial step is to make the complex picture visible and to let others make up their own minds. To quote J.C.C. Mays again, from his valuable essay on 'Brian Coffey's Work in Progress':

> Given the restricted awareness of Coffey's work, it is difficult to estimate its final worth. Not that wide acceptance seems to matter to him, and he has probably been better off without it. I suspect that the association of his name with that of Beckett and Devlin, in Ireland, has not done him much good.[19]

The grouping of Coffey, Devlin, Beckett, Thomas MacGreevy, George Reavey, Charles Donnelly and others as 'the Thirties' poets was at one time necessary and pedagogically meaningful. I have used the phrase as critical shorthand during twenty-five years of introducing the work of the 'Modernists' to a graduate seminar at Trinity College Dublin. Many of these students, who come from all over the world, understandably want to progress to the internationally recognized Irish names, particularly those of more recent years. They are often impatient, sometimes bewildered and occasionally hostile, to what appears to be seriously marginal, and marginalised, poets.

But to be truthful to the literary past means more than a passing history lesson. Reading these poets in the context of their better-known and more accessible peers and younger contemporaries makes the past much more exciting and exacting. As Derek Mahon remarked in a letter to the *Irish Times* in 1987, poets, critics and readers of poetry need to be vigilant and resist the easy stereotypes and caricatures of Irish literary history. 'Artistic success is the only kind that matters', Mahon remarked, 'and it eludes us all.' He went on, 'I ... agree that Irish "modernist" poets like MacGreevy and Devlin have received less than their due; and I, for one, rate both of them higher than any "Movement" poet ... nobody wants to hear the more complex truth'.[20]

It is that 'more complex truth' which we need to transfer to a wider audience, along with the necessary skills and instincts to decide for themselves what is personally more meaningful as poetry, what matters. It seems to me that the sense of *needing* to make a special case for poets such as Coffey has diminished somewhat in the twenty years since Mahon's letter appeared. As a result, the individuality of each poet is beginning to find his or her critical space. I also think we are beginning to see the critical contexts widening sufficiently to accommodate the work of Brian Coffey on his own terms. Towards that end it would be good to see new selected editions of the poems of these poets, updated and presented in attractive, reader-friendly formats.

An anthology or reader of critical texts might also help in the long run and open the door on what these poets wrote about their art and about each other. One would like to see in print Coffey's reviews and interviews with Augustus Young and Michael Smith, for instance, along with selected scholarly workings from his extensive archive, and also MacGreevy's monographs and unpublished memoir, as well as George Reavey's – the list goes on – revealing a history of which we actually know very little. Indeed, it sometimes seems that we have not even *started* to write an adequate literary, social and cultural history of twentieth-century Irish poetry. Now that Ireland is seemingly such an 'European' country, it surely makes sense to discover more about those men and women who in artistic and cultural terms led the way seventy and more years ago.

More immediately, it should be possible to *hear* more of Brian Coffey's work and what better way of honouring him than to broadcast a new performance of *Death of Hektor*? I cannot think of a more appropriate and timely text to reflect and reflect upon the life of our times. Encountering Brian Coffey in this one way would bring his work in contact with a new audience from what he called 'home ground'. And we should not forget in all the necessary critical and literary exegesis, Brian Coffey's declared view, in an interview with Parkman Howe, that 'a person is at their best if they're on home ground. I have always regretted that I haven't been able to remain in Ireland, because we could have had some fun.'[21]

NOTES

1. *Irish University Review: Brian Coffey Special Issue*, vol. 5, no. 1 (spring 1975).
2. J.C.C. Mays writing in his introductory essay to the *Irish University Review: Brian Coffey Special Issue*, p.16.
3. Ibid., p.17.
4. *Lace Curtain*, no. 5 (spring 1974), pp.16–32. *Lace Curtain*, no. 4 (summer 1971) was dedicated to the 'Thirties' generation, including Brian Coffey.
5. Douglas Dunn, ed., *Two Decades of Irish Writing: A Critical Survey* (Cheshire: Carcanet Press, 1975), pp.59–80.

6. Michael Smith, 'Irish Poetry Since Yeats: Notes Towards a Corrected History', *Denver Quarterly*, no. 5 (1971), pp.l–26.
7. *Irish University Review*, vol. 5 , no. 1 (spring 1975), p.19. See also 'Passivity and Openness in Two Long Poems of Brian Coffey', *Irish University Review*, vol. 13, no. 1 (spring 1983), pp.67–82.
8. See, for example, Parkman Howe, 'Time and Place: The Poetry and Prose of Brian Coffey', Ph.D thesis (University College Dublin, 1981); Jack Morgan, '"Missouri Sequence": Brian Coffey's St Louis Years, 1947–1952', *Éire-Ireland*, vol. 28, no. 4 (winter 1993), pp.100–14; Stan Smith, 'Against the Grain: Women and War in Brian Coffey's *Death of Hektor*', *Études Irlandaises*, no.8 (December 1983), pp.165–73.
9. M.Phil. in Anglo-Irish Literature dissertations, School of English, Trinity College Dublin. Sally Devlin, 'Silence in *Advent* and *Leo*' (1991) and Sandra O'Connell 'The Europa Poets' (1994).
10. Patricia Coughlan and Alex Davis, eds, *Modernism and Ireland: The Poetry of the 1930s* (Cork: Cork University Press, 1995).
11. Gerald Dawe, *Against Piety: Essays in Irish Poetry* (Belfast: Lagan Press, 1995).
12. *Tradition and Influence in Anglo-Irish Poetry*, ed. Terence Brown and Nicholas Grene (London: Macmillan, 1989), pp.119–42.
13. Dónal Moriarty, *The Art of Brian Coffey* (Dublin: University College Dublin Press, 2000).
14. Alan Gillis, *Irish Poetry of the 1930s* (Oxford: Oxford University Press, 2005).
15. Ibid., p.114.
16. Ibid., pp.118–19.
17. Brian Coffey, 'About the Poetry of Denis Devlin', *Poetry Ireland*, vol. 2 (1963), p.79.
18. Anthony Roche, ed., *The UCD Aesthetic: Celebrating 150 Years of UCD Writers* (Dublin: New Island Press, 2005), pp.94–95.
19. J.C.C. Mays, 'Brian Coffey's Work in Progress', in *Krino 1986–1996: An Anthology of Modern Irish Writing*, ed. Gerald Dawe and Jonathan Williams (Dublin: Gill and Macmillan, 1996), pp.332–41.
20. Derek Mahon, letter to the editor, *Irish Times*, 16 July 1987, p.9.
21. Parkman Howe, 'Brian Coffey: An Interview', *Éire-Ireland*, vol. 13, no. 1 (spring 1978), p.122.

CHAPTER FOUR

'Well-made things are worth songs': The Music of *Third Person*

MARIA JOHNSTON

'There are several reasons for reading Brian Coffey's poetry. The best reason is you will like the way it sounds and like it so much you won't worry if it leaves you little to say'[1] writes J.C.C. Mays in his preface to Coffey's *Poems and Versions,* and this provides a crucial point of entry into Coffey's work, the same 'key' perhaps that the *TLS* reviewer of *Third Person* in 1938 found so 'wanting' in what he termed this 'riddling' body of work.[2] Mays concludes by stressing the 'recommendation that Brian Coffey's *voice* be heard', as 'the way he makes sounds echo in your head is where his meanings begin'.[3] As this chapter will show, Coffey is the most musical of poets, attentive to the sounds of words, the phonological effects of language, and this musical element has not escaped the more perceptive of Coffey's critics and readers. Augustus Young too, in his obituary for Coffey, recognised how throughout Coffey's seven major books of poetry, 'the use of word, syntax, and topography produced a unique sound and rhythm that reverberates like a verbal free jazz'.[4] Young's account of aiding Cyril Cusack through his difficulty with interpreting *Death of Hektor* for a BBC programme in 1983, also testifies to the poetry's deeply musical sense: 'Exasperated I advised Cyril to close his eyes and listen to them and all would be clear. I emptied my mind, reading the text like music notation, while Cyril repeated the words with extraordinary effects.'[5]

Coffey is a poet dedicated to the aural and rhythmic qualities of language – the music of poetry – composing rhythms in his poetry that are, as he declared, 'somewhat different from the iambic rhythms that are common in English'. He goes on to explain further that 'the sources of my rhythms are very various, partly French, partly English, partly Irish, partly my own body. Things that move in my own body are part of my own rhythm, you see.'[6] Further elucidation is given in his 'Note on Rat Island' in which he remarks how

> words demand consideration in those of their properties which are not matters of sense and meaning but, instead, affairs of sound and sensuality and, as such, moving in themselves and impelled of themselves towards groupings and patterns of beat and stress and rhythm.[7]

His writings on other poets also display this overriding preoccupation with the centrality of sound and rhythm to the practice of composing poetry. Although he regarded the figure of Yeats as poetic precursor as problematic, he did value him as 'a man fascinated by words as sounds' who 'has left us an incomparable legacy of verbal rhythmical pattern: we Irish poets may perhaps do very well for ourselves if we listen to Yeats's English, remembering that the prize is the poem, perfect sound for perfect sense'.[8] As Coffey asserts in the same piece, echoing Mallarmé's views on the nature of poetry, 'Poems are made of words, are made, to put it crudely, out of sense *and* sound.' It is interesting to remember too that Coffey himself played the violin and his passion for music extended from Franz Schubert to Bob Dylan, the latter's 'Positively 4th Street' humorously rendered by Coffey in Seán O Mórdha's documentary 'Brian Coffey: A Visual Record'.[9]

Coffey's *Third Person* (1938) is a collection of poems constructed out of intricate arrangements of sounds, and its fourteen poems, unified as they are by motifs and aural repetitions, may be compared to songs within a song cycle. Within these poems the words sound as freely as musical notes. Unhampered by punctuation, comprising silences and slippages and never fixed to one meaning only, they invite endless interpretive possibilities and are thereby richly expressive of the reality of contingency, ambiguity and uncertainty that is human existence. The musical resources of the poetry offer an abundance of sound devices, including onomatopoeia, rhyme patterns, assonance, alliteration, syntactical parallelism, phonetic links, mouth sounds, throat sounds, repetition, echoes, syllabic timbre as well as tonal and timbral variations. Dónal Moriarty has attested to the acoustic of Coffey's *Third Person* in his sensitive study *The Art of Brian Coffey*, suggesting that 'their sounds and rhythms are effortlessly absorbed by the memory and reverberate there long after the act of reading has finished' (*ABC*, p.21).

It is precisely the richly musical nature of *Third Person* that in 2005 prompted me to initiate a collaborative project with the young Irish composer Scott McLaughlin. McLaughlin became so drawn to the musical possibilities of the work that he began thinking through a setting of the poems to music in a song cycle for voices and small instrumental ensemble. The collaborative approach is one that Coffey would surely have endorsed, having been himself immersed in artistic collaborations between poetry and visual art and also being an interdisciplinary scholar expert in the fields of science and the arts. The collaborative enterprise was also, of course, central to Modernist art; Pound and Eliot in particular worked across the boundaries between poetry and music, bringing them together through the idea of the 'auditory imagination' or 'auditory memory'.[10] The 'music of poetry', as Eliot famously put it, 'is not something which exists apart from the meaning' and further, 'a musical poem is a poem which has a musical pattern of sound and a musical pattern of secondary meanings of the words which compose it, and that these two patterns are indissoluble and one'.[11] To date three settings of the poems have been recorded and performed as a work-in-progress for a highly responsive audience at the 'Continuings' symposium celebrating the life and work of Brian Coffey at Trinity College Dublin in October 2005.[12] Thus the poetry has been heard anew in this evocative and exploratory way. The process of working with the poetry through music, with the music being built out of the structure and sounds of *Third Person*, testifies to the deeply musical quality of Coffey's poetry.

The first phase in this collaborative project was to give the composer as thorough an understanding as possible of the workings of the poems and so I, as reader, prepared for him a detailed guide to the particular sound devices employed within them. One of the most interesting points regarding this analytical reading phase was the fact that McLaughlin's work had, up until this point, never engaged with texts, due to the composer's confessed difficulty in approaching poetry as a genre. It was very important, therefore, to give him a deep understanding of how poetry's sense is embedded in its sound and structure, these being terms that he was very much alert to as a composer interested in structural procedures and in pure sound. This provided an illuminating point of comparison between poetry and music that the composer was able to develop and draw on through his own creative process. In thinking of the deep affinity between poetry and music, the words of Basil Bunting, a musician, singer and music critic as well as a poet, were an inspiring point of departure: 'Poetry like music is to be heard. It deals in sound – long sounds and short sounds, heavy beats and light beats, the tone relations of vowels, the relation of consonants to one another which are like instrumental colour in music.'[13]

McLaughlin quickly came to see how the sound texture of Coffey's work is one of echo and reverberation, as certain pivotal words and motifs resound throughout, making for resonant verbal contrasts. To give one example, the word 'eyes' is sounded fifteen times in all, appearing in 'Dedication', 'I Can Not See With My Eyes', 'A Drop of Fire', 'Spurred', 'Thirst', 'The Enemy', 'Patience no Memory' and 'Gentle' and, of course, its homonym 'I' appears time and again. All of these aural patterns were explored, leading the composer to a new insight into the poetry and the way in which this weave of complex sound effects and rhythms enacts meaning in a profoundly expressive way. The first stanza of 'A Drop of Fire' provides a compelling example of the workings of sound and structure throughout *Third Person*. The poem opens with a persuasive alliteration, 'The stars are standing in the sky', the repeated strong *st* sound of 'stars' and 'standing' mimetic of the stable position of 'standing'. The sound and syntax in the next three lines also perfectly captures the sense as:

> Gentlemen I *see* you smile
> *Stars rise* and stars *fall*
> And *fall* and *rise stars* on the *sea*.   (PV, p.29)

Evident from the first is the assonance contained in the word '*Gentlemen*' and the internal rhyme between 'smile' and 'rise', as well as the intricate pattern of repeated words that embodies the sense of the lines. Here, the words create a retrograde pattern – 'see', 'stars', 'rise', 'fall': 'fall', 'rise', 'stars', 'sea' – a mirror effect which is itself mimetic of the same upward and downward movement of the rising and falling stars and of the reflection of the stars 'on the sea'. Also, the fluid enjambment of 'fall / and fall' as well as the hypnotic falling repetition conveys their relentless downward thrust. The line builds to a climax as the repeated 'and' produces an increase in energy and momentum with the lift of the spondee 'stars rise' producing a rise in vowel sound, emphasised further by the striking *st* of 'stars'. Here too, the interim words 'on the' connect 'stars' and 'sea' in a lilting, rocking movement linked further through sibilance and long vowels. Thus sound and structure articulate meaning at the deepest levels, creating a sensuous music throughout.

Music and poetry have long been regarded as sister arts and poetry itself was traditionally composed to be sung to an audience. In the twentieth century, Modernist practices have combined the two forms in profoundly enriching ways.[14] On this point it is instructive to invoke the words of Bunting once more: 'music and poetry are twin-sisters born of the primitive dance. By studying one, you can understand much about the other.'[15] For Bunting, brought up on the folk-songs and ballads of the north-east of England, music was integral to his sense of what poetry is. Indeed, Bunting's lectures from 1968 and 1974, collected in Peter Makin's *Basil Bunting on Poetry*, highlight the centrality of music in the work of poets across the centuries, from Wyatt and Spenser to Pound and Zukofsky. The setting of poetry to music has through the ages engaged poets and musicians alike. Most notably, perhaps, the German *Lied* tradition of the nineteenth century affirmed the interrelation between poetry and music through the work of Schubert, Schumann, Mahler and Wolf.[16] The twentieth century alone has seen the work of poets – such as Walt Whitman, Emily Dickinson, Robert Lowell, James Joyce, Dylan Thomas, Elizabeth Bishop, William Carlos Williams, T.S. Eliot, W.H. Auden, Ted Hughes and John Ashbery – set to music by various composers in very different ways. Although the setting of texts to music will always inspire debate concerning the supremacy of one art form over the other, there remains the potential for mutual enrichment between music and poetry. A setting may well bring out musical aspects of the poetry in new ways, as the poem is fused with music and transmuted into song, in whatever form that may take. As the composer Steve Reich has written, in praise of Luciano Berio's *Circles*, a setting of poems by e.e. cummings:

> Here was an Italian who clearly understood that cummings's poetry was largely 'about' the individual syllables of which it was made. The first syllable of the first word 'stinging' was separated into a very long held 'ssss' followed by 'ting' and finally 'ing' by the soprano whose sibilance on 'ssss' was answered by two sandpaper blocks rubbed together by a percussionist. The marriage of instrumental timbre with syllabic timbre went exactly to the heart of cummings's poetry. It was a lesson in text setting without need of a classroom.[17]

It is interesting to note that Coffey made a cassette recording of himself reciting poems by cummings, no doubt appreciating a kindred attentiveness to sound and typographical invention in cummings's poetry. Coffey also recorded poems by Dylan Thomas, another craftsman possessed of a resounding reading voice and entirely devoted to the sounds and rhythms of poetry. Thomas began work collaborating on an opera with Igor Stravinsky in 1953 only for it to be ended abruptly by his untimely death later that year.[18]

One of the poets most concerned with the relations between music and poetry was Stéphane Mallarmé, a poet whom Coffey regarded

highly. Coffey's introduction to *Poems of Mallarmé* (1990) lauded
Mallarmé as 'the man who went further than any other in exploring
the nature of poetry, and attempting to say what it is and how to make
it',[19] and his intimate knowledge of Mallarmé's work is displayed
through his work on translating *Un Coup de dés* and other versions of
Mallarmé's poems. Coffey attests to the seductive quality of sound in
Mallarmé's poetry in the following remark on *Un Coup de dés*:

> As a result [of producing a translation of *Un Coup de dés*] I got
> the thing together and felt that I had at least one grip of this
> poem. And always bits of it remain in my mind. Usually words
> which carry with them the sound of the sea and the sound of the
> wind – that sort of thing.[20]

Mallarmé's influence on artists in the twentieth century has been widely
acknowledged and one of the composers he has most inspired is Pierre
Boulez. Boulez' *Pli Selon Pli* (published 1958–89), subtitled 'A Portrait of
Mallarmé', is a homage to the poet, a setting of five sonnets by Mallarmé
for soprano, small ensemble and orchestra, which, according to Boulez,
'represents a number of solutions to the problems posed by the alliance
of poetry and music'.[21] His other compositions based on work by
Mallarmé also include an unfinished setting of *Un Coup de dés* (begun
circa 1950) as well as the *Troisieme sonate pour piano*. Boulez has
written extensively on Mallarmé's poetry and on his engagement with it
as a composer, and his comments are particularly acute and useful
in respect of McLaughlin's settings of *Third Person*. Boulez has
emphasized, in an interview in 1972, his fascination with the poetry of
Mallarmé, its 'formal density' and the 'syntax itself, the arrangement of
words and their cohesion and sonority', which prompted him to set about
finding 'a musical equivalent'.[22] Mallarmé is, as Boulez puts it, a poet
who 'entirely rethinks French syntax in order to make it, quite literally,
an original instrument', making a poetry that is 'dominated by the strict
demands of quantity and the rhythm of the sound values implicit in each
word, so as to achieve a fusion of sound and meaning in a language of
extreme concentration'.[23] His deep understanding of the way Mallarmé's
poetry works is evident as he describes his work on *Pli Selon Pli*: 'The relationship between poem and music is not only on the plane of emotional
significance: I have tried to push the alliance still further, to the very roots
of the musical invention and structure.'[24] Boulez recognizes how 'all
poetry was originally designed for singing, and the evolution of poetic
forms was inseparable from the corresponding musical process'.[25]
Appropriately too, Boulez was one of Coffey's favourite composers.[26]

Many examples of settings of poetry by contemporary composers were considered by both myself and the composer as this project got underway, but ultimately McLaughlin went beyond these approaches to text settings, pioneering one that is very new by using contemporary compositional techniques. As a composer of the twenty-first century, he focuses on pure sound as material, influenced by the Spectral composers of the seventies (Gérard Grisey in particular) and also by the music of Alvin Lucier, which concentrates on the development of singular acoustic phenomena. It is fitting that Coffey's work, so innovative in itself, should have enabled McLaughlins's entry into text setting. Having reached an appreciative awareness of the structure and formal devices of Coffey's *Third Person*, McLaughlin then began to engage with the poems as a composer. As McLaughlin has stated: 'I was surprised to find myself so open to Coffey's poems; the myriad phonetic patterns are almost organic in the way they bloom and are then replaced.'[27] Careful to eschew a musical approach to the poetry that would attempt to impose one interpretation on the words, the phonetic quality of the words was his main focus and he began by translating the different vowel sounds into a pitch contour. Hard and soft consonants were also a determining factor in this process; the pitch material was generated from the sound and structure of the poem itself, with the rhythm matching that of the poems in terms of patterns of stress and silence. In setting the first poem, 'Dedication', McLaughlin chose to carry out a purely instrumental rendering of the text to convey the workings of the poem's structure at a pure level of sound and rhythm. The music is played on violin and the bow technique makes for particular sound qualities as low vowels are muted, articulated *sul tasto*; high, bright vowels are played *sul ponticello* and for hard consonants a grating sound is produced by increasing the bow pressure. The anaphora and repetition of words and phrases in the poem are foregrounded here and serve as a fitting prelude to a work that calls attention so provocatively to its own seductive sounds and that is unified through sonic links:

As with all poetry and music, this setting is composed to be heard. At its performance at the 'Continuings' symposium, several audience members responded very positively to McLaughlin's setting, suggesting that the desired effect of music capturing the aural qualities of the poem had indeed been achieved.

The setting of the second poem, 'White', is perhaps a more conventional one, as here the words are enunciated by a soprano. A second vocal part in the harmony reinforces certain phonetic sounds within the poem's text, bringing out the sound patterns. Again, the phonetic sounds were translated into a pitch contour that was then used as 'scaffolding'. In the first line of 'White' – 'They do not move as we do' – the stressed 'we' sounds strident, coming as it does between a series of long vowels on *oo* that echo the 'whom' of 'Dedication'. McLaughlin saw how the first four words set up a pattern moving around long vowels; 'as' brightens the sound slightly more, while 'we' leaps to the top of the vowel register. Musically, then, the opening four words have a stable tonality (oscillating around a simple minor triad) moving to the mild and preparatory plagal dissonance of the fourth scale step for 'as' then leaping wildly to the out-of-key F on 'we' and plunging back down a minor ninth to the original root of E, all the while putting tonal stress on the repeated *oo* as the vowel-tonic of the phrase. As McLaughlin explains, 'Tonal areas are used in this setting as a point of stability but, as in the poem, the view of what is a stable referent is constantly shifting.' In this way, the music sets out to match the indeterminacy of the words. The music is attentive too to every stress, pause and silence in the poetry; the space between stanzas for example is equalled by a bar's rest in the music:

This pronounced *ee* sound of 'we' returns in the third line of 'White' on 'see' and 'seen', set on F and F sharp respectively. The final 'seen' produces a dissonance in this context as the F-natural here breaks the

B minor tonality of the melodic contour 'they see they are not' (B-F#-B-A-G) mirroring the semantic dissonance in the poetry where the polyptoton of 'see' and 'seen' – the latter preceded by a harsh-sounding 'not' – offers different connotations thus necessitating markedly contrasting inflections.

The line 'empire to empire not the same' places both instances of the recurring word 'empire' on a delicately falling glissando. This is one of the very few examples of traditional word-painting in this compositional technique – suggestive obviously of the falling Empire – but also serving to link the repetition of the word through this repeated musical gesture:

The chromatic line that begins the third stanza is similar to that which opens the second, but has been slightly reordered to follow the vowel contour. As the dark tones of the second stanza are here left behind for bright vowels and soft consonants, the register breaches upward on the word 'light'. The word 'light' always occupies the highest register in the music and is punctuated further by the addition of the harmony voice. This enforces the repetition of the bright vowel sounds along with the symbolic significance of the word itself. Here too, the mirror effect and symmetry of the phrases 'light to light' and 'light from light' is captured in the music as 'to light' is on 'F# to A' and 'from light' is the inversion 'A to F#'. The word 'open' literally opens up, rising on the syllables from G to B-flat and then leaping up to a high A on 'light':

In the fourth stanza beginning 'no shadow in the white shadow', the repetition of 'shadow' is reflected in the music but the context is changed by the dissonant treatment of the intervening 'white' on C-natural. This serves both to emphasise the word 'white' in itself as a stress point and to bring out the semantic tension between 'shadow' and 'white'. This jarring effect on 'white' also links it back to its rhyme 'light'. Sounds are constantly echoing back and forth in this way.

The fragment 'rise on wind' sounds on a whole-tone pitch collection in the melody to lend a heightened sense of expectation after the chromaticism of the preceding line. 'Rise' is suitably given the highest pitch of the stanza. Also, the pitches used here – D-Ab-C in the melody along with F in the harmony – make up a half-diminished chord that should resolve, but does not in this instance, making for an effect of ominous, heightened uncertainty that complements the, rising wind. Furthermore, the melody line itself is a whole-tone scale that lacks a tonic as a stable reference point, adding to this effect.

In the last stanza the pitches plunge down to a low F-sharp for the repeated negatives in the closing lines and the final point of rest on 'no soul':

The setting of the final poem, 'One Way', is interesting in the way that it employs an electro-acoustic element, developing further the evocative sound-world of the work. Scored for piano and recorded voices, it again generates pitch material from the poem's structure and so recurring words such as 'light', 'see' and 'seen' echo back to 'White'. This echoic texture binds the whole musical work just as it does the poetry of *Third Person*. Here a male and female voice sing in unison, which is highly apt for what is a collection of poems that explores the mystery 'why one person loves another',[28] and is furthermore built around the movement of the varying pronouns 'he' 'she' 'we'. The music is held together entirely by the structure of the poem. Each chord represents a syllable of the poem and, as McLaughlin explains: 'the chords chosen were constructed by mapping the vowel sounds and morphology of the syllable to pitch'.

One Way

In Coffey's words, 'well-made things are worth songs',[29] and it may be said that the achievement of Coffey's *Third Person* lies in the ways in which it has resonated with a composer and musician who was, and continues to be, guided by the sound and structures within the poetry towards a new approach to text-setting, creating a persuasive work that, in its very deliberate engagement with the text, reveals the intrinsic music of the poetry. This collaborative project is ongoing and is at this point still in the early stages of what is expected to develop into a more large-scale work in the future. As a living work-in-progress and an experimental one, it is a fitting commemoration to Coffey himself and his dynamic, original use of form and language, in poems that conspicuously resist being fixed to a single meaning. Indeed, John Coffey, the son of the poet, having been among the audience who first heard the recording of this work-in-progress in 2005, commented on how Coffey himself would have approved of the setting because, unlike many settings of poetry by composers, it refuses to impose one interpretation on the text.

Working on the project has, through its interdisciplinary methodology and its close consideration of the poetic strategies of Coffey's work, restored a necessary focus to the importance of sound and structure in Coffey's *Third Person* and its vibrant musical aspect. The composer's attention to sound highlights the poetry's pre-existing technique, a technique that has confounded many literary critics. The interpretive act itself has greatly illuminated the inherent musicality of Coffey's poetry, a musicality that must now be regarded as central to any interpretation of *Third Person*. In all, this collaboration between reader and composer, between poetry and music, signals valuable possibilities for understanding the complex technique of Coffey's poetry and the breadth of his poetic resources. Not only does it offer a new way of experiencing the poetry as a form, revealing its artistic scope and reach, it also stands as a vital testament to the deeply musical procedures of the poetry itself and calls much needed attention to the fundmental relationship between sound and sense in *Third Person*.

NOTES

1. J.C.C. Mays, preface to Brian Coffey, *Poems and Versions 1929–1990* (Dublin: Dedalus, 1991), p.5.
2. *Times Literary Supplement*, 3 September 1938, p.574.
3. Mays, preface, p.7.
4. Augustus Young, 'Music and Mantras', *Guardian*, 21 April 1995, p.T21.
5. Ibid.
6. Parkman Howe, 'Time and Place: The Poetry and Prose of Brian Coffey', Ph.D thesis (University College Dublin, 1981), p.279.
7. Brian Coffey, 'A Note on Rat Island', *University Review*, vol. 3, no. 8 (1966), p.27.
8. Ibid., p.28.
9. See Seán O Mórdha, 'Brian Coffey: A Visual Record', RTÉ television broadcast, 28 April 1986.
10. See T.S. Eliot, 'The Auditory Imagination' and 'The Music of Poetry', in *Selected Prose of T.S. Eliot*, ed. Frank Kermode (London: Faber & Faber, 1975). See also, Ezra Pound, *Ezra Pound and Music: The Complete Criticism*, ed. R. Murray Schafer (London: Faber & Faber, 1978). Of interest too is Coffey's acknowledgement of Eliot in Howe, 'Time and Place', p.278: 'Now Eliot agreed with me that one thing for certain was that in seeking a good poet to translate, it was a good idea to seek poems which included rhythms which were ones favoured by oneself also.' Dónal Moriarty recognizes echoes of Eliot's poetry throughout *Third Person* in his study.
11. Eliot, 'The Music of Poetry' in *Selected Prose*, pp.110–13.
12. The recording of the music for *Third Person*, complete with scores and a commentary, can be heard online at http:www.lutins.co.uk/coffey.
13. Basil Bunting, 'The Poet's Point of View (1966)', reprinted in *Three Essays*, ed. Richard Caddel (Durham: Basil Bunting Poetry Centre, 1994), p.34.
14. For a detailed commentary on the relationship between poetry and music through

Modernism see *Modernism and Music: An Anthology of Sources*, ed. Daniel Albright (Chicago, IL: University of Chicago Press, 2004).

15. Bunting, 'Thumps', in *Basil Bunting on Poetry*, ed. Peter Makin (Baltimore, MD: Johns Hopkins University Press, 1999), p.19.
16. For a helpful exploration of the interrelation between poetry and music in the German *Lied* see Deborah Stein and Robert Spillman, *Poetry into Song: Performance and Analysis of Lieder* (Oxford: Oxford University Press, 1996).
17. Steve Reich, *Writings on Music 1965 – 2000*, ed. Paul Hillier (Oxford: Oxford University Press, 2002), p. 203.
18. See *The Collected Letters of Dylan Thomas*, ed. Paul Ferris (London: J.M. Dent, 1985), p.913. Stravinsky later produced the chamber work 'In Memoriam Dylan Thomas', a setting of Thomas' poem 'Do Not Go Gentle into That Good Night'.
19. Brian Coffey, 'Introduction', in *Poems of Mallarmé: A Bilingual Edition* (London and Dublin: Menard Press/New Writers' Press, 1990), p.5.
20. Parkman Howe, 'Brian Coffey: An Interview', *Éire-Ireland*, vol. 13, no. 1 (spring 1978), p.118.
21. Pierre Boulez, *'Pli Selon Pli'*, in *Orientations: Collected Writings*, trans. Martin Cooper, ed. Jean-Jacques Nattiez (London: Faber & Faber, 1986), p.174.
22. Boulez, quoted in Joan Peyser, *Boulez: Composer, Conductor, Enigma* (London: Cassell, 1977), p.144.
23. Boulez, *'Pli Selon Pli'*, p.175.
24. Ibid.
25. Boulez, 'Poetry – Centre and Absence – Music', in *Orientations*, p.186.
26. Thanks to John Coffey for providing this information.
27. This and subsequent comments on his work by Scott McLaughlin are from personal correspondence with the author.
28. See Howe, 'Coffey: An Interview', p.121.
29. Coffey, 'Note on Rat Island', p.26.

CHAPTER FIVE

Eight Lines of Coffey:
A Note on Prosody

GEOFFREY SQUIRES

Coffey's prosody is both influential and inimitable: influential in that it contributed to the general opening up of prosodic possibilities that has been a feature of late Modernist poetry, but inimitable in the particular configuration of sound and movement that constitutes his unique voice. As the final chapter in Moriarty (*ABC*, pp.87–118) clearly demonstrates, I am not alone in being fascinated by what Coffey does, as distinct from what he says, but I hope to illuminate some more aspects of his prosody in this brief note. To do this, I shall have to extract lines from their textual context, thus losing the sense of their place in the whole, but I think it is worth paying this temporary price to show what is going on within each one.

'The mare shelters in the barn' ('Missouri Sequence', *PV*, p.69)

The vowels could almost be Heaney, whom incidentally Coffey thought well of, but it is not. The line comes from the beginning of 'Missouri Sequence', published in 1962. The prevailing tone of this long poem is narrative, conversational, even confessional, with an easy control of pace and modulation of line:

> The weather last month was not winter weather:
> warm wind, gentle sun in sky,
> cool, not cold, clear moonlit nights –
> weather such as one does not at first enjoy,
> readied as one is for north wind, freezing rain.
> But mild day followed unseasonable mild day   (*PV*, p.74)

This fluency is somewhat surprising in a poet who some years, even decades, earlier had written lines such as 'sad far so various menacing' ('You', *PV*, p.60) or 'he she we you they' ('Third Person', *PV*, p.36) or 'Nothing nothing nothing nothing nothing' ('Thirst', *PV*, p.31), the last of which would reappear in *Death of Hektor*. The early work shows the influence of Modernism, but it is precisely that: an influence which, despite the interest of the poems' convoluted syntax and striking disjunctions, has not yet been properly absorbed and made his own. And in 'Missouri Sequence' too, there are sudden shifts into a different prosodic gear, more rhetorical and in places archaic, as if the big themes – love, poetry, politics, religion – somehow demanded big writing. The effect is typically inflated, intrusive and unsettling: see for example the passages beginning 'There was a man was told a secret' (*PV*, p.75) or 'Tides of silk bruised the woman' (*PV*, p.78) or 'Once long ago' (*PV*, p.84). Coffey had not yet found his distinctive voice; when he did, it would be utterly novel and yet wholly assured.

'Often I dream this strange and searching dream'

Coffey could do a straight iambic pentameter when he wanted to, witness the start of this version of Verlaine.[1] The rhythmic inversion of the first foot gives the line a small initial bound, but the alliteration and repetition that follow create an aural complacency which is then rudely disturbed in the next line:

> of a woman unknown whom I love who loves me

The adjectival inversion (not *unknown woman*) both gives rhythmic weight to *unknown* and a feeling of translation, which of course this is, but Coffey's sometimes strange word order often creates a wider sense of linguistic distancing, as if one was reading a language that was not quite English. The packing together of the two relative clauses (without *and*) will also become a typical Coffey device, contributing to the sense of compression that one often finds in his verse. The next line is:

> and each time is neither quite the same

What? The immediate effect is to pull us up short, an arrest which is then resolved in the fourth line ('nor quite another') and which goes on to complete the sequence of thought ('and who loves me and takes me in'). These four lines exemplify the interplay of both rhythmic and syntactic regularity and irregularity in Coffey's verse. One does not have to look far to find other examples of this rhythmic resolution, for example in *Advent*:

> one day yes the barque will glide out of long night seas
> slide into yellow sand at break of day   (*PV*, p.111)

or *Death of Hektor*:

> One would have had to watch out ten thousand years
> to notice change between the nodal crests   (*PV*, p.154)

or amid the broken questioning of 'The Prayers' the beautiful, truncated

> For why go probe whose heart   (*PV*, p.217)

Coffey's syntactic strangeness is well recognised, but the point is that he is not 'difficult' all the time; it is the peculiar alternation of the expected and unexpected that gives his verse its characteristic mix of ease and unease.

'Why is it when we venture far in among ancient beeches (*Advent* II, *PV*, p.117)

Not why but *why is it*; not among but *far in among*. This run of little words is suddenly halted by the vatic, open vowels of the next line: *hush we say*. Here we see Coffey's control of pace, which is further exemplified in the continuation:

> what greets a sudden presence

> As if we had been waited for ... expected

> We so twisted back upon ourselves who have forgotten
> old gods rivers peaks trees that see us born and die   (*PV*, p.117)

First, the letter and line spaces slow down the text, mimicking its internal questioning, approximating, searching ('waited for expected'). This is followed by the syntactic interpolation in the next line, with its separation of *we* and *who*, and the rapid enumeration of the subsequent one ('old gods rivers peaks trees'). In this way, the pace and movement of the writing do what the writing is saying, namely contrast a wise receptivity with unnatural or pathological action. Later in the section we have the line:

> We do now so often as it were dream back those golden realms
> (*PV*, p.118)

The interpolation of 'as it were' does two things: it adds an element of doubt or provisionality; but it also prosodically adds to the length of the line, which now has fifteen syllables. I can think of few twentieth-century poets in English who can handle a long line as well as Coffey; indeed, I think this is integral to his verse. Why? One might speculate that his deep familiarity with French poetry, with its long Alexandrine, led him beyond the typical five English feet. But the length seems necessary also for two other reasons. One is to accommodate internal qualifications or interpolations such as 'as it were'. To read Coffey is to participate in a process, one in which destinations are arrived at, if at all, by often diversionary or uncertain routes: each long line is itself a project, a journey. The other reason is quantitative, the stacking up of substantive words, which has the cumulative effect of piling up reference and meaning.

'Point-light-studded velvet-black' (*Advent* V, *PV*, p.133)

There are occasional examples of hyphenated word compounds in Coffey's earlier work: 'scant-lit' and 'ice-heart jade-leaf contra-sol' in 'How Far from Daybreak'; 'bone-sore' and 'finger-touch' in 'Missouri Sequence'. However, it is in *Advent* that they become a salient feature of his verse. Here we have, in addition to the above example, many others including: 'statue-shades'; 'wake-light'; 'ten-thousand-welcoming'; 'treacly-tempting'; 'drum-beat sole-slap heel-click'; 'wind-born feather-fall'; 'yellow-brown-nearblack-red-socalled white'; 'sky-blue pollen-haze slight-swallow high'. The following passage from *Death of Hektor* is interesting in this connection:

> Rise and fall   earth and water
> to and fro   waves of sea
> climate not weather to shelter land from fire
> sun-glow shapes cloud-cover   fills air
> all is benignity   swan-down for cygnets   (*PV*, p.152)

There are two things to note: first, the absence of any articles, definite or indefinite (i.e. not *the* land or *the* air). This is a common feature of Coffey's prosody, which gives it a characteristic jerkiness, but more importantly creates a sense of compression. Secondly, the word-compounds (*sun-glow, cloud-cover*) compound this sense. The density of writing recalls in some ways Chinese poetry, but the effect is uniquely Coffey, partly because of the stacking up of meanings in the long lines, but also because of the characteristic syntactic symmetries, as in *Hektor*:

> seldom clear-sky clear-say
> blindways night rubble earthquake residues
> the all too often often the all too much   (*PV*, p.153)

In *Hektor* also we have the beautiful 'slowly-swiftly' (*PV*, p.151) and
the memorable

> belly-ripper head-splitter neck-lopper   (*PV*, p.157)

The last exemplifies the enormous energy that such compounds can give,
which finds a remarkable outlet in the theme of war. *Hektor* is, I think,
one of the few successful war poems, not simply in its moral treatment
of heroism and codes of conduct (and what could be more relevant these
days?), but in its recognition that, as the American General Patton once
said, war is one of the great human enterprises:

> Doom for Troy had been ships a thousand dressed on the sea
> feigning a clutching hand stretching in from the west   (*PV*, p.161)

The superb evocation of violence, the 'little souls sent shrieking' (*PV*,
p.159), is paradoxical in a man as pacific as Coffey, but it is not the
only paradox.

'Time ere poems   Time ere plighted troth' (*Death of Hektor, PV,*
p.154)

I have already mentioned the strand of archaism in Coffey's work,
typified by the above line from *Hektor*, and I want to focus here on an
aspect of his prosody that seems to me unfortunate. Apart from the
prosaic, narrative element in 'Missouri Sequence', which works well in
its own right, Coffey is a rhetorical poet: that is to say, he uses heightened rather than everyday language. Nothing could be more different
from the relentless demotic of (say) the Movement poets, and this goes
some way to explaining his marginalisation in terms of the dominant
poetic register. When this rhetoric is successful it results in a form of
expression that is both charged and unique. But sometimes the strain
of the endeavour results in something else, a kind of false rhetoric that
relies heavily on both archaic syntax and diction, as for example at the
end of 'Missouri Sequence':

> Any loving soul may share
> what the rose does declare ...
>
> Never was despair imperative,

> never are we grown so old
> we cannot start our journey
> bound to find
> an eternal note of gladness
> in loves true for men,
> the source whence they flow,
> the ocean whither they go.   (*PV*, pp.86–87)

The inversions of 'never' and the use of 'whence' and 'whither' have none of the muscularity that we find in the best Coffey, where reading a line is sometimes like doing a linguistic workout in the gym. The final lines of *Advent* also collapse under the burden of intention:

> in poverty wealth
> sickness health
> on the better tack
> or the worser
> between womb and grave
> face to polar cold
> right in storm of fire
>
> for us surely
> where friend gives greatest gift
>
> so be it   (*PV*, pp.149–50)

It may be significant that both these examples come at the end of their respective poems, where the effort at finality is greatest; and while the end of *Hektor* avoids this, it is oddly tangential. It is as if when Coffey wanted to pull out all the stops, it sometimes went wrong; and those stops, as noted earlier, relate to the big themes of love, art and religion. Here, my reading of Coffey probably diverges from some others'. I do not think he is particularly successful in dealing with these themes, indeed the sense of strain that is evident when he does implies to me something false: not morally or intellectually, but artistically false. Like many, what Coffey wanted to write was not the same as what he could write, and the intention protrudes all too obviously in places. I have already said that I consider him to have written one of the few great war poems. I want now to turn to another theme of which he is also surely a master.

'a world of its own   fulfilled   utterly fulfilled' (*Advent* I, *PV*, p.112)

Of all the features of Coffey's prosody, it is the within-line pause that most clearly demarcates his mature work from his earlier work. From *Advent* on, it becomes an integral feature of his writing, as exemplified by the above line. The pause is used in various ways; to reinforce an initial statement or respond to an implied question:

> no change   sign signal far flame whatever   none   (*PV*, p.111)

or make a sudden transition:

> and on the piazza busy men no longer   thin statue-shades   (*PV*, p.111)

or to act out what the words say:

> one waited   no reason to wait   (*PV*, p.112)

But one of its most powerful uses is to express the sense of wonder, the Greek *thauma*:

> Home base and
> how behind summer heat-veil
> Earth could give one pause   Earth strange
> like the stranger grown from one's child   (*PV*, p.133)

> A day so perfect one found oneself
> asking   of whom   for a cloud in the sky   (*PV*, p.133)

> Earth since early savannahs ours   all ours   (*PV*, p.134)

These examples, all from *Advent*, show Coffey's profound feeling for the natural world. The environment is so much a part of our consciousness now that it is hard to realize just how far Coffey was ahead of his time in this. Long before the term eco-poetics became fashionable, he expressed a reverence for the planet and dismay at how man was despoiling it: 'Oh out of what depths of inattention must we crawl' (*PV*, p.135). The idyllic vision of the earth before humankind's intrusion – 'innocent days before conflict' (*PV*, p.117) – 'saurian ease' (*PV*, p.112) – is the backdrop for his anger at human pride and greed. Here, I think, we are close to the moral centre of his work. Against 'such a place of passionate symbiosis' (*PV*, p.118) Coffey issues a dystopian warning:

> Not for us that natural use of taking yielding
> We rip the fruit untimely from the womb sing no filial praise
> Rapers peepers whippers cheaters thieves one and all

stick the boot cold play like murder into stripped girl

They wreck what is not theirs work their spite against flesh   (*PV*, p.118)

Coffey, the poet of the earth, is here also the poet of the natural order, including the natural order of the body.

'Nor see how one performs freely the long foreseen' (*Death of Hektor*, *PV*, p.152)

Coffey's long line allows him, among other things, to contain contradiction, as in this quotation from *Hektor*. And this brings me to the last theme in my analysis, which returns to the old, hackneyed topic of 'difficulty' in his work. I hope I have said enough to show that Coffey's work is not difficult to read as long as one moves with the prosodic movements, the bunching and pauses, the interplay of long and short lines, the dense word-compounds and so on. As has been noted by others, his is an intensely physical writing, halting and flowing, gritty and lapidary by turns. But in a far more important way he *is* a difficult writer in that he expresses real difficulty: the difficulty of the world, of our existence in it and of our faith beyond it. This returns us to a prosodic issue that has surfaced periodically in this chapter, namely the length of his line. Taking his work as a whole, there is a long-term progression from shorter to longer lines. Of course, this is by no means consistent or without exception, and some of the most powerful effects come from their juxtaposition, at the extreme in *Hektor*

> And
> Doom now in the air like a cloudy mushroom swags above Troy
> (*PV*, p.160)

I have sometimes wondered why I find the final section (VIII) of *Advent* unconvincing and have concluded that it has something to do with the reversion to shorter lines, after the expansiveness of the preceding sections. In the short line (sometimes) I hear Coffey dictating to himself; in the long ones, I hear him following himself, through all the shifts, reversals, turnings and resolutions of his being.

'inside become without' ('The Prayers', *PV*, p.220)

And yet 'The Prayers' uses mainly a short line again. In this late, unfinished poem, the idyllic naturalism is now remote, the post-positioned *none* a repetition of despair: 'berries none nuts none verdure none but blighted' (*PV*, p.217). The pain has Coffey reaching for strange devices, such as the use of a refrain in three six-line stanzas ('wear away wear away', *PV*, p.219), which are part of a deliberate echoing of *Hektor*. But the dominant effect is of the verse turning in on itself, a merciless reflexivity or implosion:

> Here each stares each
> in each self stares self   (*PV*, p.219)
>
> lump make limp make lump   (*PV*, p.219)
>
> one theirs them unloving   (*PV*, p.220)

through to the recognition that 'One had not known oneself' (*PV*, p.222). The poem ends, as *Advent* began, with a question: 'What hand what care saves here' (*PV*, p.222). I do not want to judge this unfinished, perhaps abandoned, piece, only to make a final brief comment about its prosody. Despite the syntactic and semantic compression, I am not convinced by much of the short-line movement of the poem, not because I hear Coffey telling himself what to write here, but because many of the lines are simply too short to bear their own terrible burden, e.g. 'final frontier', 'self-abyss and null', 'no escape elsewhere' (*PV*, p.221). The artistic question is why Coffey resorted or reverted to such short lines when under extreme pressure; perhaps it was the not uncommon, though dubious, assumption that economy guarantees intensity. But for all its attractions to and influences on him, Coffey was not a natural minimalist; his writing found its best expression in a longer, more complex, expansive line. If I have been harsh on Coffey in places, it is because his best is the very best and I am distressed by his aberrations, and I cannot but think that isolation for him exacted a heavy price. I wish he had had his Pound.

NOTES

1. See Coffey's version of Verlaine, 'My Familiar Dream', *Irish University Review: Brian Coffey Special Issue*, vol. 5, no. 1 (spring 1975), p.74.

CHAPTER SIX

Brian Coffey and George Reavey: A Friendship of Lasting Importance

SANDRA O'CONNELL

I THE PARIS CONNECTION

When Brian Coffey was invited to pay tribute to the Irish-Russian poet George Reavey (1907–76) for a commemorative issue of the *Journal of Beckett Studies,* he described their enduring alliance as a 'friendship of no public importance which had lasted a lifetime'.[1] The friendship between Brian Coffey and George Reavey did span a lifetime – from their first meeting in Paris as young ambitious poets in the early 1930s to Reavey's death in New York in 1976 – yet their camaraderie transcended the personal realm on many occasions and was marked by significant periods of artistic collaboration, resulting in several outstanding publications of lasting importance.

A few years before Reavey's death, Brian Coffey published one of his friend's key poems, *The Seven Seas* (1971), in his newly founded Advent Books series, as well as ensuring Reavey's presence in Michael Smith's *Lace Curtain* magazine whose Summer 1971 issue focused on Irish Modernist writers of the 1930s.[2] Coffey selected seven poems, ranging from Reavey's early Surrealist-style work to more recent poems, including 'In Memoriam: JFK' (1964), written shortly after the assassination of the iconic American president. Their most intense period of collaboration occurred, however, in the years leading up to the publication of Brian Coffey's collection *Third Person* in 1938 through Reavey's enterprising Europa Press. From the beginning of their friendship – Coffey had arrived in Paris in 1930 to study physical chemistry under Jean Baptiste Perrin – Reavey provided a profound influence on his companion's literary interests and development.

To the circle of Irish friends – Brian Coffey, Samuel Beckett, Thomas MacGreevy and Denis Devlin – who shared Paris as a creative base during intermittent times in the 1930s, Reavey represented, undoubtedly, a considerable literary force and catalyst. The most cosmopolitan among this circle of Irish friends, Reavey was born in Vitebesk, Belarus to a Northern-Irish father and a Polish mother, and spent his childhood travelling between Russia, central Europe and Belfast, where his adventurous father pursued a career in the flax spinning industry. Reavey's pan-European identity and wide-ranging literary interests allowed him to move effortlessly in Paris between his close Irish friends, Russian *émigrés*, American expatriates, French Surrealists and other members of the international avant-garde. Moreover, in a remarkably short period of time in Paris, Reavey had made the transition from unknown poet to prolific publisher and literary agent and generously used his contacts and influence to provide introductions for close friends like Brian Coffey. The English Surrealist poet David Gascoyne, who came to Paris in 1933, for example, acknowledged that 'it must have been largely through George Reavey ... that I first made the acquaintance of many people who continued to play a role in my life for some time to come'.[3]

Although Reavey had spent his first year outside Paris near Fontainebleau, tutoring the son of a British newspaper magnate, his move to Montparnasse in 1930 and his friendship with the influential American editor and publisher Samuel Putnam catapulted him into the heart of Left Bank activity. Reavey's debut in Paris's coveted expatriate journals came with his prose piece 'Io Lo Sognai' in the pages of *transition*, which dedicated, in June 1930, an entire section to the Cambridge student review *Experiment*, of which Reavey had been a founding member. This was followed by regular contributions to *This Quarter*, a journal edited by the influential American publisher Edward Titus, including the commission for 'Some Russian Notes by George Reavey', when Titus and his assistant editor Samuel Putnam released a special Russian number.[4]

However, it was Reavey's associate editorship of an ambitious anthology of European postwar writing, *The European Caravan*, that earned him the regard of Brian Coffey, Samuel Beckett and the circle of Irish friends.[5] Although Reavey had passed the role of editor of the 'England and Ireland' section to Cambridge student friend and *Experiment* contributor, the poet Jacob Bronowski, his considerable influence is evident in the inclusion of Thomas MacGreevy and Samuel Beckett. Reavey and Beckett are also specially acknowledged in Putnam's foreword 'for loyalty and help that cannot be repaid with words'.[6]

By the early 1930s Reavey had established a busy literary agency, the Bureau Littéraire Européen, which he ran with his business partner, Russian *émigré* Marc Slonim, from rooms above a shop on Rue Bonaparte in the heart of the Left Bank. Reavey's close friend the British print-maker and artist S.W. Hayter recalled that 'between the two [Reavey and Slonim] they had complete access to almost all European languages' and that their scope 'at the time must have been unequalled'.[7] The Bureau's objective was to place foreign authors with English-language publishers and vice versa. Among the impressive client list were contemporary French writers Georges Duhamel, André Malraux, Louis-Ferdinand Céline and André Gide, whose insightful account of a stay in the Soviet Union, *Retour de l'U.R.S.S.*, had taken France by storm, as well as the philosopher Jacques Maritain, who became a major influence on Coffey's development as a writer and philosopher.

Through the Bureau Littéraire Européen, Reavey supplied his friends with small but regular commissions for translations, offering Brian Coffey, for example, Jacques Maritain's essay 'Avec le peuple'.[8] He also introduced Coffey to Gide's *Retour de l'U.R.S.S.*, which Coffey perused in the French original and considered a 'most interesting read', requesting 'any cuttings from French reviews' from Reavey.[9]

II 'THE AIR YOU NEED TO LIVE': BRIAN COFFEY AND BORIS PASTERNAK

Under Reavey's influence, Brian Coffey's literary interests began to extend to Russian literature, including to the writer Boris Pasternak, whose work Reavey had championed through his critical study 'A First Essay Towards Pasternak' in the Cambridge review *Experiment*.[10] Reavey had been corresponding with Pasternak since the publication of this essay in 1930 and a friendship had started to develop. In 1932 Pasternak also entrusted his autobiographical novel *The Safe Conduct* to Reavey for translation and publication.[11] Reavey had started to share Pasternak's work with Coffey and other close friends and when Boris Pasternak, as part of the official Soviet delegation, attended the Congrès des Ecrivains (International Congress of Writers) in Paris in July 1935, Reavey and, it seems, Coffey were among the delegates.

In the years leading up to Stalin's Purges (1937–38), when thousands of artists, writers and intellectuals were murdered or condemned to the Gulag, the political pressures on Boris Pasternak had already begun to mount. His novel *The Safe Conduct* had been banned by the censor and Reavey later expressed surprise that Pasternak had even been chosen by the Soviet Writers Union to join the 'Stalinists, Trotzkyists, Surrealists, Traditionalists [and] Independents' at the congress, who were 'fighting each other tooth and nail'.[12] To everyone present, it was obvious that Pasternak struggled amidst the tension of the congress to make his plea for the independence of poetry, arguing that poetry 'will always be too simple to serve as a matter of discussion at assemblies'.[13] Reavey, who witnessed Pasternak's emotional address, later recalled that the atmosphere was 'heated and tense' and that Pasternak 'physically and mentally ... seemed to be labouring under great tension. On the platform he gasped for breath and uttered an extraordinary moaning sound which made the blood tingle and led one to conclude that he must be suffering deeply.'[14] Brian Coffey marked Pasternak's unforgettable address with a poem that vividly recalls his mental and physical struggle on the podium. Coffey's highly visual depiction strongly suggests that he too attended the congress in Reavey's company and was deeply affected by these extraordinary events:

Congrès Des Ecrivains Pour La Defence De La Culture
Juillet 1935

... the poor fellows who live by it ...
You'll not be in it long,
Boris Pasternak.
For when you breathe in
The air you need to live
There occurs such agony
Of tissue swollen with disease
You produce such noise
As makes these writers laugh.[15]

Coffey appears to have written the poem soon after the congress, during the summer of 1935, and discussed an early version with Reavey while still in Paris. Following Coffey's return to Dublin in early 1936 (after having passed his licentiate examination at the Institut Catholique), he redrafted the poem and posted it to Reavey, writing 'if it pleases you still as much as it did when I read you the first version may it be dedicated to you when it shall be published?'[16] Although the poem was not included in the collection *Third Person*, Coffey nevertheless considered it of importance, having sent an earlier version of the poem also to his friend Thomas MacGreevy.[17]

The short poem sets out to capture Pasternak's legendary appearance at the International Writers Congress, which has since become symbolic for the ensuing oppression and purges that led to the murder of thousands of Russian intellectuals and the silence of Pasternak and many others. Coffey openly questions the possibility of producing literature in a climate that causes not only ridicule ('as makes these writers laugh') but deprives the human being of the very essence of life – 'the air you need to live'. Most importantly, Coffey's poem reiterates Pasternak's categorical refusal for poetry 'to serve as a matter of discussion at assemblies'.[18]

Throughout his life, Coffey would maintain his view of the essential separation of poetry and politics, arguing in 'Concerning Making' that 'the political use of words kills the capacity to use words to make poems'.[19] Pasternak's plea for an understanding of poetry as an integral part of the human condition – the essential 'organic function of a happy human being'[20] – and his apparent physical struggle under the pressures of his coerced appearance at the International Writers Congress, seems to reverberate in Coffey's argument that

> for poets a word partakes as much of the bodily conditions of moving breath and unconscious mimetic reflexes of one's body in speech, as of all that emanates from the *heart* (hebraic sense of the term) in order to shape and individualise the breath of the body.[21]

At the time, Pasternak's and Coffey's argument that poetry should not be misused to serve a political cause, but belonged to a different aesthetic, was part of a wider debate in French Surrealism. In 1933 the influential Surrealists Paul Éluard and André Breton had been expelled from the French Communist party over disagreements with the more politically driven Louis Aragon. However, Pasternak's memorable appearance at the International Writers Congress in 1935 may well have provided the catalyst for Coffey's lifelong argument that 'the political use of words kills ... poems', as he emphatically stated in 'Concerning Making'.[22] For Coffey, a marked contrast to the increasing dominance of politics over poetry was the tragic suicide of the Russian poet Vladimir Mayakovsky in 1930, allegedly not caused by political pressures but by an unrequited love affair. Coffey chose the hard facts of the poet's death – 'on April 14, 1930, at 10.15 a.m. Mayakovsky shot himself' – as part of his central argument that poetry was an affair of the heart, writing: 'there was someone [Mayakovsky] alone between heaven and earth'.[23] Reavey's influence on Coffey's literary choices is once again palpable, as he had extensively translated the Russian Futurist, championed him among his Irish friends, and dedicated poems to Mayakovsky and Pasternak in his 1935 collection *Nostradam*.

George Reavey's comprehensive 1933 *Soviet Literature: An Anthology*, which he co-edited with his business partner Marc Slonim, constituted a critical resource for Coffey's interest in Russian poetry. The anthology contains several poems by Mayakovsky and Pasternak, translated and with biographical notes by Reavey, who described Mayakovsky's suicide as 'both a loss and a tremendous shock to Soviet Literature'.[24] Although there is undoubtedly a political dimension to Coffey's later poetry, such as *Death of Hektor* (1979) – which submits the historic example of a noble and honourable Greek hero to a contemporary and personal analysis – Coffey argued all his life for a wider humanist (non-political) view, as can be found in the apolitical poetry of Pasternak and Mayakovsky. Coffey described these views in a letter to Thomas MacGreevy, following a talk he gave on his poetry in London on 14 October 1962:

> I introduced my own views in favour of a poetry non nationalist, not tied to England, human and universal, drawing on all the literary resources available and speaking uncommittedly politically or religiously to all men and involving a far greater understanding of the act of creation itself than is ever the case in English or most of the so far Irish examples.[25]

III BRIAN COFFEY: EUROPA POET

Reavey's and Coffey's literary collaborations reached a new level in 1935 when Reavey launched his Europa Press in Paris. He later described his publishing ambitions in an interview with James Knowlson:

> I think I was very fed up with English publishers at the time. They were always turning down books of poems, not only by me, but by various other of my poet friends. So I decided to see what I could do about it myself.[26]

Reavey had involved Brian Coffey from the start in these plans and Coffey became one of the first authors to sign up to a contemporary poetry series – the Europa Poets. The supportive Coffey also took on the role of informing his circle of Irish friends of the newly founded press and invited submissions on Reavey's behalf. As early as March 1935 Coffey wrote enthusiastically to Thomas MacGreevy:

> Reavey has been suggesting a series of books by various people ...

Sam Beckett is one. Denis another. Myself a third possibly. We were wondering if you have another book of poems ready. It might be possible to produce a series of Irish poets.[27]

With the exception of MacGreevy, who had published his collection *Poems* in the previous year with William Heinemann in London, Beckett, Coffey and Devlin all agreed to contribute books of poems to the series. In May 1935 Reavey formally introduced the Europa Poets concept to his readership, when he announced, in his second collection *Nostradam*, a numbered series of six titles:

– *Nostradam* by George Reavey
– *Image At The Cinema* by Brian Coffey
– *Signes D'Adieu* by George Reavey
– *Echo's Bones And Other Precipitates* by Samuel Beckett
– *Poems* by Denis Devlin
– *Quixotic Perquisitions* by George Reavey

Over the next years, Reavey would see books by all four authors into publication, albeit, in some cases, with different content and under new titles: Denis Devlin's *Poems* were released as *Intercessions* in 1937 and Brian Coffey's poems *Image At The Cinema* were replaced by a new manuscript, *Third Person*, in 1938. The four Irish Europa Poets that had constituted Reavey's original list – Beckett, Coffey, Devlin and Reavey – were later joined by Paul Éluard and Charles Henri Ford, whose collection *The Garden of Disorder* (1937) was introduced by William Carlos Williams.

Central to Reavey's editorial concept, and an essential part of the Europa Press's enduring legacy today, was the idea of a contemporary poetry series illustrated by artists and engravers, which Reavey had defined as 'Limited editions – Poets illustrated by Various Engravers' in his 1935 collection *Nostradam*. The majority of the illustrations for the Europa Poets series came from the British print-maker S.W. Hayter[28] and from artists who had studied at his influential print-making studio Atelier 17 in Paris, including Max Ernst, Pablo Picasso, Roger Vieillard and John Buckland-Wright. The German-born Surrealist painter Max Ernst – a close friend of Paul Éluard – provided the striking cover design for Éluard's *Thorns of Thunder*, while Pablo Picasso contributed a portrait of Éluard in charcoal as frontispiece to the book. Roger Vieillard, a French artist who collaborated in the late 1930s extensively with Jack Kahane's Obelisk Press, provided an original engraving for twenty special edition copies of Reavey's love poems

Signes d'adieu (1935) and subsequently illustrated Apollinaire's poem 'Salomé' from his collection *Alcools*. The New Zealand-born engraver John Buckland-Wright illustrated Reavey's *Quixotic Perquisitions* (1939), the last book in the Europa Poets series. The impressive list of contemporary artists was joined by the Russian painter Pavel Tchelitchew, who provided a portrait of his lover, Charles Henri Ford, as frontispiece for *The Garden of Disorder* (1938).

S.W. Hayter was a close friend of Reavey and provided engravings for his collections *Faust's Metamorphoses* (1932) and *Nostradam* (1935), describing their collaborations as 'a happy combination'.[29] Reavey's introduction of Brian Coffey to S.W. Hayter marked the beginning of an equally fruitful artistic collaboration and lasting friendship, which was reaffirmed when, in 1979, Coffey and Hayter collaborated once more and the artist provided a series of engravings for the cycle *Death of Hektor*. Back in 1938, on the advice of Reavey, Coffey showed the manuscript of *Third Person* to Hayter, who, according to Coffey, 'is very enthusiastic about them and wants to do an engraving for the signed copies'.[30]

Hayter's engraving for *Third Person* (reproduced in this volume) – with 25 numbered copies featuring an original – depicts a central fluid, feminine figure against a backdrop of fragmented angular shapes, which dissolve into a horizon that appears to be both desert and sea. The figure's head is turned towards a ship's mast in the image background and towards the horizon, where torn sails appear to metamorphose into birdlike shapes. Further fragmented pieces are arranged in the picture foreground and seem to constitute a distorted shadow or a mirror-like reflection of the main scene. In his engraving, Hayter appears to have been clearly inspired by the concluding stanza of Coffey's poem 'Gentle':

> And let her stand beside the sea
> with the desert behind the reeds
> and let her mind be white sails
> that her eyes follow
> and let her smile out strength
>
> Eyes hair birds lips garden girdle of steel   (*PV*, p.35)

S.W. Hayter's illustration captures the themes that are central to Coffey's *Third Person*; themes that seem to arise from a preoccupation with an inner reality and the subconscious. These can also be found in the poetry of Paul Éluard.

IV 'AN OUT-OF-LOVE WORLD': THE INFLUENCE OF PAUL ÉLUARD

In fact, the greatest unifying interest and influence between the poet friends Brian Coffey and George Reavey was the love poetry of French Surrealist Paul Éluard. Reavey deeply admired Éluard, whom he described as a 'genius' and 'one of the few genuine love poets writing in an out-of-love world'.[31] Most significantly, he published, edited and part-translated the first ever English-language edition of Paul Éluard's love poetry, *Thorns of Thunder* (1936), through the Europa Press. Coffey shared Reavey's admiration of Éluard as a great love poet, and later commented in 'Concerning Making' that Éluard 'principally survives in love-lyrics which simply declare themselves ... continually worth one's attention'.[32] And just as Coffey related to Boris Pasternak's apolitical stance, he identified with Éluard's refusal to commit to a strict party line, despite his intermittent membership of the French Communist party. Most importantly, Éluard's Surrealist love poetry had a profound effect on the poetic development of Brian Coffey, in particular on *Third Person*.

It is likely that, as in the case of S.W. Hayter, George Reavey provided the introduction between Brian Coffey and Paul Éluard, with whom Reavey had become acquainted through his literary agency and close contacts with the French Surrealist group. By late 1935 or early 1936, Reavey had signed up the leading French Surrealist for the publication of translations of his love poems. The collection coincided with the opening of the First International Surrealist Exhibition at the New Burlington Galleries in June 1936. Reavey, who had relocated the Europa Press to London in early 1936, was a member of the organising committee, which was headed-up by the Paris-based Surrealists Paul Éluard, André Breton and Man Ray as well as English artist Roland Penrose. Reavey was in charge of a public Surrealist reading on 26 June 1936 at which Paul Éluard read from his poems, followed by renditions of other Surrealist works by Humphrey Jennings, E.L.T. Mesens as well as the young poets David Gascoyne and Dylan Thomas.

For the content of *Thorns of Thunder*, Reavey called once more on his core group of Irish friends, as translations of key Éluard poems by Denis Devlin, Samuel Beckett and Reavey himself account for a critical section of the book. Samuel Beckett's translations, for example, had been originally commissioned by Edward Titus and Samuel Putnam for the 'Surrealist Number' of *This Quarter* and had been praised by Titus as 'characterizable only in superlatives'.[33] Denis Devlin believed that Reavey initially considered Coffey for the role of editor, with Coffey later withdrawing when he heard of the involvement of the English art critic and editor, Herbert Read, whom the Irish circle intensely disliked:

> Brian was to edit this Éluard [*Thorns of Thunder*], give some translations himself and Sam and I were to give the rest. In his letter to me, Reavey mentioned that Herbert Read was to do an introduction, Picasso an engraving. I demurred at Read then I found that R. [Reavey] had not told Br. [Brian] and Sam about Read. Anyhow Br. + Sam refuse to appear with Read and I too.[34]

Reavey's invitation to Herbert Read to write the preface for *Thorns of Thunder* was undoubtedly a strategic move, as Read was an influential member of the English Surrealist organising committee and Reavey's objective was to establish the Europa Press in London's tight-knit literary scene. Their acquaintance was later instrumental when the publishing house Routledge & Sons, for whom Herbert Read acted as a reader, accepted Samuel Beckett's novel *Murphy* (1938) from Reavey, after over forty rejections of the manuscript.

Despite Devlin's and Beckett's reluctance to contribute to *Thorns of Thunder*, Reavey pressed ahead with their inclusion, sparking off temporary rows between the poet friends. The book appeared in time for Reavey's Surrealist reading in June 1936, with translations by Samuel Beckett and Denis Devlin – alongside David Gascoyne, Eugene Jolas, Man Ray, Ruthven Todd and Reavey himself – and marks one of the Europa Press's most significant achievements. The first ever English-language edition of Éluard's love poetry brings together a considerable body from Eluard's collections *Capitale de la douleur* (The City of Sorrow), 1926; *L'Amour la poésie* (Love Poetry), 1929; *La Vie immediate* (The Immediate Life), 1932; and *La Rose publique* (The Public Rose), 1934. The book also constituted the single biggest Europa Press print run – 600 copies, with 50 signed by the author. Reavey also prepared a special copy of the edition, *No.1*, which was printed on handmade paper and contained Picasso's original drawing of Éluard and an original MS by Paul Éluard. This commemorative copy was signed by the author, the artist and the translators.

Although Brian Coffey did not contribute to *Thorns of Thunder*, he extensively translated Paul Éluard and a selection of his translations was later included in the *Brian Coffey Special Issue* of the *Irish University Review*.[35] The reason for his omission is that Brian Coffey's renditions of Éluard date primarily to work published after the June 1936 publication of *Thorns of Thunder*. Among these are the poem 'Novembre 1936' – a political poem commemorating the resistance against Franco dur-

ing the Spanish Civil War – as well as poems written by Éluard during
and after the Second World War, including 'La Dernière nuit' (1942).
For Coffey, translation was not only a way of 'working with words between the times when poems come', as he wrote in 'Concerning Making', his deeper engagement with the work of others also had a
profound effect on his own writing.[36] J.C.C. Mays believes that 'to
consider his original work and his translation separately would be a
mistake'.[37] In fact, Coffey's poems in *Third Person*, a manuscript he
prepared in 1937, are clearly marked by the French poet's influence
and echo in their sensuality the intense emotions of Éluard's love poetry. We see this affinity, for example, in Éluard's poem 'L'Amoureuse',
which Reavey chose, in the skilful translation of Samuel Beckett, as
'Lady Love' for the opening poem of *Thorns of Thunder*:

L'Amoureuse	*Lady Love*
Elle est debout sur mes paupières	She is standing on my lids
Et ses cheveux sont dans la miens,	And her hair is in my hair
Elle a la forme de mes mains,	She has the colour of my eye
Elle a la couleur de mes yeux,	She has the body of my hand
Elle s'engloutit dans mon ombre	In my shade she is engulfed
Comme une pierre sur le ciel.[38]	As a stone against the sky[39]

In Éluard's poem, the consuming passions merge lover and beloved into
one being: 'She has the colour of my eye / She has the body of my hand
/ In my shade she is engulfed'. Éluard's concept of an all-encompassing
sexual and spiritual union enters the Surrealist domain, as the resulting
image no longer reflects outer reality but has become an inner vision of
the poet: 'She is standing on my lids'. In Brian Coffey's title poem, the
desire for the union of lover and beloved is taken a step further, as both
are merged into an even more consuming entity – 'one part of all' – that,
perhaps, represents the omnipresent yet abstract 'third person' of the
poem:

> She is one part of all
> as I am as I hold all
> as no stone does
> mine in her way
> hers in mine
> By glens of exile
> if she turns
> love was needed   ('Third Person', *PV*, p.36)

Although Coffey's dreamlike imagery and soothing rhythm appear to enter the Surrealist realm, he remains at a sceptical distance and questions, at the same time as he creates, the free-flowing associations of lover with 'stone', 'lilac' or 'bird' that are so typical in Éluard's Surrealist mode, where the lover has become 'engulfed / As a stone against the sky':

> She is no stone no lilac
> no bird more beautiful than stars
> takes what she takes by right of grace
> to make hearts equal
> unequal were strange
> Her fingers play in silk hair
> she wishes wounds   ('Third Person', *PV*, p.36)

Coffey's denial of the lover being compared to 'stone' or 'lilac' is evidence of his inherent distance and later abandonment of Surrealism. Stan Smith believes that Coffey rebels against the 'Romantic cult of the image',[40] which Surrealism took a step further still by delving deep into the unconsciousness for its imagery. And J.C.C. Mays argues that *Third Person* constituted a mere 'flirtation with Surrealism'.[41]

Despite these arguments, Coffey's poetry is clearly indebted to Surrealist ideas, in particular the abandonment of an outer reality in favour of an engagement with an interior world and the subconscious. Coffey found these influences not only in the poetry of Paul Éluard, but also among his close circle of Irish friends, such as Beckett's poems *Echo's Bones and Other Precipitates* and Reavey's cycle *Signes d'adieu*, which were released by the Europa Press in 1935 and predate *Third Person* by three years. Both collections deal with the loss of a lover and the resulting sense of inner withdrawal.

George Reavey had written *Signes d'adieu* – a cycle of intensely interior poems, described by himself as 'poems on the edge'[42] – after the death of his French lover Andrée Conte. His deep-felt loss sparked off a period of intense creativity, as Reavey quickly wrote a series of twenty-eight poems between 24 November and 23 December 1932.[43] While these poems, entitled *Frailties* or *The Frailty of Love*, have never been published as a collection in their original English, Reavey selected fourteen poems for the French edition *Signes d'adieu* in the translation of Pierre Charnay. Reavey shared these poems among his group of Irish friends in Paris and later recalled that 'Beckett admired them very much'.[44] The poems remained of lifelong importance to Reavey and were, in 1973, set to music by the internationally renowned American composer Barbara Kolb and premièred at an arts festival at the University of Wisconsin, Milwaukee.

The book's title, *Signes d'adieu*, is taken from the penultimate poem of the collection, in which Reavey's poetic voice compares – with the same intense sensuality as Éluard and Coffey – the affections of women to the 'farewell of dying stars' ['signes d'adieu d'étoiles mourantes'], only to arrive resignedly at 'the inconsequence of all' ['l'inconséquence de la plupart']:

> Femmes si réelles votre réalité n'est pas sûre
> quant à ce qui est des caresses
> signes d'adieu d'étoiles mourantes
> apposition des mains mésintelligence
> des lèvres et des yeux
> l'enchaînement de certains moments
> et l'inconséquence de la plupart[45]

The women in Reavey's poem are as fugitive as Coffey's absent third person or the ghost-like dissolving figure of S.W. Hayter's etching for that collection. Both poets compare the lover to stars, emphasize her elusiveness and ultimately question her very existence. The separation and absence of the lover is, again, a recurring theme in the poetry of Paul Éluard, as in the poem 'Their Eyes are Always Pure', which Reavey translated for *Thorns of Thunder*:

> Their wings are my wings, and their flight
> Is all I know as it stirs my woe,
> Their flight of star and light,
> Their flight of earth, their flight of stone,
> Upon the billows of their wings.[46]

Both Coffey and Reavey borrow in *Third Person* and *Signes d'adieu*, respectively, stylistic innovation from Éluard. Éluard's use of repetition and his complete disregard for punctuation (which causes deliberate syntactical ambiguity) finds echoes, for example, in Coffey's poem 'Gentle', with its uninterrupted flow of words, leading to startling new associations: 'Eyes hair birds lips garden girdle of steel' (*PV*, p.35).

Éluard, in turn, had adopted this technique from Guillaume Apollinaire (1880–1918), one of the first Surrealists, who is credited with having coined the actual term 'Surrealism'. Apollinaire's life had been tragically cut short when he succumbed to the Paris influenza epidemic and died in November 1918, aged only 38. His famous love poem 'Le Pont Mirabeau' breaks from stylistic convention by omitting almost all

punctuation, relying heavily instead on the use of repetition to emphasize the transitory nature of love: 'Love runs away like running water
flows / Love flows away'.[47] The pain experienced by the loss of the
lover is so intense that the poetic self refuses to re-immerse himself in
the flow of life but remains fixed and motionless like the bridge. The
central phrase – 'Let the night come: strike the hour / The days go past
while I stand here' ['Vienne la nuit sonne l'heure / Les jours s'en vont
je demeure'] is repeated over and over again, while the static elements
of the poem – Le Pont Mirabeau and the lover – are contrasted with the
movement of the water and the fleeting emotions of the beloved:

> Under the Pont Mirabeau the Seine
> Flows with our loves
> Must I recall again?
> Joy has always used to follow after pain
>
> > Let the night come: strike the hour
> > The days go past while I stand here
>
> Hands holding hands let us stay face to face
> While under this
> Bridge our arms make slow race
> Long looks in a tired wave at a wave's pace
>
> > Let the night come: strike the hour
> > The days go past while I stand here
> > ('The Pont Mirabeau')[48]

Both *Third Person* and *Signes d'adieu* engage with the recurring themes
of Éluard's and Apollinaire's poetry – lost love, otherness and separation. Dónal Moriarty believes that, in Coffey's case, the separation is
self-inflicted, arguing that '*Third Person* plainly shows that ... people
will always be attracted to others, form relationships and subsequently
sever or endanger them for reasons they do not fully understand'
(*ABC*, p.24). In the poem 'Gentle', separation is not the outcome but
a precondition of the relationship between lover and beloved and the
lover's desire for a union is futile from the start:

> She lives in pure loss alone
> minds in silence
> the charm of secret
> You shall not find to give her
> the form of touch she needs   ('Gentle', *PV*, p.34)

In *Signes d'adieu* the relationship is prematurely terminated by the lover's death, with the resulting pain appearing all the more immediate. But Reavey arrives at the same conclusion as Coffey; the ardent desire for a union that cannot be achieved. The theme of unfulfilled love is re-iterated throughout *Signes d'adieu* and emphasized through the use of repetition (as in the case of Apollinaire). For example, in the poem 'O ma soeur des jours noirs', a soothing dreamlike atmosphere is created as the fleeting lover is compared, again and again, to a brief illumina-tion – like a flash of light – of the sky ['Lumière brève d'un ciel']:

> O ma soeur des jours noirs
> Lumière brève d'un ciel
> Qui chante le cantique d'une fin
> Soeur cri de nos jours
> Je veux prendre ta main légère
> O ma soeur des jours noirs
> Lumière brève d'un ciel[49]

While Reavey uses punctuation sparsely in the English-language orig-inal, thereby allowing the poems to find their own rhythm, Charnay's French translation almost completely omits punctuation. The reader finds only an occasional question mark to reiterate the central motif of lost love as, for example, in the poignant but rhetorical question of the opening poem: 'où donc est mon amour?' ['oh where then is my love?'].[50]

Coffey creates an equally soothing sound and rhythm in *Third Per-son* through the use of repetition and the uninterrupted flow of the poetic voice. For critic J.C.C. Mays, who wrote the preface to *Poems and Versions*, the way Coffey's poetry 'sounds' is essential to its un-derstanding: 'It can engage a reader at levels where the mind moves with the same pulse as in the author who wrote the lines' (*PV*, p.5). For example, in the poem 'Dedication', Coffey imposes a severely re-stricted palette of words, yet the subtle variations in the verb 'turn' – from past ('turned'), present ('turn') and imperative/future ('must turn') – gives the poem a sense of infinity ['again and after'] of ever-lasting loss and pain:

> *Dedication*
>
> For whom on whom then
> and before
> whose eyes desired turned

For whom on whom now
each now
whose eyes desired turn

For who on whom then
again and after
whose eyes desired must turn

For whom pain is not loss
For whom loss of is not pain
For whom want of is pain of loss   (*PV*, p.23)

Dónal Moriarty believes that Coffey deliberately 'suspends any sense of temporal progression' in *Third Person* in order to render emotional experience as a constant state of mind (*ABC*, p.25). On occasion, temporal progression is even reversed, as in the poem 'One Way', where the poetic self 'sees what he has not seen' and 'hears what he has not heard' (*PV*, p.29). Again, we find parallels in the work of Paul Éluard, who suspends time in the 1932 poem 'On a New Night' to create an everlasting (erotic) fantasy – 'Red gloves, a red mask / And black stockings / ... you quite naked' – from past, present and future lovers: 'Women with whom I have lived, / Women with whom I live / Women with whom I shall live / The same woman always'.[51] Although Coffey's poetry lacks Éluard's expressed eroticism, the sensuous effect of a heightened awareness and a new state of mind remains the same. While Coffey's poetic voice achieves a new reality of lasting otherness and separation, Éluard's poetic self loses all sense of time and place in the ecstasy of his fantasy.

Many of the parallels in Brian Coffey's *Third Person* and Reavey's *Signes d'adieu* can be traced back to the mutual influence of Paul Éluard, the French Surrealists and the close collaboration and friendship between Reavey and Coffey. These collaborations would continue for some time; for example, at Reavey's request, Coffey provided a poem on the Belgium painter Geer van Velde for a catalogue to coincide with the painter's show at the Guggenheim Jeune gallery in London in 1938. Both Reavey and Beckett had been instrumental in persuading Peggy Guggenheim to mount an exhibition of their friend's work in her newly established gallery and prepared the material for the catalogue, which appeared in the *London Bulletin*.[52] Reavey and Coffey were also able to revive their friendship after the Second World War, when Reavey had settled in New York and Coffey significantly contributed to the later appreciation of Reavey's work.

V BRIAN COFFEY AND GEORGE REAVEY: THE 'NOMAD BLAZE'

However, there is another unifying but more elusive element to Coffey's and Reavey's poetry, which reaches beyond the realm of mutual influences and artistic collaborations. Both Coffey's *Third Person* and Reavey's *Signes d'adieu* radiate an overwhelming sense of existential loneliness, as perceptively embodied in the solitary figure of S.W. Hayter's engraving for *Third Person*. Stan Smith emphasizes the overwhelming feeling of exile in Coffey's poetry and argues that in 'Coffey's thought ... exile is not so much a social condition as an ontological given, the necessary ground for existence'.[53]

This is perhaps illustrated in the following extracts from Coffey's title poem 'Third Person' and Reavey's 'How Many Fires'. The latter poem formed part of the original manuscript of *Frailties* (1932), was later reworked by Reavey, and posthumously selected by Edward Germain for an anthology of *English and American Surrealist Poetry* (1978):

Third Person	*How Many Fires*
Who shall bend	How many fires
sails white wings	what horizons
the sun with the sea	strangeness of the sky
soothe them with south hand	human face stranger
until ice melt	where shall I stake
heart flame	the flame of my hands
rains of fulfilment	where stay a firebrand heart
bless the cedar tree *(PV*, p.37)	in its nomad blaze[54]

Coffey's and Reavey's poems in *Third Person* and *Signes d'adieu* are ultimately interior and placeless. Their poetry radiates a profound sense of exile and homelessness, as the poetic self is either engulfed in a 'nomad blaze' or finds himself cast among 'sails white wings'. The effect of such estrangement and otherness is further emphasised in both poems by the juxtaposition of irreconcilable opposites – 'ice' and 'flame' and 'stay' and 'nomad'. While Coffey's poem hints at a resolution of this inherent conflict – 'rains of fulfilment' – Reavey continues to search for a place that allows the possibility to create and be creative – 'where shall I stake / the flame of my hands'. Both poems are different expressions of a mutual experience of exile. In Brian Coffey's case, as J.C.C. Mays argues, this exile differed from the other Irish expatriates in being largely 'involuntary',[55] while Reavey was driven by an inherent restlessness, which may have had its origins in his traumatic childhood exile from revolutionary Russia followed by years of nomadic existence.

However, this sense of homelessness and otherness equally permeates the poetry of fellow Irish 'Europa Poets' Samuel Beckett and Denis Devlin, who both published collections in the 1930s in Reavey's Europa Press. Gerald Dawe argues in his essay 'An Absence of Influence: Three Modernist Poets' that exile can also be read as a 'metaphor of artistic space that embraces a spectrum of experience' and refers in particular to Denis Devlin, who spent most of his nomadic life as a diplomat in foreign territories, as the 'poet of separation' and the 'poet of distance'.[56] And although the urban settings of Beckett's *Echo's Bones* (1935) and Devlin's *Intercessions* (1937) are far more recognisable than the largely interior landscapes of Coffey and Reavey, a shared sense of inner exile and alienation from their outer surroundings is common to them all. The poems of Beckett's *Echo's Bones* are populated with fugitive voices and exiled creatures on seemingly erratic journeys around the city of Dublin, where recognisable places are dissolved and metamorphosed through free-flowing mental associations into surreal inner worlds, such as in the poem 'Enueg II', where the poetic voice finds himself:

> lying on O'Connell Bridge
> goggling at the tulips of the evening
> the green tulips
> shining round the corner like an anthrax
> shining on Guinness's barges[57]

The poetic voice in Denis Devlin's *Intercessions* experiences a similar sense of alienation and exile from his environment. The poet's solitary and stagnant position in the poem 'Liffey Bridge' (which invokes the abandoned lover of Apollinaire's 'The Pont Mirabeau') is juxtaposed with the 'trailing' movement of the unknown passer-by: 'The young with masks and / The old with faces / Such an assassin / Such a world!' The poetic self feels utterly distanced from his environment and is visibly repelled by the prevailing sense of decay in both buildings and human beings:

> In limp doorways
> They try out their heaven
> They grind at love
> With gritted kisses
> Then eyes re-opened
> Behold slack flesh
> Such an assassin
> Such a world   ('Liffey Bridge')[58]

For Devlin, the only reaction against this stagnant and decaying environment is one of 'flight', as the poetic voice turns away from static 'deaf quay walls' and joins instead the liberating forces of wind and water: 'Wind weave / Try to weave / Something or other / From flight and water'. This sense of alienation, detachment and inner exile expressed in the poem 'Liffey Bridge' forms a recurring theme in the poetry of Denis Devlin, and Susan Schreibman concludes that 'foreigners, foreignness, being a foreigner in one's own land, being a foreigner abroad, being foreign to those one loves and is loved by, as well as one's self, is central to Devlin's œuvre'.[59]

When reading the poems of the Europa Poets alongside the work of French Surrealists Paul Éluard and Guillaume Apollinaire or the Russian Futurists like Vladimir Mayakovsky, it becomes clear that the foreignness and existential homelessness of the poetry of Coffey, Reavey, Beckett and Devlin was a shared experience and places these writers firmly at the heart of the Modernist movement. Although their individual experience of exile and homelessness is a different one, their poetic response is unified by a *zeitgeist* of profound angst, born out of the spiritual chaos left by the First World War, followed by revolution, economic crisis and the rise of totalitarian regimes. For the tormented poet Vladimir Mayakovsky, this existential angst expressed itself (in the translation of George Reavey) as a form of inner exile – the 'pavement / of my trampled soul' as 'I go / and solitary weep'.[60] Paul Éluard, who lived through the horrors of two world wars – having fought in the trenches of the First World War and joined the French Resistance during the Second – experienced an everlasting sense of 'otherness', as in the poem 'In Order To Live Here', selected here in the skilful translation of Brian Coffey:

> I lived in the single noise of crackling flames,
> In the perfume only in their heat;
> I was like a ship sinking in land-locked water,
> Like a corpse I was all of one kind.[61]

By a strange coincidence Paul Éluard's haunting image of a 'ship sinking in land-locked water' (in Coffey's translation) evokes once again S.W. Hayter's powerful engraving for *Third Person*, where a solitary ship mast is engulfed in a haunting setting of both desert and sea. *Third Person* – a powerful collaboration between Brian Coffey, George Reavey and S.W. Hayter, which is deeply marked by the poetry of Paul Éluard and the prevailing *zeitgeist* of existential homelessness – is therefore testament to a key matrix of influences, collaborations and shared experiences of exile in Irish and European Modernism.

NOTES

1. Brian Coffey, 'Tributes to George Reavey', *Journal of Beckett Studies*, vol. 2 (Summer 1977), p.8.
2. *Lace Curtain*, no. 4 (summer 1971), edited by Michael Smith with the assistance of Brian Coffey (Dublin: New Writers' Press). Republished as *Irish Poetry: The Thirties Generation*, ed. Michael Smith (Dublin: Raven Arts Press, 1983).
3. David Gascoyne, *Collected Journals 1936–1942* (London: Skoob Books, 1991), p.343.
4. George Reavey, 'Some Russian Notes', *This Quarter*, ed. Edward Titus, vol. 3, no. 1 (Summer 1930), pp.12–19.
5. Samuel Putnam, ed, *The European Caravan* (New York: Brewer, Warren & Putnam, 1931). *The European Caravan* was compiled and edited by Samuel Putnam (Spain) with Maida Castelhun Darnton (Germany), George Reavey (Russia) and Jacob Bronowski (Ireland and England) acting as associate editors for the individual sections. The unpublished Russian volume was later reissued by George Reavey and Marc Slonim as *Soviet Literature: An Anthology* (London: Wishart & Co., 1933).
6. Putnam, *European Caravan*, p.x.
7. S.W. Hayter, 'Tributes to George Reavey', *Journal of Beckett Studies*,vol. 2 (summer 1977), p.6.
8. Brian Coffey, letter to George Reavey, 4 March 1937. Box 48, folder 2 (Reavey Collection), HRHRC, University of Texas at Austin.
9. Ibid., box 48, folder 2, HRHRC, University of Texas at Austin.
10. George Reavey, 'First Essay Towards Pasternak', *Experiment* vol. 6, ed. G.F. Noxon (October 1930), pp.14–17.
11. George Reavey, 'How I first Discovered and Then Met Boris Pasternak', in *The Poetry of Boris Pasternak 1917–1959*, trans. George Reavey, ed. George Reavey (New York: G.P. Putnam, 1959), pp. 49–50.
12. Ibid., pp.52–53.
13. Ibid., p.53.
14. Ibid.
15. The poem is included in a letter from Brian Coffey to George Reavey, 14 February 1936. Box 48, folder 2 (Reavey Collection), HRHRC, University of Texas at Austin.
16. Brian Coffey in same letter to George Reavey, 14 February 1936. Box 48, folder 2 (Reavey Collection), HRHRC, University of Texas at Austin.
17. As is made apparent in a letter from Brian Coffey to Thomas MacGreevy, 2 February 1936. MS 8110/22, Trinity College Dublin. Letter includes a typescript of the poem.
18. Reavey, 'How I first Discovered and Then Met Boris Pasternak', p.53.
19. Brian Coffey, 'Extracts from "Concerning Making"', *Lace Curtain*, no. 6 (1978), p.31.
20. Reavey, 'How I first Discovered and Then Met Boris Pasternak', p.53.
21. Coffey, 'Extracts from "Concerning Making"', p.32.
22. Ibid., p.31.
23. Ibid., p.32.
24. George Reavey, 'Revolution and Proletarian Poets – Vladimir Mayakovsky', in *Soviet Literature: An Anthology*, p.360.
25. Brian Coffey, letter to Thomas MacGreevy, 16 October 1962. MS 8110/55, TCD.
26. George Reavey in an interview with James Knowlson on 6 August 1971 subsequently transcribed, edited and published by Knowlson in the *Journal of Beckett Studies*. James Knowlson, 'George Reavey and Samuel Beckett's Early Writing', *Journal of Beckett Studies*, vol. 2 (Summer 1977), p.10.
27. Brian Coffey, letter to Thomas MacGreevy, 15 May 1935. MS 8110/18, TCD.
28. The British artist S.W. Hayter moved to Paris in 1926 where he met the Surrealist painters Yves Tanguy and Max Ernst as well as the group's leader, the poet André Breton. Hayter, who while in Paris began to experiment with dry-point, woodcuts and aquatints, set up his first studio in 1927 to develop print-making as an art form. When he moved his studio to number 17

rue Campagne-Première in Montparnasse in 1933, it took on the legendary name of *Atelier Dix-Sept* (Atelier 17).

29. Hayter, 'Tributes to George Reavey', p.6.
30. Brian Coffey, letter to George Reavey, 29 April 1938. Box 48, folder 2 (Reavey Collection), HRHRC, University of Texas at Austin.
31. George Reavey, 'Editorial Foreword', in Paul Eluard, *Thorns of Thunder: Selected Poems*, ed. George Reavey (London: Europa Press and Stanley Nott, 1936), p.vii.
32. Coffey, 'Extracts From "Concerning Making"', p.34.
33. Edward Titus, 'Editorial', *This Quarter: Surrealist Number*, vol. 5, no. 1 (September 1932), p.6.
34. Denis Devlin, letter to Thomas MacGreevy, undated, postmarked envelope 16 March 1936. MS 8112/9, TCD.
35. Brian Coffey's translations from the French of Paul Éluard can be found in the *Irish University Review: Brian Coffey Special Issue*, vol. 5, no. 1 (spring 1975), pp.99–103. See also Coffey's translations from French poets (including Éluard) in the *Etruscan Reader VII*, featuring work by Alice Notley, Wendy Mulford and Brian Coffey (Newcastle under Lyme: Etruscan Books, 1997).
36. Coffey, 'Extracts from "Concerning Making"', p.35.
37. J.C.C. Mays, 'Introductory Essay', in *Irish University Review: Brian Coffey Special Issue*, p.22.
38. Paul Éluard, *Selected Poems*, trans. Gilbert Bowen (London: Calder, 1998), p.38.
39. Paul Éluard, 'L'Amoureuse', trans. Samuel Beckett, *Thorns of Thunder*, p.1.
40. Stan Smith, 'On Other Grounds: The Poetry of Brian Coffey', in *Two Decades of Irish Writing: A Critical Survey*, ed. Douglas Dunn (London: Carcanet, 1975), p.60.
41. J.C.C. Mays, *Irish University Review: Brian Coffey Special Issue*, p.16.
42. George Reavey in an interview with James Knowlson, *Journal of Beckett Studies*, p.11.
43. The poems are dated in handwriting from 24.11.32 to 23.12.32 in an unpublished typescript of *Frailty of Love*. Box 14, folder 5 (Reavey Collection), HRHRC, University of Texas at Austin.
44. George Reavey in an interview with James Knowlson, *Journal of Beckett Studies*, p.11.
45. George Reavey, *Signes d'adieu*, translated into French by Pierre Charnay (Paris: Europa Press, 1935), p.21.
46. Éluard, 'Their Eyes are Always Pure', translated by George Reavey, *Thorns of Thunder*, p.10.
47. Guillaume Apollinaire, *Selected Poems*, trans. and intro. Oliver Bernard (London: Anvil Press, 1986), pp.32–33.
48. Ibid.
49. Reavey, *Signes d'adieu*, p.20.
50. Ibid., p.9.
51. Éluard, *Selected Poems*, p.41.
52. Brian Coffey, 'The Painter Geer van Velde', *London Bulletin*, vol. 2 (May 1938).
53. Smith, 'On Other Grounds', p.59.
54. Edward B. Germain, ed., *English and American Surrealist Poetry* (Harmondsworth: Penguin, 1978), p.130.
55. J.C.C. Mays, *Irish University Review: Brian Coffey Special Issue*, p.16.
56. Gerald Dawe, 'An Absence of Influence: Three Modernist Poets' (1989), in *The Proper Word, Collected Criticism*, ed. Nicholas Allen (Omaha: Creighton University Press, 2007), pp.142, 149.
57. Samuel Beckett, *Collected Poems in English and French* (New York: Grove Press, 1971), pp.13–14.
58. Denis Devlin, *Collected Poems*, ed. Brian Coffey (Dublin: Dolmen Press, 1964), p.95.
59. Susan Schreibman, 'Denis Devlin (1908–1959)', in *The UCD Aesthetic: Celebrating 150 Years of UCD Writers*, ed. Anthony Roche (Dublin: New Island, 2005), p.100.
60. Reavey, *Soviet Literature: An Anthology*, pp.360–61.
61. Paul Éluard, 'In Order to Live Here', trans. Brian Coffey, *Irish University Review: Brian Coffey Special Issue*, p.100.

CHAPTER SEVEN

Le Livre d'artiste
Mallarmé, Reavey, Coffey

THOMAS DILLON REDSHAW

In the early 1970s Michael Smith's little magazine *Lace Curtain* countered the antiquarian drift of Liam Miller's Dolmen Press by championing the accomplishments of the Paris Modernists – Thomas MacGreevy, Samuel Beckett, Denis Devlin and Brian Coffey.[1] Excepting young poets then closely associated with Smith's New Writers' Press – Augustus Young, Trevor Joyce, Gerard Smyth – few Irish poets and critics then welcomed this invitation to Modernism.[2] Despite an efflorescence of interest in the poetry of these Continental Modernists of the interwar decades – especially after the 1995 publication of *Modernism and Ireland: The Poetry of the 1930s* – the least examined of them has nevertheless remained Brian Coffey.[3] Excepting Dónal Moriarty's *The Art of Brian Coffey* (2000), many extended readings of Coffey's poems share a preference for 'Missouri Sequence' (1962).[4] First published in the *Irish University Review* and then gathered into the New Writers Press' edition of his *Selected Poems* (1971), 'Missouri Sequence' chronicles Coffey's sometimes fraught American sojourn on the western bank of the Mississippi at St Louis University, a Jesuit institution. Coffey makes the turns of the sequence's four parts accessible with almost confessional expressions of exilic sentiment, and he leavens each part by wrangling with the role of the poet and the nature of poetry in the context of his neo-Thomism. 'Missouri Sequence' constitutes, as well, an energetic prolegomenon to the best of Coffey's later work – chiefly *Advent* (1975) and *Death of Hektor* (1979). And it was after the former poetic sequence that Coffey named his own experiments in letterpress printing beginning in 1966.[5]

The chapbooks that Brian Coffey printed in London under his Advent Books imprint – for example, *The Time The Place* (1969) and its two-colour lithograph or *Bridget Ann* (1972) and its linocut – convincingly express his enduring interest in the interplay of written word with visual image. Late in his career Coffey gave that interest free range in one of his 'mean smiles', a satiric farrago titled *The Big Laugh* (1976). Judging from more easily available examples of his poetry – like *Selected Poems* (1971, 1983) or Coffey's *Poems and Versions 1929–1990* (1991) – many readers would not credit this later bent of Coffey's sensibility.[6] That may be especially so if casual readers recall in only a stereotypical way Coffey's Thomist learning and the influence of his studies with Jacques Maritain. The 1975 *Brian Coffey Special Issue* of *Irish University Review* provides the handiest record of Coffey's engagement with the visual arts in the sequence *Leo* (1975) – another of his 'mean smiles' – and its colloquy with drawings by Geoffrey Prowse, not to mention the typographical experiments of *Advent*, or Coffey's own stylized bird emblem on the review's cover.[7]

The austere letterpress presentation of the Menard Press's 1982 printing of *Death of Hektor*, his most durable long poem, hints at Coffey's connection with the gravure of Stanley William Hayter (1901–88) in two factual notes – one in the colophon and the other in the 'select bio-bibliographical note'.[8] An artist of great discipline and inventive energy, Hayter created nine engravings for Coffey's *Death of Hektor*, turning the poem into a *livre d'artiste*.[9] Coffey's connection with Hayter had come through George Reavey's Europa Press in Paris, where Coffey had his *Three Poems* (1933) printed by Adrienne Monnier in Paris.[10] In 1927 Hayter founded an open studio in Paris to explore methods of gravure, which he named Atelier 17 after moving to rue Campagne-Première in the fourteenth arondissement in 1933. In 1936, following International Surrealism, Reavey removed his press to London. Three years later, with the coming of the Second World War, Hayter moved to London and thence to the United States, where he set up Atelier 17 in New York at the close of the war in 1945.[11] An early advocate of Hayter's work, Reavey issued Coffey's *Third Person* (1938) in London in the uneasy months during the Munich crisis. *Third Person* was the eighth of nine Europa Press printings dating from 1932. Its signed edition came, in Reavey's words, 'illustrated with an original engraving by S.W. Hayter'.

Between the wars Paris had become the locus of a displaced avant-garde including, of course, the Joyce circle to which the Irish Modernists of the 1930s were tangentially aligned.[12] Through Thomas MacGreevy, Coffey was introduced to Joyce at the bedside of Samuel Beckett, who had been the victim of a stabbing incident.[13] Beckett's

impression of Devlin and Coffey's poems was not altogether sympathetic. Writing to MacGreevy, Beckett complained that he did not 'get
much kick out of Coffey and Devlin, their pockets full of calm precious poems', and he later found Coffey 'very *fort* on his subject but
the poetry is another pair of sleeves'.[14] Coffey's 'subject' was not chemistry, which he had come to Paris to study in 1930, but the neo-Thomist
aesthetic and criticism of Jacques Maritain (1898–1975), with whom
he studied between 1933 and 1936, returning in 1937 to write his *doc-
torat* on Thomas Aquinas and the idea of order. Even so, in his 1934
review for Dublin readers, 'Recent Irish Poetry', Beckett approvingly
linked Coffey and Denis Devlin by asserting their reaction against the
'*Gossoons Wunderhorn*' of the Revival's romanticization of Ireland.[15]
What Beckett recognized in MacGreevy, Devlin and Coffey was their
efforts to counter, in Terence Brown's phrase, the 'absence of that urge
to make it new' in Irish poetry.[16] That MacGreevy, Beckett, Devlin and
Coffey left Ireland after the Irish Civil War for the cosmopolitan milieu of Paris underscores, of course, their own artistic and intellectual
ambitions. Their time on the Continent in the 1920s and 1930s hints
at their sense of Ireland's cultural claustrophobia and the enervation
of those Modernist attributes that had characterized the Literary
Revival.[17]

A similar sort of cultural exhaustion may explain, as well, why
Michael Smith's advocacy of these poets and of Modernism in the *Lace
Curtain* in the early 1970s – at the outset of the Northern Troubles –
then found so little cultural purchase in Ireland.[18] In 1971 Michael
Smith's New Writers' Press and not the Dolmen Press published the
Selected Poems that Brian Coffey had offered to Liam Miller in July
1965, two months after the publication of *Dice Thrown Never Will
Annul Chance*.[19] Contrary to Coffey's expectations, Miller never committed the resources of the Dolmen Press to Coffey's own œuvre –
preferring rather, to keep to the work of Denis Devlin.[20] Indeed, it was
Miller's interest in republishing the *Irish University Review* edition of
Devlin's *Collected Poems* (1964) that led to his association with Coffey. On 21 September 1963, when the *Irish University Review* was in
press, Coffey wrote to Miller from London offering an edition of Devlin's *The Heavenly Foreigner* and his translation of Mallarmé's typographical poem. Coffey sent over his translation on 13 October 1965.
Replying with enthusiastic promptness, Miller let Coffey know that he
had met Reavey in New York City, reminding Coffey that Reavey had
published Coffey's *Third Person* in Paris. Reavey had hinted to Miller
that some sheets of *Third Person* remained in storage, and so Miller

now suggested to Coffey that Dolmen might have an interest in reis-
suing *Third Person* (1938). In doing so, Miller suggested also that Dolmen might become the medium for Coffey's return to the parish of
Irish poetry that was stirring to life in the mid-1960s.[21]

What Coffey had sent to Miller was his manuscript translation of
Mallarmé's 21-page poem *Un Coup de dés jamais n'abolira le hasard*
as printed in the 1914 Pléiade edition of Mallarmé. Characteristically,
Miller seized upon this text as if he had discovered a new formal and
visual concept. Miller's enthusiasm for the typographical jigsaw of Coffey's typescript derived as much from his delight in the printerly challenge it represented as from the translation itself.[22] Coffey followed
this manuscript with a letter explaining

> I wrote it out, preserving, as you will see the spacing of N.R.F.
> edition. N.B.
> the unit & 'a stating minim darkling'. Mallarmé intended a
> reference to minion (?) type – can the type affect the poem at this
> point?[23]

Note Coffey's initial emphasis on the verb 'wrote'. Coffey's actual
manuscript possesses, as well, the characteristics of a transcript of the
original text. Painstakingly, Coffey carefully printed out in pencil his
English wording according to the situation of the words on the page
in the French text, and then he lettered in the words in ink, rendering
his final text as a twice-removed calk (*calque*) of the original. The manuscript makes evident the exacting care that Coffey took to replicate
the visual character of the original's visual display.[24] Miller had
this transcription typed in the Dolmen offices and returned a copy to
Coffey.[25]

Coffey's 1964 introduction to his translation of *Un Coup de dés*
proposes that Mallarmé's poem 'is the ultimate evidence of Mallarmé's
sustained effort towards original utterance'.[26] At Liam Miller's suggestion, Coffey followed his own introduction with a translation of
Mallarmé's preface to the first printing of the poem in *Cosmopolis*
(1897).[27] Mallarmé begins diffidently – 'I would rather this Note were
not read' – but ends by proposing that the text of any poem constitutes
a visual 'score', thus raising the printed page to the condition of
music.[28] While the idea of the poem that Mallarmé bequeathed to
Modernism circulated fruitfully through the immediate postwar
decades in Paris right through the Beat 1950s in San Francisco, *Un
Coup de dés* itself has had less currency. It is not just humility that leads
Coffey to identify the difficulty of Mallarmé's accomplishment by

asserting that his 'present translation offers ... an approximation to a *calk* of *Un Coup de dés*' (*DT*, p.5). Rather, Coffey recognizes in the term 'calk' the belatedness of his own effort, mindful that his contact with Mallarmé's poem came in Paris during his studies with Jacques Maritain in the 1930s, when he was keeping at a tangent from the environs of the Joyce circle.[29] Alluding in detail to Joyce scholarship of the 1950s, Coffey recirculates the suggestion that, more than the actual text, the notion that Mallarmé's poem had played a role in Joyce's composing of *Finnegans Wake* and earlier, perhaps, in the writing of *Ulysses*.[30] Coffey closes the preface with this assertion: 'The present translation follows the text and, thanks to Mr Liam Miller, the typographical lay-out of the 1914 edition of the poem' (*DT*, p.6).

Coffey's twice hand-inscribed translation does not always 'follow' the typographic display or score of *Un Coup de dés* as laid out in the definitive setting that Mallarmé approved for the Pléiade editon of his work. Indeed, that Coffey departed from it is a signal point of Dónal Moriarty's characterization of Coffey's accomplishments as a practitioner of 'deviant translation'. In Moriarty's detailed exegesis, the adjective 'deviant' is a positive one because it highlights those points at which Coffey's practice of translation reveals the deepest themes – and inner contentions – of his own poetry (*ABC*, pp.53, 57, 59). And Moriarty resorts first to a Bakhtinian and then to a musical analogy – 'dialogic' then 'polyphonic' – so as to underscore the importance of *Dice Thrown* in Coffey's work (*ABC*, p.69). He cites a number of Coffey's swervings, deviances, polyphonic responses to Mallarmé's 'original utterance' (*DT*, p.5), but locates as key or 'clew' (*DT*, p.7) the clustering of lines under '*THE NUMBER*' (*DT*, p.23) and grouping together three of Mallarmé's four subjunctive assertions rendered by Coffey with 'MIGHT'. Moriarty observes: 'It is no error that this opening should feature the only significant departure from the layout of the original poem' (*ABC*, p.79).[31] Miller set *Dice Thrown* as exactly as the resources Dolmen allowed at the time and exactly in accord with the manuscript of the translation that Coffey had twice inscribed – once in pencil and over that in pen, rendering the final manuscript itself a 'calk'.[32] Tellingly, when Moriarty comes to Coffey's later work, he links it to the example set by Mallarmé and simulated by Coffey. Moriarty supplements his discussion with illustrations of two facing pages from *Death of Hektor* in the Menard Press printing, just as if they constituted two open pages of a 'score', two open leaves from *Un Coup de dés* (*ABC*, pp.106–07).

Working from London, Coffey's efforts to represent the œuvre of

Denis Devlin by means of the Dolmen Press culminated in his 1967 edition of *The Heavenly Foreigner*. The publication of his translation of Mallarmé constitutes a likewise guarded reassertion of his own presence as well as the culmination of his effort to use his translations – of Baudelaire, Nerval, Claudel – to help Irish poets, in Coffey's words, 'on their difficult paths' (*ABC*, p.53).[33] That Coffey did so through the medium of Mallarmé recapitulates not only his own experience in the 1930s but also one of the nationalist emphases of high Catholic culture in Saorstát na hÉireann – the effort to overlook Britain in favour of the Continent. By reaching back to the 1890s with *Dice Thrown* and retrieving an early Modernist experiment, Coffey also reached back to a particularly French genre of the book that came to prominence as a vehicle of Modernism in the twentieth century. This, of course, is the *livre d'artiste*; and in the instance of Coffey's *Dice Thrown*, the artist's book as a type of verbal expression that relies on language for 'its material properties and linguistic resonance'.[34] Here, also, appears one of the links back from Coffey's later work, like *Death of Hektor*, through the privations of wartime England and his American sojourn to his earlier poetry as epitomized in *Third Person* published by George Reavey's Europa Press.

Probably the most influential title of the seven issued by the Europa Press is Paul Éluard's *Thorns of Thunder* (1936), issued to complement the International Surrealist Exhibition at the Burlington Galleries in London in June 1936.[35] The advent of *Surréalisme* in Britain had its handbook in David Gascoyne's *A Short Survey of Surrealism* (1935).[36] Surrealism's poetic exemplar came in George Reavey's English edition of Éluard's poems, which includes versions by Beckett and Devlin, but not Coffey.[37] Reavey's editorial foreword made claims for Éluard, linking him back to French poets of interest to Coffey – to 'Nerval and Baudelaire, Rimbaud and Lautreamount'.[38] Moreover, for example, Coffey later published a translation of Éluard's 'Novembre, 1936' in 1938.[39] Certainly, then, Coffey could have contributed to *Thorns of Thunder*.[40] Indeed, Coffey's affection for Éluard's poetry endured and found its best expression in *Poèmes d'amour* (1983), a portfolio of Coffey's translations and Hayter's gravures.[41] That he did not registers his wariness about Surrealism, its politicized milieu, and about, for example, the rhetorical flamboyance of such figures as André Breton.[42] Surrealism's Romantic celebration of individual interiority and its elevation of the material fetish of the aesthetic object, as Alex Davis has noted, posed afresh for Coffey the same problem he encountered in Mallarmé's idealization of *Le Livre*.[43] Despite his sympathies with Mallarmé – sympathies that drew him back to Mallarmé repeatedly – in the 1930s Coffey founded his philosophical stance on Maritain's teaching that the proper realm of art lies within the realm of making, and that making enables the real presence of what Maritain termed 'transcendentals' in the created world.[44]

Reavey was abetted in the Éluard project by the firm of Stanley Nott, in London's Fitzrovia, the district of literary pubs and publishing houses centred around Fitzroy Square. *Thorns of Thunder* is not in any sense a small press book, though the press run of 500 copies was small. Reavey aimed at high, if conventional for the period, production values for the trade edition of *Thorns of Thunder* – linen-sewn signatures of laid paper, for instance.[45] This reflects Reavey's increasingly sophisticated sense of book design, however conventional the book may appear today. The lilac wrap of *Thorns of Thunder* features designs by Max Ernst and the frontispiece is a drawing by Picasso. The very first copy off the press was printed on hand-made paper, included a manuscript in Éluard's hand and the original of Picasso's drawing, and was signed by Éluard, Picasso and the translators. These elements make of *Thorns of Thunder* a *livre d'artiste* whose informing concept originated in Reavey – in the editor acting as *régisseur* – rather than in Éluard or in the translators and the artists represented.

The origins of Europa Press lay in Reavey's desire to publish his own experiments in poetry in the cosmopolitan milieu of Paris in 1932. However, with the publication of Beckett's *Echo's Bones* in 1935, Reavey had become more interested in acting on behalf of the young writers and artists with whom he had become acquainted. From the start he had an interest in Hayter's gravure. Reavey's own *Faust's Metamorphoses* (1932) and *Nostradam* (1935) featured graphics by Hayter, as did Brian Coffey's *Third Person* (1938). Other artists were recruited for Europa publications, including John Buckland-Wright and Roger Vieillard, both linked to Hayter. Hayter and Atelier 17 also provided links to international Surrealism – and to Picasso, Pavel Tchelitchew and Max Ernst. While some Europa Press printings – such as Beckett's *Echo's Bones* – lack frontispieces, they share many design traits and production values that Reavey carefully noted in each book's colophon. All were limited editions; all were further limited in the issuance of signed copies. The titles produced in France make use of artisanal papers, though their actual construction is fussy and impractical. Beginning with *Thorns of Thunder* (1936), the books Reavey produced in London display more expert production. They are designed to be read rather than viewed. Even so, Reavey sought letterpress quality printing for each title. He best achieved this in his own *Quixotic Perquisitions* (1939), which was printed by René Hague and Eric Gill. Taken all together, the Europa Press titles comprise attempts to achieve the difficult aesthetic ideal of Mallarmé's *le Livre*. Failing that, of course, they comprise a *livre d'artste* in seven fascicles and they portray Reavey in the role of editor-as-artist.

Published in the summer of the Munich crisis and the subjection of Prague, Reavey's presentation of *Third Person* displays confidence in fine printing in its 'ordinary edition' – elegant blue wrap, neat red-linen binding and text on deckle-edge paper.[46] Reavey provides two statements of the Europa Poets list of 'limited editions in collaboration with modern artists and engravers' – including forthcoming titles by Reavey himself and by Dylan Thomas.[47] The twenty-five signed editions of *Third Person* include a thematically fitting, even allegorical engraving by Hayter (reproduced in this volume).[48] In contrast, Devlin's *Intercessions* (1937) offers no frontispiece. Coffey was pleased with the book, as signed copies sent to his family in Dublin attest. What most probably appealed to Coffey about the 'ordinary edition' – the edition that most interested readers would encounter – is the chaste presentation of the collection's fourteen poems as texts on the page. Most other readers would agree. Furthermore, most readers would have a difficult time distinguishing it from other examples of London book-making of the 1930s – from, for example, the Faber edition of Louis MacNeice's *Poems* (1935). In that context, *Third Person* seems to be a conventional example of careful design and production, rather than a *livre d'artiste*.[49]

Yet, all the qualities of Reavey's Europa Press output – from the social to the aesthetic – encourage us to read Coffey's *Third Person* as a *livre d'artiste*. Fittingly, the paradoxes raised by doing so point up continuing tensions latent in Coffey's poetry. As Coffey's commentators note, and none more persuasively than Alex Davis, the fourteen lyrics of *Third Person* arise from a personal, biographical occasion – Coffey's engagement and marriage in 1938 – but they rise in the midst of his studies with Maritain. Working from Aquinas, Maritain argued the other side of the coin from Marxists, but to the same effect, that the aesthetic should not and could not be divorced from its 'conditions of existence, the sum of which is: humanity'.[50] In following Maritain, Coffey countered with his own strain of Dedalian romanticism. At the end of the first decade of the twentieth century, Joyce's Stephen Dedalus had found in the trinity of '*integritas, consonatia, claritas*' the reasoning for the *fin de siècle* romanticism of his *villanelle* to Emma Cleary – scribbled on a torn open cigarette packet.[51] Two decades later,

Coffey found in Maritain a counter to that Dedalian subjectivity and to its extension in Surrealism.

Consequently, in its pursuit of the Mallarméan ideal as embodied in *Un Coup de dés*, the *livre d'artiste* as proposed by Reavey would seem an aspiration contrary to Coffey's philosophical convictions. Reinforced by familial duty and economic necessity, those convictions had led him to set aside the making of poems for nearly two decades.[52] Yet, when Coffey begins again the practice of poetry in the 1960s, he chooses to do so just at the margins of the fine letterpress movement of the late 1950s and 1960s. Despite their actual aesthetic differences, in both Britain and the United States practitioners of the craft claimed counter-cultural status on the basis of the credit they gave to the idea of the book beautiful.[53] As with *Un Coup de dés* and *Dice Thrown*, it is the printing – the typography registered on the page – rather than the frontispiece, text paper or binding of *Third Person* that signals clearly and cleanly that Coffey is the *artiste* of the *livre*.

Regrettably, the colophon on the verso of the title page of *Third Person* does not attend to specifying the typeface that Reavey's Guernsey printers offered him. For Coffey's particular lines he chose Monotype Bembo, with bold initials to head each poem.[54] Even in the most densely lined of Coffey's poems – 'A Drop of Fire' or 'Gentle'– the clarity and weight of the typeface draw attention to the particularity of the words – and to Coffey's wording. The visual display of the type encourages the reader to respect that wording by attending to each word in its singularity. Reavey's management of *Third Person* convinces the reader's gaze that Coffey is the *artifex* here. And this is where Dónal Moriarty's redemptive reading of *Third Person* has its start. Contrasting the oracular, baroque surrealism of Devlin's *Intercessions* to Coffey's lines, Moriarty nicely observes that 'Coffey … proceeds by selection and careful placement. The relationship between his short, spare lines and stanzas is more oblique and is determined by a deep impulse to explore aural rather than visual resonances' (*ABC*, p.9).[55] Moriarty's wording here – 'proceeds by selection and careful placement' – calls to mind Coffey, thirty years later, deliberately tracing first in pencil and then in ink the visible siting of each word in his novel translation of Mallarmé. And Coffey's later sequences and satires do exploit – but not always effectively – visual parody and play upon the page.[56]

In preferring the aural to the visual, Moriarty's ultimate characterization of Coffey's artistry calls for complementary amendment. In the lyrics of *Third Person*, Coffey deploys a range of discrete effects in order to articulate the amatory occasion of his engagement to Bridget

Baynes in 1938, thus distilling the motives of an epithalamion into a *Moderne* mode.[57] Because that pursuit takes place in the milieu of his studies with Maritain, the emotional moment also engages the metaphysical concerns that have led commentators to insist overmuch on the Eliotic cast of these fourteen poems. Coffey's compositional resources range from such ordinary rhetorical figures as syllepsis and polyptoton to imagism and colour symbolism. More particularly, Moriarty insists that Coffey's thematic effort in *Third Person* engages an 'awareness of sound as the primordial matter of language' (*ABC*, p.33). The vocalic contrasts thus obtained are brought about, in part, by Coffey's equally noticeable suspensions of usual expressive syntax, which registers right away in 'Dedication':

> For whom on whom then
> and before
> whose eyes desired turned   (*PV*, p.23)

If, to use Moriarty's terms, Coffey takes 'dislocation and aporia' to be 'the ontological givens of the human condition', then his eschewing of the usual continuities of English syntax proves an apt correlative for that assumption (*ABC*, p.45). Suspending those continuities also permits a narrowness of diction that creates a nimbus of allusivity from which the reader may draw Coffey's emotional connections to his themes – and to Dante or Fichte, to Eliot or Rilke (*ABC*, p.26). Not incidentally, doing so enables Coffey also to evade 'the questionable rhetorical strategies of "Anglo-Irish"' (*ABC*, p.24). It has, however, a complementary effect, for it focuses the reader's effort on Coffey's visible situation of the word in the line on the page. Coffey's accomplishment of logopoeia, or at least his lines' incitement of it, owes as much to the visual sitting of his words on the page as to their echoic, aural character. Unexpected, visually heightened lapses in conventional syntax enable Coffey's imagery and license his close and distant allusions. They do so by emphasizing the singularity of word that Coffey has traced upon the page and which the typography has impressed on the reader's attention, as in 'Patience No Memory':

> In the ice field it is one
> the rock the lake the tree
> never is nothing here
> burning is light cold
> patience the lost word unsaid   (*PV*, p.33)

That technique allows Coffey to frame the echoes in 'Patience No

Memory' by calling attention to the words themselves, and, thus, to the poet's role in placing them on the page. The words may be images or pronouns, but their 'syllables enjoy a rare autonomy' (*ABC*, p.45). In that self-denying way, Coffey steeled himself to be the *artiste* of *Third Person*.

Likewise, most readings of Coffey's suite of fourteen lyrics recognize their contrapuntal internal elements and emphasize their integrity as a whole – as a *livre*.[58] The impulse towards this exploit does not prove to be quite so neo-Modernist, as Coffey's advocates sometimes suggest. *Third Person* hardly resembles either the Beaux Arts *livre d'artiste* of the 1890s or the graphic collations typical of the decades after World War I. Yet, as published, *Third Person* does embody Coffey's willingness to risk temptation to pursue a Mallarméan ideal, even while his philosophical convictions were leading him away from it.[59] Coffey followed Maritain away from the absolute aestheticism of Modernism and into the twenty-five years of poetic reticence. He ended that reticence with both 'Missouri Sequence' and his 'deviant translation' of *Un Coup de dés* in 1965, which registered both his continuing attraction to and contention with aesthetic absolutism. In the closing decade of his writing life, Coffey reasserted the inciting, if contrary presence of Mallarmé in his imagination by publishing *Salut: Versions of Some Sonnets of Mallarmé* (1988) and *Poems of Mallarmé* (1990).[60] Indeed, Coffey's effort in *Third Person* to reconcile the amatory occasion, with philosophical conviction, and Christian ethos has a motive in that residue of Dedalian romanticism present through the 1940s in the culture of Dublin's *haute bourgeoisie*.[61]

NOTES

1. This essay in book history owes much to Coffey's commentators, especially Alex Davis and Dónal Moriarty, and to the helpful e-mail advice of Harry Gilonis, James Hogan and Ben Keatinge.
2. A similar lack of regard for these Paris Modernists marked populist Irish poetry of the Left in the 1930s. In 1936 Leslie Daiken noted that Beckett, Devlin and Coffey had 'trekked' to Paris 'driven by the psychology of escape, then become a cult, across the wastelands of interiorization, and technical experiment, [where] they eventually found a mecca in a sort of essentially-celtic surrealism – as far from Ireland as they could get, in art.' Leslie Daiken, 'Introduction', *Good-Bye Twilight: Songs of the Struggle in Ireland*, ed. Leslie H. Daiken (London: Lawrence & Wishart, 1936), p.xii.
3. Preferring MacNeice and Charles Donnelly, A.T. Tolley and Valentine Cunningham offer Beckett and Devlin – but not Coffey – only glancing attention in their standard surveys of Anglophone poetry of the 1930s. See A.T. Tolley, *The Poetry of the Thirties* (New York: St Martin's Press, 1975), and Valentine Cunningham, *British Writers of the Thirties* (Oxford: Oxford University Press, 1988).
4. Alan Gillis' survey *Irish Poetry of the 1930s* (Oxford: Oxford University Press, 2005), pp.109–19 focuses on *Third Person*. Treatments of Coffey's life and writing range from Gerald Dawe's

'An Absence of Influence: Three Modernist Poets', in *Tradition and Influence in Anglo-Irish Poetry* (1989) to Alex Davis' 'The Irish Modernists and Their Legacy', in *The Cambridge Companion to Contemporary Irish Poetry* (2003) and to Stan Smith's recasting of his 1974 *Lace Curtain* essay in *Irish Poetry and the Construction of Modern Identity: Ireland Between Fantasy and History* (2005).

5. James Mays, 'Biographical Note', *Irish University Review*, vol. 5, no. 1 (spring 1975), pp.10–11. An early advocate of Coffey's poetry, Mays edited this special issue devoted to Coffey's work and introduced *Poems and Versions, 1929–1990* (Dublin: Dedalus Press, 1991).

6. Michael Smith published Coffey's *Selected Poems* as a New Writers' Press book in 1971. Later, uncased copies of this printing were given new covers by Dermot Bolger's Raven Arts Press, which issued the book again in 1983 as a Belacqua Series of Irish texts.

7. Coffey prefaces *LEO* with this note: 'The words and drawings were brought together in London, Winter 1968'. Brian Coffey, *Leo, Irish University Review*, vol. 5, no. 1 (spring 1975), p.113.

8. Brian Coffey, *Death of Hektor* (London: Menard Press, 1982), pp.2–3.

9. *Death of Hektor* was first issued as a *livre d'artiste* in 1979 by Circle Press in a printing of 350 copies. The colophon suggests that this project began in 1976 with Hayter's engravings in response to Coffey's text. The printer and designer of the whole – including four of Hayter's nine gravures, Coffey's text and binding – was Jack Shirreff of 107 Workshop. Hayter executed five of the gravures in Paris. *The Prints of Stanley William Hayter* (1992) does not distinguish which gravures were executed in Paris by Hayter and which were printed in Surrey by Shirreff.

10. Bridget Baynes had spent time with Hayter in Paris at Atelier 17 in 1937–38. Harry Gilonis, personal communication to the author, 1 November 2006.

11. 'Atelier 17, A Collaborative Laboratory of Creative Printmaking: Paris 1927—1939', in Duncan Scott, *Twentieth-Century Master Prints: Some Atelier 17 Connections* (London: Royal Society of Painter Printmakers/Bankside Gallery, n.d.), pp.7, 11. 'Biographical Notes', in *The Renaissance of Gravure: The Art of S.W. Hayter*, ed. P.M.S. Hacker (Oxford: Clarendon Press, 1988), p.106. 'Biographical Note', in *S.W. Hayter: Catalogue of an Exhibition of Paintings, Drawings and Engravings from 1927–1957* (London: Whitechapel Art Gallery, November 1957), pp.8–10.

12. For a swift survey of the Free State's affiliations with France and French culture, see 'The French Connection' in Brian Fallon, *An Age of Innocence: Irish Culture 1930–1960* (Dublin: Gill & Macmillan, 1998), pp. 123–32.

13. Patricia Coughlan and Alex Davis, 'Introduction', in Patricia Coughlan and Alex Davis (eds), *Modernism and Ireland: The Poetry of the 1930s* (Cork: Cork University Press, 1995), pp.3–4.

14. Samuel Beckett, letters to Thomas MacGreevy, 9 October 1933 and 9 January 1935. Quoted by Patricia Coughlan in '"The Poetry is Another Pair of Sleeves": Beckett, Ireland and Modernist Lyric Poetry', in Coughlan and Davis, *Modernism and Ireland*, p.185.

15. Paradoxically, Beckett conclusively pairs Devlin and Coffey as having submitted themselves 'to the influences of those poets least concerned with evading the bankrupt relationship referred to at the beginning of this essay … ', Samuel Beckett, *Disjecta: Miscellaneous Writings and a Dramatic Fragment*, ed. Ruby Cohn (New York: Grove Press, 1984), pp.75–76. See also Alex Davis, *A Broken Line: Denis Devlin and Irish Poetic Modernism* (Dublin: University College Dublin Press, 2000), p.17.

16. Terence Brown, 'Ireland, Modernism and the 1930s', in Coughlan and Davis, *Modernism and Ireland*, p.27. Brown notes that the Irish Civil War began in the hallmark year of high Modernism, 1922, when both Joyce's *Ulysses* and Eliot's *The Waste Land* were published.

17. This exhaustion may well explain why the Modernist Dublin magazine titled *The Klaxon* (1923–24) failed, appearing as it did toward the close of the Irish Civil War. See Tim Armstrong, 'Muting the Klaxon: Poetry, History and Irish Modernism', in Coughlan and Davis, *Modernism and Ireland*, pp.43–47.

18. The eight-year span of turmoil and conflict in Ireland from the 1916 Rising to the close of the Irish Civil War in 1924 both excited and called into question domestic cultural production. Likewise, the eight-year span of change and conflict from the Yeats Centenary of 1965 and the fiftieth anniversary of the Rising through the advent of the Northern Troubles and the crises of 1973 also excited and called into question Irish cultural production.

19. Brian Coffey, letter to Liam Miller, 21 September 1963, Wake Forest University, Z. Smith

Reynolds Library, Rare Books and Special Collections, Dolmen Archive, B47 F19.

20. Despite the scarcity of Devlin's *Lough Derg and Other Poems* on readers' shelves in Dublin, his elegized exemplification of the Continental poet appealed to the aspirations of Catholic high culture of the period and to Liam Miller. One sign of this appeal is the observations of and allusions to Devlin in John Jordan's critical prose culminating in 'Amor Fati Sive Contemptus Mundi', a 1978 *Crane Bag* essay, in *Crystal Clear: The Selected Prose of John Jordan*, ed. Hugh McFadden (Dublin: Lilliput Press, 2006), pp. 250–51. Jordan never mentions Coffey.

21. Coffey responded to Miller's suggestion at length. He asserted: 'I want to make sure that ther'll [*sic*] be a chance of having published the poems I am working on <u>now</u> and which I feel are the best I shall ever do'. Brian Coffey, letter to Liam Miller, 21 October 1964, Dolmen Archive, B47 F19.

22. Liam Miller, letter to Brian Coffey, 19 October 1964, Dolmen Archive, B47 F19.

23. Brian Coffey, letter to Liam Miller, 16 October 1964, Dolmen Archive, B47 F19. The parenthetical question mark is Coffey's. 'Minion' is an antique type size in French and English printing lore approximately equivalent to 7 picas.

24. The manuscript consists of 34 pages, 32 x 25.2 cms, in Coffey's hand, each lettered first in pencil and then in ink. Coffey marked the left edge of each recto page and the right edge of each verso page with pencil registration marks so as to keep the lines of his English aligned as in Mallarmé's original. Miller marked up this manuscript indicating font and type size. Pasted in on pages 3–5 is Coffey's typescript of his introduction. Dolmen Archive, B47 F19.

25. Marked up in blue pencil by Miller, the Dolmen copy text is a typescript on foolscap with a stapled edge titled *Dice Thrown*. Dolmen Archive, B47 F19.

26. Stéphane Mallarmé, *Dice Thrown Never Will Annul Chance*, trans. Brian Coffey (Dublin: Dolmen Press, 1965), p.7; hereafter cited parenthetically, thus (*DT*). Miller issued other translations from French poetry of the same period: Villiers de l'Isle Adam, *Axel*, trans. Marilyn Gaddis Rose (Dublin: Dolmen Press, July 1970) and Guillaume Appolinaire, *Zone*, trans. Samuel Beckett (Dublin: Dolmen Press, July 1972).

27. In production in 1897, the second printing of *Un Coup de dés* was to have been a *livre d'artiste* conceived by Ambroise Vollard with lithographs by Odilon Redon. In an eleven-page, illustrated but unpublished article the typographer Neil Crawford gives a detailed account of the printing history of Mallarmé's poem. See Neil Crawford, 'A Typographic Translation of Stephane Mallarmé's *Un coup de dés*', unpublished article, courtesy Harry Gilonis.

28. Mallarmé extends the trope in Wagnerite terms: 'one must add that from this naked use of thought with withdrawals, extensions, evasions or its very design, results, for whoever wish to read aloud, a score. The differences of type between a preponderant motif, a secondary motif, and adjacent ones, prescribes its importance in the delivery and the stave, the median, at the top, at the bottom of the page, marks the rise and fall of intonation.' The aesthetic dimension of this experiment reaches out of *fin de siècle* France to the Mauve Decade in London and to W.B. Yeats' experiments with the psaltery. See Edward Malins, *Yeats and Music*, Yeats Centenary Papers XII (Dublin: Dolmen Press, May 1968) and Matthew Spangler, '"Haunted to the Edge of Trance": Performance and Orality in the Early Poems of W.B. Yeats', *New Hibernia Review*, vol. 10, no. 2 (summer 2006), pp.140–56.

29. Moriarty opens his masterful chapter on Coffey's *Dice Thrown* with a strong portrayal of Coffey's engagement with French literary culture: 'The reviews [Coffey] wrote for Eliot's *The Criterion* reveal an encyclopaedic knowledge of French literature, especially nineteenth-century poetry, much of which he had committed to memory' (*ABC*, p.52).

30. When referring to Joyce, by borrowing the Dedalian trope of the 'artificer' from *A Portrait of the Artist as a Young Man*, Coffey also chooses one congruent with Maritain's thinking. He suggests: 'Perusal of the following pages [his translation] may perhaps stimulate a memory related to such ignorances in friends still living of the Irish artificer' (*DT*, p.6).

31. Noting Coffey's Joycean scruples, Moriarty concludes: 'This is an important gesture, at once expressive of Coffey's trust in the existence of truths which are accessible to the virtue of those faculties bestowed on man by God – a sense conveyed by the choice of verb form that could also express aspiration – and of his need to signify his resistance to the far-reaching implication of Mallarmé's proposition' (*ABC*, p.79). Crawford confirms this departure in 'A Typographic Translation of Mallarmé's *Un Coup de dés*', p.9.

32. While Miller did succeed in turning Coffey's twice-inscribed manuscript into type, other aspects of his design of the book hazard Joycean parody by running counter to the character of both

Mallarmé's and Coffey's thematic interests. Miller chose the typographic conventions of turn-of-the-century placarding for the title page and, especially, the display capitals of the wrap. He had the book bound in quarter vellum with black boards and endpapers. In contrast, the wrap Miller designed for Devlin's *Collected Poems* (1964) is a straight neo-Bauhaus exercise in the Moderne. The interior text is another matter. Its recapitulation of the *Irish University Review*'s fussy setting of the poems constitutes a triumph of impoverished convention over invention. His setting of Coffey's edition of Devlin's *The Heavenly Foreigner* (December 1967) succeeds better.

33. Coffey and Miller planned to publish a selection of Coffey's translations from the poetry of Paul Claudel (1868–1955) as a *livre d'artiste* with art by Eduard Ardizzone. Brian Coffey, letters to Liam Miller, 16 November 1964 and 31 March 1965, Dolmen Archive, B47 F19.

34. Johann Drucker, *The Century of Artist's Books* (New York: Granary Books, 2004), p.227.

35. Thomas Dillon Redshaw, '"Unificator": George Reavey and the Europa Poets of the 1930s', in Coughlan and Davis, *Modernism and Ireland*, pp.254–5. For example, moving between Ireland and France in the 1960s and 1970s, the Irish poet John Montague kept this edition of Éluard with him and, on occasion, recommended it to his students.

36. See '1929–1937: "Elephants are Contagious"', in Gérard Durozoi's synoptic *History of the Surrealist Movement*, trans. Alison Anderson (Chicago, IL: University of Chicago Press, 2002), pp.189–337.

37. Gascoyne gives three translations from Éluard in *A Short Survey of Surrealism* (London: R. Cobden-Sanderson, November 1935), pp.147–52, 157–59.

38. Paul Éluard, *Thorns of Thunder: Selected Poems*, ed. George Reavey (London: Europa Press and Stanley Nott, 1936), p. vii. Reavey's list of translators appears on the title page: Samuel Beckett, Denis Devlin, David Gascoyne, Eugene Jolas, Man Ray, Reavey himself and Ruthven Todd.

39. Éluard's poem responded to the outbreak of the Spanish Civil War in 1936. Coffey's translation appeared in a French political leaflet titled *Solidarité*. James Mays, 'Biographical Note', *Irish University Review*, vol. 5, no. 1 (spring 1975), p.10.

40. Quoting a 1936 letter from Denis Devlin to Thomas MacGreevy, Sandra O'Connell shows that Coffey's antipathy to Herbert Read led him to decline the opportunity to edit *Thorns of Thunder*, despite his admiration for Éluard. See Sandra O'Connell's essay in this volume.

41. See *Prints of Stanley William Hayter*, pp.372–79, 428–39. Like *Death of Hektor* (1979), Éluard's *poémes d'amour love poems* (1984) was executed by Hayter in Paris and by Jack Shirreff at his 107 Workshop, Shaw, Wiltshire.

42. Alex Davis, '"Poetry is Ontology": Brian Coffey's Poetics', in Coughlan and Davis, *Modernism and Ireland*, pp.167–68. Coffey's philosophically informed wariness helps distinguish his work as neo-Modernist in the sense set out by Frank Kermode in his wide-ranging review essay 'The Modern', in *Modern Essays* (London: Collins Fontana, 1971).

43. Davis, '"Poetry is Ontology"', pp.152–53.

44. See: Francesca Aran Murphy's chapter 'Beauty, "The Cinderella of the Transcendentals": Jacques Maritain's Philosophy of Art', in her *Christ the Form of Beauty: A Study in Theology and Literature* (Edinburgh: T. & T. Clark, 1995), pp.37–67; Leland Ryken, 'Formalist and Archetypal Criticism', in *Contemporary Literary Theory: A Christian Appraisal*, ed. Clarence Walhout and Leland Ryken (Grand Rapids, MI: William B. Eerdmans, 1991), pp.1–23.

45. Thomas Dillon Redshaw, '"Unificator": George Reavey and the Europa Poets of the 1930s', in Coughlan and Davis, *Modernism and Ireland*, pp.273–74.

46. Sandra O'Connell notes that Reavey planned to issue a collection by Coffey titled *Image at the Cinema* as early as 1935. See Sandra O'Connell's essay in this volume.

47. Reavey lists Thomas' *The Burning Baby*, which never was printed despite Reavey's two attempts to have it set, and his own *Quixotic Perquisitions*, which was issued in 1939.

48. Executed at Atelier 17 in Paris, Hayter's engraved frontispiece (reproduced in this volume) depicts a figure facing away from the viewer and posed between, on the left, a decomposing edifice and, on the right, shards of shadows. The figure faces towards a sail rising away from its mast and boom. Thus the gravure seems to depict a moment of choice and attraction. Writing to Gwynedd Reavey, Coffey commented that 'Hayter's engraving is queer, quietly right'. Coffey, letter to Gwynedd Reavey, 27 May 1938, Reavey Archive, B48.F2, HRHRC, University of Texas at Austin. See also: Peter Black and Désirée Moorhead, *The Prints of Stanley William Hayter: A Complete Catalogue* (Mount Kisco, NY: Moyer Bell, 1992), no. 124, p.141.

49. The 'ordinary editions' of *Thorns of Thunder*, Charles Henri Ford's *The Garden of Disorder* and *Quixotic Perquisitions* are not so ordinary. They offer as frontispieces photographic re-

productions of art by, respectively, Picasso, Tcheltichew, and Buckland-Wright.

50. Maritain quoted by Davis, "'Poetry is Ontology'", p.153.

51. James Joyce, *A Portrait of the Artist as a Young Man*, ed. Chester G. Anderson (New York: Viking Press, 1964), p.212. From 'The Beautiful Mabel Hunter!' in chapter 1 through to his sighting of Emma Cleary at the National Library, Joyce links Stephen's subjective romanticism to his aestheticizing of experience and aspiration.

52. Citing an article by Jack Morgan, Davis observes that, during his years at St Louis University, Coffey revealed his endeavours in poetry only to his colleague Leonard Eslick. Davis, "'Poetry is Ontology'", p.171. For an extended account of Coffey's time in the United States and of the autobiographical grounding of 'Missouri Sequence', see Jack Morgan, "'Missouri Sequence': Brian Coffey's St Louis Years, 1947–1952', *Éire-Ireland*, vol. 28, no. 4 (winter 1993), pp.100–13.

53. For an account of bibliophilia, the 'book beautiful', and the fine press movement in the United States, see Megan L. Benton, *Beauty and the Book: Fine Editions and Cultural Distinction in America* (New Haven: Yale University Press, 2000), especially the second chapter, 'On Sacred Ground: The Theory of the Ideal Book', pp.32–56.

54. In the 1920s Stanley Morison revived Bembo, among other typefaces, for the British Mono-type Corporation. For a short account, see Simon Loxley, *Type: The Secret History of Letters* (London: I.B. Tauris, 2004), pp.123–35.

55. Moriarty takes pains to argue against the 'uncritical coupling of Devlin and Coffey that one often finds in narratives of twentieth-century Irish poetry', asserting that *Third Person* 'possesses no analogue in Irish writing' of the period (*ABC*, p.9).

56. That Coffey remained preoccupied with the poet's act of putting the word on the page is underscored by the manner in which he first published *Advent*. On 20 June 1974 he issued the typescript of his 28-page poem in twenty-five numbered presentation copies as an Advent Book (Special Collections, University of Delaware Library, Brian Coffey Papers, B1 F2). See also Brian Coffey, *Advent* (London: Menard Press, 1986).

57. Moriarty refrains from proposing a biographical interpretation of *Third Person*, but Coffey's letters to Reavey about the book suggest that he saw the poems as autobiographical. Writing from Paris to Reavey in London, Coffey twice insisted that he was not to show the poems of *Third Person* to Peggy Guggenheim, with whom Coffey had an affair in 1938, and who had introduced Coffey to Bridget Baynes. Brian Coffey, letters to George Reavey, 23 May 1938 and 6 August 1938, HRHRC, Reavey Archive, B48 F2. The tale of Coffey's affair is well attested to in the biographies of Beckett by Deirdre Bair and Anthony Cronin, but see James Knowlson, *Damned to Fame: The Life of Samuel Beckett* (New York: Simon & Schuster, 1996), pp.262–63.

58. Alluding both to Coleridge and to Mallarmé, Moriarty asserts that 'What defines *Third Person* as a collection is the way all its elements are dedicated to a specific project'. He later varies that assertion: 'Of all the Europa poets, Coffey was the only one to seize the opportunity to stake a claim for the "poetry collection" to be considered as a genre in itself' (*ABC*, pp.39, 47). Assuming that Coffey acts as *artifex*, then the thing of his making is *le livre* and an attempt at the Mallarméan ideal.

59. Though incited by Coffey's efforts to 'dizzy and destabilize' received language as underscored by the typographic display of *Third Person*, Gillis remains none the less unconvinced by the effort in his *Irish Poetry of the 1930s*, p.118.

60. See Brian Coffey, *Salut: Versions of Some Sonnets of Mallarmé* (Dublin: hardPressed Poetry, 1988); Brian Coffey, *Poems of Mallarmé* (London: Menard Press, 1990).

61. Joyce encapsulated that romanticism in the lyrics of *Chamber Music* (1907), which he dictated to his brother Stanislaus. Although Joyce half-aestheticized it and half-mocked it in the crooning of Stephen Dedalus to 'EC' in *A Portrait*, the poetic conventions endured through the 1960s in much undergraduate Irish poetry, owing both to the example of Yeats' early lyrics and to the *aisling*, as Stephen's revision of 'Darkness falls from the air' to 'Brightness falls from the air' may betoken. *A Portrait*, pp. 232, 234.

CHAPTER EIGHT

Brian Coffey's Review of Beckett's *Murphy*: 'Take warning while you praise'

J.C.C. MAYS

I

*M*urphy was famously difficult to get accepted and at first something of a flop. A catalogue of publishers turned it down until Routledge took a gamble. The reviews, when they came, were for the most part puzzled or unenthusiastic and relatively few copies sold. The three different bindings that command different prices of the first edition suggest that the disappointed publisher either made copies available only when need arose, or was constrained by wartime shortages. The legend that 750 copies were destroyed by enemy bombing appears to be supported by the fact that the book went out of print about the time the war ended, having produced relatively small royalties. Its fame came later, not with the French translation published by Bordas, which sold exceptionally poorly, but when it was reprinted in New York after the success of *Godot*.

There were only two good reviews. Kate O'Brien's pleased Beckett most and Dylan Thomas's was perceptive. O'Brien in the *Spectator* communicates her enjoyment and made it her book of the week, praising its 'gladdening, quickening' spirit. She admitted there was much she failed to understand, but insisted this did not matter: 'Rarely, indeed have I been so entertained by a book, so tempted to superlatives and perhaps hyperboles of praise.' Thomas in the *New English Weekly* differs from others who balanced praise with blame. He straightforwardly called the book 'wrong' but, in explaining how its qualities are at variance, demonstrates that he took Beckett's literary methods seriously.

Austin Clarke wrote the only review to appear in Ireland, anonymously in the *Dublin Magazine* a year after the book appeared, and damned it with circumspection. The remaining reviews were negative and un-interesting. All the more pity, then, that the most informed and most engaged review written at the time is published only now.

It was written by Brian Coffey, who had been born in Dublin a year earlier than Beckett. Both their backgrounds were what the English would describe as first-generation upper-middle-class, but they moved in different circles – Coffey being the son of Denis J. Coffey, a profes-sor of medicine whose family came from County Kerry, who served as President of University College Dublin from 1908 to 1940. Coffey spent the last year of his secondary education in France, earned de-grees at UCD in maths, physics and chemistry, commenced research in physical chemistry in Paris in 1930 and, after three years, transferred to the Institut Catholique to study philosophy mainly under Jacques Maritain. He had published poems in an undergraduate magazine and in a jointly authored small volume with his UCD contemporary, Denis Devlin, in 1930. He picked up with Devlin again in Paris, through whom he met Thomas MacGreevy and later (in London, summer 1934) Beckett. George Reavey contracted with Devlin and Coffey to publish collections of their poems as early as 1935, but Coffey found composition difficult. He meanwhile passed his licentiate exam in phi-losophy in 1936, and the following year registered as a doctoral stu-dent working on the idea of order in Aquinas. His response to Beckett had been immediate, and he wrote to MacGreevy following the ap-pearance of *Echo's Bones* (not all of whose allusions he understood at first reading) affirming his sense of Beckett's gentleness ('as sweet as butter-milk').[1]

Their friendship began during the period when Beckett moved from London back to Dublin and then made an extended trip through Ger-many, that is, when *Murphy* was being completed and revised. Coffey remained based in Paris until summer 1936, when he returned to Dublin hoping to find a job, and returned to Paris as a doctoral student in October 1937. Their meetings during this period were not frequent, although they met when Coffey passed through London in 1935 and Coffey helped Beckett with Spinoza when both were back in Dublin during the following summer.[2] They met again when Beckett returned to Dublin in 1937, each of them living somewhat uncomfortably with parents who hoped their sons would grow up and find regular em-ployment without further delay. Thus, Coffey was privy to the emer-gence of *Murphy* as a completed text, before it began the tedious round of publishers. He was in Dublin to accompany Beckett through the traumatic Sinclair-Gogarty libel trial, and was part of the welcoming party when Beckett returned to Paris shortly afterwards. The period of their closest friendship extended through the following months, between the acceptance of *Murphy* by Routledge and its appearance in print. Soon after that period began, Beckett was stabbed in the street and hospitalized; by the time first reviews began to appear, each of them was beginning to head in a different direction.

It is easier at first to demonstrate what Coffey got out of the friendship than Beckett, at least with respect to *Murphy*. The principle intellectual sources of the book had been accumulating from the time Beckett arrived at the École Normale, and anything Coffey might have added can only have been incidental. Beckett's fellow Normalien, Jean Beaufret – Lucien of *Dream of Fair to Middling Women* – had guided Beckett's reading of the later Cartesians and the Presocratics,[3] and Coffey came in on the novel after its main lines were set. However, at that stage his analysis of the intellectual problem the novel presented, and transposition of it into his own terms, where the same problems had some kind of answer, was of enormous benefit for his own thinking. It enabled him to finish the stalled volume contracted to Reavey. This collection, *Third Person*, is written in dialogue with both the novel and *Echo's Bones*, and against the background of the two writers' shared relationship with Peggy Guggenheim. Beckett, for his part, gave the completed collection its title and, as if to acknowledge their overlapping concerns and clarifying discussions, made Coffey a present of the manuscript of *Murphy*. I have described Beckett's contribution to this turning-point in Coffey's emergence as poet in another essay,[4] and the purpose of the present remarks is to underline the importance of Coffey's review for Beckett.

The review was completed in Paris in March 1938, the month *Murphy* was published, but it was not taken up and then set aside and forgotten. The only known fair copy is among the Reavey–Coffey papers connected with the production of *Third Person* now at Texas. Coffey remembered writing the review, and retained a pencil draft that is now at Delaware, but he had lost any duplicates he possessed by the 1970s or before. He is likely to have approached Reavey, who had acted as Beckett's agent for the novel, and asked him to place it. If this was the case, Reavey very likely put it on one side, reckoning that it needed revision (simplification) if it stood a chance of being accepted, which Coffey – involved as he was in arrangements for his own book and simultaneously for his forthcoming wedding, in addition to completing his dissertation and establishing a viable financial future – was too busy to undertake. His manner rivals Beckett's in allusiveness and would have puzzled all but the most hard-bitten readers of avant-garde little magazines, of which there were then a rapidly declining number, but its interest is the greater now. It cuts to the heart of Beckett's book with total understanding and sympathy. It takes the core issues seriously, even as Coffey makes clear that his own understanding of them is different.

At this point I should present the review, which fills two and a quarter pages of typing paper. I have corrected spelling mistakes and typos, but allowed some period idiosyncrasies to remain. I have also revised some punctuation, specifically by inserting commas to mark parentheses. This last is the only change over which I have misgivings, but there is no point in further distressing a reader who struggles to make difficult connections. The shelfmark at the Harry Ransom Humanities Research Center, University of Texas at Austin, is MS | Reavey, George | III. Miscellaneous. Box 71, Folder 2. The folder contains the following review and two proof copies of *Third Person*.

The shelfmark of the pencil draft at Special Collections, University of Delaware Library, is MSS 382 | Box 2 | F26. It is signed and dated 28 February 1938. It is written on four pages of lined foolscap, and there are revisions in pencil and ink, the most extensive revisions occurring at the close of paragraph 5. It clearly served as the basis of the typescript, in which Coffey made some minor stylistic adjustments as he copied.

II

MURPHY. By Samuel Beckett. (Routledge, London. 7s 6d.)
One locust points to panic. Here, there, everywhere amazed eyes multiplying the monster, they numbered little foxes. See the *Mémoires de Trévaux* or in Pfaff, *De Egoismo*. To this day no one knows where he lies who forgot the world. We remember – 'Rien n'existe qu'avec la connaissance: je veux dire qu'il y a contradiction qu'on puisse attribuer l'existence à un être auquel on ne pense point' – the white flame where there was nothing before, the incredible beginning. One might have kicked Berkeley into salvation. Brunet grasped, lord of the panopticon, in himself at once kick, kicker and kicked. Solipsist. Alone in being. Fear derided his predicament. He was viewed a sect. He has been put away for Christiana's victim, whose reasons, shadow then now clear, swell the debate without end. Glory in the memory of man.

Give them their way. His *Projet d'une métaphysique* that was never a project – no this and later that, no then and after now, perfect end in finished birth, Thales struck by water – since lost, was the egocentric port, greenest apple of the idealist garden in the west; and a universe beside. Brunet's was a unique predicament, like the order of art.

Let us take a luncheon example, a little pleasure in the daily round. Buy a pot of Youghourth, a banana, a knife. Eat the curds. Lay the pot on its side on a table. Hold the banana tail down by the stalk. Split the skin with the knife several times. When done correctly you should have a knob of stalk with pendant eight slips of skin, if the fruit has been abstracted with care. Lay the knife along the mouth of the pot. Place the skin so that the knob sits on the top edge above the mouth, six strips spread starwise, one rests curled inside, one coils in protective or deadly possession around the knife. You can see, reward of industry while you feed on fruit, a cold pearl diver detained where the saffron squid attends. A low order. Skin, pot, knife undigested assert themselves. The compleat madman will bring them too to heel. Down receding grades, until mind is bled white, far below the sisterhood of oleanders, the touch of order will change things to art's things. One thinks of a board of plain deal at an immense remove from stone, inchoate, the need that takes the artist in a groundswell. He will come to know his own, the blue no other eye had dropped on. Toil in himself below the light of day. Toil from day to year, the long step from Manon to Celia whom patience brings the sun to shine upon. Unintelligible to unintelligible, anguish to anguish in the dark before light, in the dark after light, two pains the spider does not feel, while the others play from first seen to seen last with the febrile coherence of the dark-house, text to text. The poet, from the night of eyes learning to the night when ruined eyes retire, all attempted, all laid aside, fights against a board of plain deal, the matter that would stultify the cause, as base weds acid, to forestall a stone-change. What he has not known he may not use. What he makes he must not have seen. He sights the untold, cousin as much of his fibres as of the earth, spoil of conflict. We do not see as he does. We must trust our eyes, pay tribute to a one-fold grasp, a manifold design, this time no Venetian hair of tempered glass sliding into the sacred fount but the gash of the dirk, the hard new style.

'The sun shone, having no alternative, on the nothing new.'

I shall not project the plot onto a plane. This red-clawed world, Miss Counihan, will chase Murphy always to the door of the next. I cannot condense the meaning to an attar of pain. Murphy will seek

the best always in himself. I shall not distinguish raindrop from raindrop in the pool. Stavroguin at Bartholomew Fair mentioned *The
Counterfeiters* to Belacqua from whom he got little. The time. The
place. Athens was the focus of the islands. The Wylies, the Nearys will
ever be rushing from Dublin to London and back, wrenched two ways
by the whirling ensign. The language and so on, the imagery and so
forth, the relative ease in the balanced mind, such may be left safely to
scholars. Read for yourself, careful reader. Learn how the heart finds
the living heart behind grotesque features and salutes. I shall have my
own way in four moments to admire.

Who is Murphy? The world gives little credit for detached labour.
Here there is no excuse for pleasurable misreading. *Murphy* did not
drop like an apple from the tree. No work ever did to please Saint-
Beuve who had the vice of the gossip. Murphy, like all poetic objects,
has made previous appearances not just as. On the contrary. One
would need four pages to assign his name to Murphy. '*Les affections
de l'homme sont un abîme d'avidité.*' Obermann would have greeted
a world stripped of each exact image, dissolved in some metaphysical
dew of which the caress would accomplish the soul's desire. There are
origins, laws of development, inevitable death in art for the Murphy
type. Time and the card-index will make it all drear. The careful reader
will be sure, even now, unaided, that Murphy is not his author, for a
simple reason. Samuel Beckett walks on Murphy's scene to judge the
little world where Murphy does not stir, flying from being. French
skill.

What then is Murphy as he sees himself? He is given, whole and entire, wrapped in his own mysterious quality, a drawing fire. He drools
no memories of days past. We sense a musical ear, an eye for colour,
conscience, learning lost in better times. But why should he seek the
new life described in section six? A man may fall from vision, Saint
Augustine says. *Et fit rei non transitoriæ transitoria cognitio.* Through
what seven ages of loss must Murphy seek his rest who comes into our
view blasted, spavined song-maker to dead Laura fleshed in pitiful imitation, and as Alastor, his wan eyes gazing

'on the empty scene as vacantly
As ocean's moon looks on the moon in heaven.'

Unmanned by who shall not come back he holds to manhood in his
mind. No Brunet wondering and sure, Murphy complains for quiet to
descend. Numbed by the initiation, his honesty is his manhood, to
cleave to the setting of the pearl. The archetypal journey from the cave
to the house across water binds him from hope; his hope to despair.

Consilium proprium. The greater leprosy. The intellectual love with which he loves himself is a drowning attention to contradiction, threshold of nothing. In retreat since asters nodded, he moistens where unequal blades grind and rend, breast against thorn. '*Madre del nulla*', she will guide him attended by her theory of daughters while the Ephesian, he smothered in dung, breaks the mind. 'Fire is want and surfeit'; Murphy goes away backward to the incredible beginning. Home and the darkness before the gift. The Mothers come down from boxes where they have been knitting to bring the small ballet dancers home. Murphy beats his hands on his own walls for a time to say, 'I am if I am not', the rational mind rebelling against the half-light.

Where the fibre is strong a man will retrieve the fields of tulips, the blue no other eye has seen. When the sloth is deeper he will sun himself to repose in the central plain. Murphy, who wants indifference, is not Oblomov. Five different biscuits may be taken in one hundred and twenty ways. Saved from all desire for this one or that, in the faith that the lower of the joined vessels, obeying extension's laws, will harmonise unaccountably with the upper, Murphy in ideal weather would not suffer the pain of choice, the ass that did not die. *Propria voluntas*. The lesser leprosy. He does not remember the day he chose, poor man. If only the street-cry did not touch the ear, or one's heart need, one could journey back, sight America, land. Who shall cleave a waterspout with his sword now? Earth's voices. Return, Murphy, where pride sheaths with grace, fear.

In the Magdalen Mental Mercyseat, 'kneeling at the bedside, the hair standing in thick black ridges between his fingers, his lips, nose and forehead almost touching Mr. Endon's, seeing himself stigmatised in those eyes that did not see him, Murphy heard words demanding so strongly to be spoken that he spoke them, right into Mr. Endon's face, Murphy who did not speak at all in the ordinary way unless spoken to, and not always even then,

> "the last at last seen of him
> himself unseen by him
> and of himself."'

Communication – the crash together in space of two granite blocks – ends at the finger-nails. He does not undesire but through pain of loss. The experiment failed again. Fear had been rising from the start out of the undiscoverable ground, always first as a white living spot no bigger than a weasel. Portent of universal languor, foretaste of wrath, the first locust that comes when the corn is green, he shall flourish in days of withering light, reason's drunken mood bearing monsters. Take the warning while you praise. These images have suffered reason.

The end. Draw the blind on no stars; Murphy has entered fire. From cabs the avid pour to the inquest, to chatter above the ripped carpet, to draw the world together again. The white point drops behind. In the old way signs nourish unnatural babel. So time tells. Who shall judge him? The anatomist does not know the vibrant lash of the medusa. The soul of another is dark and dark the root of the flame. Brian Coffey. Paris. March, 1938.

III

Even before a reader begins to try to make sense of the above, it is evident that Coffey writes from a more privileged position than any other of Beckett's reviewers. Kate O'Brien's generalized enthusiasm is replaced by someone who does not apologise for what is difficult: Coffey does not offer himself as mediator, postponing understanding, but pays the higher tribute of matching Beckett's style. While Dylan Thomas chose to write from the perspective of a writer, arguing that the book 'is not rightly what it should be', Coffey writes from the position of someone who takes ideas seriously too: he engages with Beckett's philosophical predicament, but tactfully resists turning the occasion into a statement of his own answer to life's problems. From the outset, he makes plain that this is not a retort from a customer who feels he has not been served, nor an apology from a kind, approving reader who feels she is not quite up to the task today, nor an alternative novel by a writer who thinks he could have written a better book, but that this is a dialogue between equals. The worked-over draft and the connected web of images – of locusts, whiteness, stone and fire/flame – are an index of the care with which the statement was crafted. I leave someone else to trace each particular reference and allusion, but a gloss on the movement of the argument as a whole will assist some further observations.

The opening paragraph, following passing references to the *Journal de Trévoux* [sic] *ou Mémoires pour l'histoire des sciences et des beaux-arts* (Paris, 1701–67) and to Christoph Matthäus Pfaff's *Oratio de Egioismo nova philosophia heresi* (Tübingen, 1722), presents a figure who does not appear in *Murphy* but who embodied its central argument in its purest form: the seventeenth-century French physician, Claude Brunet, who is the subject of Coffey's several floating pronouns. Beginning from Descartes' *cogito*, Brunet earned a place in history as

the only major philosopher to advocate solipsism seriously. His expo-
sition is strikingly coherent and he lived by his beliefs. He was ridiculed
at the time and afterwards forgotten in favour of Descartes ('Christiana's victim'). His reputation has recovered a little, if not much, but
the effect of Coffey's gambit is to establish the reviewer as equal master of the material Beckett discovered or that Beaufret recommended.
Put another way, Beckett's allusions to Geulincx and others are
trumped by naming the supreme 'seedy solipsist', the exemplar of
whom Beckett was apparently unaware. Coffey claims the right to play
this game on his own, the proper terms.

One should remember that Coffey and Beckett played against each
other at golf – on the idiosyncratic Carrickmines course – when their
visits home coincided. Coffey's opening references to voluminous and
obscure sources – the *Mémoires* are in sixty-seven volumes, the *Egoismo* in twenty-seven pages – are one-upmanship in a game between
friends, but his greater knowledge of the history of philosophy, even
though the area Beckett has drawn upon was not his specialism, is
more seriously applied in the figure he concentrates on. Brunet's complete solipsism – 'in himself at once, kick, kicker and kicked', as in
Murphy chapter 6 – defines the order of art that Beckett's protagonist
aspires to. Paragraph 2 elaborates, first by restating Belacqua's lunch
preparations in the opening story of *More Pricks Than Kicks* so that
emphasis is thrown on to the remnants that cannot be digested,[5] and
then, by means of allusions to Heraclitus and Ovid (to Echo's bones
that turned to stone), formulating the ultimate predicament of the
artist: 'What he has not known he may not use. What he makes he
must not have seen.' This is what Beckett's 'hard new style' aims to
express and what it will fail to express for reasons that are more honourable now they are restated and clearly understood – more honourable because of the 'compassion' that Coffey recognised in Beckett
from the first.

From a position of authority thus established, Coffey dismisses ordinary questions about the book in short order. The plot and surrounding characters are unimportant: 'The language and so on, the
imagery and so forth, the relative ease in the balanced mind, such may
be left safely to scholars.' Similarly, the character on which the plot
turns, together with his literary antecedents (to which Coffey adds Sé-
nacourt's Obermann, which is interesting): 'Time and the card index
will make it all drear.' The point, Coffey insists, is that 'Samuel Beckett walks on Murphy's scene to judge the little world where Murphy
does not stir, flying from being. French skill.' These two paragraphs –

numbers 3 and 4 – compress and set aside what other reviewers felt bound to complain of, and they bring the central issue into focus: how Murphy sees himself and the moment of crisis when, confronting the little world of complete solipsism, he turns away. Paragraphs 5 and 6 move from these wrong ways to read onward to the way Coffey recommends, and they are the heart of his argument.

Paragraph 5 provides a metaphoric commentary on the larger part of the book's action. It is contrived by a quotation from St Augustine that escaped Beckett's attention (*De Trinitate* XII 23: note that Coffey substitutes 'cognitio' for Augustine's 'cogitatio') and further allusions to Heraclitus. It summarises Murphy's dilemma in Cartesian terms – 'I am if I am not' – as if this had taken him only halfway on his journey, to a point where he could still return from where he had arrived. Paragraph 6 describes a further level of alienation in which Murphy's anguish is more subtle but no less powerful. 'Earth's voices. Return, Murphy, where pride sheaths with grace, fear.' The advance from one paragraph to another is signalled by the Thomist distinction between *consilium*, a specified stage in deliberative reasoning, the term being borrowed from the language of politics, and *voluntas* which, combined with *intentio*, unifies human action and enables human freedom and responsibility towards God. They mark levels of alienation and interiority – greater and lesser leprosy, the greater being the more outwardly marked, the lesser being systemic – less visible but more pervasive. At this deeper level of evaded choice, 'Who shall cleave a waterspout with his sword now?'

Paragraph 7 pursues the intellectual plot to its denouement, where, at the Magdalen Mental Mercyseat, Murphy gazes into Mr Endon's eyes, 'seeing himself stigmatised in those eyes that did not see him'. He speaks what he does not understand and retreats from the little world. Coffey's imagery of colliding antinomies is borrowed from a poem centred on the same theme by his and Beckett's mutual friend, Devlin ('Est Prodest').[6] 'The experiment failed again. Fear had been rising from the start out of the undiscoverable ground.' Coffey's carefully positioned keywords return in a rush. The little cloud promising salvation becomes the weasel-shaped cloud of Polonius:[7] 'These images have suffered reason.'

The concluding paragraph rounds out the argument, where praise and warning are supported and excused by engagement and sympathy. Murphy's collapsed dialectic is not to be salved by indifference: Guggenheim's Oblomov diagnosis, which Beckett had been eager enough to embrace. Coffey turns the emphasis on to the eye that

observes Murphy and the cause of his author's failure at the show-
down moment, the recoil of a passionate humanity. 'So time tells. Who
shall judge him?' As the Thomist references make clear, Coffey comes
to the question of solipsism and volition from a different direction
than Beckett, who found Schopenhauer more congenial, but the issue
is not pressed: 'Draw the blind on no stars.' Coffey left the development of his counterstatement to his own *Third Person*, which came together as a volume in tandem with his review. In his poems, the image
of fire deployed throughout the review with Heraclitan overtones is
transposed into an Hegelian context and a secular (materialist) dialectic is critiqued by a Trinitarian (Catholic) system of belief. Coffey's
idea of *poesis* is based upon the exact same predicament that he sums
up in the second paragraph of the review but the predicament is differently understood. 'The soul of another is dark and dark the root of
the figure.' Only the one-way Hegelian images of self-consuming flame
carry forward.

Coffey added the following poem to the thirteen that make up his
collection at the very last moment, deliberately acknowledging another
way that was not his way as well as Beckett's unswerving purpose:

One Way

Giving what he has not given
he sees what he has not seen

Taking what he has not taken
he hears what he has not heard

No worst fear
no best light
constraint constrained
to work himself out

he breasts tide's breast[8]   (*PV*, p.38)

IV

Coffey's review of *Murphy* was the best review the book never had.
One must suppose that he showed it to Beckett and/or elaborated his
views in conversation, and one might fairly ask what effect the review
had.

It is important that, while Coffey was part of a circle of Irish writers in Paris, he was not close to Beckett in the way Joyce or MacGreevy

were. Beckett was drawn to Joyce by fascination with his already enormous achievement and was honoured to assist with *Work in Progress* (*Finnegans Wake*). MacGreevy was, from the time Beckett went to the École Normale, a trusted confidant with whom Beckett shared his troubles and hopes as with nobody else. Coffey's way to Beckett was through MacGreevy and Devlin, for both of whom he had great regard and enormous affection. He met Joyce in person relatively late, at the injured Beckett's bedside in December 1937 and then again only once again shortly afterwards.[9] As I suggested above, his contribution to the writing of *Murphy* was at the stage of revision rather than of construction, and minimal at that: he assisted Beckett with his reading of Geulincx,[10] and the help with Spinoza was more bibliographical than intellectual. After all, in 1935–36 he was still a neophyte in philosophical matters. If he had been in a position to assist the composition of *Murphy* in a material way, he would surely have introduced Brunet, the chestnut he produced from his sleeve, at an earlier stage.

Coffey's review, then, results from a friendship that had previously been casual and had suddenly become intimate. For Beckett, it was a limbo period between the acceptance and publication of a book he had written a while ago; for Coffey, it was the moment when his own stalled writing suddenly came together as a result of thinking about Beckett's. It was also a time when events in their personal lives became intimately entangled. Coffey succeeded Beckett as Peggy Guggenheim's lover, for a spell, with unhappy results. Two members of a loose group of friends were thrown close together by accident and reacted to the moment in different ways. Coffey's review and poems contain his sense of Beckett's response to Guggenheim as well as his own response that led to a different outcome. He saw his poems into print within six months and, during the same time, proposed and married. Documentation is difficult in the case of Beckett because his state of mind was caught up in the fortunes of his novel in a complicated, diffused way. He told Lawrence Harvey that the period was one of 'apathy and lethargy'; James Knowlson describes it as a period of meeting people and reading books.[11]

Beckett's gift of the manuscript of his novel none the less shows his appreciation of Coffey's appraisal: the review shed clear light on the book into which he had put so much. Together with *Third Person*, the illumination came from a position Beckett would not wish to share but that mattered less. No other reviewer, no other friend with a close interest in his previous writing, had the same technical equipment that enabled him to cut to the core of the onion. His earlier philosophical aid, Jean Beaufret, had moved on to a different life by 1938. Old Tom MacGreevy, to whom Beckett made some concessions at the revision stage, shared Coffey's beliefs but not his particular information or razor mind. I suggest that Coffey's review, coming as it did in a way for which Beckett cannot have been wholly prepared, gave him a clearer understanding of the impasse he was in and at the same time left him the more unsure how to resolve the impasse on his own terms. In short, the best review *Murphy* never had must have left him feeling more lost as well as cheered.

Beckett's biography and the chronology of his writings do not contradict this supposition. He did many things next – composing in French, returning to write occasional poems, beginning to translate *Murphy*, comparing the predicament he shared with painters and musicians – in a way that makes evident that he knew he was in a cul-de-sac. The war pre-empted any extended focused effort, and the aptly named *Watt* served to keep his hand in, but the following years were years in limbo. I remember Coffey saying – with some delicacy – that Beckett's French was really not as good as his when Beckett began writing in French, and I can imagine that some of Beckett's reading in early 1938 was suggested by Coffey: it would be in character for him to urge a kindergarten manual of science on the medal-winning arts graduate from TCD. It is on record that Coffey lent him more serious reading – for instance, Maritain's *Humanisme integrale* – and was a sounding-board for his essay, *Les Deux besoins*, written in 1938.[12] Coffey thought in French as readily in as in English at the time, as notes on English books in French and formulations of his ideas in French preserved among his papers at the University of Delaware testify.[13] Some curious misspellings in the *Murphy* review are reverse testimony to his French education.

Les Deux besoins was undertaken at the urging of Beckett's long-standing friend from TCD, Alfred Péron, and it incorporates material from lessons learnt at that time. But it makes equal if not more sense as a response to the ideas contained in Coffey's review. Coffey's review clarified the dilemma of the artist with stunning clarity – 'What he has not known he may not use. What he makes he must not have seen.' – and Coffey's response as developed in *Third Person* was founded upon religious belief, which was unavailable to Beckett. All he had was the imperative Coffey acknowledged in 'One Way' and was to be reaffirmed at the close of *The Unnamable*: 'you must go on, I can't go on, I'll go on.' *Les Deux besoins* is the first, confused formulation of an intellectual position that was afterwards clarified in relation to a number of painters: 'there is nothing to paint and nothing to paint with.'[14] It set the parameters of Beckett's writing when he picked up again in French after the war, and so remained until the reformulation of the same concerns in drama turned Beckett's perception of the argument around. Though he never bought Coffey's line on intention, *Murphy* was the last book he wrote in the old style. Henceforward he wrote without any such preparation as contained in the *Dream* and *Murphy* notebooks now at Reading: he wrote out of ignorance, intentionally will-less.

Beckett gave Coffey the *Murphy* manuscript but never publicly acknowledged his help. The review, after all, had not been published during the muddled moments of spring 1938. Coffey later returned to France with his wife, Bridget, to live near Dampierre-en-Yvelines, where he and Beckett continued their conversations at weekends, but war overtook them. Coffey left, via Dublin, to teach in a boarding school in Yorkshire; Beckett migrated to the Vaucluse. The two of them met by accident in a Dublin hotel when each was visiting parents in Dublin in 1945, but, after Coffey gained his doctorate from Paris in 1947, he moved from school-teaching in London to become a professor of philosophy in Missouri. He did not pick up again with Beckett until several years later, after he returned from America.

The renewed contact in 1957 took Coffey back to a conjunction of events on which his idea of poetry and his long and happy marriage were founded. Significantly, the long letter he wrote to Beckett at that time, reminiscing about their prewar days,[15] coincided with the beginning of a revival of his ambitions as a poet. His later writing, *Advent* and what followed, is best understood as an attempt to build on the argument the review assumed and that *Third Person* magically sketched. Specific allusions to passages in Beckett's trilogy of novels in his later writing are not adventitious: they serve as starting point and measure. Later, the example of Beckett's *Still* led him back to the engraver Stanley William Hayter, whom Reavey had persuaded to supply a frontispiece to signed copies of *Third Person*, so that Hayter came to illustrate Coffey's *Death of Hektor* and a volume of translations from Éluard.[16] The relationship for the busier Beckett, on the other hand, eventually became an annual Christmas card, which is not unimportant either. Coffey was not a young author who needed to be encouraged. He was a tie with the past that was no less precious as the past receded. In short, the later relation between Beckett and Coffey rested on the acknowledgement of earlier friendship and a singular moment retrieved after a significant interval. No less and no more.

Two further, incidental points are relevant here. First, Coffey's doctoral dissertation and philosophical publications in the *Modern Schoolman* overlap Beckett's interests minimally, but, by 1938, Coffey was well acquainted with the German Idealist tradition. Forty years later, in retirement, I found him supervising a University of London doctorate on Hegel – and still able, I might add, to quote medieval philosophers in Latin by the yard. Another of Coffey's interests that we discussed at the later time was the continuity of the Idealist tradition through Nietzsche, Coffey then being particularly interested in the application to W.B. Yeats and the establishment of the Irish Free State. The continuity of the same Idealist tradition was something Beckett had previously followed up, in his way, in Gaultier's handbook of the same title,[17] but I do not know if his early interest owed anything to Coffey or Coffey's later interest owes anything to Beckett.

I mention these coincidences because it need not be supposed that Beckett's and Coffey's conversations were limited to conventional neo-Thomist topics or authors. Far from it, I should guess, and, as one important instance, the allusions to Hegel in *Third Person* suggest a shared currency for discussion. Coffey suggested that the Descartes of Beckett's *Whoroscope* could be interpreted through Hegel,[18] and is very likely to have been ahead of Beckett in his technical understanding of Being and Non-Being. The application of a dialectal solution to a dualist problem in *Third Person* suggests as much, and it is something that might have provided a bone to worry over during those walks through the Île-de-France countryside in 1939. Commentators who find Hegelian structures embedded in the articulation of Beckett's later novels may not be importing ideas that were never in the author's mind, therefore, and I confirm that Coffey was aware of the Hegelian Master-Slave relationship in *Godot* several years before it began to be publicly discussed. The appendix to *Watt* and the oddly angry put-down of Father Ambrose in *Malone Dies* are reminders that Beckett did not feel he had to buy Coffey's neo-Thomist package or anything like it, but the irritation is of a kind one finds other instances of, occasionally, in his earlier writing.

Secondly and related, it is worth remarking that Arland Ussher was the only other Irishman with philosophical pretensions with whom Beckett discussed philosophical matters. Indeed, Beckett corresponded with Ussher throughout the period when *Murphy* was written, leaving a paper-trail that is often lacking in Coffey's case. But Ussher lacked Coffey's trained background, was always more *belle-lettristic*, and Beckett's estimation of his abilities grew less as he himself came to know more. The vague existentialism Ussher promoted in earlier years can be measured by his published writing. I attended some of his 'conversational evenings' much later, when he was more interested in the tarot pack, and found him still unconvincing. Only sweet Arthur Power, who introduced me to him, was forever impressed and I can confirm that it was difficult to tell if Ussher had read any of Beckett's books or not.[19] I knew Ussher and Coffey in relative old age, but the difference between the mental powers of each of them was immense.

V

What effect might the review have had if it had been published in 1938? It is doubtful if it would have saved *Murphy* from the short-term fate it suffered. It was, like the book itself, too far ahead of its English readers and war was imminent. In Ireland, De Valera had already closed the country down and the Emergency arrived only to seal an unwelcoming situation. Beckett was best known for his part in the recent court case in which he had been publicly described as the 'bawd and blasphemer' from Paris, and one should remember that the review he liked best came from a writer who had also been banned.[20] No review, unless a favourable review had been written by the Archbishop of Dublin in very simple language, could have retrieved the situation. Coffey was only known in England to readers of the *Criterion*. He had used French printers for a couple of semi-private publications, but had no reputation in Paris outside a circle of Irish friends and French postgraduates. In the minds of most Irish readers he wrote himself off as too clever by half even before he left Dublin, and the style of the review would not have persuaded them otherwise. His college contemporary, Brian O'Nolan, spoke for the man at the Dublin bus stop when he parodied the pretensions of Joyce's experimental writing, and when *Third Person* received its only Irish notice – by Austin Clarke, on the state radio programme – the collection was summarily dismissed. In short, publication of Coffey's review would have served to confirm existing prejudices – appearing like more manure from the same stable – although publication might have lifted Beckett's spirits, slightly.

If Coffey's review had been available when Beckett's earlier writing was discovered after the success of *Godot*, on the other hand, it could have prompted a different kind of engagement from one that we are only now beginning to recover from. As things turned out, Hugh Kenner's suggestion that Descartes was the key to this difficult author, reinforced by an essay from Samuel Mintz,[21] turned Anglophone readers off into an enjoyable detour. Kenner's coinage of the phrase 'Cartesian Centaur' lodged in the memory and became a key that closed as many doors to understanding as it opened. Coffey's starting point – which takes for granted that the structure of the novel displays a distrustful critique, not hilarious celebration, of Cartesian dualism – is the more profitable one.[22] Similarly, the way Coffey's review incorporates references to the Presocratics accurately conveys their subordinate position in the overall argument. They play a supplementary role, and, if Beckett's irony is obscured by the relish with which he observes his puppets, Coffey is not confused. He isolates the issue on which the intellectual plot turns: Murphy's confrontation with what Mr Endon represents, as observed by the author, the qualification being all-important. The resulting dilemma is one, Coffey demonstrates, that the author does not resolve but can only upstage with delicate humanity. In short, the review could have helped enormously at the crucial moment when academic discussion of Beckett began to accumulate. It might also, as a result, have drawn greater critical attention to Coffey's own writing, although he has never been forgotten by a small number of Irish poets.

The summary conclusion rests on a point I have reiterated, that Beckett gave the manuscript to Coffey. It is the ultimate acknowledgement that Coffey was the most sympathetic of the book's early readers and the one from whose different understanding of the same themes Beckett learned most. Subsequent readers might have learned something sooner, too. Future learners also have something to learn from the open exchange between two exceptional minds who understood each other so well.

NOTES

This essay previously appeared in *The Recorder* (New York), vol. 18, nos. 1 and 2 (Fall, 2005), pp.956–114.

1. Brian Coffey, letter to Thomas MacGreevy, Paris 6 December 1935. MS 8110/20, TCD.
2. James Knowlson *Damned to Fame: The Life of Samuel Beckett* (London: Bloomsbury, 1996), p.219, quoting letters to MacGreevy at TCD. Knowlson is the source of all undocumented references to Beckett's biography in the present essay.
3. Described by Knowlson, *Damned to Fame*, pp.96–97, 152–53, 219.
4. J.C.C. Mays, 'Brian Coffey (1905–1995)', *The UCD Aesthetic: Celebrating 150 Years of UCD Writers*, ed. Anthony Roche (Dublin: New Island, 2005), pp.87–98. I never saw the *Murphy* manuscript. Coffey's son, John, remembers trying to decipher the writing of the holograph notebooks in which it is contained, in about 1959, before they were sold to a private collector sometime during the 1960s (personal communications: 21 February and 6 April 2005).
5. Symbolism was a feature of Coffey–Beckett meal arrangements. See Brian Coffey 'Memory's Murphy Maker: Some Notes on Samuel Beckett', *Threshold* (Belfast), vol. 17 (1962), pp.28–36 at p.33. The physical haphazardness here is deliberate.
6. Published in *Intercessions* (London: Europa Press, 1937), pp.51–57.

7. Compare I Kings 18:44 with *Hamlet* III.ii.396–7.
8. In conversations at Southampton during August 1974, Coffey glossed the Hegelian themes in *Third Person*, and his critique of them as well as the Beckettian theme of 'One Way'.
9. Recorded from Coffey's point of view in 'Joyce! "What Now?"', *Irish University Review*, vol. 7, no. 1 (spring 1982), pp.28–31.
10. Coffey, 'Memory's Murphy Maker', p.29.
11. Knowlson, *Damned to Fame*, p.295. Knowlson p.762, n.166 provides the reference for Harvey referring to a Dartmouth College Library MS.
12. For the loan of Maritain and Coffey's part in *Les Deux besoins* see Deirdre Bair, *Samuel Beckett: A Biography* (New York: Harcourt Brace & Jovanovich, 1978), p.292 and p.295.
13. There is a classified list of Coffey manuscripts held at the University of Delaware at http://www.lib.udel.edu/ud/spec/findaids/coffey.
14. Samuel Beckett and George Duthuit, 'Three Dialogues: III. Bram van Velde', *Disjecta: Miscellaneous Writings and a Dramatic Fragment*, ed. Ruby Cohn (London: John Calder, 1983), p.142. *Les Deux besoins* and Beckett's other essays on painters and painting from the same period are collected in the same volume.
15. Beckett's response is quoted by Bair, *Samuel Beckett*, pp.479–80. I have not located the original.
16. Hayter's illustrations of all these titles are most conveniently to be found in Peter Black and Désirée Moorhead, *The Prints of Stanley William Hayter: A Complete Catalogue*, (London: Phaidon, 1992).
17. Jules de Gaultier, *De Kant à Nietzsche*, 10th edn (Paris: Mercure de France, 1930). See *Beckett's 'Dream' Notebook*, ed. John Pilling (Reading: Beckett International Foundation, 1999), #1143 *et seq.*
18. Coffey, 'Memory's Murphy Maker', pp.28–29.
19. Beckett's earlier correspondence with Ussher is in HRC MS | Beckett, Samuel | Series 2. Correspondence (box 9, folder 5). The later correspondence between the two, now preserved in TCD MS 9031/41–77, is relatively perfunctory and personal. For Beckett's later opinion of Ussher, see his comments to Aidan Higgins in letters dated 30 August 1955 and 24 March 1959 (HRC: ibid., box 8, folder 9). Ussher's earlier philosophical essays were collected in *Postscript on Existentialism* (Dublin: Sandymount Press, 1946) and *The Twilight of the Ideas* (Dublin: Sandymount Press, 1948).
20. *Mary Lavelle* (1936) was the first of several novels by Kate O'Brien to be banned by the Irish Censorship Board.
21. In the same journal, *Perspective*, vol. 11, no. 3 (autumn 1959), pp.132–41 and pp.156–65 respectively. Kenner's essay became a chapter in his book on Beckett published by Grove Press in 1961.
22. As C.J. Ackerley notes in his *Demented Particulars: The Annotated 'Murphy'*, 2nd edn (Tallahassee, FL: Journal of Beckett Studies Books, 2004), p.18.

CHAPTER NINE

More and/or Less than Fifty Years Ago

BRIAN COFFEY

EDITORS' NOTE

As a young man Samuel Beckett was a keen golfer, even playing in solitude on occasion, hitting two golf balls round the course at Carrickmines, County Dublin, where he was a member. Playing from a handicap of seven, Beckett in fact represented Trinity College Dublin at golf during his student years (1923–27).[1] Written in 1984 and published here for the first time is a brief, impressionistic reminiscence by Brian Coffey concerning his lifelong friendship with Beckett, in particular a number of rounds of golf played by the pair in the 1930s and 1940s.[2] First introduced to each other in 1934 by Thomas MacGreevy, their paths crossed a number of times in London, Paris and Dublin. They moved in the same circles in Paris in the late 1930s, with Coffey even returning to Ireland with Beckett for his appearance as a witness in Harry Sinclair's libel action against Oliver St John Gogarty in 1937.[3] It is therefore curious that many such aspects of the friendship are completely omitted in Coffey's own essay here. John Coffey, the poet's son, has said that his father always displayed a certain reticence in talking about his Paris years, a time when he saw Beckett regularly.[4] Such reticence could perhaps account for their non-appearance here. Furthermore, the wry, ironic tone of the piece, echoing the tone of the satirical works that Coffey was composing in the 1970s and 1980s, would seem to indicate that the essay be read in a less than strict manner. This tone explains the idiosyncracies of the text, most of which we have allowed to remain as they appear in the typescript, while we have silently amended only the most problematic grammatical errors. Despite its omissions and the brevity of the piece, it is none the less of significant value, if only for its demonstration of the genuine affection held for Beckett by its author.

I

One saw some of the work before one had met the man. That was in 1930, in Grafton Street, Dublin, in Combridge's,[5] a bookshop where the manager, Mr. Nairn, has just received copies of *Whoroscope*, a poem by Samuel Beckett which was selling at more than a Dublin student could then afford.[6]

After the more than fifty years since the events related in this part of this piece were being undergone one still remembers having been struck by the word 'potatoey' occurring in an aggressive text.[7] Spuds in your eye, dear reader!
Soon after, one had left Dublin for Paris, entering finally the less than fifty years ago and the start of the second part of the piece.[8]

II

To continue, informally now, one becoming me, and using a term as near as one remembers a term due to Beckett, written possibly *kkrrit-tikk*,[9] shortened hereforth to K (plural: Ks), to refer to that choosy class of literary eunuchs that dislike journalistic biographers who discover facts they haven't, I met Beckett via Tom McGreevy's introduction near Edith Street in Chelsea.[10] We then went to the Six Bells[11] for a drink and a chat among all the actors who then talked a lot about the mission of carrying Shaw to those noticed by W.B. as 'coming up through the bookclubs'.[12]

We arranged to meet again in Dublin and some weeks later played our first of many games of golf at a mountain links, Carrickmines,[13] near Beckett's home. There, we always played good golf, which included making eagles at the long (520 yards) third.[14] We did not know then, and later it was denied that there had ever been any, but there we were dead centre in those good old days now gone without recall. Beckett, at other moments of that stretch was busy writing *Murphy*. He allowed both Denis Devlin and I to read the completed typescript. Both of us admired and loved in particular the Mozartian sound of Beckett's prose and when, eventually, the published book was reviewed in a Sunday paper by a well known K we both shared Beckett's pain and grief at the treatment his work received at the pen or more likely the dictation – abuse and malicious name-calling – of a truly conservative discritic.[15]

During the winter of that year Beckett left Dublin for Paris and was invited to write something in French but this first attempt (which I remember as showing many traces in advance of Beckett's later French) lost itself in geometrical items which reminded a reader of *A Vision*.[16] Beckett may have begun a sequel to *Murphy*, of which the only remaining part may be the initial passages of *Watt*. When I met Beckett in 1945 or 1946 in Dublin, on the same occasion as his return from Paris, wasted away to bones, he said: 'I've brought a book back', and this was the book offered to a large number of London publishers to no avail and disappearing while Beckett wrote the trilogy and *Godot*. But finally *Watt* did appear.[17] But I'm going back to our golf. About 200 yards from the fourth tee where our Dunlops[18] lay we found a withered spore-filled large puffball. It reminded us of the Baudelairean *Sein Martyrisé* which stands also for civilization.[19] With a pre-celtic name like Cobhthaigh I could be impassive.[20] Not so Beckett who turned pale and reacted like a man nauseated, but he said nothing and went on to make a bogey.[21]

Later, on the way towards today I did often remark a barometer setting towards worse worsening in the manner discovered by numerous Ks. There was a time when one of them used to talk of Joyce in terms of *Ulysses* as an *Inferno*, *Finnegans Wake* as a *Purgatorio* and so on to a future *Paradiso*. Literary hermeneutics should include a caution not to write off a life or work as endless night until 'the poor old chap is dead'. And now for part three.

III

Beckett was in London some time after the fall of Heath, vetting a production of one of his later plays at the Old Vic.[22] He approached me from the front of the building, about 50 years off, in his black and white herringbone coat, the well-known, slim figure, menacing, suggesting a jaguar, the lethal in person. Into the pub, bitter, sandwiches and chat, no break due to years of absence in the free talk. He told me about his happy meeting with East German players and of cleaning up *Godot*. Then we started to walk towards Holland Park. As it had been. The walking, the quiet, the noting, remarks, seeing. In such a setting I saw what I had never seen, unsuffering happiness in the Beckett the Ks have made the man himself into.

We were on a bridge, lake waters each side. A mother was placing bread crumbs on her about five year old daughter's head, above which the birds, gulls and pigeons planed and hovered. The child was awaiting the alighting of airborn feet, webbed or scratching, the small face of expectation and concern. I heard Sam exclaim: 'Look. Brian, look!' And I looked to see the scarred, wrecked and still beautiful features declaring his delight, his happiness at another like human sharing the feelings that had been his own much more than fifty years before. *Ever the same anew.*[23] The real Beckett, missed by all the brick-red word spinners, by all the self-assured plundering Yale-birds,[24] who has discovered compassion and loving in the night of agony, in the man-made midden of malice.

NOTES

1. Beckett's sporting interests are well documented in James Knowlson's biography, *Damned to Fame: The Life of Samuel Beckett* (London: Bloomsbury, 1996). According to Knowlson, Beckett 'joined Carrickmines Golf Club as a student member and, during the holidays, would often complete as many as seventy-two holes in a day. Golf was for him, he told Lawrence Harvey, "all mixed up with the imagination", with the impact on him of the ocean which one could see from the local course, and the landscape of the Dublin foothills.' Returning to Dublin after the war (and on the threshold of his great creative period), Beckett 'spent his days playing golf by himself at Carrickmines Golf Club' and, in the clubhouse, drinking 'double whiskeys with his old golfing coach'. For details of Beckett's golfing career, see pp.33, 61, 344, 368, 439.
2. Original typescripts are held at the University of Delaware Special Collections, box 2, folder 25.
3. See Knowlson, *Damned to Fame*, pp.275–80. Details of Coffey and Beckett's friendship are dealt with at greater length elsewhere, in particular by J.C.C. Mays in this volume and in his essay on Brian Coffey included in *The UCD Aesthetic: Celebrating 150 Years of UCD Writers*, ed. Anthony Roche (Dublin: New Island, 2005), pp.87–98.
4. In conversation with the editor, 29 July 2005.
5. Then a well-known bookshop on Grafton St, Combridge's also appears indirectly in James Joyce's *Ulysses* where mention is made of 'Combridge's corner'. See James Joyce, *Ulysses*, Bodley Head edition, introduced by Declan Kiberd (Harmondsworth: Penguin, 1992, 2000), p.214.
6. Samuel Beckett's first published poem. Awarded a prize of ten pounds for the best poem on the given subject of Time in a competition judged by Richard Aldington and Nancy Cunard at the Hours Press, it was published in 1930 in an edition of 100 signed copies at a price of five shillings and 200 unsigned at one shilling each. See Knowlson, *Damned to Fame*, pp.111–13.
7. 'Whoroscope', lines 8–9:
   We're moving he said we're off – Porca Madonna!
   the way a boatswain would be, or a sack-of-potatoey charging Pretender. (Samuel Beckett, *Collected Poems 1930–1978* [London: John Calder, 1984], p.1).
8. Coffey moved to Paris in 1930 to begin research studies in Physical Chemistry under Jean Baptiste Perrin.
9. *Waiting for Godot*, Act II:
   VLADIMIR: Sewer-rat!
   ESTRAGON: Curate!
   VLADIMIR: Cretin!
   ESTRAGON: [*with finality.*] Crritic!
   VLADIMIR: Oh!
   [*He wilts, vanquished, and turns away.*] (Samuel Beckett, *The Complete Dramatic Works* [London: Faber & Faber, 1986], p.70).

10. Thomas MacGreevy (1893–1967) changed his surname mid-career from McGreevy to MacGreevy. Coffey uses the earlier version here.
11. Beckett took lodgings at 48 Paulton's Square, Chelsea from January 1934 until August of that year. In September he moved into a bedsit at 34 Gertrude St, also in Chelsea. The Six Bells, located at 197 Kings Road, was then known for its artistic clientele.
12. Probably an anachronistic reference to the prologue from an 'Old Man' in W.B. Yeats' last play *The Death of Cuchulainn*, (1939): 'I am sure that as I am producing a play for people I like, it is not probable, in this vile age, that there will be more in number than those who listened to the first performance of Milton's *Comus*. On the present occasion they must know the old epics and Mr Yeats' plays about them; such people, however poor, have libraries of their own. If there are more than a hundred I won't be able to escape people educating themselves out of the Book Societies and the like, sciolists all, pickpockets and opinionated bitches.' See *The Collected Plays of W.B. Yeats* (New York: Macmillan, 1952), p.438.
13. Carrickmines Golf Club is a nine-hole course located about eight miles south of Dublin city. It would have been only around a mile from Cooldrinagh, Beckett's family home in Foxrock, Co. Dublin.
14. Either a lapse of memory on Coffey's part or a figment of his imagination, since his description of the third hole on the Carrickmines course is inaccurate. The third hole is, in fact, a 320-yard par 4. An eagle (2 under par) would be virtually impossible for an amateur golfer.
15. Possibly a reference to Dilys Powell's review in the *Sunday Times*, which, according to Deirdre Bair's biography, Beckett found particularly irritating. See Deirdre Bair, *Samuel Beckett: A Biography* (London: Jonathan Cape, 1978), p.285.
16. W.B. Yeats, *A Vision: The Original 1925 Version*, in *The Collected Works of W.B. Yeats*, vol. 13, ed. Catherine E. Paul and Margaret Mills Harper (New York: Scribners, 2008). The work by Beckett referred to here is probably 'Les Deux besoins', a short essay on art written, according to Deirdre Bair, in 1938 or 1939 with the encouragement of his friend Alfred Péron. It was collected in Beckett's *Disjecta: Miscellaneous Writings and A Dramatic Fragment* (New York: Grove Press, 1984), pp.55–58. Beckett's inclusion of a geometrical diagram to illustrate his ideas were no doubt the source of the comparison with Yeats. See Bair, *Beckett: A Biography*, pp.294–95.
17. *Watt* was published in 1953.
18. A brand of golf clubs and equipment.
19. A reference to Charles Baudelaire's poem 'Au Lecteur' in *Les Fleurs Du Mal*:
    Ainsi qu'un débauché pauvre qui baise et mange
    Le sein martyrisé d'une antique catin,
    Nous volons au passage un plaisir clandestin
    Que nous pressons bien fort comme une vieille orange.
    Translated by Roy Campbell:
    Just as a lustful pauper bites and kisses
    The scarred and shrivelled breast of an old whore,
    We steal, along the roadside, furtive blisses,
    Squeezing them, like stale oranges, for more.
    From Roy Campbell, *Collected Works II*, (Craighall: A. D. Donker Publishers, 1985) , p.61.
20. Cobhtaigh is the Irish version of Coffey.
21. A 1 over par in golf.
22. Edward (Ted) Heath, Prime Minister of the United Kingdom from 1970 to 1974 and leader of the British Conservative Party from 1965 to 1975. He fell from power in 1974 after the seven-week miners' strike and was succeeded as leader of the party by Margaret Thatcher in 1975.
23. This line is cited from part one of Brian Coffey's *Advent* (*PV*, p.112).
24. A reference to the Yale school of literary criticism, which in the 1970s included Paul de Man, Geoffrey Hartman, J. Hillis Miller and Harold Bloom.

CHAPTER TEN

'Missouri Sequence' and the Search for a Habitat

BENJAMIN KEATINGE

The writing of 'Missouri Sequence' and its publication in 1962 mark an important episode in Coffey's creative development. Following the publication of *Third Person* by George Reavey's Europa Press in 1938, Coffey wrote little and published less. From 1947, with a growing family, Coffey worked as an academic philosopher and teacher at the University of St Louis, Missouri and his career as a poet was held in abeyance as he concentrated on earning a living and developing his academic career. This changed when, in 1952, Coffey resigned from St Louis in a dispute over 'academic principle' with his Jesuit employers.[1] However, even before this (as it transpired) decisive break with the academic world, Coffey's poetic instincts were stirring. In a letter of July 1950 to Thomas MacGreevy, Coffey writes:

> Poetry is again filling my private thoughts, after some years, and I may perhaps get a chance to do some verses. If I don't I'll burst. As for the old country, it still looks as good as ever, especially those Kerry sea-shores with the lovely cool waters coming in in September. Alas, alas.[2]

We see here the precise genesis of 'Missouri Sequence' in a renewed creative impulse and a sense of dislocation and homesickness as Coffey reminisces about the Ireland he knew and wished to return to. Unlike Samuel Beckett, whose hostility to Irish conditions dictated his move to France and unlike Denis Devlin, who willingly joined the Irish diplomatic service 'to get out of Ireland',[3] Coffey always regretted his enforced exile. His letters to MacGreevy are full of schemes by which he might return to Ireland and live and work there. So Coffey exhibits an unreconciled stoicism towards his exile while Denis Devlin and Beckett

willingly embraced theirs. As for Thomas MacGreevy, he reconciled
himself to the cultural claustrophobia of his native land to become in
1950 Director of the National Gallery of Ireland and he remained in
Ireland until his death in 1967.

In a poignant letter to MacGreevy, following the death of Devlin in
1959, Coffey expresses his regret at the *émigré* status of their circle:

> I thought a lot about those days in Paris when we were all
> together, surprised to find how close it all was to my heart, as if
> of yesterday – one's best times timeless or unaging rather. I
> have always been sad about the accidents that scattered us, as it
> seemed, we could have been more 'useful' at home. I am in fact
> still quite unreconciled to the role of foreigner here, exile from
> there and so on, at this late hour.[4]

This letter expresses a certain anguish of exile and in 'Missouri
Sequence' themes of exile, home and belonging are prominent. The
breaking of Coffey's poetic silence involved a re-engagement with his
native land that testifies to the struggles of emigration and expatriation
and to the lure of Ireland as both a geographical and imaginative
homeland.

In some ways, 'Missouri Sequence' is the least typical of Coffey's
poems, adopting as it does a conversational style and using the vocabulary of place and social life in more obvious ways than do *Third Person*,
Advent or *Death of Hektor*. Its formal accessibility (as compared with
Coffey's elliptical style elsewhere) is complemented by its themes of
exile and displacement, which address a core Irish experience, that
of migration. The economic hardship behind Irish emigration also
forms a context for the poem. The circumstances of the Coffey family
following Brian Coffey's resignation from his lecturing post in 1952
were, as the poet admits in a letter to MacGreevy of 5 August 1952,
'desperate',[5] with the family surviving on an average income of 45
dollars per week. Despite numerous applications for other academic
positions in America, Coffey found himself without an income to
provide for his large family. In a reversal of roles, Coffey's wife Bridget
was able to earn money through fabric design to help them through
this difficult period, while Coffey kept house, cooking and looking after
the children. It was in these inauspicious circumstances that Coffey's
return to poetry took place beginning in July 1952, after which he
'wrote steadily' through to June 1953.[6] Seeking a 'less elliptical line',
Coffey adopted 'a five accentual base-line going down to two and up
to seven accents, with rhyme and no rhyme at pleasure, and quite a lot

of "spondees" to help things out. Very plain diction, little or no complex metaphor, and a close relation to personal experience.'[7]

So the poem is partly a biographical meditation through which
Coffey relates his own circumstances to the common experience of
migrants, those who have 'drifted in here from the river / Irish, German,
Bohemian' (*PV*, p.69) in the cycle of displacement and resettlement
which characterizes Irish and American experience. A brief look at
Missouri's history shows the Coffey family's situation to be representative of migrant lives:

> The first settlement was made at Ste Genevieve in 1735 by the
> French, and the second by the French at St Louis in 1764. The
> Spanish also came up the river in search of gold, and St Louis
> was soon a busy trading centre … From the eastward soon came
> emigrants from other states – especially Kentucky, Tennessee, and
> the Virginias – and later came the emigrants from foreign shores,
> particularly the Germans, Irish, and some Scotch … There are
> settlements of Italians, Hungarians, and Bohemians, but on the
> whole these nationalities make up only a small part of the popu-
> lation. St Louis is a cosmoplitan city, but the predominant strains
> of foreign blood are German and Irish.[8]

Historically, a large proportion of immigrants to Missouri were
Catholic, many being of Irish origin, and Coffey was aware of these
facts. Coffey even wrote to MacGreevy in August 1952 to suggest the
rather far-fetched scheme of an Irish government-sponsored study of
this pattern of migration:

> I have discovered that there is a great amount of lore about the
> Irish immigrants in Missouri, which has not been written up in
> a way which would li[n]k up the present Ireland with the Irish
> here. Would our government be willing to sponsor a writer to
> collect the material and write up the story of the Irish in the
> States? Or would it be possible for me to be put in touch with
> some of the rich Irish in the East, who might be willing to spon-
> sor a similar effort?[9]

While a large-scale study of Irish immigration to the United States
would have probably been beyond Coffey's interests, he is most certainly meditating during the composition of 'Missouri Sequence' on
Irish migration patterns and the 'lore' of immigration into Missouri.

The poem also engages with Missouri landscape and community,
features which gain in particularity when seen through the eyes of

an exiled Irishman. This concentration on communal surroundings is particularly noticeable in an unpublished poem entitled 'Old Gravois Road', which stands as a kind of prolegomena to 'Missouri Sequence'. 'Old Gravois Road' may have originally been envisaged as the first part of a five-part 'Missouri Sequence' (instead of the existing four sections) in which local lore would have played an even greater role than in the existing poem.[10] This discarded first section underlines the history of travel and displacement found in the published text via reference to a particular local byway, an 'old gravel road', named after a French family since dispersed or deceased.[11] It is 'a discard' which is 'passed beside' (OGR, 6–7) by the new highway, but it still stands as a reminder of those lost generations of migrants whose early struggles echo those of the present generation. Coffey's own family participate in the sense of adventure American frontier history abounds in:

> We had come from overseas,
> driving southwest from the Mound City,
> exiles, not the first, not the last,
> remembering home, forseeing no return.   (OGR, 8–11)

The sad resignation of the published poem 'Pain it was to come, / pain it will be to go' (*PV*, p.72) is mirrored in this earlier draft with the concluding lines 'the changing will not hurt us / though we grieve' (OGR, 221–22). The attempt to put down roots in a new community only to be uprooted again reverberates painfully. The natural cycle of seasons, the particular local climate are juxtaposed in 'Old Gravois Road' (as they are in the published poem) with the enforced displacement of new beginnings, the return in the Coffeys' case to the old world from the new:

> Six years have passed since we first saw
> cedars standing upright on brown hills,
> six years of winter, spring, summer and fall
> recurrent seasons never twice the same.
> In this seventh year we must move on again.   (OGR, 16–20)

Likewise, the parallel Coffey maintains between Irish conditions and those in Missouri is 'apprehended at first mainly in difference' (OGR, 44), which nonetheless belies a solidarity of purpose expressed through communal living which, Coffey imples, is common to both Irish and American communities. The 'love of Ireland / withering for Irishmen' (*PV*, p.70) is formulated, in the published poem, through an identification with people and place:

> ... the hills behind Dublin,
> those white stone cottages,
> grass green as no other green is green,
> my mother's people, their ways.   (*PV*, p.70)

The road of 'Old Gravois Road' is a kind of unifying principle that links the disparate farmhouses of House Springs into a real community. The road 'goes past Les Weber's farm / goes past Matt Brouk's / skirts a stream soon to be lost in sand / under the bluff by Bear Creek' (OGR, 25–28). It acts as a kind of natural viaduct of communal feeling shown to be common to Irish and Missourian circumstances. The 'continual surprise' (OGR, 42) of a new environment becomes, over time, a sense of home and belonging comparable to Coffey's identification with Ireland and Irishness. A balance of attachments is thus formed which runs through both 'Old Gravois Road' and the published 'Missouri Sequence' and which stimulates direct comparisons between the two homelands:

> Your trees show the strain of harsh seasons,
> ours are touched by gentler heat and cold.
> Our grasses – you do not know what grass is –
> your corn – corn will not head out in Ireland.   (OGR, 47–50)

Indeed, as Coffey confesses, 'I am distracted by comparisons' (*PV*, p.69) between the old world and the new and as 'Missouri Sequence' shows, conditions of exile lead to complex meditations on identity and belonging.

The concept of a 'habitat' is one which helps to elucidate the exile's dilemma in his search for a viable home, but it also encompasses the search for an imaginative space, intellectual affinity, the sense of relatedness not just to immediate surroundings, but to one's homeland, one's contemporaries, indeed to the whole public sphere understood as dealings with others in the broadest sense, or even with oneself. Coffey's meditations on exile are just one strand in a wider search for a habitat that requires a flexible and nuanced definition of what it means to belong, not just to a place, but to any form of human fraternity. We are accustomed to distinguishing the public and private spheres where public denotes the political and communal aspects of social life (anything from national politics to the local bus service) while the private denotes immediate family, friends and one's individual private space. There is thus a definite distinction made, in everyday thinking, between what is properly ours and what is shared with others. However, this definition, I suggest, is inadequate for discussing 'Missouri Sequence', which merges what are traditionally viewed as public and private realms so that a broader definition of social relationships is required, one which redefines belonging in terms of social and familial habitat.

'Missouri Sequence', of course, addresses private concerns, but it does so in a particular social and communal context rendering it an essentially social poem. The confiding and lyrical voice of the poem is interwoven with its public voice so that Coffey's own dilemmas transcend private experience by continual reference to shared experience. In its four sections, the published poem takes the form of verse letters addressed to Coffey's friends; but these are not wholly private missives since, as a published poem, 'Missouri Sequence' is a public document accessible to any reader.[12] Also, Coffey's circumstances in 1952 are inextricably linked to the public sphere – to the House Springs community, to St Louis University, to his own family – all of which cease, in the poem, to be wholly private concerns and enter into a publicly enunciated search for a poetic habitat. There is, then, a broad communal context for the poem that includes the immediate environs in Missouri but also people far away (like Thomas MacGreevy), historical figures like Su Tungpo and even imaginary beings (the fleeting Muse of section 3). The poem also reveals a metapoetic anxiety over the communicative function of poetry itself, so that the search for a habitat is not just the need for a physical home but also an imaginative need, a search for origins and destinations, a quest for belonging in the broadest possible sense.

In this connection, it is worth dwelling on some remarks made by Seamus Heaney on the poetry of Patrick Kavanagh. Kavanagh is, of course, well known for his championing of the parochial over the merely provincial in relation to his native County Monaghan. In 'The Placeless Heaven: Another Look at Kavanagh', Heaney argues that Kavanagh's early poetry uses the townland of Inniskeen as a 'real topographical presence' in the poetry,[13] while in the later poetry, Heaney suggests, we find Kavanagh inhabiting a homeland of the imagination where the locality of his birth exists as 'luminous spaces within his mind … transfigured images, sites where the mind projects its own force'.[14] There is an evolution, then, according to Heaney, from Kavanagh's earthy evocations of Inniskeen in the early verse, to a more imaginative procedure in the later verse. One could argue that Coffey employs both procedures in 'Missouri Sequence', where Missouri is the tangible and topographical locality, while Ireland becomes an imaginative homeland equated with more distant parallels, like Su Tungpo's China or the unreachable Muse figure. Clearly, Coffey's search for a habitat encompasses two modalities, the real and the imaginary, and they co-exist in complementary ways, neither being less luminous than the other.

This search for a habitat finds useful expression in the work of W.H. Auden, a poet not often associated with Coffey. Auden's well-known poem 'Thanksgiving for a Habitat' articulates the importance of a creative space for any writer, which encompasses, but is not limited to, the precise living space of the author. Auden's widely recognized gifts at describing private and public tensions (in such famous poems as 'September 1, 1939' and *New Year Letter*) are also relevant to Coffey's concerns in 'Missouri Sequence'. Auden's historical consciousness may be more expansive than Coffey's, but his search for 'A common meditative norm'[15] from which to survey the present moment involves the same type of elision of public and private spaces. Auden's poem 'Thanksgiving for a Habitat' celebrates domestic comfort in a house he acquired in 1957 in Austria and, in a local and precise way, it articulates that same process of orientation which his more famous, earlier poems also describe. In Auden's work, a habitat can take many forms, ranging from simple domestic arrangements to broader social obligations as well as matters of religious conviction or personal linkages of love and friendship. According to Auden, in all these various spheres, the poet is part of a community that defines itself in various ways, as a household, a neighbourhood, a religious congregation or a university department. While the poet may feel displaced in relation to his historical moment, and is often alienated from the society he lives in, the act of writing poetry implies an audience of sympathetic readers and hence a poetic community. The verse letter parades this fact by having an identified recipient, as do Auden's *New Year Letter* and each section of 'Missouri Sequence'; these poems are both private and public, being both personal communications and open letters for anyone who cares to read them.

It may seem somewhat arbitrary to draw a comparison between Auden's communal theories and 'Missouri Sequence', given Coffey's well-known antipathy towards his English contemporary. Coffey seems to have disliked Auden's poetic versatility as well as his left-wing rhetorical urgency. He even refers to Auden, in an interview with Parkman Howe, as 'that fearfully competent rhymer with practically no scruples at all'[16] and in a letter to Denis Devlin, praising Devlin's work, Coffey also disparages Auden:

Even now you have some pieces to your credit which anyone

would wish to have written, and you have an immense superior-
ity over Auden – who shows more versatility in rhyming that you
have yet bothered to show – though you could – in that you lack,
thank the Lord, his obtrusive hinting that he knows what makes
us all tick. He's too slick. You have the innocence of the mind
accepting mystery.[17]

Be this as it may, Coffey and Auden do find common ground in their
public voicing of private woe and, as I will argue, Auden's communal
themes help to elucidate Coffey's poem.

In his essay 'The Virgin and the Dynamo', from *The Dyer's Hand and
Other Essays*, Auden postulates three types of 'pluralities' summarised as
'crowds, societies and communities'.[18] A crowd is simply a loose assem-
bly of unconnected individuals; a society is an organized grouping with
defined interrelationships; and a community is a group of like-minded
individuals united, as Auden puts it, 'by a common love of something
other than themselves'.[19] The poet uses language, Auden suggests, in
order to turn a loose aggregate of unconnected experiences into an
organised linguistic unit amounting to a poetic community. He writes:

> The subject matter of a poem is comprised of a crowd of recol-
> lected occasions of feeling, among which the most important are
> recollections of encounters with sacred beings or events. The
> crowd the poet attempts to transform into a community by em-
> bodying it in a verbal society. Such a society, like any society in na-
> ture, has its own laws; its laws of prosody and syntax are
> analogous to the laws of physics and chemistry.[20]

By marshalling his experience through language, the poet enacts a
kind of social synthesis which is effected linguistically. Poetry is a social
act that implies an ideal community through the perfection of language
and also implies a real, human community in a group of sympathetic
readers. As Coffey reminds us, 'Poetry becomes humankind' (*PV*, p.86)
and 'The habit of withholding love / unfits us for poetry' (*PV*, p.86).

'Missouri Sequence' envisages different types of community or 'pluralities' along the lines suggested by Auden. The 'sacred beings or
events' mentioned by Auden resemble Coffey's imaginative processes
as he strives towards poetic perfection only to find it compromised by
the realities of his life in Missouri; the perfections of language and the
imperfections of life are sharply juxtaposed. By dwelling on the word
'perfect', referring to the 'never perfect work' (*PV*, p.80) and asking
'is one ever perfect here and now?' (*PV*, p.76), Coffey evinces an

Audenesque sense of the inevitability of creative and practical compromises. However, the poem also suggests that poetry can transcend
the contingencies of life. The 'Deepest winter perfect now' (*PV*, p.73)
that Coffey refers to in part one, 'Nightfall, Midwinter, Missouri', implies a mystical moment of achieved perfection that is interrogated as
the poem progresses. The poem turns on Coffey's tussle with imaginative and worldly dilemmas and his search for a true habitat involves
facing questions that he would 'rather not' (*PV*, p.70) face. On one
level, there is Coffey's care-worn anxiety about how to face the future
on a practical level, but also a cosmic dislocation played out on the
imaginative plane. It is the quest for what Coffey calls the 'true muse'
(*PV*, p.80) which directs him towards a poetic habitat or refuge. But,
as the poet is aware, 'he must not escape / from here and now' (*PV*,
p.81) and overlook worldly cares. The mystical enchantment of section
three, 'Muse, June, Related', is fleeting and transitory and is soon displaced by more mundane realities, but this juxtaposition creates a dialogic anxiety between real and imaginary planes.

Stan Smith, in his pioneering essay 'On Other Grounds: The Poetry
of Brian Coffey', has argued for the 'casualness' of Coffey's exile in
America, pointing out the 'circumstantial' attitude of the poet towards
his place of residence.'[21] Smith argues that this stands in contrast with the
more definitive break that exiled writers such as Joyce and Beckett made
with Ireland. Coffey's stated preference for a life in Ireland confirms
that he never made a programmatic rejection of his home country.
In these respects, his experience chimes with emigrant experience in
general and indeed Smith underlines this provisionality, arguing that:

> What the poem celebrates is a natural and inevitable vagrancy,
> rather than exile, which presupposes some determining locus
> in space and time. Drifting together, drifting apart, men live; all
> settlements, of the spirit or of the body, provisional, a making
> over of the self in the making of a home.[22]

Smith sees a link between 'the genesis of personal identity' and the
uncertain status of the exile/vagrant in 'Missouri Sequence'.[23] There is
certainly an ontological side to Coffey's search for personal, poetic
and social identity, something which Smith argues convincingly for.
However, it is equally clear that Coffey's poem participates, first and
foremost, in 'familiar categories of residence and expatriation'[24] as a
premise and occasion for wider questions of personal identity. These
'familiar categories' are never fully transcended; rather, 'Missouri
Sequence' participates in such categories in a far more obvious manner

than the lofty rejectionism of Joyce and Beckett, so that we *can* identify a 'determining locus in space and time' running through the poem. This process of orientation is based on locales of self which take their stimulus from real places and people so that Coffey's experience does fall within fairly well-defined categories of exile. The poem's sense of dislocation has a strong communal context, which grounds its more universal anxieties.

Indeed, Coffey obsessively ruminates on ideas of place and community, highlighting his solidarity with the Irish diaspora who have settled on the 'worn Ozark hills' (*PV*, p.70) of Missouri. The accidental pattern of migration amongst the 'Many Irish souls' (*PV*, p.70) who have found their way to 'Byrnesville' (*PV*, p.70) exhibits exilic casualness. Coffey speaks of the 'bitter necessity' (*PV*, p.71) that afflicts his family alongside others in a universal cycle of want and displacement which has 'no monopoly of Irish soil' (*PV*, p.71); socioeconomic woes are shared by all who have 'drifted in here from the river' (*PV*, p.69). There exists, then, a makeshift community in Missouri of those forced to consolidate themselves in a new environment. And in broader terms, Coffey's descriptions of Irish migrants are not far from our current ideas of an international Irish identity. The 'familiar categories of residence and expatriation', referred to by Stan Smith, would seem to include the Irish diaspora, those who for economic reasons have left Ireland and settled elsewhere, but who still form part of the Irish nation, broadly conceived.

If we take Auden's definition of a community as a group united 'by a common love of something other than themselves',[25] then the community of Byrnesville may seem excluded by this definition, as they are united by little else than the 'bitter necessity' (*PV*, p.71) of which Coffey speaks. However, the religious dimension to Coffey's communal sense consolidates the poem, bringing it closer to Auden's notion of a unified love of something other than the self. The last lines of section one, where Coffey describes

> the only Ireland we love
> where in Achill still
> the poor praise Christ aloud
> when the priest elevates
> the Saviour of the world   (*PV*, p.75)

show Coffey's identification with home-grown Catholicism. By foregrounding the strong communal sense of rural Ireland united around the Catholic faith, Coffey praises what Kavanagh and others excoriated as the pietistic conformity of rural Ireland, a view perhaps strengthened by his long absence from Ireland. Coffey also points to communal religious faith in America, reminding us of the 'Irish graves' (*PV*, p.69) at Byrnesville, a parish administered by a Cork-born priest known to Coffey. The local solidarity of 'Irish souls' (*PV*, p.70) in Coffey's parish is thus linked to their Catholic identity, which is local as well as international.

Coffey is also highly conscious of the secular aspects of communal life in Missouri, praising his 'honest, practical and kind' (*PV*, p.70) neighbours and honouring their friendship. The negative side of Auden's 'pluralities' finds voice in the rancour aroused by Coffey's resignation from St Louis University:

> celtic anger ruined me.
> Busy men see
> what it profits to see,
> malice in them as hard to prove
> as asininity.   (*PV*, p.83)

Coffey understandably prefers the easy familiarity of neighbours to the dubious manoeuvres of his academic employers, and the Coffey family participate in aspects of American life, adopting the ideals of self-reliance and self-sufficiency which are softened, but not eliminated, by neighbourly co-operation. Coffey's children 'know nothing of Ireland' and 'grow American' (*PV*, p.70) and the Coffey family celebrate Thanksgiving and Independence Day, participating in American customs and traditions. Thus Coffey's poem interweaves versions of communal life from both Irish and American experience, uniting common elements and drawing parallels across the Atlantic.

In the dedication of section one, 'Nightfall, Midwinter, Missouri' to Thomas MacGreevy, and section three, 'Muse, June, Related' to the memory of Denis Devlin, we see Coffey reaching out to a distant poetic community who form part of his audience. The anguished intimacy of Coffey's address to MacGreevy –

> Dear Tom, in Ireland,
> you have known
> the pain between
> its fruiting and the early dream
> and you will hear me out.   (*PV*, p.70)

– demonstrates, once again, Coffey's regretful attitude towards the scattering of his poetic contemporaries. Coffey's return to poetry was tentative, in need of affirmation from his peers, a point well made by James Matthew Wilson in this volume in relation to Coffey's mentor, Jacques Maritain. The so-called Irish 1930s modernists (Coffey, Devlin, Beckett, MacGreevy, Reavey) may not hold together as a group; as J.C.C. Mays argues, 'None of them, at any time – except perhaps Brian Coffey retrospectively – thought of themselves as members of a group.'[26] But this is an important exception in respect of 'Missouri Sequence'. If the loose association between these writers has been exaggerated in the past, it remains the case that Coffey himself *did* see something communal in the *émigré* status of his contemporaries, united by their very dispersal.

Susan Shreibman has argued, in relation to Devlin, that 'Foreigners, foreignness, being a foreigner in one's own land, being a foreigner abroad, being foreign to those one loves and is loved by, as well as one's self' is central to his work.[27] Coffey's deliberate seeking-out of an audience, his perhaps wishful sense of solidarity with his peers, belies this overriding sense of estrangement. Coffey's 'warring wishes' (*PV*, p.72) express an anxiety as if to confirm his underlying lack of belonging. The poet retracts into himself, 'cowering bone-sore, / combating retractile fear / with bankrupt self' (*PV*, p.76), just as he simultaneously reaches out in search of compensatory affirmation. The social currents of the poem act as a deliberate counterpoint to Coffey's feelings of isolation.

Just as the public and private spheres are blurred in relation to issues of community, so the inner and outer life of the poet is enacted as a living dichotomy. Coffey dramatizes the act of composition, portraying it as an interactive dynamic between the poet and his muse. Poetry, Coffey states in 'Extracts from "Concerning Making"', 'involves a self-aware obedience to the precious stream or flow of interior life always moving always vanishing but out of which alone arises the beginnings of a poem'.[28] In metapoetic fashion, 'Missouri Sequence' depicts this process and section three, 'Muse, June, Related', is about this relationship between inner and outer life:

> He did not know, not yet,
> him hers, his elements
> scattered on shore and shore
> where he must run, must implore
> her veiled features in desperate race
> to recapture such a grace   (*PV*, p.80)

Thus the 'always moving always vanishing' muse is personified and objectified so that the poet *can* communicate with her in a way which resembles a social relationship, a reaching out towards embodied inspiration, 'The true muse fleshed' (*PV*, p.80).

This dialogic relationship with the muse figure reflects Coffey's views on creativity in which he sees the muse as the stimulus for the poem rather than the direct agency of its composition; as he states in 'Extracts from "Concerning Making"': 'The Muse initiates the beginning of the movement, the poet labours towards the poem.'[29] This formulation reflects Coffey's view of the poet as a 'makar', a craftsman who works towards poetic perfection in an artisanal rather than transcendent way.[30] The poet seeks inspiration from an elusive muse, but he does not embody that inspiration himself; he labours towards perfection only to come up against 'The never perfect work' (*PV*, p.80). Such a view reflects Coffey's profoundly Thomistic outlook on life and creativity in which human activity defers to a social and theological hierarchy. Coffey had, after all, written his doctoral thesis on 'The Notion of Order According to St Thomas Acquinas'. As James Matthew Wilson argues in this volume, Coffey's neo-Thomist aesthetics steer a middle course between what Jacques Maritain describes as the 'sin of materialism' and the 'sin of the angels'. So when Coffey writes 'Poetry becomes humankind' (*PV*, p.86) and 'The habit of withholding love / unfits us for poetry' (*PV*, p.86) he is expressing a clear sense of poetry's place in a social order which is subject to a divine order. Coffey's children 'make their friendships' (*PV*, p.71) and 'learn to love God' (*PV*, p.71), thus acquiring a dual allegiance to a human community and to Catholicism. The poet inhabits a defined space in God's hierarchy, he is both abstract and concrete, both angelistic and material, part of a divine and a social order. Poetry offers a possible transcendence within the temporal realm, but it too is full of compromises, a reflection perhaps of 'twisted man' (*PV*, p.86) and his imperfections. 'But is one ever perfect here and now?' (*PV*, p.76), asks Coffey, only to reply 'One is all too sure that one is not' (*PV*, p.76). The 'future labour' (*PV*, p.80) of the poet can only lead to the 'never perfect work' (*PV*, p.80) and Coffey is constantly aware of the frustrations this imperfectibility brings.

Of course, in Missouri Coffey's poetry could find no immediate outlet. Apart from his wife Bridget, only Leonard Eslick, a university colleague (and dedicatee of part two of 'Missouri Sequence'), knew that Coffey was a poet who was writing again. With this artistic isolation in mind, it is perhaps inevitable that Coffey should find his 'own reward' (*PV*, p.80) in the poems and claim they should be judged on 'other grounds' (*PV*, p.77) than the particular audiences which surrounded him. There is a supra-individual context for his writing, a 'flight from where one is' (*PV*, p.72) which does not depend on the 'here and now' (*PV*, p.81) and which envisages spiritual communion as much as human fraternity. A necessary internationalism is linked to the poem's spiritual 'cry in the wilderness', which balances the 'equation between God's will and mine' (*PV*, p.71). The aura of acceptance at the conclusion to 'Missouri Sequence', anticipating the 'so be it' of *Advent* (*PV*, p.150), suggests a reconciliation with poetic and personal destiny.

It remains significant that 'Missouri Sequence' marks Coffey's return to poetry and the re-embarkation point on a career of making which would last until the poet's death in 1995. His declaration in 'Missouri Sequence' that 'nothing exact is said' (*PV*, p.86) except through poetry was acted upon. The intensity of the poetic vocation is as 'withering' (*PV*, p.70) as the poet's love of Ireland and the quest for a 'poem born aright' (*PV*, p.84) is worth the temporal and spiritual frustrations associated with its composition. The involuntary aspect of poetic composition, the need for poetry, which Coffey so vividly describes, is linked to his search for an ideal habitat and ideal community. As Stan Smith has commented, the poet is 'impelled to find in the impalpable community of language a home he could not locate in any specific time or place'.[31] Poetry becomes a refuge, with the 'poem born aright' (*PV*, p.84) resembling Auden's notion of a 'verbal society'[32] and acting as a shelter or habitat for the poet. Language becomes the true habitat, an authorial shelter and linguistic fraternity that provides a fulcrum around which the displaced self can find identity and belonging.

The local detail of 'Missouri Sequence' and its exilic concerns are thus closely related to its metapoetic and abstract concerns. In both his life and his work, Coffey is searching for a space, a place of belonging and a creative habitat. The search for creative identity is inseparable from the search for an ideal community in language, in God, in family life and in human fellowship. 'Missouri Sequence' operates, then, around these communal clusters. The perfect poem, like the ideal habitat, may be aspirational, but the search for it provides ample poetic sustenance for Coffey and for his readers.

NOTES

1. There were a number of issues at stake in Coffey's resignation. Foremost was the question of remuneration, which was inadequate for Coffey's large family (he wrote to Jacques Maritain saying he resigned 'on the salary question'). There was also a pedagogical issue over the necessity of teaching Aristotelean philosophy of nature prior to metaphysics, on which Coffey held strong views, which he outlines to Maritain in the same letter (which is cited in full by

James Matthew Wilson in chapter 11 below). In the background to this was the Jesuits' distrust of Coffey's cosmopolitan past and especially his admiration for Éluard, who represented atheistical Surrealism in the eyes of Coffey's employers. The view that Coffey resigned on a matter of 'academic principle' (as suggested in the 'Biographical Note' to the Coffey special issue of the *Irish University Reveiw* [vol. 5, no. 1, spring 1975]) is therefore only partly true.

2. Brian Coffey, letter to Thomas MacGreevy, 7 July 1950. MS 8110/35, TCD.
3. Michael Smith, 'Interview with Mervyn Wall about the Thirties', *Lace Curtain*, no. 4 (summer 1971), p.82.
4. Brian Coffey, letter to Thomas MacGreevy, 10 September 1959. MS 8110/43, TCD.
5. Brian Coffey, letter to Thomas MacGreevy, 5 August 1952. MS 8110/36, TCD.
6. Brian Coffey, letter to Denis Devlin, 5 October 1953, in which he describes his family's struggles in 1952–53. Box 28, folder 22 (Brian Coffey Papers), Special Collections, University of Delaware.
7. Brian Coffey, letter to Denis Devlin, 5 October 1953. Ibid.
8. *The Catholic Encyclopedia* (1911), volume 10, entry for 'Missouri'. Available on line at http://www.newadvent.org/cathen/10398a.htm (accessed by the author 10 January 2007).
9. Brian Coffey, letter to Thomas MacGreevy, 5 August 1952. MS 8110/36, TCD.
10. A typescript of 'Missouri Sequence' held at TCD comprises a five-part sequence with 'Old Gravois Road' as the first section. This little studied version forms part of the Denis Johnston Papers and resides in the Early Printed Books Department of TCD Library without a formal MS number. There is also a fairhand copy of 'Old Gravois Road' alone, as a discrete poem, held amongst the Brian Coffey Papers at the University of Delaware, Special Collections, box 2, folder 29.
11. In relation to 'Old Gravois Road', I will cite line numbers from the TCD typescript, hereafter referred to in the text as OGR. 'Old gravel road' quoted above is from line 5. The poem confirms that the 'Old Gravois Road' is named after early French settlers: 'We were told / the road was named / for a family now died out, / farmers far from the river settlement / in a manner quite unusual / among the gregarious french', lines 68–73.
12. The poem was first published in the *Irish University Review*, vol. 2, no. 2 (1962), pp.29–46.
13. Seamus Heaney, 'The Placeless Heaven: Another Look at Kavanagh', in *The Govenment of the Tongue* (London: Faber & Faber, 1988), p.5.
14. Ibid.
15. W.H. Auden, 'New Year Letter', in *Collected Longer Poems* (London: Faber & Faber, 1968), p.79.
16. Parkman Howe, 'Brian Coffey: An Interview', *Éire-Ireland*, vol. 13, no. 1 (spring 1978), p.122.
17. Brian Coffey, letter to Denis Devlin, 5 October 1953. Box 28, folder 22 (Brian Coffey Papers), Special Collections, University of Delaware.
18. W.H. Auden, 'The Virgin and the Dynamo', in *The Dyer's Hand and Other Essays* (London: Faber & Faber, 1963), p.63.
19. Ibid., p.64.
20. Ibid., p.67.
21. Stan Smith, 'On Other Grounds: The Poetry of Brian Coffey', in *Two Decades of Irish Writing: A Critical Survey*, ed. Douglas Dunn (Manchester: Carcanet, 1975), p.59.
22. Ibid., p.74.
23. Ibid.
24. Ibid., p.59.
25. Auden, *The Dyer's Hand*, p.64.
26. J.C.C. Mays, *N11 A Musing* (Clonmel: Coracle Press, 2006), paragraph 6.1.1.
27. Susan Shreibman, 'Denis Devlin (1908–1959)', in *The UCD Aesthetic: Celebrating 150 Years of UCD Writers*, ed. Anthony Roche (Dublin: New Island Press, 2005), p.100.
28. Brian Coffey, 'Extracts from "Concerning Making"', *Lace Curtain*, 6 (August 1978), p.34.
29. Ibid., p.31.
30. Coffey expresses this view of creativity in an interview with Parkman Howe: 'the Scots are nearer the mark when they call the poet a "machar," [*sic*, makar] a maker, rather than a creator. There seems to me to be too much conceded to oneself when one speaks of one's creative work.' Howe, 'Brian Coffey: An Interview', p.119.
31. Stan Smith, '"Precarious Guest": The Poetry of Denis Devlin', in *Modernism and Ireland: The Poetry of the 1930s*, ed. Patricia Coughlan and Alex Davis (Cork: Cork University Press, 1995), p.232.
32. Auden, *The Dyer's Hand*, p.67.

CHAPTER ELEVEN

Brian Coffey, Jacques Maritain and 'Missouri Sequence'

JAMES MATTHEW WILSON

I THE FIGURE OF THE PHILOSOPHER

As a young poet and aspirant student of philosophy, Brian Coffey, like many Catholic intellectuals of his day, looked to the great French Thomist philosopher, Jacques Maritain (1882–1973) for inspiration and guidance. While still a young man himself, Maritain had shown that the thought of Thomas Aquinas could refute the popular but irrational modern philosophy of Henri Bergson, while also resolving with reason the many problems voiced in that philosophy. *La philosophie bergsonienne; études critiques* (1913) savaged his former professor, but earned Maritain himself the lasting admiration of the Vatican.[1] Shortly thereafter, Maritain would become the unofficial philosopher of conservative Catholic France as a colleague of Charles Maurras in *L'Action française*. But his influence was neither limited to the Catholic hierarchy nor the French monarchists. In a Parisian milieu where André Breton and the Surrealists, and André Gide and *La Nouvelle Revue Française* identified the experimentation of modern art and literature with the agenda of the political left, Maritain argued for the contrary. In his short treatise *Art et scholastique* (1920), he contended that the self-consciousness and spiritual ambition of modern art indicated its ontological value; that is, art was a means of exploring the depths of being, and 'being' must be understood in terms of the philosophical tradition of St Thomas Aquinas. Having convinced the likes of Jean Cocteau that Surrealism was a pseudo-theology and that art complemented Thomistic philosophy and theology, Maritain established himself (literally) as the godfather of much of the Parisian avant-garde and, shortly thereafter, as an intellectual cornerstone of T.S. Eliot's *Criterion*. The growth of Maritain's reputation seemed to be strong evidence that Catholicism, Thomism and modern art were all conjoined as an avant-garde unto themselves, searching not for the merely new, but to recapture the (metaphysically) real, wherever it may be found, in its most permanent form.[2] In *Anti-moderne* (1922), Maritain would claim that Thomism

> overflows infinitely, in the past as in the future, the limits of the present moment; it does not oppose itself to modern systems, as the past to that which is actually given, but as something peren-nial to something momentary. *Anti-modern* against the errors of the present time, it is *ultra-modern* for all truths enveloped in time to come.[3]

This claim for a philosophy at once contemporary and permanent, and the implications Maritain had shown it to have for art, clearly gripped Coffey's imagination. While his friend Denis Devlin, in *Intercessions* (1937), would seek to reconcile Surrealist automatic writing with the Christian search for God's presence in the soul, Coffey consistently rejected any such attempt on Maritainian grounds. Art was the perfection of a made thing, Maritain had shown with the apparatus of Aquinas.[4] To defend this 'practical' definition of art was also to preserve the larger scholastic system to which it belonged. As late as 1964, when Coffey edited Devlin's collected poems, he carefully affirmed that, while the early work may have drawn on Surrealism, it was not, for all that, an example of automatic writing.[5]

Maritain's synthesis of modern aesthetics and scholastic thought seems to have stirred Coffey to write to the philosopher years before he arrived in Paris to study with him at the Institut Catholique. In October 1930 Coffey sent Maritain the small book of poems he had co-authored with Denis Devlin, writing, 'J'ose vous présenter ces poèmes écrites par mon ami Denis Devlin et moi, et j'espère qu'elles vous plaisont. Je pense souvent à vous et combien sympathetique vous avez été aux idées d'un jeune homme.'[6] The second sentence of this brief note suggests Coffey had established contact earlier, though this is uncertain. In any case, we can be sure that Coffey sought out Mari-tain not merely as a potential mentor for his philosophical studies, but also as someone whose artistic approval he coveted. As we shall see, over several decades Coffey admired both Maritain's aesthetic judgement and his distinctive advocacy of Thomist metaphysics as a development on, and continuation of, Aristotle's philosophy of nature. Coffey sought Maritain's advice and drew on his metaphysics and philosophy of art alike in his prose essays for the *Modern Schoolman* and, no less crucially, in two of his most important poetic works, *Third Person* and 'Missouri Sequence'.

Coffey corresponded with Maritain in subsequent years, begging advice on more academic matters, including, in 1935, whether he should pursue his studies at the Institut Catholique and whether the Marxist interpretation of science might prove a fit subject for his thesis. A note to Maritain from 1937 solicits a letter of recommendation for a philosophy post at the University of Swansea, where he would teach alongside the Aristotle scholar and translator, W.D. Ross. Coffey confides that Swansea is a 'Protestant' milieu, in which it would prove difficult to discuss Thomist philosophy. Ross, for instance, never mentions Aquinas in his own work on Aristotle's *Physics* and this, Coffey and Maritain alike, would have found unconscionable since they believed (as we shall see) the philosophy of nature was a necessary stepping-stone to the study of metaphysics and theology.[7] That is, they believed that *Physics* provided a common conceptual foundation that allowed Catholics, Protestants and non-Christians alike to discuss philosophy intelligibly with one another, even if they did not share subsequent premises that followed from it.

Coffey's letter indicates he had absorbed Maritain's teachings in *Eléments de philosophie I. Introduction générale à la philosophie* that the philosophy of nature should be taught before metaphysics, and that he accepted those in *Distinguer pour unir ou les degrès du savoir* arguing for a metaphysical hierarchy of knowledge in which the study of nature flows logically into that of mathematics and metaphysics as one moves from more simply apprehended modes of being toward those that cannot be apprehended at all, but only known by reason.[8] If one could only establish this proper ordering of study and knowledge, previously intractable problems of communication between persons of different religions or backgrounds could be lessened through the use of a common philosophical language (one grounded in the concept of Aristotelian being rather than post-Cartesian consciousness). Coffey's concerns about Ross as a Protestant Aristotelian therefore indicate an underlying unease about his philosophical convictions. If Ross excluded Aquinas from his study, his work was probably suspected by Coffey as irrationally sectarian rather than truly philosophical.

I dwell on this point because, in the year following this letter, Coffey published his short collection of poems, *Third Person*. As I have argued elsewhere, this collection shows the profound imprint of Maritain's conceptual realist metaphysics (especially as detailed in *Les degrès du savoir*) on Coffey's poetry. The poems, like Maritain's Thomism, seek to appreciate the reality of things – of substantial beings – as existing independently of human subjectivity and to demonstrate that one can proceed logically and experientially from this encounter with the 'thingness of the thing' (a phrase borrowed from Martin Heidegger) to a natural knowledge of God as the ground of all being.[9] Maritain had argued for the renewed distinction in philosophical discourse between things and objects. Post-Kantian idealism and Husserl's phenomenology both attended only to reality as it was perceived by a human subject, and therefore ignored things *per se* in order to explore them only in their relation to a subject. Such a project 'will try to reabsorb the thing and its existentiality into transcendental subjectivity, one function of which will be to constitute the thing inside the self. But that is just another way of suppressing the thing in the authentic meaning of the word, the extramental or metalogical thing.'[10] Coffey's *Third Person* sought to represent human subjects as substantial beings, reducing them, as it were, to things in order to liberate them from the solipsistic trap of subject–object relations.

The poems do not stop there however. Again following Maritain, Coffey tried to illustrate how recognition of the full subjectivity of other beings, and of the subject–subject relations that emerge from that recognition, lead both to true human love and to a natural knowledge of the God of love. The poems give an austere depiction of men and women in love in terms of their independently existing essences, and the relations that obtain through that love which lead to a Trinitarian vision of man, woman and God. As Maritain expressed it, as one came to understand the first-person 'I' and the second-person 'thou' as things independent as to their existence and yet related by love, one discovers a third person between, within and beyond them:

> And what do all these things, that 'I' address familiarly as 'thee' and 'thou', say to me? 'The third person is the one of whom we speak.' He is on every lip; all things speak of Him. And as long as I have not known Him for myself, I only hear the voice of creatures talking among themselves about him. But when I know Him for myself – without any intermediary other than the light and propositions of faith, – then it is Thou, yet more hidden, more mysterious and freer than anything that can be created and every person that can be created, it is Thou I hear.[11]

Meditation on the essence of subject–subject relations, Maritain's philosophy and Coffey's poems suggest, gives a natural intimation of God's presence, which faith must complete. Sound metaphysics led to the divine, but the only good metaphysics was that Aquinas had built upon Aristotle's philosophy of nature. Ross would be blind to this, Coffey seems to have feared, as if he read Aristotle *sola scriptura*, as other Protestants read the Bible, immune to the developments of tradition as consummated in Aquinas's writings. Even in 1937 it is clear that Maritain stood as the model philosopher, judge of poetry, as well as metaphysical source for Coffey's first major poetic enterprise.

Alex Davis has demonstrated in his valuable essay, '"Poetry is Ontology": Brian Coffey's Poetics' that Maritain's influence was not limited to his Thomist metaphysics and did not cease with *Third Person*. Indeed, Davis only briefly mentions that book in order to concentrate on the impact Maritain's two most important treatises on art, *Art et scholastique* and the late masterpiece *Creative Evolution in Art and Poetry* (1953) made on Coffey's poetry from 'Missouri Sequence' through to *Death of Hektor*.[12] He argues, as I shall consider below, that Maritain's exploration of the tension between the drive of art to purity through a scorn of matter, and the origin of the work of art in the mind of an embodied human person, who must reify his idea in sensible matter, must be carefully balanced so that one recognizes 'the impossibility of achieving – and the dangers of yearning for – the absolute in pure art'.[13] Maritain believed art should embrace its modern 'self-consciousness' in order to rise to great spiritual heights and to explore the depths of being; as such, his writings on art frequently resolve into the contemplation of being *per se* as it is revealed through the artwork. This quest is analogous to the religious quest of the mystic for infused contemplation of Being Itself in the beatific vision, but, as Maritain observes in his essay 'Concerning Poetic Knowledge', theology must save the artist from thinking this artistic quest more than an analogy.[14] The artist must recognize the personal and material components of art as essential, falling prey neither to the 'suicide of the angels' in the quest for pure spirit or the 'sin of materialism,' which pretends – as the French neo-classicists had – that art itself is simply an assemblage of practical techniques for manipulating words or matter. As Davis elaborates, Coffey's later writings seek to maintain this balance and to explore the ethical dimensions of the life of poetry in terms akin to those of Maritain.

This influence of Maritain on Coffey is more certain than perhaps Davis realized. After 1937, as is well known, Coffey fell silent as a poet for more than a decade. During that time he established himself as a minor light in the American branch of the revival of Thomist philosophy as a professor at St Louis University, publishing articles in the *Modern*

Schoolman that employ a Thomist philosophy of nature, and Maritain's writings in particular, to expose the insinuation of the errors of philosophical positivism into the natural sciences. His most prescient work in this regard occurs in his debunking of the Kinsey Report, where he exposes the unstated philosophical presuppositions A.C. Kinsey makes while claiming his conclusions to be purely scientific, and where he also demonstrates the incompetent scientific method used to gather evidence for the controversial report on American sexual proclivities. He accomplishes this with specific reference to *Les degrès du savoir*.[15] After these productive years of philosophical work, however, Coffey was forced to resign his professorship. The accompanying poverty and sadness, in the old cliché, hurt him into poetry once more. Jack Morgan has elegantly traced the biographical origins of 'Missouri Sequence', demonstrating how immanent the recent struggles of Coffey's life were to the composition of the poem.[16] Soon after the completion of that poem, Coffey briefly resumed his correspondence with Maritain, sending a letter dated 9 August 1953 that testifies to the 'indirect' source of the poem in the philosopher's writings on art. 'Missouri Sequence' is, as Davis claims, a poem partly about the embedded nature of poetry in a human environment, and this Coffey emphasizes to Maritain. The letter's biographical interest transcends the purpose it serves in my argument – a definite connection between Coffey's poem and Maritain's philosophy of art – and so I quote it in its entirety here.

Dear Monsieur Maritain,

I am writing to you with much diffidence, because the enclosed manuscript consists of poems of mine which I should very much like that you would read and pass judgement on. Most of them, with three exceptions, have been wrtitten since July last year (1952), during a period of hardship and worry which followed on my resignation from St. Louis University. I resigned on the salary question, but without having taken the precaution of finding other work. The inevitable result was that I found no work, with the exception of a short job in a small factory printing textiles. My wife was able to support us, doing art-work at home, while I gradually began to practice verse-making again, after a lapse of many years during which it had been impossible to find any time for such an occupation. Well, I came to another period of my life, as [*sic*] short time ago, convinced that I have to give up hopes of another university post possibly finally, and I have found a small job in a surveyor's office, where I shall have to learn a new trade.

It seemed a good moment to collect together all that had been written during the preceding months, and I cannot but feel that what I have written is good. But as I live here in conditions of isolation, and see no one who might read and criticize my work, and because I should like to have someone else's judgement before seeking publication, I am sending the poems to you. I thought of you because you love poetry and understand it better perhaps than anyone else living, and because, once, when you gave me a copy of *Frontières de la Poésie*, you asked me to tell you what I thought of your work. I never did, because of my slowness in reaching exact judgements. But I do think that now, in some of my poems, you will find, indirectly, an expression of what I have thought of your writings on poetry. Indirectly, I say, because what I have written I found by thinking about my own poems. But I think it true to say that there does not seem to be too great a gap between the things I have managed to say and what you have so perfectly expressed in your analyses of poetry.

I shall be very, very grateful, if you can find time to read my work and if you will tell me what you think it worth. Would I be altogether a fool, were I to reorganize the rest of my life so as to have some time for writing more, or am I wiser saying: enough?

The verse form I use is developed from Apollinaire, in an indirect way. I made an almost perfect translation of his *La Maison des Morts*, and in doing so found a way to use English accents and feet with a freedom limited only by sense and breath movement. I should have tended to use elliptical diction, had I followed my own bent entirely (as I did in my book: *Third Person*), but my wife asked me to write so that she could follow me, and so I did what I have done. Of the poems, the *Missouri Sequence* follows the personal pains and troubles of the last year, and I thought of it also as opening the way to a poem in which I could speak unself-consciously as a Catholic, without falling into merely Catholic rhetoric. The Poems: 'Liminal', 'White One', 'An Old Story' are addressed to my wife. 'Brigid Ann' speaks to our prematurely born daughter, now two weeks old and still in hospital.

*** [*sic*]

My differences with St. L.U. ended in my resignation, after I became angry. The main issue was the salary one, important for a large family. There was, I think, also an issue which was never mentioned, but which did I think affect adversely any possibilities of reinstatement. I held, and hold, that one teaches the Philosophy

of Nature before one teaches Metaphysics, and I am confident that
that is the true teaching of St. Thomas. I'm sure it is foolish, for
administrative and dilutive reasons, to attempt to start students
off with a course in metaphysics, especially some courses. Any-
way, a mess developed, and my irascibility overcame me. Later I
remembered hearing you, one evening, remark to Dalbies that
'un philosophe ne doit pas s'émouvoir', but afterwards was too
late.

I do hope that I shall not have bored you with such personal
troubles. And if you will let me know what you think of the
poems, I shall be delighted.

Hoping that you and Madame Maritain keep very well,

> Yours sincerely,
> Brian Coffey[17]

Coffey seeks to ally himself with Maritain once more, noting an
'unmentioned' conflict over the order of teaching natural philosophy
and metaphysics reminiscent of his worries sixteen years earlier
regarding the 'Protestant' faculty at Swansea. While insisting on the
merely 'indirect' influence of Maritain's writing on his poem, he tries
to establish a firm connection between them as philosophers. Indeed,
the letter makes Coffey's manifold intellectual debt to Maritain so
apparent that it seems worth returning to 'Missouri Sequence' to
examine more closely how the poem confirms this debt even more
surely than Davis has contended.

II POETRY AS THE FLESH OF WORDS

I have noted that *Third Person* made a unique contribution to modern
poetry by using Maritain's metaphysics to affirm the existential reality
of things independent of a subjective gaze. But when he wrote 'Missouri
Sequence', Coffey stood on the other side of Pound's *Cantos*, the rise
of objectivist poetry and William Carlos Williams' dicta, 'No ideas / but
in things.'[18] He could scarcely have avoided sensing his poetry now
demanded not affirmation of the reality of extramental objects, or
things, but the reconciliation of authorial subjectivity, and its provincial
limitations, with the transcendental of being. Coffey's first volume
of poems privileges 'thingness' but without the anti-intellectualism
inherent in Williams' phrase. And Coffey almost certainly agreed with
Devlin that to take the side of things *against* the highest power of the
human person, the intellect, should have been 'one of [Ezra] Pound's

1. Engraving by S.W. Hayter for limited edition of *Third Person*. S.W. Hayter, courtesy of DACS, imaging by University of Delaware Library, Special Collections.

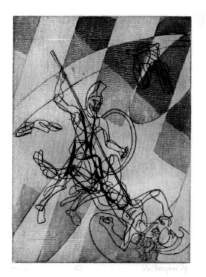

2. Four engravings by S.W. Hayter for limited edition of *Death of Hektor*. S.W. Hayter, courtesy of DACS, imaging by University of Delaware Library, Special Collections.

Paris
22. 2. 74

SAMUEL BECKETT

Dear Brian

Thanks for yrs. of Feb. 15.
Delighted at thought of your
reading me at Cambridge Festival.
Jean has had a gruesome time,
but seems now to be coming
round. Playwriting again.
I marvel at your vitality
& variety of interests and
doings. The here over may
give you some idea of mine.

Loin dans le néant
au bout de quel affût
l'œil crut entrevoir
remuer un instant
la tête se calma disant
ce ne fut que dans ta tête

affectionately to you all.

Sam

3. Postcard from Samuel Beckett to Brian Coffey, 1978, with one of Beckett's *mirlitonnades* inscribed. Courtesy of the Estate of Samuel Beckett and the University of Delaware Library, Special Collections.

TELEPHONE
TUDor 0701

13 Elms Avenue,
Muswell Hill,
London N.10.

10th September,'59.

Dear Tom,

John has just returned and has told me
that you have not been having good health;I was
very sorry to hear about it, and hope that there
will be an improvement-I'm sure you do too much,
and should insist on resting more, in spite of
the calls on you which must be so very numerous.
It was kind of you to takean interest in °ohn, who
was very impressed by you.I had wanted him to meet
you and had told him a lot about you, but wondered
if he would overcome shyness sufficiently to call.
As things turned out, he made good use of his visit
to Dublin and carried away a varied and good first
impression of many things.

It was very sad to hear of the death of
Denis.Moya sent me a wire on the day he died, and
an earlier letter of Don's and one even earlier of
Denis's had prepared me for the rst. I thought
a lot about those days in Paris when we were all
together, surprised to find how close it all was
to my heart, as if of yesterday-one's best times
timeless or unaging rather.I have always been sad
about the accidents tht scattered us, when as it
seemed, we could have been more"useful" at home.
I am in fact still quite unreconciled to the role
of foreigner here, exile from there and so on, at
this late hour.Moya tells me it was a gentle and
orderly going out, as he liked things. I

Well, take care of yourself, people can
always wait day or two to be told what they want
to know.Bridget joins me in sending you our
affectionate good wishes,

4. Typewritten letter from Brian Coffey to Thomas MacGreevy (1959) expressing regret over the death of Denis Devlin (TCD MS 8110/43). Courtesy of the Board of Trinity College Dublin.

5. A youthful Brian Coffey, c.1935, courtesy of John Coffey.

6. Coffey family photo taken in Muswell Hill , 1956, courtesy of John Coffey.

7. Brian and Bridget Coffey with John F. Deane (Dedalus Press), Ursula Foran and President Mary Robinson, 1991. Photograph by Niamh Foran, courtesy of John F. Deane.

8. Brian Coffey with Michael Smith of New Writers' Press. Courtesy of Michael Smith.

9. George Reavey as a young man. Photograph by John Albert, courtesy of the Harry Ransom Humanities Research Center, University of Texas at Austin and the Estate of George Reavey.

10. Thomas MacGreevy at the Ecole Normale, Paris in the 1920s. Courtesy of Margaret Farrington and Robert Ryan and the Thomas MacGreevy Archive, University of Maryland.

11. Brian Coffey from front cover of his *Selected Poems* (New Writers' Press, 1971). Courtesy of John Parsons.

bad jokes'.[19] In rejecting such closed practices, Coffey's 'Sequence' sought to escape the privileging of the art object as pure, as angelistic and cut off from matter and history. In this important respect, Coffey succeeds in writing a poem that answers the challenges Maritain had made for an art perfectly actualized *qua* art, but which did not conceal its origin in the human person. 'Here poetic "making" is not fueled by the desire to "escape" the matter of art', Davis tells us. 'Coffey fore-goes pure art's aim of somehow *representing*, in Renato Poggioli's words, "a state of beatitude and grace, a condition of perfection and stasis fixed forever, by the severe ethos of form."'[20] The poem can bear the scars of its making and be no less a poem. If, according to Maritain, the end of art is perfection of the thing made, all made things are made by flesh and bone, by human beings, and to deny, denigrate or even conceal those origins is a kind of betrayal.[21] In addition to absorbing Maritain's critique of the suicide of the angels manifest in pure art, Coffey may also have come to see *Third Person* as overly ontological and discursive in form, ignoring the act of poetic making in favour of an act of dry speculation.[22] Poetry could not afford contempt either for individuated matter or human maker, nor could it relieve itself of the essential qualities of the made poem that differentiate it from the discourse of philosophical investigation. And so 'Missouri Sequence' begins by enunciating its first-person localization, striking a note both human and safely within the tradition of the meditative lyric. Its poetry insists upon the reality – the very domestic reality – of the poet:

> Our children have eaten supper,
> play Follow-my-Leader,
> make songs from room to room
> around and around;
> once each minute
> past my desk they go.   (*PV*, p.69)

In the midst of the financial and domestic difficulties Coffey detailed in his late letter to Maritain, he may have come to feel that a depiction of human relations, and their relation to God, might not be realizable in a poetry that is as purely ontological and concerned exclusively with essences, as was *Third Person*. To be real, most essences require form and matter; beyond that they must *also* have existence. Once one has acknowledged that, the history of form and matter constituted entitatively in time requires a dignity that poetry of pure ideas, Pla-tonic or otherwise, may often ignore. Coffey's close friend, Thomas MacGreevy, had emphasized in his monograph on Jack B. Yeats that true Catholicism was not universalism exclusively, but a synthesis of the provincial and the universal, the individual and the totality that is capable of respecting both.[23] Coffey, Davis rightly argues, had appreciated a similar spirit in Maritain's philosophy of art. In his treatise, the French philosopher insists that

> art does not reside in an angelic mind; it resides in a soul which animates a living body, and which, by the natural necessity in which it finds itself of learning, and progressing little by little and with the assistance of others, makes the rational animal a naturally social animal. Art is therefore basically dependant upon everything which the human community, spiritual tradition and history transmit to the body and mind of man. By its human subject and its human roots, art belongs to a time and a country.[24]

Davis represents Maritain and Coffey as contending with this facet of art as an ethical imperative. Pure art is founded, as it were, on a hatred of matter and extension, on a kind of misanthropy that rendered much modern art subject to accusations of manifesting either escapist or totalitarian sympathies – two tendencies Maritain would subsequently decry as the 'suicide of the angels'. Maritain's own rhetoric on the transcendent purity of art at least once got away from him and resulted in the unfortunate claim that compared to art, 'creatures have no savour'.[25] However, his philosophy of art gives little support to that phrase, and he appended an apologetic footnote in the 1935 edition of *Art et scholastique*:

> One must have little experience of created things, or much experience of divine things, in order to be able to speak in this way. In general, formulas of contempt with regard to created things belong to a conventional literature that is difficult to endure. The creature is deserving of compassion, not contempt; it exists only because it is loved. It is deceptive because it has too much savour, and because this savour is nothing in comparison with the being of God.[26]

Whether Coffey's misgivings about being a poet stemmed from just such a tendency to devalue the imperfect human person we cannot say for certain. Davis has suggested that they did, at least in part.[27] It is clear, in any case, that Coffey's 'Sequence' moves from the ontology of general essences seen in *Third Person* to the treatment of concrete beings in their essential and contingent attributes. That is, he attempts to understand the historical relation between individual beings in the universal order.

A fitting project indeed. One of the many articles he wrote for the *Modern Schoolman* was a summary of his thesis on the notion of order in St Thomas.[28] That article outlined four kinds of *ordo*: gradation, destination, relation and rank.[29] The poem's four sections offer four ways of looking at the individual's life within the human and divine order. In the space remaining, I would like to consider the exploration of this order the poem exhibits in the light of Maritain's early writings on art, and of the natural attachment to place, nation and history – all of which Coffey's earlier poetry had seemed to ignore.

The first section, 'Nightfall, Midwinter, Missouri', from which I have just quoted, registers the historical fate of the poet, and of all Irish. His mother grows old in Ireland, but, 'Five miles away, at Byrnesville, / the cemetery is filled with Irish graves' (*PV*, p.69). That is, when one comes from a nation that has been subject to mass emigration, one cannot retain a sense of national identity strictly de-pendant on physical proximity to the native soil. Indeed, Coffey would probably reservedly agree with Arjun Appadurai's observation that the experience of emigration and exile is *one* condition of possibility for profound national attachment.[30] The imagination, as Appadurai understands it, makes possible the formation of group identity quite in-dependent of those material structures normally supposed to support it. Coffey's poem acknowledges the way in which this identity-making works co-operatively with the making of a new, post-emigration home. He writes of Byrnesville,

> People drifted in here from the river,
> Irish, German, Bohemian,
> more than one hundred years ago,
> come to make homes.   (*PV*, p.69)

This passage, which might seem to anticipate the clichés of American immigration-as-assimilation, in fact prefaces a stabilization, or harden-ing, of group identity. 'Many Irish souls have gone back to God from Byrnesville', he writes, and 'many are Irish here today / where cedars stand like milestones / on worn Ozark hills' (*PV*, p.70). Coffey expresses his love of both the beauty of Dublin and the countryside. He then ex-presses his love of France and England, implying that one need not love one place, one nation exclusively, while also that they must remain for-eign affections, 'a love apart' (*PV*, p.70). The section is dedicated to MacGreevy, and Coffey makes clear that the motive for the dedication is that both poets, through exile, have been forced to understand that a nation is both more and less than contemporary Irish nationalists like

Daniel Corkery had made it out to be. National identity, but perhaps especially 'postcolonial' identity, represents hope inscribed within the experience of disappointment:

> Dear Tom, in Ireland,
> you have known
> the pain between
> its fruiting and the early dream   (*PV*, p.70)

We can love and suffer for the communities and lands in which we are born, or where we by necessity live, but we must not make of the local or locale an idol. It is contingent, and our attachments are often conditioned by suffering and separation rather than a tenacious clinging to a hypostatized nation-state. In Coffey's Thomistic Catholicism, only Christ is omnipresent and, as our Final Cause, structures our progress and our end. This knowledge puts in question contingent identities, as Coffey proposes in asking, 'Does it matter where one dies, / supposing one knows how?' Yet the incarnation does not annihilate but rather guarantees the importance of the contingent realm, permeates its unnecessary conditions with the drama of divine necessity: 'The truth is, where the cross is not / the Christian does not go' (*PV*, p.71). The narrative that reveals itself through the fragmentary strophes of the poem is continuous from birth in Ireland, exile in America, to the later return to England and, finally, to the afterlife. It tells us of a single order, a seamless movement of which no part is inessential, where the divine always promises to manifest itself among the most ostensibly inconsequential of peoples, for example, in Achill, where

> The poor praise Christ aloud
> When the priest elevates
> The Saviour of the world.   (*PV*, p.73)

'March, Missouri', dedicated to his colleague at St Louis, the Thomist philosopher Leonard Eslick, negotiates between the local and the universal in a distinct way. Eslick would have known Coffey's life in the States, but not that in his native land. Coffey, in turn, tells a parable of 'Su Tungpo' (*PV*, p.74), whose historicity is irrelevant – only his Oriental exoticism matters, because he thereby has common national experience with neither the poet nor his dedicatee. In the Enlightenment tradition deployed by Oliver Goldsmith in *The Citizen of the World, or, Letters from a Chinese Philosopher* (1762), the figure's otherness makes him universally representative, because he stands at one remove from the local prejudices and assumptions of the intended audience's culture. The allegory is of exile, of course: '"Where is my home now," he cried, / "I have no home," ... ' (*PV*, p.74). Coffey offers a typology of exile. Human experience is patterned, has archetypes; it has seasons and essences that can be grasped if enfleshed in the language of narrative. Hence Su Tungpo's story is followed by still another allegory of a man with a 'silver key for lock of gold' (*PV*, p.75). Like the Aristotelian-Thomistic philosophy of nature, allegories (of *our* nature) allow us to communicate across localized, cultural divides. They do not, however, negate the reality of these divides. If the local is by definition less than the universal, it paradoxically transcends it as well (much in the way that the universal 'being' transcends the individual, even though to know an individual existence is more than just to know that it has being, or exists):

> And all again begins again,
> each time other, each time same,
> cycles of rising and resting
> which do not fit our bounds.   (*PV*, p.77)

The individual's destiny, because it is part of the total structure of creation, lies beyond either the specific or universals we can conceive; province and universe are reconciled, yes, but only because they are transcended eschatologically. Finally, in relation to this claim, the allegorical narrative insists upon our mode of knowing. We perceive and experience only particulars. They are necessarily more immediate to consciousness than the knowledge resultant of reasoning. Hence there is an epistemological priority of the particular, of the local (physics), that engages without contradicting the elevated universality toward which allegory points (metaphysics or theology). This section of the poem moves fluidly between levels of generality and specificity, universality and locality in order to admit them all to the communicative act between author and Eslick.

The tone of this section, however, is melancholy. Necessity forces Su Tungpo, like Coffey, to abandon his well-furnished homestead, and we are asked to consider that a life of particulars, because contingent, is inherently unstable. As in Boethius, we see the universal schemes of providence crosshatched with the immanent movements of fortune, and this calls for a certain stoicism: 'To greet unwisdomed change of season / is to fail the unexpected / test, ruin completed' (*PV*, p.75). As in the philosophy of Spinoza or the great wheel of Yeats' *A Vision* (1925), Coffey's Christian stoicism suggests the universal as a compensatory narrative for the frequently unhappy stories of individuals.

The cycles of death and rebirth of nature, in all these systems, affirm that present sorrow will be reconciled with a higher purpose. The section concludes with just such benign resignation: 'any weather is good weather / for the loving soul' (*PV*, p.77). Curiously, several years earlier, Devlin had mocked this very position as it was found in the poetry of Robert Lowell and John Frederick Nims, who, perhaps a little like Coffey, 'have the rather boisterous cynicism which many Catholic poets affect, in a mistaken zeal, presumably, to qualify as retired worldlings'.[31]

'Muse, June, Related' is fittingly dedicated to Devlin, whose poetry more than most in the twentieth century depended upon a 'muse' figure. The poem addresses the bodily localization intrinsic to being *man* and the temptation to transcend matter as *poet*. Of this as an ethical problem I have already spoken. But taking on Maritain's dicta that art is the dance of the intellect among the senses, Coffey gives voice to the conventional understanding of poetry as the concretion of absolutes. Here, we need only recognize that, through it, Coffey insists that art need not be the manifestation of man's desire to transcend matter; it also can serve as an apology for matter because, again, following Maritain, art offers a different kind of knowing. The universal or absolute cannot be experienced, only known, *qua* universal or absolute concepts. But through its necessary cohesion to the concrete, art can represent those concepts under the mode of the contingent and particular: 'All the passions meet at the dinner table, / all men's history ever was or will be / uncoils its features while we serve the food' (*PV*, p.78). The experience of individuated beings, of the individuated artwork, can communicate – sometimes almost intuitively – mysteries from the ontological depths. In still another allegorical passage, this section considers the question of a male lover 'questing' for his beloved muse. Her precise significance is indiscernible, save that she serves as 'stimulant' for a difficult labour of perfection:

> Muses, casual stimulants,
> have short lives.
> The true muse fleshed
> nor was, nor shall be,
> is a torment of oneself,
> cannot be done without.   (*PV*, p.80)

The first sentence, with its abrupt ending in the second line (just when it might seem on the verge of making a sweeping claim), registers the slightly comic anachronism of muse figures in modern verse. And yet, what follows acknowledges the incommensurable role they play as well. How else to represent the creative passion, to render the absolute in the concrete, which defines art for Coffey and Maritain alike, save through the analogy to heightened erotic passion that the image of the muse makes possible? Coffey's children 'in their scrambling play' (*PV*, p.80) interrupt his own musing, and thus guarantee the whimsicality with which he judges Devlin's efforts to harness the Dantesque lady/muse in his own work. However lightly he may take those efforts, Coffey by no means dismisses them. The section concludes:

> This much is certain:
> he will not forget her beauty,
> he must not attempt escape
> from here and now.   (*PV*, p.81)

Rather than cast the idea of the muse aside, these lines acknowledge how she makes possible the persistence of art in the concrete. Her beauty, which is figurative and spiritual, makes possible an art of the embodied 'here and now'. To abandon it is to lose the sensual and the particular in favour, once more, of discursive flights of abstraction or angelistic contempt for human reality. Contrary to claims that the stereotyped muse figure hypostatizes the female as object rather than subject (a concern Coffey's early work brilliantly addressed), the connection between female and artistic beauty vouchsafes the latter's responsibility to the world of form and matter.

The final section of the poem, 'Missouri, Midsummer, Closure', might almost be considered an iteration of the ontology of love found in *Third Person* in the terms of the more personal, first-person poetic. Dedicated to his wife, Bridget, its pages highlight that any love we have must be for *this person there*, not simply a generalized object. Similarly, the path through life we take, though it be based upon some universal pattern - as of course the poem takes pains to show – is always *my* path or yours. Hence the confession, 'I have grown slowly into poetry' (*PV*, p.82). A life's narrative perforce lingers behind its reified productions, including poetry, and so even the hypostatized muse figure of the previous section has her roots in flesh and bone. As Maritain had insisted in *Art et scholastique*, the artwork is always the work of human hands, or at least of the human intellect, and therefore has its life of and within a human life. Once again, Coffey embraces the contingent concrete in its history as essential to any knowledge of the abstract absolute. His slow growth in craft is therefore drawn into relation with the suffering of Bridget as a result of the dearth, poverty and necessity of repeated emigration. As the quoted letter indicates, Coffey's career at St Louis was brief and hardly marked by great happiness or prosperity. He refers (rather than alludes) directly to those conditions and his dismissal from the University: ' ... if I am victim, / as I judge, of men / who owed me respect' (*PV*, p.83). Following this, however, he tells an almost Yeatsian parable of a 'queen of a pale people', who serves allegorically as the universal woman who eases the suffering of her subjects in maternal fashion, and typologically as Bridget herself (*PV*, p.84). Only if the queen signifies *both* does her meaning become intelligible. She speaks directly to Coffey, in his contemplation of his own experience, as well as to the very condition of humankind – to those who must live in a world of suffering and consolation – all of which is rendered meaningful, once again, through the understanding of its teleological nature, its destiny in God. It is in accepting the movement of suffering and consolation, of failure and redemption, that Coffey's poem ends:

> Never was despair imperative,
> never are we grown so old
> we cannot start our journey
> bound to find
> an eternal note of gladness
> in loves true for men,
> the source whence they flow,
> the ocean whither they go.   (*PV*, p.87)

Coffey's poetry only gradually came to address the contingent and historical, trusting to the virtue of hope that looks beyond human experience but does not eschew it. Each of the poem's four sections establishes the order of the local and universal in relation to that eschatological hope. As the final line makes clear, he also followed MacGreevy's praise of Jack Yeats' painting, by trusting to an identification of the particular experience of the Irish (in this case, that of the diasporas) with that of human life as a whole. His personal and poetic narrative of freedom, directing itself in the light of necessity, strikes an 'eternal note' common to all persons.

When Davis noted more than a decade ago certain continuities between Coffey's poetry and Maritain's philosophy of art, he struck upon what is arguably the crucial intellectual background to that poetry. Not only did Maritain's metaphysics inform *Third Person*, but the ordering of knowledge between the natural and the supernatural, between *Physics* and metaphysics, would ground the embodied poetic of 'Missouri Sequence', Coffey's best-known, most accessible and humane work. Indeed, given the poem's origin during a period when Coffey was still publishing frequently on Thomist philosophy, one might be tempted to say that the 'Sequence' is Coffey's most significant contribution to that philosophical tradition and cannot be fully understood apart from it. The 'Sequence' did not mark a permanent shift in Coffey's style, of course. His later poems frequently exhibit clipped and fragmented language reminiscent of *Third Person*, and so may also exhibit a return to the early ontological explorations. If Coffey did not abandon his early techniques, he did not necessarily cease to be influenced by Maritain's philosophy either. As Jack Morgan has observed, certain lines of *Advent* (1975) derive from a short essay of Leonard Eslick's in the *New Scholasticism*.[32] And it is possible that the meditations on the meaning of a work of art across massive historical change in *Death of Hektor* (1979) owe something to Maritain's similar meditations in his essay 'Sign and Symbol' and his major work, *Creative Intuition in Art and Poetry*.[33] It would be reductive to propose that the work of one thinker – even so prominent a philosopher as Maritain – could be the source of so long and varied a career in poetry as Coffey's. It is clear, however, that Maritain influenced Coffey greatly and that this influence has yet to be fully explored.

NOTES

1. J. Barré, *Beggars for Heaven*, trans. Bernard Doering (Notre Dame, IN: University of Notre Dame Press, 2005), p.127.
2. For the most comprehensive account of Maritain's French influence, see S. Schloesser, *Jazz Age Catholicism: Mystic Modernism in Postwar Paris, 1919–1933* (Toronto: University of Toronto Press, 2005).
3. Quoted in F.J. Sheen, *God and Intelligence in Modern Philosophy* (Garden City, NY: Image Books, 1958), p.23. Italics in original.
4. Jacques Maritain, *Art and Scholasticism and the Frontiers of Poetry*, trans. Joseph Evans (Notre Dame, IN: University of Notre Dame Press, 1974) pp.6–7.
5. Brian Coffey, 'Introduction' to *Collected Poems of Denis Devlin*, ed. Brian Coffey (Dublin: Dolmen Press, 1964), p.xi.
6. Brian Coffey, letter to Jacques Maritain, 13 October 1930. Kolbsheim Archive, France.
7. Brian Coffey, letter to Jacques Maritain, 23 June 1937. Ibid.
8. See Jacques Maritain, *Eléments de philosophie I. Introduction générale à la philosophie* (Paris: Pierre Téqui, 1920) and *Distinguer pour unir ou les degrès du savoir* (Paris: Desclée de Brouwer, 1932).
9. See 'Brian Coffey, Jacques Maritain and the Recovery of the "Thing"', forthcoming in *The Maritain Factor: Taking Religion into Interwar Modernism*, ed. Rajesh Heynickx and Jan De Maeyer. See also my dissertation, 'Catholic Modernism and the Irish "Avant-Garde"' (University of Notre Dame, 2006), from which some of this discussion derives.
10. Jacques Maritain, *The Degrees of Knowledge*, trans. G.B. Phelan (Notre Dame, IN: University of Notre Dame Press, 1995), p.99.
11. Ibid., p.117.
12. See Alex Davis, '"Poetry is Ontology": Brian Coffey's Poetics', in *Modernism and Ireland: The*

Poetry of the 1930s, ed. Patricia Coughlan and Alex Davis (Cork: Cork University Press, 1995), pp.150–72.

13. Ibid., p.153.
14. Jacques Maritain, *The Situation of Poetry* (New York: Philosophical Library, 1955), p.60.
15. Brian Coffey, 'The Philosophy of Science and the Scientific Attitude: I', *Modern Schoolman*, vol. 26, no. 1 (November 1948), pp.1–35. See p.29 for Coffey's reference to Maritain.
16. See Jack Morgan, '"Missouri Sequence": Brian Coffey's St Louis Years', 1947–1952', *Éire-Ireland*, vol. 28, no. 4 (1993), pp.100–14.
17. Brian Coffey, letter to Jacques Maritain, 9 August 1953. Kolbsheim Archive.
18. W.C. Williams, *Selected Poems* (New York: New Directions, 1985), p.145.
19. Denis Devlin, 'Twenty-Four Poets', *Sewanee Review*, vol. 53 (1945), pp.457–66.
20. Davis, '"Poetry is Ontology"', pp.160–61.
21. Maritain, *Art and Scholasticism*, p.74.
22. Maritain warns against poetry as mere versified intellectual discourse in *The Situation of Poetry*, p.60.
23. Thomas MacGreevy, *Jack B. Yeats* (Dublin: Victor Waddington, 1945), p.6.
24. Maritain, *Art and Scholasticism*, p.74.
25. Ibid., p.36.
26. Ibid.
27. Davis, '"Poetry is Ontology"', p.150.
28. Brian Coffey, 'The Notion of Order According to St Thomas Aquinas', *Modern Schoolman*, vol. 21, no. 1 (November 1949), pp.1–18.
29. Ibid., p.18.
30. Arjun Appadurai, *Modernity at Large* (Minneapolis: University of Minnesota Press, 1996), pp.21–22.
31. Devlin, 'Twenty-Four Poets', p.461. Devlin may in fact have applied these criticisms to Coffey. It is not clear that Coffey's admiration for Devlin's poetry was reciprocated to the same extent on Devlin's part.
32. Jack Morgan, '"Missouri Sequence"', p.103.
33. See Jacques Maritain, 'Sign and Symbol', in *Ransoming the Time*, trans. Harry Lorin Binsse (New York: Charles Scribner, 1941), pp.217–54, and *Creative Intuition in Art and Poetry* (New York: Meridian Books, 1957).

CHAPTER TWELVE

Brian Coffey's Metaphysics of Love

AENGUS WOODS

The metaphysical desire tends toward *something else entirely*, toward the *absolute other*. (Emmanuel Levinas)[1]

'Poetry' means, not a literary genre as such, but the limits of 'literature', of 'writing', where nothing is written but the coming of a presence, a coming that can never be written or presented in any way. The edge on which writing writes only its own limit, exposed to … (Jean-Luc Nancy)[2]

'She' he says and not define
nor circumscribe and yet abide
not in ignorance   (Brian Coffey)[3]

I

In his introduction to *Poems and Versions 1929–1990*, J.C.C. Mays, in qualifying what might sound like a condemnation, indicates the depth of ambition of Brian Coffey's poetry:

> None of Brian Coffey's poems 'succeed', but, if I have made myself clear, it will be evident that success in poetry is provisional and local. Nor are they oppressed by failure: there is room for sorrow and anger but not disgust. They make up a poetry of intention. (*PV*, p.6)

To say admiringly of a poet that his work fails is a curious statement, though perhaps less so for readers of Samuel Beckett, where the question of literature is only ever a question of failure.[4] There the attempt to find comfort in a comfortless world and, by extension, to express oneself adequately (expression itself being a possible source of comfort) is in a certain sense damned since, for Beckett, the results are intolerable.[5] In his work the recurrent expressive drive leading to failure – the attempt to 'fail better' – reveals itself to be pure compulsion, an inability to stay still rather than any hope for success, tenuous or otherwise.[6] However, Mays' characterization of Brian Coffey's poetry in terms of *intention* decidedly shifts the aim of the work away from any such notion of 'failing better' and toward a very definite refusal to accept the failure of poetry. That Mays would indicate a long sequence called 'The Prayers' as paradigmatic of this intention is telling. Prayer necessarily involves belief, communication and a giving or offering up, while the notion of intention itself has a religious dimension in its reference to 'any object for which a prayer or intercession is said'.[7] Yet there is also a philosophical, phenomenological dimension to intentionality that complements this notion of prayer in Coffey's usage, providing grounds for understanding the sense in which his poetry both approaches and refuses failure. Intentionality in the phenomenological sense may be understood as that feature whereby consciousness is always a consciousness *of something*.[8] This 'something' is usually understood simply as any object of or within consciousness, but it can also be taken to indicate, as Jean-Luc Marion puts it, the fact that consciousness 'is not first consciousness of itself, but of something other than itself, that is always outside itself – alienated, so to speak'.[9] Thus to take a Coffey poem as intention, understood in this phenomenological sense, is to see it as aiming toward someone or something other, a desire for what is other than oneself. The difficulty, the risk of failure that presents itself for such a poetry is the risk of objectivation, or the reduction of something exceeding consciousness to merely an object for that consciousness. Taking the measure of this risk and of Coffey's means of articulating and facing such a task provide the most appropriate way in which to appreciate the love poetry of his later years.

The introduction of a philosophical register to characterize Coffey's poetry is neither casual nor accidental. A philosopher by training, it is key to understanding the aspiration, the content and the originality of Coffey's mature work, in particular, his significant body of love poetry. At first glance his love poetry can appear opaque, a particular feature being its apparently impersonal nature, lacking the specificities of the private relationship that makes a love poem like 'The Skunk' by Seamus Heaney so appealingly intimate.[10] There Heaney gives us the rich evocation of his own location, 'refrigerator whinnied into silence. / My desklight softened beyond the verandah', while sharing a recollection of deep intimacy: 'Your head-down, tail-up hunt in a bottom drawer / For the black plunge-line nightdress'. Coffey's love poetry displays no such concern with recollection of specific historical moments or the evocation of private feelings. Rather, his concern is with the broader philosophical significance of love, its impact upon one's existence and its consequences for how life is lived.[11] None the less, while Coffey was of course a philosopher and while one might object that such an approach is to be expected from a person who, it seems, had forsaken poetry for philosophy completely in the 1940s and 1950s, his verse is not simply the poetic expression of his philosophical opinions.[12] As Dónal Moriarty rightly observes of Coffey's poems, 'philosophers are not referred to by name; they are rarely invoked by way of quotation and very few passages of his poetry can be adduced as an example of this or that thinker' (*ABC*, p.15). Moriarty characterizes the influence of philosophy upon Coffey's poetry as informing the poet's perspective rather than providing subject matter. This is true but even so, the philosophical significance of his work is not to be underestimated. However, as I will argue, this significance lies in the form as much as in the content of Coffey's poetic work. Specifically in the later published verse, poetic form itself comes into play as an integral part of how we can discuss love and how we may express it. In this way poetry becomes an essential vehicle for the articulation of the philosophical dimensions of love, an articulation that, I will suggest, is not available to philosophy for reasons concerning the fundamentally conceptual nature of philosophy itself.[13]

While Coffey wrote numerous love poems, the focus here will be restricted to just three – two long sequences, 'Mindful of You' (1962), 'For What For Whom Unwanted' (1977) and a lyric poem, 'Answering Mindful' (1962).[14] These works are paradigmatic for Coffey's love poetry as a whole in that the trajectory traced between them maps out the development of Coffey's own notions of love as they mature and deepen, incorporating the lessons learned through years of marriage. 'Mindful of You' is a sequence of eleven cantos charting the dynamics of gain and loss that for Coffey are essentially operative in the experience of love. 'Answering Mindful' by its title indicates that it is a response to the former sequence and to that extent can be read as clarifying and elaborating a number of issues raised in it. 'For What For Whom Unwanted' is, I suggest, Coffey's attempt to integrate a number of the insights from 'Answering Mindful' into the framework of 'Mindful of You'. Such an interpretation is justified by the poem's mirroring eleven-canto structure and the strategic recurrence of key themes and images from the earlier sequence.

II

Love opens up the world in its richest sense to us. This is the central claim of Coffey's later love poetry and the notion that distinguishes these poems from his earlier works in *Third Person*. In that 1938 collection the dynamics of love are displayed in terms of a mutual reciprocity within a tripartite structure. This triad alternates between filial love – mother, father, child – and erotic love, which for Coffey involves the unity of lovers through a third factor – God, the Holy Spirit and as such would be a manifestation of *agapic* or divine love. The centrality of triadic structures and motifs in the poems has led some critics, J.C.C. Mays and Dónal Moriarty in particular, to rightly detect the presence of German Idealism within the collection, especially Hegelian metaphysics, albeit filtered through a specifically Christian lens. In his identification of a philosophical dialogue between Coffey and Beckett through their work, Mays points to a spirituo-religious dialectic operative in Coffey's collection, a dialectic whose *aufheben* – sublation or resolution – is achieved in the religious, Trinitarian figure of the third person.[15] Mays distinguishes this from a secular, materialist dialectic in Beckett's *Murphy* between self and world, inner and outer that precisely as secular cannot find resolution. Moriarty, in his close attention to Coffey's form and composition, identifies Hegelian dialectics operative throughout the movement of the poems and discerns traces of Gottlieb Fichte's theory of recognition, itself taken up and decisively developed by Hegel in his master–slave dialectic, whereby 'the self could only develop through its recognition *by* others and *of* others in human society' (*ABC*, p.29; my emphasis). With this understanding of intersubjectivity – the constitutive relations between people, the one and the other – the dynamics of this relationship are given in terms of reciprocity, mutuality and unity. Thus applying these notions to *Third Person* one can read the poems as outlining the relationship between a number of figures – lovers, parents, child – as to be constitutive of the fundamental nature of these figures through reciprocated acts of mutual determination. Thus the child determines the parent and vice versa, while through erotic love the self finds its validation and actualization in the eyes of another. The resultant unity, precisely love itself, would then be the articulation and concretion of the third person of the title – the Holy Spirit, God.

This Hegelian reading of the notion of love in *Third Person* is, on the whole, consistent with the trajectory of the collection. However, the views of love expressed in the latter poems published after the

1950s depart from these in a very definite manner, a manner which allows us to align the views expressed in the latter poems with a strain of French philosophy that matured contemporaneously with Coffey himself, and which grew out of a critical stance toward Hegel and the insistent drive towards unification within the framework of his metaphysics. In the later poetry, the role of love in the constitution of the self is radicalized even while the loved one will no longer be described as abiding in reciprocal relations, but will be seen to maintain distance, avoiding any pure unification and so drawing attention to the limitations and finitude of the self. The elevation of alterity or otherness and rejection of unity or reciprocity is a defining feature of much French post-structuralist thought, in particular that of Emmanuel Levinas, whom we shall consider below and whose notion of metaphysics as a desire for the other, for what is *meta*-physical or beyond ourselves, provides the ultimate sense in which we shall use the term *metaphysics* with regard to Coffey here.[16] By understanding Coffey's mature love poetry as an investigation into the experience of love that takes a critical stance towards the kind of Hegelian metaphysics identified in *Third Person*, and outlines an alternative account that rejects reciprocity and emphasizes disunity, we can identify a philosophical position that is not derivative but contains in embryonic form an original metaphysics of love.

That a position opposed to Hegel would become necessary for Coffey should not be surprising when we bear in mind that, despite the dialectic features of *Third Person*, the collection also contains a decisive rejection of any form of idealism. In the *Encyclopaedia of the Philosophical Sciences*, the mature statement of his thought, Hegel makes clear the full extent of his 'absolute idealism':

> Mind [*Geist*] is, therefore, in its every act only apprehending itself, and the aim of all genuine science is just this, that mind shall recognize itself in everything in heaven and on earth. *An out-and-out Other simply does not exist for mind.*[17]

As a Catholic, such a position is untenable for Coffey and his rejection of idealism is made clear in 'White', where the final verse can be read as both a riposte to Beckett's Cartesian leanings and as a dismissal of any notion of reality constituted by thought alone:

> Think no flower a surface
> no smile no extreme star
> think you can see no soul   (*PV*, p.24)

While Descartes was not an idealist, both idealism and Cartesian-inspired solipsism share a fundamental propensity to undermine the irreducible nature of whatever we normally take to exist outside of the mind, be that a material object or another person. In his *Meditations on First Philosophy*, Descartes argues that we can always doubt the product of our senses – those ideas and perceptions we have about the exterior world and so that world's existence – but that we cannot doubt at the very least, even within this doubt, that we are thinking.[18] With the indubitability of the act of thinking alone comes the indubitability of my existence. Thus he achieves a separation between mind and world that for Descartes can only be bridged by Divine guarantee.[19] Cartesian solipsism, then, is simply this doubt about the exterior world and is thus predicated on the notion that thinking can be detached from material conditions, precisely the position we find Murphy aiming towards in Beckett's novel.[20] Thus, for both solipsism and idealism there is a necessary recourse to a foundational subjectivity, since pure alterity – the possibility of an exterior world, the possibility of another person's independent existence – is problematized in the former case and relativized in the latter. However, as 'White' makes clear, Coffey sees both of these positions as false. If we lose the independent existence of what is beyond us – flowers, surfaces, the face of another person – then we lose life itself. The necessity of this rejection of idealism becomes more pronounced in the later works where Coffey will come to describe the loved one precisely as an 'out-and-out Other', a separate living being that precedes oneself in the world, awakens one's consciousness to the world and by virtue of their separation, even in love, always exceeds any complete comprehension.

III

In both 'Mindful of You' and 'For What For Whom Unwanted' Coffey provides an account not only of the condition and significance of love, but also its genesis. The approach of the loved one is the advent of an absolute other who comes, not on one's bidding but by their own accord, bringing to an isolated self nothing less than the world itself. In the earlier poem, existence is initially characterized as a barren desert. However, with the arrival of the other person the poet now finds himself in an infinitely richer world of growth and light: 'There was a desert I had raged in / flowered of sudden rain' (*PV*, p.92). What was a desolate, impoverished world is now fertile, not only richer in substance but infinitely ripe in possibility – a 'land without end' (*PV*, p.93). 'For What

For Whom Unwanted' radicalizes this account by indicating that the love of the other not only awakens the one to the world, but also awakens one to oneself. The other, and the love they inspire, is now placed as the very foundation of our consciousness. Whereas in 'Mindful of You' the self is capable of activity, albeit only a 'futile raging', by 1977 Coffey has come to see the primordial condition of the self as passive. This passivity in the absence of the other amounts to an unthinking form of self-absorption and solipsism: 'backward staring' (*PV*, p.171). Unconscious and unwaiting, none the less with the appearance of the face of the other, indicated phenomenologically by the other's 'bright eyes', their gaze coaxes the self out of its narcissistic self-absorption, turning it outwards in the direction of the world. This world, as in 'Mindful of You', takes on a quality of richness indicated by images of abundance, 'bright flowers' stirring as the self is stirred from hibernation (*PV*, p.171). In effect, the world takes on its plenitude and worldliness for the self only by virtue of the appearance and activity of the other.

This changes the reciprocal dynamics of *Third Person* considerably. The self cannot be brought into the fullness of existence without the advent of the other, but Coffey refuses to extend this into an account of mutual recognition or co-determination. In the later poems Coffey elevates the other, the loved one, to so great an extent that they now have no need of what the self can bring to them. However, the other awakens need in the self, a need moreover that cannot be satisfied and so exists rather as pure desire. This is a desire for the other, or what we call love. With this Coffey provides the grounds for what will be the defining feature of his late metaphysics of love, one which decisively distinguishes him from any idealism or Hegelianism. This is the absolute singularity and unknowability of the other.[21] In 'Mindful of You' the image of circling dust in the first canto indicates that attraction can never result in the complete union of two distinct terms:

> Never forever
> though in mine yours
> and in yours mine
> random should stray   (*PV*, p.91)

Unity, either of essence or understanding, ontological or conceptual, is impossible; the notion of a 'single sight' is an illusion. The unknowability of the other is indicated phenomenologically or in concrete terms as the experience of uncertainty regarding the future of any relationship with the other. Thus the other can, and will as both of the long

sequences indicate, disappear without warning both for motivations unavailable to us, or as the final cantos of 'For What For Whom Unwanted'
suggest, through our own periodic, misguided return to self-absorption.

'Answering Mindful', published in the same year as 'Mindful of
You', also deals with this issue and is crucial for understanding the
longer poem's significance for Coffey since it precisely re-examines
the notion that the ones we love are so separate and different from
us as to be unknowable. Of the three poems under consideration, it
is arguably the most immediately satisfying for its blend of abstract
reasoning and appeal to experience based on two decades of marriage.
In the opening verse Coffey's ambiguous phrasing achieves an effect
similar to that which Dónal Moriarty has identified in his reading of
the poet's translation of Mallarmé's *Un Coup de dés jamais n'abolira
le hasard*, whereby Coffey produced deviations from the original text,
slight but significant enough to maintain two opposing views within
one text, that of Coffey's and that of Mallarme's.[22]

> You ask if we from your kind differ so
> no Darby wholly sees his Joan
> no Joan her Darby
> Not true not trim
> what thrives on facts by all of us allowed[23] (*PV*, p.198)

Here Coffey attempts to inscribe within the same lines both a challenge
to his own earlier claims and a response to that challenge. The two
readings hinge on whether we read 'Not true' to refer to the claim of
unknowability, or whether it indicates that there are indisputable facts
that provide us with knowledge. These facts or readily accessible truths
are outlined in the second verse as insights gained from hard experience: bodies grow old, spontaneity succumbs to the easy satisfactions
of habit, basic needs of comfort and sustenance must be met and it
is an absolute certainty that families will quarrel. Coffey's response
is to acknowledge this, as indicated by the lack of change in register
between the second verse and the third, but he goes on to restate his
claim: 'Do not doubt deep the difference / lacking which two make no
one' (*PV*, p.198). The poet cannot accept with certainty that mere facts
amount to a complete knowledge of another person. The best one can
arrive at is a 'guess if you dive at a void / not to be bridged between
two' (*PV*, p.198). Thus in the final verse Coffey pledges both humility
and commitment in the face of the unknowable and an acceptance of
the priority of the other's will. This is a moral response to the condition of love. It is in fact love's moral dimension, the meaning of an

oft-used term in Coffey's work, *patience*, a humility and commitment that will be clarified further in 'For What For Whom Unwanted' as not only the acceptance of mortality and loss but also the price of freedom:

> Where goes his love
> How should he know
> This way of liberty
> is hard   (*PV*, p.173)

Particularly towards the second half of the sequence, 'Mindful of You' is already concerned with the possibility of loss that can give love its painful dimension. There, the loss of the other results in a return to bare existence that is exacerbated by the awareness of what one no longer has. However, the violent conclusion to that poem ('she shall not assuage / though he be torn apart') indicates, in spite of the narrator's return to a world shared with his love, the constant threat of dissolution resulting from subjection to the vagaries of an other. The account of loss and pain in 'For What For Whom Unwanted' places it more concretely in the context of marriage and old age. Gone is the storm and stress of the earlier poem, to be replaced with an all too real awareness of death and the space in which pointless regret about the past can surface. The pain of approaching death, hers and his, and the pain of loneliness become intertwined until both are but modalities of the loss of the other. The need to patiently accept death's inevitability is a burden relieved by the other's presence:

> O miseries of so-called life
> why will not one leave drab
> and dross behind
> tear out withered heart
> go naked smiling into light
> fairly call her love
> wait on her answering call   (*PV*, p.177)

All three poems, then, amount to a sustained attempt to outline the significance of love for human existence. To this extent, it could perhaps be characterized in Heideggerian terms as an existential analysis of love, its concrete features and its role in the constitution of the self. However, Coffey's insistence upon the centrality of the other moves his account away from the existential analytic of Martin Heidegger and, somewhat surprisingly for a professed neo-Thomist or Maritainian like Coffey, closer to the post-structuralist ethical thought of Emmanuel Levinas.[24]

Almost exact contemporaries, one year before Coffey published 'Mindful of You' and 'Answering Mindful', Levinas published *Totality and Infinity*, which outlined in strikingly similar terms to Coffey, an account of existence that stressed the centrality of the other person. In *Totality and Infinity* Levinas argues that the significance of the other has been systematically overlooked by philosophy. Without the acknowledgement of a radical other he claims, there is only philo- sophical idealism as all difference vanishes, leaving only a unified field of consciousness, relating to nothing beyond itself, precisely the kind of absolute idealism identifiable in Hegel. The other, whom we encounter concretely in the experience of the face of another person, is absolute and unknowable, constantly exceeding any fixed notion or concept that might be applied to comprehend them: 'The relation between the Other and me, which draws forth in his expression, issues neither in number nor in concept.'[25] Furthermore, Levinas argues that the other is at the source of the very identity of the self, by dragging the self out of its own unreflective consciousness and inaugurating its self- conscious engagement with the world.[26] As such the other for Levinas is at the root of worldly meaningful existence.

Because the other exceeds all categories of knowledge, Levinas attempted to develop a non-conceptual terminology to talk about the other that would not distort it by conceptualization or categorization. This discourse concerning the self as *hostage* to the other, the extreme *passivity* of the self and the characterization of this passivity as patience mirrors in many respects the terms that Coffey uses in his love poetry. This does not indicate on either side the possibility of influ- ence but rather, I would like to suggest, a case of two philosophers coming from a similar intellectual background, attempting to commu- nicate a fundamentally similar insight.[27] Furthermore, it indicates that one would be overly reductive to assume that Coffey was lacking in original philosophical thought or that he was essentially transcribing insights gleamed from studying Hegel, St Thomas Aquinas or Jacques Maritain. Rather, what we see here are two thinkers, independently working from similar concerns and offering strikingly similar descrip- tions of the metaphysics of human interaction.[28]

IV

Coffey's love poems are frequently self-reflexively aware of their own status as love poems. Throughout all three poems here, frequent reference is made to praise, song and 'the words that name her his love' (*PV*, p.173). Such reflexivity is a common feature of Modernist work, but Alex Davis has suggested that Coffey's silence as a poet during the 1940s and 1950s can be, at least partly, attributed to increasing doubts about how to reconcile the demands of an experimental Modernist outlook that increasingly reified poetry as pure form with the humility and acceptance of the Catholic faith.[29] It should come as no surprise, then, that much of Coffey's later poetry will, to varying extents, attempt to assess its own source, worth and function. Davis convincingly argues for the influence of Jacques Maritain and his notion of the poem as a material object of craft on Coffey's notion of the form and parameters of poetry in general. This emphasis on poetry as *poesis*, literally 'making', in Davis' reading points to 'Coffey's rejection of art's autonomy, and his concomitant emphasis on the artwork's connections with the author's and readers' life worlds [which] constitute an implicit critique of the post-Kantian separation of science, morality and art'.[30] Art then is not separate from life. The poem is part of the very stuff of living and Coffey's poetry is both formally and materially grounded in the concrete conditions of existence. Thus within the specific context of the love poem, Coffey's notions of its worth and function are grounded in his account of the significance of love and in a secondary movement poetry itself comes to play a central role in the dynamics of loving. Poetry thus becomes a material aspect of the loving relationship, being both an attempt at loving communication and an analogue of the experience of love. This movement can be traced in both of the long poems under consideration here.

That poetry itself is at stake in 'Mindful of You' is indicated in the second, four-line canto. The desire to 'tell all' is contrasted with its impossibility due to the interconnected factors of time and mortality. However, not until the sixth canto does this desire become embroiled in the dynamics of gain and loss that make up love. Midway through, in his state of isolation, the poet suddenly declares to his love that 'I wish you kind' (*PV*, p.93). The sentiment is followed by a series of well-wishes until the place of isolation becomes a location for the composition of poetry – a place 'where I reiterate / the way of heartbreak' (*PV*, p.94). From this point on, the declaration of love becomes both a way of coping with the solitude of separation and also a plea for help. The plea itself indicates the insights gained in the process of gain and loss:

> Seek not your eyes in mine
> as I would not seek mine in yours   (*PV*, p.94)

To think solely of oneself is to condemn oneself to isolation, even when in the presence of the other. Existence becomes inward-looking, and with this our engagement with the world impoverished, while the clear and true engagement with the other brings to us the infinitely rich world of sensation – 'when seeing is to breathe, to hear / to touch to tell to be' (*PV*, p.94). The movement of the last four cantos back into the realm of shared full existence attests to the power of poetry. The hope needed to survive the pains of life and the anguish of its brevity can only be summoned through communication:

> Pain sower of hope
> none in heart
>
> Yet did appear
> did speak   (*PV*, p.94)

In 'For What For Whom Unwanted' the notion of commitment underpins poetry. Commitment is meaningful because it is achieved on the basis of uncertainty, freely chosen and subject to the absolute freedom of the other. Commitment here becomes synonymous with poetry, thereby deepening the sense of the genesis of love poetry in 'Mindful of You'. Poetry is material and temporal, making it a tangible offering of the poet's love:

> what he gives time and place to
> the words that name her his love
> the words that make him hers   (*PV*, p.173)

His 'song', constituting the eighth canto, takes on a Heideggerian resonance in its emphasis on and repeated utterance of the word 'You' (*PV*, p.175). Thus his song, and by extension the poem as a whole is both celebration and a statement of the continuous offering of self to other, of the poet to his lover, even in the face of mortality:

> to glorify the day he dies in
> declaring her all
> all he would be with   (*PV*, p.176)

However, Coffey's commitment to love poetry alongside his conviction that the other is unknowable requires that he develop a way of speaking about the other that would not distort the concrete experience of the other by applying concepts and categories. Since the unknowability of the other can be attributed to its transcendence of all categories of knowledge, a linguistic device for paradoxically indicating that which is beyond language is required.

V

The identification of a parallel notion of alterity within the work of Levinas and Coffey reveals a factor that comes to play a determining role in the latter's poetry at the level of form. It must be acknowledged that if Coffey's love poems were to remain at the level of merely indicating this notion of a non-conceptualizable other, they would be susceptible to the same fundamental problem faced by Levinas in his account of alterity. Since the other is essentially unknowable, any attempt to conceptualize the other ultimately distorts and misrepresents. This renders even the task of elucidating a philosophical account of the other problematic, as it must inevitably say that the other is 'such and such' or provide linguistic, conceptual content to the signifier, 'the other'. However, I would suggest that it is Coffey's application of a scholastic theory of analogy to poetic composition which allows him to overcome this problem. This makes itself apparent in the poems at a formal level. In Coffey's love poetry it is the trajectory or actual experience of reading the poem that communicates meaning as much as the conceptual claims contained within the words. Structurally the poems become an analogue for the experience they wish to communicate. Thus it is the interplay between analogy and poetic form that allows Coffey to go some way towards dealing with the problem of philosophical accounts and in doing so indicates further the reach and scope of poetry.

The medieval scholastics, most notably Aquinas and Cajetan, outlined a theory of analogy to explain how we can use the same terms in a variety of senses, such as 'wise' or 'good' for both God and earthly things without equating one with the other.[31] In particular, the latter's theory of proportionality in analogy can provide a way of understanding how poetic utterances relate to the reality they are indicating. The basic form of the proportional analogy would be A is to B as C is to D. In the case of a poetic analogy, the proportion between the terms contained in the poem can be used to make sense of the reality that the analogy is indicating. Thus, in 'Mindful of You' the proportion of difference between a desert and a lush garden would indicate the difference between isolated existence and shared existence. This theory of analogy can also be applied to the form and structure of many of Coffey's poems. In James Hogan's 1983 BBC documentary about Brian Coffey, the narrator draws attention to the way in which the poems often enact rather than describe their themes.[32] He rightly points to the 1975 long poem *Advent* as the apotheosis of this, but it is also apparent in the two long poems discussed here. In each poem the opening canto strikes the most lyrical note of the sequence and contains hermetically within it all the issues and concerns raised in the rest of the poem. The cantos proceeding from it can be understood as the deepening of these issues through an enactment of the processes implicated around the moment the first canto alludes to. In this manner the reader is invited to witness or more precisely experience the events given in the narrative arc of the poems rather than merely grasp a series of categorical claims in rigidly conceptual terms. Hence the movement in 'Mindful of You', for example: from isolation of the self to the advent of the other, her subsequent loss, the realization of pain which accompanies the subsequent isolation until the reappearance of the other and the final position of non-unifying co-existence. The progress of the poem is an analogical relation to the reality it refers to and the success of the poem is based on the extent to which it is experienced before it is conceptualized.

The formal structure of 'Mindful of You' is thus essential to the poem's progress as an analogical enactment of the dynamics of loving existence. It is for that reason that the insights gained from its companion poem 'Answering Mindful' needed to be reinscribed within a formal structure identical to the earlier poem to produce 'For What For Whom Unwanted'. As such, the latter poem follows the same trajectory as 'Mindful of You' but with the crucial difference that the concluding position of non-unifying co-existence has inscribed within it the acceptance of death and loss, gained through the patient giving of oneself to another in marriage and parenthood. Taken together, the three poems amount to a non-conceptual account of the metaphysical significance of loving existence. They indicate the manner in which the human subject is awoken to self-conscious existence within an infinitely rich world, the essential intertwining of pain in love and also the intimate role played by poetry in the dynamics of love and human interaction.

VI

The love poems of Brian Coffey neither fail nor succeed, or perhaps in a more Hegelian mode we might say that they both fail and succeed, but for intrinsic reasons – reasons that do not diminish their worth, but rather to the contrary, make us all the more aware of what is at stake in the work. The poems succeed precisely by refusing to admit defeat in the face of the impossible challenge they set themselves. The poems attempt to say something about loving existence, about that other whom we find ourselves in love with and whom we find loving us, without recourse to conceptual language with its rigid determinations and its implicit prioritizing of the self's point of view. The difficulty of this is acute when working within the resources of philosophical discourse, a conceptual language through and through, but it is also a difficulty inherent in language *per se*. The attempt to describe, to ascribe even or simply to identify carries the risk of dissimulation, of an alteration of the other's nature, of committing an act of injustice toward the other.

It is this paradox that holds the meaning and the force behind Coffey's intent as a love poet, by which he uses the resources of poetic form to overcome or sidestep the inherent limitations of language underpinned by conceptuality. The resulting poetics therefore express a profound ambition, one that moves Coffey beyond his usual position as a footnote in twentieth-century Irish poetry or as merely another Modernist bump on an otherwise smooth trail to Heaney's skunk. As fine a poem as it is, 'The Skunk' is arguably paradigmatic of a certain kind of Irish poetry that displays on the one hand an unquestioned prioritizing of the narrator's consciousness, and on the other, a ready trust in language as it is, a belief that expression is simply a question of digging to find the right words. In contrast with this, the formal innovations of Coffey's love poems, in their attempt to say the unsayable, more properly align him with the likes of Paul Celan, George Oppen and Wallace Stevens, to name but a few, poets whose works constantly aim to express by means of language, precisely what is beyond language. Celan and Oppen in particular share with Coffey the tendency towards what we might call, after Philippe Lacoue-Labarthe, 'poetry as experience'.[33] Celan applied techniques of extreme defamiliarization in an attempt to thwart any recourse to conceptual meaning through the fracturing of line syntax, enjambment, the use of ellipsis, repetition and the coining of neologisms.[34] In a different manner, Oppen's objectivist commitments led him to compose poetry with a keen regard for the experiential dimension, the physical and visual reading of the poem.[35] As I have tried to suggest, the strategy attempted by Coffey is to make his love poems function in an analogical manner, so that by virtue of their formal composition the actual experience of reading them would transmit, in a non-conceptual mode, as much of their significance as the words themselves.

None the less, even if these poets share a certain wariness of language as a given medium and a tendency towards developing strategies that might avoid its pitfalls, their deeper concerns vary and are each their own. The central concern expressed throughout all of Coffey's love poetry remains remarkably consistent, namely that the loved one and the experience of love exceed and escape all articulation and conceptualization. For this reason, philosophy and language in general are always compromised in their attempts to describe the world. In spite of this, Coffey's love poetry is precisely an attempt to do justice to the other, to express *something* of the loving relationship between the self and other, not quite within language but by functioning, as Jean Luc-Nancy says, at its very limits. Thus the movement and trajectory of the poems are as important as what is said, the silences as meaningful as the words, the experience as important as understanding. Aware of these limits of language, poetry in the hands of Brian Coffey becomes an attempt to communicate non-conceptually, without resort to argumentation but by immersing us in the poem, as an experience that brings us to the edge of language, precisely at the point of contact between one person and another. A difficult task certainly, but one indicating that, however we might understand Coffey's abandonment of verse in favor of philosophy in the 1940s, his eventual return, after two decades, to writing poetry stands as testament to a renewed belief in its power and possibilities.

NOTES

1. Emmanuel Levinas, *Totality and Infinity: An Essay on Exteriority*, trans. Alphonso Lingus (Pittsburgh, PN: Duquesne University Press, 1969), p.33.
2. Jean-Luc Nancy, *The Birth to Presence*, trans. Brian Holmes *et al.* (Stanford, CA: Stanford University Press, 1993), pp.ix–x.
3. 'Cave', *PV*, p.211.
4. Samuel Beckett, *Worstward Ho* (London: John Calder, 1983), p.7.
5. Ibid., p.10: 'No choice but stand. Somehow up and stand. Somehow stand. That or groan. The groan so long on its way. No. No groan. Simply pain. Simply up. A time when try how. Try see. Try say. How first it lay. Then somehow knelt. Bit by bit. Then on from there. Bit by bit. Till up at last. Not now. Fail better worse now.'
6. Ibid., p.8: 'First the body. No. First the place. No. First both. Now either. Now the other. Sick of the either try the other. Sick of it back sick of the either. So on. Somehow on. Till sick of both. Throw up and go. Where neither. Till sick of there. Throw up and back. The body again. Where none. The place again. Where none. Try again. Fail again. Better again. Or better worse. Fail worse again. Still worse again.'
7. John Bowker, 'Intention', in *The Concise Oxford Dictionary of World Religions* (1997). Available online http://www.encyclopedia.com/doc/1O101-Intention.html (accessed by the author 16 March 2009).
8. Edmund Husserl, *Ideas: General Introduction to Pure Phenomenology*, trans. W.R. Boyce Gibson (London: George Allen & Unwin, 1931), p.120.
9. Jean-Luc Marion, 'The Intentionality of Love', in *Prolegomena to Charity*, trans. Stephen E. Lewis (New York: Fordham University Press, 2002), p.72.
10. Seamus Heaney, *Opened Ground: Poems 1966–1996* (London: Faber & Faber, 1998), p.176.
11. Of course, Coffey is not the only poet, indeed not even the only Irish poet, to consider the

philosophical significance of love; Thomas Kinsella in 'Echoes' and indeed W.B. Yeats ('Adam's Curse') being notable exemplars. None the less, Coffey is notable for his commitment to a philosophical exploration of the question of love in his poetry, consistently eschewing the personal and the epiphanic in favour of love's deeper significance.

12. Between 1934 and 1939 Brian Coffey studied philosophy intermittently at the Institut Catholique de Paris, then under the sway of the neo-scholastic Jacques Maritain. In 1937, after brief spells in Dublin and London, Coffey began working on his doctoral thesis 'De l'idée d'ordre d'après saint Thomas D'Aquin', under the supervision of F.A. Blanche, O.P. Delayed by the outbreak of the war, the thesis was completed and defended in 1947, after which Coffey found employment as professor of philosophy in the USA. He taught at the University of St Louis, Missouri between 1947 and 1952, when he returned to ultimately settle in England after resigning his assistant professorship following a dispute with the university.

13. It should be noted, however, that the history of philosophy is not without its accounts of love – Plato's *Symposium* and *Phaedrus*, Aristotle's account of friendship in the *Nicomachean Ethics*, right up to Harry Frankfurt's *The Reasons of Love* (2004). However I would suggest that some of the difficulties that philosophy faces when talking about love are already apparent in *Phaedrus*. There it is significant that Socrates resorts to allegory and myth to explain his ideas on love. This already suggests there are limits to a language of definition which functions by dividing its subject manner into simple parts, the better to grasp them conceptually. Indeed, the insistence with which Socrates places rhetoric under the authority of philosophy there, and also in *Republic* by condemning poets outright, indicate Plato's awareness of the threat posed by poetic expression to philosophy's realm of authority.

14. Two points need to be made. First, the dates given here are dates of publication. The manuscripts for these poems are unfortunately not dated. None the less, I think it is not unreasonable to suggest that 'Mindful of You' is a significantly earlier poem than 'Answering Mindful' and that the latter is a response to it. Furthermore, this chronology is supported thematically by the poems, the former detailing love's encounter, the latter a retrospective glance over marriage. The second point is that I have chosen to consider 'Answering Mindful' outside of the context of its positioning within a sequence of poems called 'Fidelities'. I have done so as this sequence merely draws together a number of independent poems, in contrast to both 'Mindful of You' and 'For What For Whom Unwanted', which are sequences of untitled cantos and are thus more correctly understood as long poems.

15. J.C.C. Mays, 'Brian Coffey (1905–1995)', *The UCD Aesthetic: Celebrating 150 Years of UCD Writers*, ed. Anthony Roche (Dublin: New Island Press, 2005), pp.91–93.

16. Part of Levinas' project was to alter the sense of the term *metaphysics* from simply an indication of the underlying substance/structure/reality (pick your metaphysician!) of the physical world to an indication of the self's essential enthrallment to what is beyond itself, i.e. the other person. It is thus a consequence of Coffey's own shift from a loosely Hegelian position (in many ways the traditional metaphysician par excellence) to a post-Hegelian, proto-Levinasian position (as I wish to suggest) that the term *metaphysics* cannot be used univocally with regard to his work, but must change as his position changes. Put another way, Coffey's poetry does metaphysics in the traditional sense only by ultimately demonstrating the appropriateness and necessity of the Levinasian sense.

17. G.W.F. Hegel, *Hegel's Philosophy of Mind: Part Three of the Encyclopaedia of the Philosophical Sciences*, trans. William Wallace and A.V. Miller (Oxford: Oxford University Press, 1971), §377 (zusatz), my emphasis.

18. René Descartes. *The Philosophical Writings of Descartes*, vol. 2, trans. John Cottingham, Robert Stoothoff and Dugald Murdoch (Cambridge: Cambridge University Press, 1984), pp.3–62.

19. Hence, Descartes is a dualist and his solipsism is methodological. However, if one puts aside the Divine guarantee, what one has is metaphysical solipsism, which is the position that interests Beckett and which Coffey rejects.

20. J.C.C. Mays, in the present volume, convincingly demonstrates the role and influence of other accounts of solipsism in the writing of Beckett's novel, particularly Geulincx. I am in agreement with most of his claims, particularly those pointing to Coffey's deep understanding of the issues surrounding solipsism and his critical reaction to these leanings in Beckett, apparent in the review of *Murphy*. My aim here is to suggest that this position can be read as ultimately necessitating a move away from the kind of Hegelianism that Mays detects in

Third Person, a move that will find its full expression in Coffey's later love poems.

21. It must be noted that such unknowability does not commit Coffey to the kind of solipsism we have previously discussed in regard to Beckett. Metaphysical solipsism questions the reality of anything outside the mind while epistemological solipsism questions the possibility of having knowledge of anything outside the mind. As I see it, Coffey's position does not problematize knowledge *per se*. Science and the understanding of the world is possible and real for him. Rather, the point is that absolute or complete knowledge is impossible with regard to the other person in that they will continually exceed our understanding of them. One's relationship to the other is not founded on our complete comprehension, as in idealism, but is consummated in love.

22. Stéphane Mallarmé, *Dice Thrown Never Will Annul Chance*, trans. Brian Coffey (Dublin: Dolmen Press, 1965). According to Moriarty, Coffey translated Mallarmé faithfully but none the less rejected the latter's notion that 'truth posited nothingness as the source and end of all', and leaves evidence of this divergence carefully positioned within the text, producing opposed meanings simultaneously (*ABC*, p.84).

23. A quintessentially English reference 'Darby and Joan' is generally taken to refer to an old-fashioned, reliable albeit unexciting, loving relationship. They make a number of appearances in Victorian, Edwardian and modern literature from Thackeray and Trollope to even Albert Camus. In particular, Henry James' reference in *The Golden Bowl* brings out the implicitly unsatisfying or tragic aspect to the notion of a perfect happiness: 'Their very silence might have been the mark of something grave – their silence eked out for her by his giving her his arm and their then crawling up their steps quite mildly and unitedly together, like some old Darby and Joan who have had a disappointment.' See Henry James, *The Golden Bowl* (Ware: Wordsworth Classics, 1993), p.242.

24. Heidegger did not share this emphasis on the centrality of the Other that I am attributing to Coffey. In *Being and Time*, other people are reduced to either *Mittsein* ('Being-with'), a impersonal structural necessity within the existential framework of Dasein ('There-being' or 'Being-in-the-World') or they are denigrated to the level of *Das Man*, the 'They', the milieu of idle-talk and inauthenticity. The work of Emmanuel Levinas, whose ideas share a similar trajectory to the one I am attributing to Coffey, grew in part out of a critique of this very aspect of Heidegger's thought.

25. Levinas, *Totality and Infinity*, p.194.

26. Emmanuel Levinas. *Otherwise Than Being, or Beyond Essence*, trans. Alphonso Lingus (Pittsburgh, PN: Duquesne University Press, 1998), pp.99–121.

27. Emmanuel Levinas was born in Lithuania in 1906 but moved to France to study philosophy at Strasbourg University in 1923. He fell under the sway of Heideggerian philosophy until the latter's support for National Socialism forced a critical reappraisal. As a prisoner during the war, Levinas began to read Hegel closely and after the war he taught in Paris and became familiar with the Hegelian readings of Jean Hyppolite and Alexander Kojeve. Of Coffey, on the other hand, we know from Deirdre Bair's biography of Samuel Beckett that he was reading Heidegger in the 1930s and, living in Paris, would certainly have been aware of the Hegelian currents within its intellectual circles at the time. See Deirdre Bair, *Samuel Beckett, A Biography* (London: Jonathan Cape, 1978), p.97. Also, J.C.C. Mays' chapter 8 above refers to Coffey's deep understanding of Hegel, even to the extent of supervising a Ph.D thesis on Hegel in the 1970s.

28. It must be acknowledged, however, that the shared concern with the Other in both Coffey and Levinas does not prevent them from displaying considerable divergence in other ways. Levinas' account is by far the more expansive, especially in terms of the ethical dimension of alterity, and as such many of its details would not map easily on to Coffey's concerns. I am thinking in particular of Levinas' rather Platonic interpretations of art as mere imitation and hence complicit in the dissimulation of the Other. See 'Reality and its Shadow', in *The Levinas Reader*, ed. Seán Hand (Oxford: Blackwell, 1989), pp.130–43. My point here is merely to indicate by comparison, that within his poetry Coffey worked out a legitimate philosophical position that overcame shortcomings in his earlier position and in the current philosophical notions of his time. Similarly, parallels can be drawn with other philosophers facing related issues at the time – Sartre for example and even, later on, Jacques Derrida.

29. Alex Davis, '"Poetry is Ontology": Brian Coffey's Poetics', in *Modernism and Ireland: The Poetry of the 1930s*, ed. Patricia Coughlan and Alex Davis (Cork: Cork University Press, 1995), p.151.

30. Ibid. p.167.
31. As Coffey tellingly states in the publication of part of his doctoral thesis on Aquinas, 'it must always remain a source of regret to Thomists that St Thomas did not find time to compose treatises on subjects such as analogy and participation, which must be understood thoroughly by whoever would obtain a firm grasp of Thomism'. See Coffey, 'The Notion of Order according to St Thomas Aquinas', *The Modern Schoolman: A Quarterly Journal of Philosophy*, vol. 28, no. 1 (November 1949), p.2. None the less, the most extensive consideration of analogy by Aquinas is to be found in the *Summa Contra Gentiles*, book I, section 32. See Aquinas, *Summa Contra Gentiles: Book One*, trans. Anton Charles (Pegis, IN: University of Notre Dame Press, 1997). Thomas De Vio, Cardinal Cajetan offers the most important medieval development of Aquinas' notion of analogy. See Cajetan, *Scripta Philosophica: De Analogia Nominum; De Conceptus Entis*, ed. P.N. Zammit, O.P., revised P.M. Hering, O.P. (Rome, Institutum Angelicum, 1934).
32. BBC Radio programme on Brian Coffey, directed by Augustus Young (James Hogan), 1983.
33. Philippe Lacoue-Labarthe, *Poetry as Experience*, trans. Andrea Tarnowski (Stanford, CA: Stanford University Press, 1986). I use the conditional here since the notion of poetry as experience has a different significance in Lacoue-Labarthe's than the one I am suggesting here in reference to the experiential, analogical dimension of reading Coffey's poetry.
34. Paul Celan, *Poems of Paul Celan*, trans. Michael Hamburger (New York: Persea Books, 1972).
35. Dónal Moriarty comes close to making the same point with regard to Oppen when, quoting him, he speaks of the manner in which Oppen's poetry aspires to the condition of 'unmediated perception' (*ABC*, p.41). This would mean precisely experience unmediated by concepts. The poem from *Discrete Series* that he cites ('Thus / Hides the / Parts ... ') therefore demonstrates an attempt to *enact* experience without recourse to concepts, in this case the perception of a soda fountain in operation. See George Oppen, *New Collected Poems*, ed. Michael Davidson (New York: New Directions, 2002), p.7.

CHAPTER THIRTEEN

Coffey/Dante/Pound: A Personal Encounter

BILLY MILLS

When Brian's *Poems and Versions 1929–1990* came out in 1991, Harry Gilonis asked me to write a review of it for a magazine he was involved with called *Eonta*. Unfortunately, I got a bit carried away, and the resulting essay was far too long for any magazine to carry. After Brian's death, Harry offered to publish my review as a booklet from his own Form Press, and it appeared in 1995 under the title 'Behind all Archetypes: On Brian Coffey'. The title of this present writing derives from a footnote to that earlier study, and, if you bear with me, I will get to it eventually. Before I do, I would like to discuss the broader topic of encountering Brian Coffey; specifically, I want to explore what it meant for a young, would-be poet to encounter Brian's poetry in 1970s Ireland. Given that the poet in question was me, this means I am going to write about myself for a while. I am also going to quote from some of my favourite poetry, so at least one of us is going to enjoy themselves.

For as long as I can remember, I have been a reader. As a child, this meant, for the most part, classic novels and popular science. Around about the age of 11, I discovered poetry via my father's old editions of Palgrave's *Golden Treasury* and Fitzgerald's *Rubaiyat of Omar Khayyam*. My favourite contributor to Palgrave was Anon, but I enjoyed Shakespeare enough to start looking for more in the public library. Even then, Wordsworth, Keats and Shelly left me cold; too many words. A couple of years later I discovered Bob Dylan; next came Ezra Pound and T.S. Eliot. Suddenly the poem was no longer just a way of weaving attractive sound patterns or telling old tales; now it began to look like a whole new way of hearing, seeing and articulating the world and me-in-the-world.

Once launched on the Modernists, I threw myself into reading everything I could lay my hands on; most of Eliot, Pound's shorter poems,

Literary Essays, Selected Cantos and, later on and after much saving, *The Cantos of Ezra Pound,* the Faber dark blue hardcover edition of Cantos 1 to 109 (I–CIX), David Jones' *In Parenthesis* and *The Anathemata* (all readily available in Dublin bookshops and libraries at that time thanks to Faber & Faber), Joyce's *Dubliners, A Portrait of the Artist,* and the wonderful Penguin edition of *Ulysses* with its striking black cover.

Reading these writers, and especially Pound, produced a list of others I wanted to move on to: Marianne Moore, William Carlos Williams, H.D., Wyndham Lewis, Basil Bunting, Louis Zukofsky, and more, many of them difficult if not impossible to come across in Dublin thirty five years ago (most still are, especially Bunting, Lewis and Zukofsky). Moore was available, again thanks to Faber, and I found the Calder editions of Lewis's *Childermass* novel sequence in the Paperback Centre in Suffolk Street (long since closed down). The Paperback Centre had a copy of the Fulcrum Press edition of *Briggflatts* on its shelves for a while, but it was sold before I could scrape the cash together. Peter Jones' 1972 *Imagist Poetry* anthology was a treasure, as was, to a lesser extent, Edward Lucie Smith's *British Poetry Since 1945* (1970), which had the full text of Bunting's long poem 'The Spoils'. Both these anthologies, being published by Penguin, were readily available. Some years later, the 1978 Martin Brian & O'Keefe edition of Hugh MacDiarmid's *Collected Poems* turned up remaindered in Fred Hanna's basement. I also bought the Temple Classics edition of Dante's *Divine Comedy,* three volumes with text, facing-page translation and notes, first published 1899–1901 (and the very edition used by Pound and others), again in Hanna's and costing a few shillings the volume. Where would you get it now?

The appearance of Pound's *Drafts and Fragments of Cantos CX–CXVII* was a great event and I can still remember the excitement of buying the handsome slim black hardback in Hodges Figgis' old shop in Dawson Street, just across the road from where they are now. Even more memorable was the immediate impact of the opening page:

> Thy quiet house
> The crozier's curve runs in the wall
> The harl, feather-white, as a dolphin on sea-brink
>
> I am all for Verkehr without tyranny
>   —wake exultant
> in caracole
> Hast'ou seen wake on sea-wall
> how crests it?

As I did not go to university after secondary school, I was free to read what I wanted, when I wanted and in the order I wanted, and so construct my own map of poetry. In retrospect, I now see that what this map showed, and what Pound, Dylan and the others represented for me, was a kind of radical dissatisfaction. The only Irish writers I encountered who were part of this were Joyce and Beckett, but I saw them as prose writers, not poets. At school, Irish poetry was, essentially, Yeats, Clarke and Kavanagh; each of them had their merits, but they weren't what I needed, they were not on my map.

Then one day I discovered a display of New Writers' Press books in the Eblana Bookshop on Grafton Street (also long gone). Wonderful books by, amongst others, Trevor Joyce, Michael Smith and Michael Hartnett. But the two titles that I just had to buy were Thomas Mac-Greevy's *Collected Poems* (1971) and Brian Coffey's *Selected Poems* (1971). These two books were a complete revelation, especially Brian's work, and most especially the two long poem sequences 'How Far from Daybreak' and 'Mindful of You'. Here, at last, I found Irish poetry that belonged to what I had learned to call the Modernist tradition, work that spoke to me in the way that I had come to expect: restless, demanding, questioning.

Over the following months and years I tracked down as much of Brian's work as I could lay my hands on: the *Irish University Review: Brian Coffey Special Issue* (1975) with the first appearance of *Advent*; books and pamphlets in the National Library; and, eventually, publications by Brian's press Advent Books that I bought once I had summoned up the nerve to write to his address in Southampton to enquire. An exciting voyage.

Probably the most exciting moment of all was the first time I read the opening lines of *Advent*, with their clear echo of an earlier, similar experience:

> Unquiet house it is   darkness solid
> like what wake-light once showed   shadows pressing
> From tumbled citadel one stared at air
> shaped by walls   rigid like speech frozen (*PV*, p.111)

Clearly Coffey knew and was responding to *Drafts and Fragments* and I was pleased to see a copy of the same Faber edition on his shelves during a visit to his home in Southampton in 1988. Given the differences in their personal circumstances, it is not surprising that Pound's house (or rather the Basilica in Torcello where the poem opens) would be quiet while Brian's would be unquiet, being, as it was, both full of people and noisy and disturbed by the death of a son. However, the parallel that struck me most forcibly was the punning use of the word 'wake' in both poems. One of the references of Pound's wake is back to the last line of the previous canto, Canto CIX, 'You in the dinghy (piccioletta) astern there!', itself a reference to the following passage from Canto II of Dante's *Paradiso* (I said we would get there eventually):

> O voi che siete in piccioletta barca,
> desiderosi d'ascoltar, seguiti
> dietro al mio legno che cantando varca,
>
> tornate a riveder li vostri liti:
> non vi mettete in pelago, ché forse,
> perdendo me, rimarreste smarriti.

Translated in the Temple Classics version as:

> Oh ye who in your little skiff, longing to hear,
> have followed on my keel that singeth on its
> way,
>
> turn to revisit your own shores; commit you not
> to the open sea; for perchance losing me, ye
> would be left astray.

Dante, approaching his poetic expression of paradise, is warning those of us who have followed in his wake that we are now entering dangerous, uncharted waters and letting us off the hook if we choose to turn back. As he set out to write the final installment of *The Cantos*, Pound also intended to write a paradise, hence his reference to the earlier attempt. Perhaps Brian, in his appropriation of much of the same vocabulary (even down to his choice of the work 'barque' for boat in the line 'one day yes the barque will glide out of long night seas' further down the opening page) is signalling a similar intention.

Writing in the context of Christianity and shared religious belief, Dante was able to draw on an unproblematic concept of what paradise might be like, an advantage that allowed him to pull off the writing of his vision triumphantly. Pound, faced with the complete discrediting of the Fascist political foundations and Social Credit economics of his proposed earthly paradise, accepted personal failure. While insisting that the *matter* of his poem was, in theory at least, susceptible to a degree of intellectual coherence to match the theological coherence which Dante could take for granted from a readership who shared this basic ideological assumptions, he was forced to the realization that it

was beyond him as a poet and as a man. The resulting fragmentary, and
more or less accidental, ending to *The Cantos* has been widely read as
reflecting the equally fragmented state of the human condition, at least
in its Western form, in the second half of the twentieth century.

Advent can then, on one level, be read as an argument with the
Pound of *Drafts and Fragments*. For Brian, a committed Roman
Catholic, even in the face of personal tragedy, faith is the key to the coherence that Pound failed to achieve. This belief in the power of faith
reaches its climax in the closing line of the poem, 'so be it', the most
common translation of the Latin word *Amen*. Brian does not ignore the
indeterminacy and fragmentation of late twentieth-century experience;
in fact he confronts it face on. This confrontation is enacted through
the poem's syntax. Look again at the opening lines:

> Who wakes now being here if not one alone

> where where lifts no sail no dew cools
> far stars of their purity presage none
> voiceless unfeatured unrapturing deep
> own the place dice dead naught to please   (*PV*, p.111)

Is the opening a question or not? Does the unknown 'who' wake from
sleep or wake the dead? Does one of the repeated 'wheres' relate back
to the 'here' of line one? Does the dew cool the stars or not? And if
not, what? Am I, the reader, to admit that this place I do not yet know
is 'dice dead', whatever that phrase, redolent of Mallarmé, might be
construed to mean? Unless they make the entirely rational decision to
abandon the poem there and then, the reader is required, on each and
every reading, to create some form of meaning out of the uncertainty
reflected in these, and the many other, questions that arise from even
these few lines. And each time, even a small shift of readerly attention
opens up whole new areas of possibility. However, as we move towards
the resolution of the poem, this indeterminancy gives way to certainty,
so that at the very end meaning is more or less imposed by the poet:

> in poverty wealth
> sickness health
> on the better tack
> or the worser
> between womb and grave
> face to polar cold
> right in storm of fire

for us surely
where friend gives greatest gift

so be it   (*PV*, pp.149–50)

As I discuss in 'Behind all Archetypes', Brian told Parkman Howe in an interview in *Éire/Ireland* (vol. 13, 1978) that the structure of the eight-part poem was originally based on the eight hours of the Church day. The following table, copied from my earlier essay, is intended as nothing more than a guideline for the interested reader:

1. Matins   The world of the isolated individual.
     (inc. *Venite* & *Te Deum*)
2. Lauds   The world of beauty and its abuse.
     (inc. *Laudete* & *Benedictus*)
3. Prime   The world of (the abuse of) history
     (followed by a reading from the *Martyrology*)
4. Terce   Idolatry, especially the worship of technology
     (it is this section of the poem that was prefigured in 'The Monument').
5. Sext   The Earth as home/mother.
6. None   Mothers and children.
7. Vespers   Death (specifically the death of a son).
     (inc. the *Magnificat*)
8. Compline   Prayer/acceptance.
     (inc. the *Nunc Dimittis*)

As a committed Catholic, Brian drew on the same Christian traditions that underpinned Dante's paradise. However, he was writing in a context where many people, including many of his otherwise most sympathetic readers, did not share his beliefs. Specifically, the ending he found for the poem as quoted above, one based on prayer and Christian acceptance, is one that many readers, including the present writer, find less than satisfactory.

This path back through Dante is, of course, only one way to slice through these two poems. Both openings refer to awakenings and both are, in their own ways, waking the dead. As always in *The Cantos*, any reference to boats and the sea also refers back to Odysseus, Homer, the fall of Troy and the House of Atreus, the original 'unquiet house' in the European tradition which is named in section three of *Advent*. And for Brian, it seems that the death of a son reverberated with the death of Hektor, the tragic Trojan hero of the epic conflict that resulted from that unquietness. On this reading, it is possible to see Brian's 1980 poem *Death of Hektor* as the true resolution of the motifs raised at the beginning of *Advent*. Here the death of the hero, son of the Trojan king Priam, opens out the personal tragedy that underpins *Advent* way beyond the Christian resignation of that 'so be it' and connects it to a much wider mythological field. Certainly, in its identification with the victim and the down-trodden, *Death of Hektor* connects fully with that radical dissatisfaction that, for me at least, underpins all the truly vital poetry of the last one hundred years.

As I stated earlier in this chapter, encountering Brian's work was a significant event for me as a poet. However, this impact was not a matter of straightforward influence; Brian's style is too much his own to be successfully adopted by anyone else and his Catholic beliefs too far removed from my own worldview for that kind of relationship with his work. What mattered, matters, to me is his integrity. All through his sixty-odd years as a writer, Brian remained impervious to the idea that writing poetry could be anything other than a necessary act; it was certainly not a career option. He was a contrary man who turned down what others might have considered irresistible opportunities to 'advance' himself. He never wrote anything with an eye to sales or grant funding. It is, for me at least, this resistance to commodification that has made, and continues to make, his writing so important.

CHAPTER FOURTEEN

Mapping Half of *Advent*

HARRY GILONIS

Brian Coffey's *Advent*, written over the course of twenty-five years, is his largest single poem (eight parts, some thousand lines) and arguably his most important. Of a more well known user-unfriendly precursor work, Ezra Pound's *Cantos*, their author declared 'I haven't an Aquinas-map', and a similar lack confronts the reader of *Advent*.[1] Furthermore, as we shall see, there is an added difficulty in that Coffey often recofigures source material in a complex and idiosyncratic manner. My intention below is to tease out some of the myriad references in *Advent*, and the implications of their use; such explication being a necessary precursor to interpretation. None the less it is only a sketch-map, hardly on the scale of an Aquinian *Summa*. Though extensive, it could easily be more detailed; other cartographers with better tools will doubtless follow. (I should say at the outset that this is but *half* such a map, dealing as it does with just the first half of *Advent* – of necessity, given the space available.)

Reading *Advent* must begin with its title. 'Advent' specifies the weeks preceding Christmas Eve, but, more importantly, what these prefigure for Catholics – the Incarnation, Christ's coming (*adventus*) in the flesh – and his *second* advent, when he shall come again to judge mankind. The *OED* allows advent 'poetically or grandiloquently' for *any* arrival; for Coffey's finest commentator, J.C.C. Mays, *Advent*'s title 'takes off from the moment of expectation when all is potential'. However, while part retrospective and part anticipatory, the poem is always uncertainly expectant. There are, after all, *false* advents; in David Jones' phrase, 'it is easy to miss Him at the turn of a civilisation'.[2]

I

Advent opens with an arrival: perceiving consciousness has awoken *to itself*, not merely *from* sleep (line 6). In epic mode we arrive *in medias res*, in an unearthly, almost Beckettian zone where all description is negated. (No concidence – Beckett was a lifelong friend of Coffey's.[3]) Dice, or chance, 'own' this voiceless place because it holds no humans; yet the dice are 'dead' because there is no one to throw them. The question, whether 'dice thrown' will 'annul chance', is yet to be asked.[4] There is 'no sail', no vessel to venture on to the 'deeps' ('unfeatured', with no one to name such features; unrapturing, with no one to be enraptured – or suffer nitrogen narcosis, 'rapture of the deep'). Yet there is inhuman otherness in the *peopled* world too – hence the echo of 'unchilding unfathering deeps', from Hopkins' 'Wreck of the *Deutschland*'. The camera eye of the poem jump-cuts between these alternatives – as Dónal Moriarty observes, the first part of *Advent* 'ranges across massive expanses of imagined time and space' (*ABC*, p.98). This is not the liberal cliché of humanity's steady progress, but rather a stultification: 'habit [is] hostile to hope'. Hopeful yearning intervenes – for 'sudden garden bell', 'far flame', 'angel' (lines 7, 9, 11, 25); yet no adventive being is specified.[5] Chance enters this now humanised domain, but 'unsafe', 'unhappy', its 'Unquiet house' threatened. This last phrase blatantly reverses Pound's description of the cathedral dedicated to the Virgin at Torcello as 'thy quiet house'. No Godless space can be thus extolled; lacking that, darkness is palpably manifest (if not actively 'visible', in Milton's phrase). This is our first example of *corrective* allusion, a crucial device in *Advent*. The term *Widerruf* (literally 'cancellation') is useful for such 'attempts at retracting, countermanding, disavowing previous poetics'.[6] Although it can refer to a point-by-point *in toto* 'refutation' of another poem, Coffey's reconfigurings are local and particular. These *Widerrufe* provide keys for correctly navigating this 'Aquinas map' and their identification is a central task of the present work.

After a three-line space a new stanza group begins. As we shall see repeatedly in *Advent*, the focus of the poem pulls back to provide an enlarged recapitulation. The spatio-temporal domain is vast – the 'planet-fall' of Earth from space, transition from Eden via the prehistoric to speeded-up human development – ancient mounds, Mesopotamian tells, Roman villas, medieval manors and Renaissance towns, ending with the modern city. This progression was prefigured: 'Early victory on the upward path after / ranges chasms dawn-grey crests beginnings' – lines adapted from Rilke (Second *Duino Elegy*, ll.10–12) – but it is unclear if this Edenic world is aware of God, the 'behind all archetypes' of line 51. It already knows war (implicit in the allusions to Xenophon in lines 41–42).[7]

What might be the Edenic creation or the eventual evolution of deciduous trees – 'the first of autumns' – presents either a world with no human beings, or at least one before language (line 62). Yet by the opening of the next stanza group we are somehow post-lapsarian, the known world has become unsatisfactory and refuge sighed-for (the classical 'Blessed Isles', their Celtic double, Tír-na-nÓg). In this state we remain fit not for a brother-who-might-be-a-saviour (prefigured by Isaiah 40:3–4), but rather reshaped for an Orwellian 'Brother Big'. 'Brother' here is a Janus word, modifying differently to its left and right; spatial play is relatively frequent in Coffey, and owes something to the greater positional freedom of French (especially unpunctuated late Mallarmé, which Coffey translated); and also to classical Chinese poetry – in which Coffey had a strong interest – where grammar is 'contextual rather than explicit'.[8] This makes demands on the reader, already supposed to be alert for *Widerrufe*; but Coffey's verse here maintains a strong onward momentum – there is no time for rest, and no space for *Eleanor Rigby*'s lonely people, 'moved on' by impulse, or police.

The next stanza group addresses wider contexts for loneliness and separation. A 'dark house' is a Shakespearean madhouse, unlit, fit location for the night vision of the 'ghost of a flea' (famously recorded by Blake), and a fine spot for administraitors (the pun is Coffey's), reductionist file-tab twiddlers who cannot grasp the complexities of being human, pretending (after *The Hunting of the Snark*) that 'What's avoided three times ain't there'. This may be a *Widerruf* of the pioneer cybernetician Norbert Wiener, who also quoted Carroll to suggest the human brain worked – like a computer – as if 'what I tell you three times is true'.[9] The section ends with a switch from the demotic to anaphora,[10] and a heightened language which contrasts with the demagogues' 'words to soothe'. Despite the Latin proverb, *verbum sapienti sat* ('a word to the wise suffices'), we, as Coffey reverse-puns, confront *saps* – the 'would-be-wise'. Asking who would be like that, slaving for material goods or dozing through life, Coffey answers: *we* are (lines 106–07). He situates humanity halfway between angel and doll: the first bodiless *anima* or spirit, the second inanimate matter, literally 'inane'; empty-headed, even soul-less. That we occupy this median position, between and yet part of both, is not merely elegant but *essential*, reflecting as it does the Catholic-Aristotelean doctrine of *hylomorphism*: living things are compounds of material and shaping form, inextricably composite, matter *and* spirit. Within this tradition angels are '*thinking substances* in the pure sense of the word, pure subsistent forms ... free from the vicissitudes of time, movement, generation and corruption'.[11] If this be taken as literal truth, then human aspiration to the order of pure spirit is illogical – and both hubristic *and* hybristic.[12] Being composites of form and matter, there are things we cannot do, and 'a zone of darkness in us which we can't get into focus' (Howe, 'Interview', p.121). To one side, the Rilkean 'dread angel'; to the other, the purely mindless puppet, which Coffey, like Rilke, distrusts.[13]

But our nature is *as it is*, not innately flawed (that required original sin); in the very dense lines that follow (lines 110–11), hylomorphism appears to be a necessary precondition for any *productive* sacrifice such as Christ's. A non-human divinity could not – logically – die to expiate our sins; and a non-divine human will inevitably die, but inefficaciously. Coffey makes the point figuratively: if humans are partly base clay, we are also kin to the emblematically spiritual eagle. However, this does not make our lives any less difficult, as the next stanza group shows. Momentary epiphanies, light on a tree-trunk, proffer a seemingly uncomplicated order of things which we cannot share; we lack both the instincts of soul-less animals *and* the innate rectitude of un-bodied angels. Maritain explicates: 'human intellect is the last of the spirits, and the most remote from the perfection of the divine Intelligence'. The Christian existentialist Nicholas Berdyaev goes further (appositely, as part VIII of *Advent* makes clear): a perfect classicism, capable of extracting from Nature an entirely happy and satisfying harmony, is impossible since the Crucifixion.[14]

Coffey shared with Blake a fondness for the arcane verb 'swag', and Blake, who made emblematic use of eagle and clay, now enters more directly. Before a nod towards his 'Tyger', he gives a 'voice to dew': Vala, protagonist of *The Four Zoas* (1797), lifts her hands to heaven and cries '"Where is the voice of God that call'd me from the silent dew?"'[15] Coffey immediately moves to the creation of art, which could, in the context, appear blasphemously parodic; but that is not how Coffey (following Maritain) saw it. For them, art *cannot* be moral, for it is the work of the 'practical intellect'. Virtuous artists might through 'creative intuition' envisage art that is also virtuous; but making has its own rules, and artists, being human, have free will. 'The mind does not have to know, but *make* 'the not yet heard', 'the not yet seen', for 'we modify what we find'.[16] This urge to create, part of our fallible nature, is within a fallible world; hence the jump to a deliberately unspecific 'real' world's death and destruction (lines 130–32).

Emerging from this backdrop is another fast-forward: this time the history of religious artworks, from the cultic Stone Age 'Willendorf Venus' through utile axe-heads via votive Bronze Age Cycladic marbles to Michelangelo's *Pietà*, Mary cradling the dead Christ; both ethically *and* aesthetically good. The list closes with Brancusi's 1920s *Bird in Space* bronzes,[17] slipping from their almost-evanescence to the (Hegelian? Christian?) 'vanishment' of art and artist. The final stanza of this group generalizes human dissatisfaction, seeming consequence of our mortality; this perhaps alludes to the fact that during Advent the Catholic faithful are enjoined to make themselves ready for Christ's final coming, as a judge. *Advent* VI and VII will offer examples of those who have – and have not – so readied themselves.

The next sub-group opens out to a major mode of (self-)satisfaction – fantasy. Coffey, ambivalent towards Surrealism, surveys Rimbaud dining on stones, sees Arctic flowers under a folkloric mountain of gold, and is unimpressed by the lure of 'what's not'.[18] Other distractions follow – mountaineering (lines 148–52) and politics (lines 153–55), both modes of false self-elevation.[19] Celtic Iseult's 'white hands' become those of Pilate: both causers of death, like warmongers, inverse alchemists who turn gold into 'lead' bullets.

Death, 'the great deed', is not the 'child's play' of fertility cults;[20] humans cannot scrub out death with a 'real return'. The following stanza paraphrases Aquinas on the possibility of *total* non-existence (*Summa Theologica* I a.2.3), returning us to where *Advent* began, perception 'thrown' into the middle of things. Now the opening question, 'Who wakes now …', is answered: *we* do. By our own analysis 'alone and unfulfilled', with multiple wants (line 166),[21] searching for an adventive being, wanted once again – in the senses of needed *and* lacked. Part I ends, as it began, questioning.

II

Part II opens with paired word-columns differently evoking movement; the left more gravity-bound – fountain-water droops like a 'rooted' willow – whilst to right poplar and raincloak arch and 'dance'. Although terms from each column recur, notably in part VII, they seem more a focus for separate contemplation than fully integrated into the poem.[22]

Perhaps the natural world is 'what has called' us into ancient woodland; it is *our* advent, we who are 'waited for expected'. Yet as before, we are not at home; perhaps because, as self-modifying 'language animals' we are no longer animal at all. (Ironically the Greek alphabet is mythically animal in origin; when Palamedes 'scried' cranes, their straggly, linear flight inspired the row of characters.[23])

Likewise impossibly far back are the first fires, predating poetry, even the Irish-Gaelic vision poem the *aisling*. In *aislingí* poets dream of a 'sky-maiden' (*spéirbhean*) personifying Ireland and bewailing her/its sorry state. Coffey borrows from two *aislingí* by Aogán Ó Rathaille (*c.*1675–*c.*1730); one, *'Gile na gile ...'* ('Brightness of brightness ...'), is the most famous of all such poems.[24] A sleeper is woken from dream – paralleling Dante's *Commedia* as well as *Advent* – to encounter 'curl upon curl' of blonde hair and vivid blue-green eyes. Coffey's sky-woman is non-specific; omitting Ó Rathaille's hints at her redeemers' identities,[25] he can more easily meld eighteenth-century 'Éire' into Roman Venus of 50 BC, as envisioned by Lucretius. His long poem *De Rerum Natura* ('On the Nature of Things') is adapted/quoted in lines 20–27.[26] Again Coffey skips temporal particulars; we don't need *details*, because both these (false) adventive visions are merely (wonderful) distractions, 'different expressions of misguided human ambition', as Moriarty puts it (*ABC*, p.93). Coffey subject-rhymes Rome and Ireland: *Alma* ('nurturing'), Lucretian honorific for Venus, becomes 'Ana', Celtic mother-goddess. *Alma* is usually reserved for Ceres, goddess of agriculture; her benificence is 'cornucopia', prompting Coffey's description of American 'corn' (maize), familiar to him from the Midwest, where his family lived for some years (see *PV*, pp.71, 79).

The next stanza group links all creation 'in passionate symbiosis' – Aristotelean categories of inanimate, rooted, mobile and rational. These appear in reverse order because the 'lower' down this chain anything is, the less capable it is of evil. For Thomists, 'Evil' is a privation of good, a negation, rather than anything active; hence both proto-ecological awareness (line 42) and opposition to abortion (line 43) emerge from a single religious stance rather than separable secular-political ones.[27] As before, the paths to error are 'high road low road': hybristic aspiration to pure spirit ('angelism'), or its opposite, collapse into unthinking puppetry. Coffey asks if we, sleep-walkers 'footing it to Babylon and basilisk',[28] know not what we do, our actions almost 'wreakful' (vengeful), though it would be hard to say why vengeance is sought, save in self-defeating 'spite' against the flesh which constrains our condition (line 46).

The curative for our wrong-headedness is obedience to God's laws, implicitly enjoined in the monostich and couplet opening the next section, with their echoes of Pauline injunctions (I Corinthians 13:12) and the 'Sermon on the Mount'. The next lines recapitulate, alluding in passing to W.E. Henley's flatulent 'Invictus' (a pedestrian poem with laboured rhyming) and to the close of Victor Hugo's 1859 'Booz Endormi', which gives a model of holy sleep: the biblical Ruth spends a night with Boaz, whom she later marries (Ruth 3:14). Is Coffey simply unable to resist local colour? Hugo describes, gorgeously, Ruth wondering at the desert sky and harvest moon: 'Quel dieu, quel moissonneur de l'éternel été, / Avait, en s'en allant, négligement jété / Cette faucile d'or dans le champ des étoiles'.[29] This is not just purple writing, though; Boaz's kindness wins Ruth's hand, and their subsequent child is grandfather to King David, hence ancestor of Christ. There are rewards for probity. (The next lines display an un-Christian converse, 'Skinner Apollo', flayer of his rival Marsyas.[30])

The following rosy-spectacled stanza is a welcome contrast to the preceding Jeremiad; but we should not be lulled. Awakening from Eden was sad, but a *felix culpa*; subsequent evocations are temporary idylls. Human beauty, natural not spiritual, is likewise a 'false advent idol' (line 75) exemplified by Laura, Petrarch's beloved.[31] Whatever her charms, they are ultimately kin to the wood and stones only heathens bow down to (line 80); joy that is futureless, unlike Ruth's.

The next stanza group opens with an epiphany requiring human participation, London tower-blocks reflecting the setting sun, which Coffey must have seen (his family lived at the top of London's Muswell Hill in the late 1960s/early 1970s). 'Coals of fire' (Romans 12:20) hints at menace; an echo of Beckett is from a poem of flight from suffering.[32] Coffey proffers an alternative: Christian faith,[33] necessitating marriage, which he embodies, curiously, in a Chinese image. The *chien* is a 'fabulous bird with one eye and one wing'; a pair must unite to fly. If the character is written twice it means such a pair: idiomatically, 'man and wife'.[34] Coffey paraphrases Maritain pertinently: God so made human nature that 'marriage is necessary in order that humanity may endure and develop';[35] successful marriages display what the broader 'we' fail at. He concludes offering glimpses of such a life, illuminated by 'small beauties', micro-epiphanies; a ladybird afloat on a leaf, a violet in 'green shade'. These matter because the world is there outside mind, and so existence has 'intelligible value, not expressible in a concept'.[36] In contradistinction to Marvell's mind withdrawing into its own world, 'annihilating all that's made / to a green Thought in a green Shade', Coffey places us – *pro tem.* – in *this* world. We are warned that such temporary Edens are perilous; but how could one not enjoy them?

The final section opens in *aisling*-esque mode, but is also a *Widerruf* of Mallarmé's 1885 'Le vierge, le vivace et le bel aujourd'hui',[37] an immensely complex and obscure poem.[38] This sonnet presents a swan trapped in ice, struggling to break free. To remain a pure poetic Idea and be deathless requires frozen stasis; a real swan would want freedom, even at the cost of immortality. Who would wish to freeze for the sake of symbolism? Not even a poetic swan. Mallarmé had a famous encounter with metaphysical nothingness,[39] subsequently substituting 'pure' words for the impure *real*, a zeal for the unencumbered artwork which is *precisely* Maritain's 'angelism' (and voiced in the same terms by Mallarmé scholarship: 'the world cannot be surpassed no matter how insistently one is called towards the absolute').[40] Coffey was torn between admiration for Mallarmé's poetry and critique of its implications (*ABC*, p.81): not merely *hybris* (line 114) but also implicit 'angelism'. We should not, then, be surprised to meet *Widerrufe*: Coffey's swan is not locked in '*stérile hiver*' (*pace* Mallarmé), but moves through broken ice. Mallarme's swan is his *creature*, animated solely by his attention; Coffey's bird, in this astonishing, richly imbricated passage, is hard to distinguish from its ground or, rather, water (Moriarty offers a fine close-reading of this passage [*ABC*, p.92]). The refusal to privilege figure over ground reflects Thomist metaphysics, wherein *realia* exist independent of a subject–object relation.[41] This provides implicit value for the extant world, which is there all the time, regardless of ourselves. In a flashback to *Advent* I, lines 162–63, we are reminded of Aquinas' refutation of the idea that all could ever be naught, in the process refuting its Mallarméan inversion, the taking of 'Naught as Source of All' – 'hybris positive'.

The following lines reiterate, substituting a real (and grey, not prettily white) gull for a *textual* swan, inviting us to 'praise beauty' – not least because it is 'matched to us' (as everything is, *pace* Genesis I:28–30). Coffey recapitulates part I's unrecorded 'millions of days and nights', offering now a positive take: nights were only silent until 'shepherd's harp gave voice to star and sky' – presumably Boaz's descendant David, shepherd and harpist. A statement that mankind is both strange and wonderful leads to castigation of human behaviour with regard to the world. One might be prepared for this by Psalm 8, wherein David the Psalmist, considering the heavens, asks 'What is man, that thou art mindful of him?' The free-standing line 127 quotes the second choric ode from Sophocles' *Antigone*: 'Many are the wonders, none / is more wonderful than man', man who 'crosses the sea', 'ploughs', snares 'the brood of the sea', having taught himself 'speech and windswift thought'. Again, this looks like (secular) ecology, but is (also) theology;[42] Coffey's concluding lines (128–31) are a point-by-point *Widerruf* of the pre-Christian Sophocles. Implicit, though, as we shall see, is his agreement with Sophocles' sole caveat: 'only against death / can he call for aid in vain'. Our good nature may be applauded in plays, but should perhaps be written only on moving water, or wind-blown sand – for reasons part III will make clear.[43]

<h1 style="text-align:center">III</h1>

Part III opens, like its predecessors, with a question; but a readily answerable one. Klio, muse of history, embodiment of its intelligibility, has been dethroned. Coffey opens with an emblem of twentieth-century horrors: 'numberless suppliant bones' facing which one wants – *lacks* – words. Falsely intelligible, 'bad history' has – as Coffey's one-time employer T.S. Eliot wrote – 'many cunning passages, contrived corridors / And issues, deceives with whispering ambitions, / Guides with vanities'[44] – and conceals the evidence of all this (as Hamlet did, hiding Polonius' corpse behind a convenient Arras tapestry).

As before, the scope widens, from personal to national, displaying a state, more rotten than Denmark, with militarist drumming and soldierly song.[45] The next stanza extends further – colonial booty got by 'carnage'. Coffey tentatively invokes 'good' history – agriculture (which feeds even soldiers), love and memorials of joy rather than war – but closes alluding again to *Hamlet* and all-too-real *Realpolitik*.

The next stanza group refines analysis of human motivation. Deliberate banalities, concisely put, reduce our sophisticated world to the level of fable, even fairy-tale.[46] A stanza break transports us to the slangy contemporary, to 'vibes' (moods induced by surroundings), in which light there is no 'hybris', no presumption against the divine: the free-market-capitalist Bullfrog's lunacy seems *conditioned*, not freely willed. Yet even the Bullfrog is no Cartesian 'angel driving a machine', but, in the then topical novelist William Burroughs' phrase, a 'soft machine', a vulnerable body.[47]

The next section opening is puzzling, with its image of an eagle in the big-top, though a 'hoop-la' ('exclamation accompanying a quick or sudden movement' – *OED*) suits the phantasmagoric emergence of a dictatorial leader – whom one might idiomatically call 'Kilroy'.[48] His speech is a composite of horrors, drawing on Paul Claudel's unap-peasable tyrant, 'Tête d'Or', as also the 'Improperia' (Christ's reproaches in the Catholic Good Friday liturgy).[49] With conventional parallelism the words come from the Old Testament: 'O my people what have I done unto thee?' (Micah 6:3). Kilroy's co-option, 'What have they done to you my people', would be blasphemous even had he not performed a *Widerruf*. The rest of his speech, complete with Hitleresque crowd manipulation, is straightforward enough. The pairing of spinifex (a coarse Australian desert-grass) with 'ice-wind' suggests a wide geographical span; 'Kilroy' presumably conquers the world (like 'Tête d'Or', or Coffey's 'Topman Ti' or 'Glutz'). Indeed, there's something of Claudel's more symbolic tyrant in 'Kilroy', but he is not wholly fictional. Coffey lived in Europe in the 1930s, and 'drum-beat sole-slap heel-click halt' clearly evokes the Nuremberg rallies (compare *PV*, p.183). That 'Kilroy' has betrayed 'my people' becomes clear when a cock crows, in both French and English. This, of course, echoes the Gospels, but also Claudel: the symbolic death of Cébès, Tête d'Or's 'good twin', is marked by a chilly violet dawn and a cry of 'Cocorico!'[50] The final stanza spirals down into a Popean 'eyeless night' via preposterous, apostate fictions: that we can act alone, that there can be empires on which the sun never sets.[51]

The pause between stanza groups allows a hiatus before the awful implications of 'my country right or wrong' are exemplified: the 'purple and gold' of military conquest (Byron's 'Assyrian', of course, after Isaiah 37), the 'stench of victory' and, as far as the eye can see, 'white crosses'. Amidst it all, a Blakean sunflower, as 'weary of time' as the victims of history should be. Coffey considers the aftermath of war (birdsong resuming after WWI trench bombardments). He explicates one phrase himself: 'When I came back to England from the States in the 1950s, I went to see [Eliot] and: "Nations never recover from war", said the Arbiter Dicter' (Howe, 'Interview', p.116). 'Sharp' and 'Seeclear', kennings for the far-sighted, try to make sense of history, scrutinizing evidence, staking claims like bets; but, as it is never clear, in logical(-positivist) fashion, that 'if p then q', then no quizzer/ enquirer, asking God for answers (*pace* Job 38:1) will ever clear their desk, fulfil their allotted tasks. Yet we live specifically 'as if' there were purpose and meaning; hence Coffey citing Hans Vaihinger, Kantian author of *Die Philosophie des Als Ob*, who says that we, unable to *know* if our systems match underlying reality, *act* as if we do: the 'philosophy of "As If"'. In social terms, this encourages herd behaviour; foolish at the level of 'what a gas',[52] insane when queuing for gas chambers. Small and large link up, 'nail clipping to holocaust'. The vast scope is signalled by Coffey's allusion to Dante, who as *poet*, not protagonist, addresses readers *outside his text*: 'O you that are in your little bark ...

following behind my ship … turn back … ' (*Paradiso* II, ll.1–4).[53] However, Coffey reverses the roles: the hopeless address a ship – the evil
Naglar, key to the Ragnarok, the Norse apocalypse just alluded to.[54]
History is a relentless cycle, '*ad infin victims dooms*'; 'justice in short
supply', suppliants 'lied to later slain', from biblical times to now, with
barely a breathing space. Coffey is extremely compact here: biblical
suppliants clung to the sacrificial altar-horn (I Kings 2:28; Psalm
118:27 [Catholic 117:27]); chancelleries are, by synecdoche, the
offices of rulers (including Hitler); Lenin's *peredyshka* ('breathing-
space' in Russian), the reintroduction of capitalism, was one of many
acts of 'bad faith' in history;[55] by mirror-play are we fooled, as in the
Hall of Mirrors where the Versailles Treaty was signed. Line 85 shows
Realpolitik at its worst: in 477 BC the Plataeans, asked by Sparta if they
had assisted her in a recent war, answered 'no'. Hundreds of men were
killed, the women enslaved, the city razed.[56]

Unsurprisingly the next stanza group opens with Klio giving no
victory crowns – partly as, banally, there are no final victors, but also
because if 'we' are to learn from history it must be through diversity.
We humans are, being each *materially* different, unique, whereas for
Aquinian Catholics, purely spiritual beings are each unique, having no
input of base matter to differentiate them.[57] Coffey generously extends
the same logic to the Muse Klio. Hence 'clear view of what we
are' comes from the inescapable panoply of unique stories, and Klio's
support is for teller, not doer: 'She is the Muse of History as Story, not
as Deed'.[58] Importantly, though, the stories must be *true*; poets are
adjured to cautious 'silence when best is guess'. And such silence, such
cautious observance, now enters history.

The scene – almost literally a Greek stage (*skene*) – is set with
Thucydides recalling how, formerly, Athenians put aside weaponry and
led peaceful lives; some, even when he was writing, wore plain linen,
fastening hair with golden grasshopper-clasps.[59] Coffey doesn't dally
with such nostalgia, moving rapidly through correctives like smoky
kitchens and irrational ritual, to leave us where Klio wants us: ready
for poets to explain history.

The next lines are, as history often is, confused; arguably unpicking
them is the opposite of what's wanted. So keen is Coffey to display
the repetitive, yet still inexplicable, that the brutally brief summaries
are (intentionally?) misleading: line 103's litany of offences in the
House of Atreus are hard to ascribe. Atreus himself is guilty of murder
(killing his brother Thyestes' children) and of incestuous rape;
Agamemnon, as line 121 testifies, forcibly married Clytaemnestra after

killing her husband. The complex, internecine tale is spelled out in Graves' *Greek Myths* (sections 110, 111, 112.*c*); but the lesson one might be *expected* to learn is simple: 'wisdom is won through woe' (Aeschylus' *Agamemnon*, line 176, reprised importantly in *Advent* VIII, line 142).

Coffey now starts to paraphrase the Aeschylus. The play opens (unsurprisingly!) with wakefulness and sleep, as a blazing beacon tells that Troy has fallen; it also warns Clytaemnestra and her lover Aegisthus (surviving child of Thyestes) of Agamemnon's imminent return. Coffey builds on the mythic cycle familiar from Eliot, Frazer and Graves, presenting Agamemnon's death conventionally off-stage. Much of this is given as quotation – as it happens, directly from a footnote in Graves:

> Agamemnon dies in a peculiar manner: with a net thrown over his head, with one foot still in the bath, but the other on the floor, and in the bath-house annexe – that is to say, 'neither clothed nor unclothed, neither in water nor on dry land, neither in his palace nor outside' … Clytaemnestra may also have given Agamemnon an apple to eat, and killed him as he set it to his lips: so that he was 'neither fasting, nor feasting' … Basically, then, this is the familiar myth of the sacred king who dies at midsummer … (*Greek Myths* 112, n.1)

If sense is to be made of all this, it can only be because poets have found a pattern; and, after laying it out in lines 119–24 (Orestes will kill his mother Clytaemnestra and be pursued by the Furies), Coffey says as much – 'So was myth worked to poet's will / to teach viewers how god heals'; he even offers Aristotelean catharsis, as we get to 'take new hearts home'. This section ends declaring such drama as unlike *other* staged events, but partaking of mysteries which are – among other things – socially integrative. This is perhaps not immediately clear; but, just as Dante spoke to us-as-readers, so Aeschylus' declaration that suffering men learn understanding is not aimed at Agamemnon, who dies too quickly thereafter to profit by the lesson, but at us, the *audience*. With curious bathos the high drama is collapsed into what tragedy is *not* like: tumbling acrobats, derived, down to the detail of the sticking-plaster, from Rilke's fifth *Duino Elegy* (Coffey translates lines 9–10 in line 136). This section is summarised – unusually for Coffey – in a small rhymed triplet verging on *sententia*.

The final stanza group opens hinting at the summation of history; the dark side of harvest. We, at the last vintage, after Christ's second

Advent, will be separated into worthwhile yield and useless weeds (tares).[60] Our failure is manifest even in the everyday realm of food – soup kitchens, the Irish potato famine (caused partly by the dominance of a vulnerable potato variety called 'lumpers'). Despite Coffey's evident personal anger (why else an Irish example?), these indistinct cycles feel mythical/symbolic – spider lairs, monster dens, building and demolishing. Coffey sums up our own existence, our larger histories, linking the officialdom of (British/Irish) Registrars of Births, Marriages and Deaths with Galileo's pungent – once heretical! – declaration of the continuing movement of the heavens: *eppur si muove*.

Coffey studied both science and philosophy, so when he writes of 'randomness' and the yen for laws of history, ways of revealing past or predicting future patterns, it is unlikely to be idle metaphor.[61] If history, a human construct, works 'against the rounded tale' then presumably the non-human – the divine – is the answer. Before that can be assayed, though, there is a retrenchment to received opinions and another slant-wise allusion to Irish history: 'envy one of history's oldest friends / till compromise partition induce civil war',[62] with results (lines 155–60) that stand for every conflict since Plataea. History may be 'earth's un-finished business', but there are things bigger than the earth. And before we consider the obvious one, God, Coffey takes an intriguing detour to consider another: those 'who are no kin of ours' (IV, line 31).

IV

We human beings are prone to human-centredness, seeing ourselves as the be-all and end-all; which equips us ill for understanding interventions from beyond our scope, which might seem as inexplicable as a 'Pryer's rod' in a crab-pool.[63] Coffey suggests that creatures work instinctively, as if computer-programmed; so – more complexly – may we (with 'no escape'). But a richer (self-)consciousness might grasp the common essence shared with animals, as Coffey hints, considering Orpheus, the poet-musician whose lyre playing moved animals – and trees.[64]

We move on to the bereaved Hamlet, who has within himself 'that which passes show' – unassuagable by 'the trappings and the suits of woe' (that last Agamemnon's word, III.109). At this point there is something of a jump via an 'I-protagonist' wondering at the constellation of Orion. Coffey here tangles an already confused web; Graves says 'Orion's story consists of three or four unrelated myths strung together', and there's neither space for nor point in untangling this.

The *details* of Orion's story – pursuing the sister-nymphs the Pleiades, who are turned into doves and become stars to escape him – are incidental to his *own* posthumous transference into the heavens; indeed, Graves suggests Orion myths derive from attempts to explain celestial events, since this otherwise prominent constellation disappears below the European horizon for part of the year (*Greek Myths*, 41). Coffey's purpose is to introduce the heavens and the unimaginably large time-spans necessary to encompass their cycles, 'stars risen stars fallen since before there were names'. One name here is particularly arcane – Laurence's, a Dublin toy shop, long, thin and 'getting darker-and-darker' as one 'vanished into it'; the relevance here, as with Jack B. Yeats', is elusive.[65]

Names were first bestowed by Adam (Genesis 2:20), and we duly move from our own commencement in the Quaternary period through another accelerated chronology – hunter-gatherers to 'recent' time. All under 'unchanting' stars, a word so peculiar one might posit a deliberate *invitation* to misread 'unchanging'. The stars are *not* unchanging in reality (there are fewer Pleiades now than in classical times – see *Greek Myths*, 41.6) nor are they unchanging in the poem – for, as the science fiction cliché has it, 'we are not alone'. In an echo of Arthur C. Clarke's *2001*, we are told Earth has been visited before, on a savannah with Quaternary tool-making proto-humans, the silver gleam of a spaceship 'too strange to remember'.[66]

This move into the widely critically disdained area of science fiction might seem a falling-off from Rilke and Aeschylus – but this is snobbism; *The Tempest* can be seen as science fiction. Although Coffey was keen enough to read widely in the genre rather than wisely (a friend reports it being a topic best avoided), readers of *Advent* should eschew ray guns and androids and consider how 'Speculative Fiction' offers an opportunity for what science calls *Gedankenexperimenten* ('thought experiments') – a way to move Vaihinger's '*Als Ob*' from present to future, consider 'what-would-happen-if'. This allows one to contemplate the non-experiential – much as theology does; which might further ratify Coffey's interest.[67]

In line 6 Coffey spoke of humans as 'kind', a race having a common origin. Now that all-inclusive grouping encounters the 'unkin' – those in every sense 'alien'.[68] The arrival of extraterrestrials prompts an awakening (not for the first time in *Advent*); everything, *pace* Yeats, seems 'changed utterly'. However, our responses are unchanged, remaining all too human: fawning deference (lines 44–45), bullying (lines 50ff.), unscrupulous conflict (lines 59ff.).[69] The alien arrival, then, is another *false* advent; they have nothing *useful* to teach us ('anti-gravity' is 'mere', such 'know-how' 'vain'). Hence instead of a description of these aliens, we are given an alienating catalogue of our *own* varieties (line 43). This is not surprising since the aliens are merely extrapolations from ourselves; speculative 'fictions' of how *we* might behave, should our world survive long enough to develop literally world-shattering technologies. (After all, 'How does one recognise an alien at sight if he/she/it is clearly a featherless biped and speaks English?'[70]) The next stanza group makes this plainer, examining the aliens' earlier history. Their long technological development parallels ours; it would take a rare imagination to invent a wholly unfamiliar technological history, and, besides, the point lies in the parallels; we should see *ourselves* – as in the foreign races Gulliver encounters. Like us, Coffey's aliens have art and are concerned with the remains of their dead. (In Coffey's view 'real aliens', being God's creation, could not be *wholly* alien; nor, in plot terms, could fictitious ones be, for one could say nothing about them.) This concentration on parallels, then, comes not from a paucity of imagination, but theological necessity.

Coffey pondered 'human policy as regards the intelligent beings ... that might be found on other planets', noting that

> Too many of those who have written of these matters believe that it is the destiny of man to spread his seed through space and time in a race against entropy for one to have much faith in the purity of the intentions of human space travellers.

Although a Cardinal Mercier thought our main business 'would be the communication of our most fundamental concepts and principles', pulpier science fiction often displayed less noble attitudes: 'The Soviets can have the Earth ... we are going to scatter the West throughout the stars'.[71] The like is *not* true of Coffey's aliens, who received an advent of their own: 'It was a voice broke sleep in them', whereupon, like the Magi, they set out on an impossibly long journey in search of news of redemption, their 'unguessed-at want fulfilled' by the scene 'where arms stretch' on 'upright frame' and our – and evidently *their* – redeemer is crucified.[72] It is surely *they* who have been truly 'changed utterly' (line 103).

Coffey's aliens set out, on the basis of a deep dissatisfaction, their loving 'a lack', bonds with their own kind 'weakened', until they had their way pointed in the stars by 'ostensive definition'. He draws here on a standard genre device, the 'space ark' (albeit in a new way, being driven by *spiritual* need, not *material* necessity). Traditionally within the genre the rationale is immanent planetary destruction: in an early example, Olaf Stapledon's 1930 *Last and First Men*, alterations in the moon's orbit threaten Earth with catastrophe. Stapledon suggests it would take centuries to devise 'a tolerable means of voyaging in interstellar space', and Coffey's aliens likewise spend 'thousands of years' preparing to leave – in what science fiction calls 'generation ships', wherein they breed and die many times over en route (lines 115 and 120). Coffey read Stapledon, 'a man whose thought is vivified by a deep religious feeling which unfortunately his mind interprets in a naturalistic sense'.[73] Naturalism is a mode of materialism that see the limits of nature as the limits of existing reality. Coffey states that it 'typified men's regression from their highest good', as, obviously, it would preclude religious sensibility.[74] Coffey's aliens are *not* in this sense naturalistic, being driven by inspiration outside natural agency – the novelty in his use of the 'space-ark'.[75] Yet despite this, their endeavours are none the less doomed; their destruction of their (still occupied) home planet in the process cannot be moral, so their journey must parallel our own fallen nature with its cycle of births and deaths (III, line 148; IV, line 121). Their arrival leaves them breathing 'recycled air', not in a spaceship but on earth, where one breathes the same molecules repeatedly, enacting the same scenarios repeatedly – as Coffey makes clear with his glance at the watchman of part I (lines 117–19 and 127). A lute needs not merely skill to sound, but also willpower;[76] hence morally insufficient endeavours will be *literally* fruitless (see line 130). The self-sacrifice – 'against culture's grain' – of the mythical but *human* Alcestis cannot alone outweigh human brutality, the Orwellian boot in the face.[77] There is cultural as well as genetic transmission forward; it is for that reason that history matters. As John Macquarrie says, history is oriented to the future; in studying it we study *man*, to learn about possibilities in store. 'We are mistaken in thinking that history is to do with the past';[78] but neither our known past nor our forseeable future seem to offer an alternative to simply sleeping on.

Advent, of course, does not end here. In brief, part V seeks to integrate history, constructed fictions of the past and speculative fictions about the future. Part VI considers, by individual example, our immediate end; as, from another (less consolatory) perspective, does part VII. Neither secular history, nor our own histories, nor the advent of far more technologically 'advanced' 'unkin' can redeem us; this requires a *different* unearthly sacrifice. Part VIII endeavours to deal with Christ's *actual* second Advent, which provides a resolution to all the previous sections (as of all worldly concerns). But there is not space to treat of this here; a survey of the second half of *Advent* must await another occasion.

NOTES

I owe an immense debt to earlier Coffey scholars, and to friends, associates and relations of the poet. Particular thanks to John Cayley, John Coffey, Philip Coleman, Peter Davidson, Alex Davis, John Goodby, James Hogan, Elizabeth James, G. Ingli James, J.C.C. Mays, Billy Mills, Sandra Andrea O'Connell, Thomas Dillon Redshaw, Anthony Rudolf, Maurice Scully, Jessie Sheeler, Michael Smith, James Matthew Wilson and, of course, the editors of this book. This chapter is dedicated to John Coffey.

1. With honourable exceptions, attention to Coffey's work has been skimpy (there are more index entries for Enid Blyton than Coffey in Declan Kiberd's *The Irish Writer and the World*). Ezra Pound, *Selected Letters 1907–1941* (London: Faber & Faber, 1950), p.323.
2. J.C.C. Mays, 'Introductory Essay', *Irish University Review: Brian Coffey Special Issue*, vol. 5, no. 1 (spring 1975), p.19 (henceforth *IUR*). David Jones, *The Sleeping Lord and other fragments* (London: Faber & Faber, 1974), p.9.
3. See *Poems and Versions 1929–1990* (Dublin: Dedalus Press, 1991), p.110, Coffey's essay 'Memory's Murphy Maker', *Threshold*, vol. 17 (1962), pp.28–36, and a 1965 letter by Coffey now in his poet-friend Thomas MacGreevy's papers in Trinity College Dublin, MS 8110/73.
4. Coffey surely alludes to Mallarmé's *Un Coup de dés jamais n'abolira le hasard*, which he translated in 1965 as *Dice Thrown Never Will Annul Chance*.
5. The beached 'barque' is not from *The Tempest*, but dreamed by Coffey. See Parkman Howe, 'Brian Coffey: An Interview', *Éire/Ireland*, vol. 13, no. 1 (1978), p.116.
6. 'Introduction' to Pierre Joris' translation of Paul Celan's *Breathturn* (Los Angeles: Sun & Moon Press, 1995), p.21. Coffey's 'Syllables for Accents' (*PV*, pp.57–58) ripostes, line-by-line, his poet-friend Denis Devlin's 'Little Elegy' (*Collected Poems* [Dublin, Dedalus Press, 1989], pp.209–10). Pound: see 'Canto CX', and Billy Mills, *Beyond All Archetypes* (London: Form Books, 1995), p.6.
7. 'The sea, the sea!' – shouted by the '10,000' homeward-bound Greek mercenaries in Xenophon's *Anabasis* – famously alluded to in *Ulysses*.
8. While Coffey was writing for the *Criterion* it published Hsieh Wen Tung's 'English Translations of Chinese Poetry', which says Chinese grammar is 'contextual rather than explicit'. See *Criterion*, vol. 17, no. 68 (April 1938), p.414. See also *PV*, pp.55 and 74, and Parkman Howe, 'Time and Place: The Poetry and Prose of Brian Coffey' (Ph.D thesis, University College Dublin, 1981), pp.1–4.
9. Coffey vehemently disapproved: 'Nothing that Professor Wiener has to say about the new computing machines provides any evidence for the opinion that it may ever be possible to dispense with human intelligence in the elaboration of a human science', 'The Philosophy of Science and the Scientific Attitude, II', *Modern Schoolman*, vol. 26, no. 4 (May 1949), p.332.
10. The anaphoric triplets may draw on T.S. Eliot, Coffey's one-time publisher in the *Criterion*; see *Collected Poems 1909–1962* (London: Faber & Faber, 1974), p.199. In Moriarty's phrase, 'allusions to Eliot subsist like watermarks' in Coffey's writing (*ABC*, p.26) – though, of course, they may well be *Widerrufe*!
11. Jacques Maritain, *Three Reformers: Luther – Descartes – Rousseau* (London: Sheed & Ward, 1928), p.55.
12. Coffey (II, line 119; III, line 26) differentiates *hybris*, 'presumption, especially against the gods' from mere *hubris* 'wanton insolence' (*OED*).
13. Rilke's phrase '*jeder Engel ist schrecklich*' ('every angel is terrible') occurs in both the first two *Duino Elegies*; contrast the Fourth *Duino Elegy* and Rilke's essay 'Some Reflections on Dolls' (German *Puppe* = doll and puppet).
14. See Maritain, *Three Reformers*, p.55; *Art and Scholasticism* (New York: Charles Scribner's, 1962), p.214. 'Wherever the soul of man turns, unless toward God, it cleaves to sorrow,

even though the things outside God and outside itself to which it cleaves may be things of beauty.' *Confessions of St Augustine*, IV.x (London: Sheed & Ward, 1944), p.53.

15. Blake, *Vala*, or *The Four Zoas*, 'Night the Ninth', line 500, in *Complete Writings* (Oxford: Oxford University Press, 1972), p. 370. Keith Tuma links 'dew' to Blake's *Book of Thel*, where it exemplifies sexuality and transience – see his *Anthology of Twentieth-Century British and Irish Poetry* (New York: Oxford University Press 2001), p.290. This excellent anthology reprints part one of *Advent* with annotations gathered by Tuma and Nate Dorward.

16. Maritain, *Creative Intuition in Art and Poetry* (New York: Pantheon Books, 1953), p.173, n.22.

17. Coffey saw one such, from the collection of his one-time lover Peggy Guggenheim, at a 1965 London exhibition – see TCD MS 8110/72.

18. Tuma (p.290) sources Rimbaud – 'Faim' (*Une Saison en Enfer*), 'Barbare' (*Illuminations*) – and ponders the Grimms' fairy-tale 'King of the Golden Mountain'; David Green suggests Humean scepticism – see 'A Return to *Advent*', *Beau*, vol. 1 (1981), p.75.

19. Mallory's justification for climbing Everest is well known. Coffey, no mountaineer, found it fascinating – and metaphorically useful (see e.g. *PV*, p.191). For Coffey on politics, see e.g. 'Leo' (*IUR*, pp.111–85), *The Big Laugh* (Dublin: Sugar Loaf Press, 1976), 'Topos' (in *Lace Curtain*, vol. 6 [autumn 1978]) and *PV*, pp.183–86.

20. Ishtar (correctly), the Assyrio-Babylonian goddess of love; Coffey would have encountered her in Graves' *Greek Myths*.

21. The repetition in I, line 166 echoes King Lear's quintuple 'never', Beckett's 1931 poem 'Enueg II', and Coffey's 1938 poem 'Thirst' (*PV*, p.31); see also *Advent* VIII, line 83.

22. Mays ('Introductory Essay', p.21) and Howe (Ph.D thesis, p.196) offer differing, incompatible, readings of these 'columns'.

23. See Robert Graves, *Greek Myths* (Harmondsworth: Penguin, 1955) section 52.*a*; also the 'Palamedes' chapter in *The White Goddess* (London: Faber & Faber, 1986).

24. For the *aislingí* used in *Advent*, see Dinneen and O'Donoghue, *The Poems of Egan O'Rahilly* (London: Irish Texts Society, 1911), pp.12–21. Coffey, who had 'Matriculation Gaelic', called the '*Gile na gile*' 'lovely'; an unpublished poem quotes it (TCD, MS 8110/24/2).

25. The 'sky-woman' is called 'Éire' in the '*Gile na gile*'; her redeemers in these *aislingí* have been identified as the Stuart 'Old Pretender' and Spain. See Seán Ó Tuama, *Repossessions: Selected Essays on the Irish Literary Heritage* (Cork: Cork University Press, 1995), pp.107–09, 113–14.

26. *De Rerum Natura* I.6–7: 'from you goddess the winds flee and the clouds of heaven / [likewise] at your advent'); Coffey misquotes Lucretius' Latin, trivially.

27. Moriarty (*ABC*, p.26) links estrangement from nature with Heidegger (whom Coffey read); but such awareness is commonplace in twentieth-century Catholicism; compare David Jones' 'Even while we watch the boatman mending his sail, the petroleum is hurting the sea', *In Parenthesis* (London: Faber & Faber, 1963), p.ix. Coffey presumably knew Pope Leo XIII's 1891 encyclical *De Rerum Novarum* ('On Capital and Labour') which, employing Thomistic natural law theory, proposed economic models dedicated to the common good; it inspired agrarian and co-operative movements. See James Matthew Wilson's Ph.D. thesis, invaluable on early Coffey, 'Catholic Modernism and the "Irish Avant-Garde"' (University of Notre Dame, 2006), pp.79–80.

28. See the lullaby 'How Many Miles to Babylon?' Babylon and basilisks both occur in Devlin; see his *Collected Poems*, pp.103–05, 188.

29. 'What god, what harvester of the eternal summer, departing, had negligently thrown down this golden sickle in the field of stars.' Anthony Hartley, *Penguin Book of French Verse*, vol. 3 (Harmondsworth: Penguin, 1958), p.73.

30. 'Skinner Apollo' *looks* like a classical epithet, however, I cannot trace it.

31. Perhaps also referring to Laura Riding, to whom Robert Graves was in thrall (Howe, Ph.D. thesis, p.199); *both* Lauras appear in *PV* (pp. 53, 72, 181), but for Coffey 'The true muse fleshed / nor was, nor shall be' (*PV*, p.80); see also TCD, MS 8110/60.

32. In 1932 Beckett wrote in 'Serena I' of a similar London view: 'I find me taking the Crystal Palace / for the Blessed Isles from Primrose Hill'. Samuel Beckett, *Collected Poems 1930–1978* (London: John Calder, 1986), p.21; see also *Advent* I, line 65.

33. See line 86; Peter Davidson informs me Christ is called Stella Vera ('Star of Truth') in the Mozarabic Breviary.

34. *Mathews' Chinese–English Dictionary* (Cambridge, MA: Harvard University Press, 1943),

character no. 833. Coffey probably met these birds in Apollinaire, who calls them 'pihi' (in 'Zone', ll. 61–62, 'Les Fenêtres', ll. 3–4).

35. Brian Coffey, 'The Philosophy of Science and the Scientific Attitude: I', in *Modern Schoolman*, vol. 26, no. 1 (November 1948), p.30.

36. John Hanke, *Maritain's Ontology of the Work of Art* (The Hague: Martinus Nijhoff, 1973), p.26.

37. See, for example, Anthony Hartley, *Mallarmé* (Harmondsworth: Penguin, 1965), pp.85–86; Stéphane Mallarmé, *Collected Poems and Other Verse*, trans. A.M. Blackmore and E.H. Blackmore (Oxford: Oxford University Press, 2006), pp.66–68.

38. 'Almost every role or interpretation has been ascribed to Mallarmé's swan.' Wallace Fowlie, *Mallarmé* (Chicago, IL: University of Chicago Press, 1953), p. 96; Elizabeth McCombie thinks a completely fixed reading *intentionally* impossible, in Blackmore and Blackmore, *Mallarmé: Collected Poems*, 'Introduction', pp.xxiv–xxv.

39. See, for example, Hartley, *Mallarmé*, 'Introduction', pp.xvi–xx; Coffey, *Poems of Mallarmé* (London/Dublin: Menard Press/New Writers' Press, 1990), p.8.

40. Fowlie, *Mallarmé*, p.97. Art attempting pure creation commits what Maritain called 'angelist suicide'; contrariwise, over-close mimicry of the world is 'the sin of materialism'. Art must *tend towards* purity, struggle against the conditions in which it finds itself (see Hanke, *Maritain's Ontology*, pp.44–45).

41. Maritain observes that the 'thing as thing exists and is able to exist for itself', in *Degrees of Knowledge* (Notre Dame, IN: University of Notre Dame Press, 1995), p.95. If things *need* no object-relation, much of Descartes is under threat.

42. 'Some men have no doubts about man being the measure of all things', Coffey observed critically in 'The Philosophy of Science ... II', p.334. See *Sophocles I*, trans. David Grene (Chicago, IL: University of Chicago Press, 1991), p.174 (translation adapted).

43. See, for example, Maritain, paralleling Benjamin: 'The Church knows that no civilisation, no nation, has clean hands: *omnes quidem peccaverunt et egent Gloria Dei* [Romans 3:23], in *Religion and Culture* (London: Sheed & Ward, 1931), p. 36.

44. While Eliot was writing these lines the Treaty of Versailles was signed, ending World War I; the 'Polish Corridor' was a bone of contention. Coffey quotes this passage in a review in *Modern Schoolman*, vol. 25, no. 3 (March 1948).

45. The 1902 'Soldier's Song', reputedly sung in the GPO during the 1916 Rising, became the Irish national anthem, placing violence explicitly within the foundation story of the new Free State.

46. The unstoppable salt-mill is from a Norwegian folk-tale, probably met by Coffey in Andrew Lang's ubiquitous *Blue Fairy Book*.

47. Perhaps even soft machines are Cartesian; Maritain said Descartes saw humans as 'a composite of two substances, each complete in itself: pure spirit and geometrical extension. An angel driving a machine'. See Maritain, *Religion and Culture*, p.24.

48. Coffey's joke is grim; not (idiomatically) 'Kilroy was', the dictator *is* here. The name Kilroy happens to be Irish. For a more Ubuesque take on dictators, compare 'Topman Ti' (in the poem 'Topos') and 'Glutz' in *The Big Laugh* – see note 19 above.

49. Coffey admired (and translated) Claudel, another Catholic modernist. See *IUR*, pp.12, 23–24, 26 and 81–82. I am grateful to Peter Davidson for alerting me to the Improperia.

50. See, for example, *Théâtre de Paul Claudel*, vol. 1 (Paris: Mercure de France, 1947), p.88. Eliot too quotes the cockerel in French, and speaks of 'violet light' in *The Waste Land*; he had doubtless read Claudel.

51. In Seán Ó Mórdha's 1985 RTE television programme on him, Coffey spoke of his wish to write specifically for Irish readers, any of whom would know the everyday Irish-Gaelic phrase meaning 'we alone' which provided the name of the nationalist political party Sinn Féin. The parallel English truism is of course put under scrutiny early in *Ulysses*.

52. Coffey noted language innovation coming from the crowd: 'The word "gas", for example, and many another. Human beings make poetry'. See Howe, Ph.D thesis, p.268. *Cassell's Dictionary of Slang* records 'gas' (an 'enjoyable, pleasant situation') as originally Irish.

53. Charles Singleton's translation. *The Divine Comedy: Paradiso 1: Text* (Princeton, NJ: Princeton University Press, 1975), p.15; see also *Paradiso 2: Commentary*, p.37.

54. Ragnarok will follow assembling sufficient nail-clippings from the dead to build Naglar, in which to attack Valhalla.

55. Mays' gloss ('Introductory Essay', p.27, n.27) of the *peredyshka* as 'Stalin's deal with Hitler'

is wrong; the term comes from Lenin's 1921 speech announcing the New Economic Policy's reintroduction of capitalism to the USSR.

56. Thucydides, *History of the Peloponnesian War*, III.68.
57. See, for example, Frederick Copleston, *Aquinas* (Harmondsworth: Penguin, 1955), p.95.
58. Stan Smith, 'Against the Grain: Women and War in Brian Coffey's *Death of Hektor*', *Études Irlandaises*, vol. 8 (December 1983), p.171.
59. Coffey may have taken this luminous detail from Thucydides (*History* I.8) via Yeats ('Nineteen Hundred and Nineteen', I). Golden bees, which Yeats adds, were, ominously, the emblem of Agamemnon's brother Menelaus, cuckolded husband of Helen (see *Advent* III, line 102).
60. See line 15, and II, line 30; also Matthew 13:24–30, 36–42. On the complex definitional relations of cockle/darnel and tares, see *OED*, 'cockle', sb. 2; importantly, on their theology, Maritain, *Religion and Culture*, p.18.
61. A place to begin thinking about Coffey's position might be his article 'The Notion of Order According to St Thomas Aquinas', *Modern Schoolman*, vol. 27, no. 1 (November 1949), which considers 'order' (*ordo*) in the senses of sequence, hierarchy, relationship and purpose. This article is part of Coffey's doctoral thesis, while the rest is unpublished.
62. After the English 'Better Government of Ireland Bill' (1919) and the consequent compromise of November 1921, an Irish delegation in London – under threat of immediate war – accepted proposals involving partition and *implicit* allegiance to the British crown. A treaty based on these proposals was ratified by the Dáil, and declared confirmed by the 1922 election; the 'civil war', arguably a continuation of the pursuit of a full 'Irish Republic', was *not* an uncomplicated result of 'compromise [and] partition'. The basis for war was 'the shadow of the oath, and not the substance of the dismemberment of the country' according to T.P. Coogan in *Ireland in the Twentieth Century* (London: Hutchinson, 2003), p.104. This is a complex matter, and neither Coffey's nor more sophisticated 'revision' has much clarified it.
63. Coffey draws on *The Waste Land* – 'The sound of horns and motors', itself pastiching John Day's seventeenth-century 'noise of horns and hunting'. Line 4's 'waxes' (in the Menard edition and *Poems and Versions*) should read 'wakes' (1974 *Advent* circulated typescript, *IUR*).
64. Coffey draws on Virgil, *Georgics* (IV.507ff.) and Ovid, *Metamorphoses* (X.86ff.). 'Zone' looks like an antique Englishing of the famous oak-oracle at Chaonia (*Metam.*, X.90).
65. Mays glosses Laurence's – see 'Introductory Essay', p.27, n.27, misspelled 'Lawrence's'; I have been unable to find it in Jack Yeats.
66. Clarke's *2001*, and its important precursor 'The Sentinel' are doubtless the best-known 'first contact' science fiction. In both, alien motivation is unclear; though they might wish to 'help our infant civilization … they must be very, very old, and the old are often insanely jealous of the young'. *The Sentinel* (New York: Berkley Books, 1983), p.149.
67. Science fiction should be 'a search for a definition of man and his status in the universe which will stand in our advanced but confused state of knowledge' according to Brian Aldiss, *Trillion Year Spree* (New York: Atheneum, 1986), pp.111–12. It is by no means invariably unrealistic in its speculations; in 'The Philosophy of Science … II' (1949) Coffey wrote of the combination of 'enthusiasm and a sort of pre-Socratic rigor' to be found among contributors to the first science fiction magazine *Amazing Stories*, noting the reducing 'gap' between their speculations and 'plain fact' (pp.334–35). Arthur C. Clarke famously foresaw geosynchronous telecommunications satellites, and nuclear weapons appear in SF from around 1913; see Patrick Parrinder, *Science Fiction: Its Criticism and Teaching* (London: Methuen & Co., 1980), p.43.
68. In May 2008 the director of the Vatican Observatory wrote in *l'Osservatore Romano* that extra-terrestrial life was neither logically impossible nor an impediment to faith. The theological implications had already been thought through in Marie George's 'Aquinas on Intelligent Extra-Terrestrial Life', in *The Thomist*, vol. 65, no. 2 (April 2001). Coffey had, half a century earlier, provided the science. In 'Notes on Modern Cosmological Speculation' in *Modern Schoolman*, vol. 29, no. 3 (March 1952) he finds difficulties inherent in the 'cosmological postulate' (that 'observed phenomena be representative of the whole universe'), which one can only posit 'at the expense of substituting for the real universe one which exists only in the region of conceptual construction' (pp.189–90). Given local variation – for which Coffey cites cosmological evidence – alien life is neither logically nor scientifically impossible; any conclusions based on the postulate must be 'conditional' (p.193).
69. Coffey underlines the point, making parallels elsewhere in *Advent*: the 'stage' of line 45

'rhymes' with Agamemnon's at III.100, and the stranded aliens are sold 'bitter salt' (line 57), previously the unwanted, super-abundant by-product of human greed (III, lines 21–23).

70. Coffey, 'Extracts from "Concerning Making"', *Lace Curtain*, vol. 6 (autumn 1978), p.33, alluding to Plato's definition of the human. Science fiction of the 1950s took such questions seriously; the film *Invasion of the Body-Snatchers*, or the stories of Philip K. Dick (whom Coffey read), posit biological and technological methods of replicating humans. Eric Mottram (in his 1989 *Blood on the Nash Ambassador*) reads such American narratives as allegorizing Communist infiltration; when in the US, Coffey was known as a former associate of French Surrealist communists in the 1930s.

71. Coffey and Mercier from the former's 'The Philosophy of Science ... II', p.335; see also James Blish, *Cities in Flight* (London: Orion, 1999), p.24.

72. The Incarnation being unique and unrepeatable, redemption for en-souled non-humans must be implicit in Christ's sacrifice – if, that is, such beings need redemption. Blish sets out a theologian's view: soul-less aliens should be 'treated with compassion but extra-evangelically'; those 'fallen' should be 'evangelized with urgent missionary charity'; but if we met the soul-endowed and unfallen, contact should consist in trying to learn of this state of grace. See James Blish, *A Case of Conscience* (Harmondsworth: Penguin, 1963), 'Foreword', pp.8–9.

73. W. Olaf Stapledon, *Last and First Men* (London: Orion, 1999), pp.225, 233; Coffey, 'The Philosophy of Science ... II', p.335.

74. Coffey, untitled review, *Modern Schoolman*, 26, 3, p.269.

75. By contrast, Coffey's 1952 'The Monument' (which parallels *Advent* IV/V) posits a 'space-ark' impelled wholly by human wants, so doomed by hubris and/or angelism: 'Perfect our reliance / on shaping matter as we willed' (*PV*, p.88). All this may seem absurdly tentative, but the 'space-ark' has now moved beyond Speculative Fiction. Stephen Hawking has stated that humanity's long-term survival is at risk if confined to a single planet, advocating the construction of what science fiction calls 'relativistic ships' travelling at just below the speed of light (speech at the Royal Society, London, 1 December 2006).

76. I am puzzled by the allusion back to IV, line 10's 'unaided lute'. Watchmen are biblical (e.g. Isaiah 21:6–12), as is failing on watch (Matthew 26:40, Mark 14:37); the uncommitted Laodiceans are rebuked in Revelations 3:14.

77. For Alcestis, see *Greek Myths*, 69. She prefigures Christ's sacrifice rather than exemplifying our behaviour: 'Euripedes insists on the unique, the extraordinary quality of Alcestis's act' – L.P.E. Barker, *Euripedes' Alcestis* (Oxford: Oxford University Press, 2007), p.liv.

78. See John Macquarrie's *Martin Heidegger*, Makers of Modern Theology series (London: Lutterworth Press, 1968), p.37.

CHAPTER FIFTEEN

Brian Coffey and the Two Fat Ladies

JOHN PARSONS

I first met Brian Coffey when I was at art school in the late 1950s, where I spent most of my time in the etching department. It was ruled and run by Dick Fozzard, a man of few words and infinite skill, who taught by example. I was quick to learn all the mysterious arcane chemistry of oils and acids, resists, deckled edges, aquatints and the art of handling the old star wheel press. I became his, almost indispensable, understudy, finally taking the subject full time.

During that period various other students would pass through on a half-day basis, and it was here that I met Mary, one of Coffey's daughters. She was deeply involved with David Chapman, a young student who leant more towards literature than art. He was heavily into drugs, which would inevitably cut his potentially brilliant life short. Mary was a lively person, she shrieked well, laughed loudly, was talented and had a wicked streak. We became friends and eventually very close, I was asked back to meet the family and her father, the poet.

13 Elms Avenue was an eye-opener. I had never seen a place quite like it. I had lived in student flats, always minimal and poorly furnished, but never seen their equivalent on such a grand family scale. Here was Bohemia in its true guise. The place seemed cavernous, acres of old linoleum and ancient wallpaper, chairs and furniture used to destruction, lashed together or poorly mended in a 'what the hell' kind of way. A dividing wall had been pulled down revealing the studwork. There were no pretensions. I was to meet Dr Coffey, mathematician, philosopher and poet and I approached the situation with some degree of nervousness.

I need not have worried, he was charming and cut a dapper figure in his green Harris tweed jacket, check shirt, grey trousers, beige woollen tie and black Oxford shoes. There must have been similar complete outfits racked up somewhere in the house, I was never to see him in any other uniform. His hair, unruly and white, floated sideways like a cloud of wire wool, above a red, very Irish, face. It smiled, the blue eyes pierced, the excited mouth dribbled slightly. There was an air of lightness, openness and humour about him, which I immediately liked, and we quickly became good friends.

The Coffey household was a thoroughfare for a huge variety of people, young and old. There was always something happening: actors, poets, artists, all passed through. Conversations were lively and boisterous, and over all this Brian ruled with wit and respect. Always smiling and encouraging, never patronising, quoting philosophy or literature or doing his famous high kicks (he would take a swipe at the ceiling with his right foot, often encouraging us all to have a go, it got plenty of laughs). Occasionally, a spontaneous excited little dance made an appearance. From the background, Bridget would give intuitive asides and add to the humour. She could be just as entertaining, and was an accomplished watercolourist and fabric designer, though I relish an image of her coming in from the garden in a beaten-up summer hat, tied under her chin, and carpet slippers, holding a handful of spring onions. Both dainty and ladylike in a large kind of way, she seemed to embody an upper class of privileged creativity. What a relief it was from my own background in the suburbs of Edmonton. I felt completely at home.

The kitchen, which lay down three or four stairs, was set beside the back room, with the dividing wall removed. It was here that amateur productions were enacted, the auditorium being the kitchen, with its splintery benches round the table. The very table at which I experienced my first game of 'Up Jenkins', with its cries of creepy crawlies, and the slamming of a dozen elbows on its surface. Everybody was encouraged to make noise and vociferate loudly. There was a great choral tradition too, of Irish and American songs. The daughters all had fine voices, one would start and the rest would follow – 'Down by the Ohio', 'Spinning Wheel' or 'Barbara Ellen' – with great enthusiasm, no shyness, everyone joined in, while Brian conducted.

Later, as part of the Coffey starving-young-artist support initiative, I was employed to decorate the outside of the house, rehang the gate and fix gutters. This, in my hippy persona, was performed in a white boilersuit, long hair and cowboy boots, or the ubiquitous flares and rainbow sweater. I introduced the Coffeys and the long-suffering neighbours to Captain Beefheart, Country Joe and Frank Zappa.

Muswell Hill was a large village, it seemed that everyone knew one another. When you walked the Broadway with Brian, both young and old addressed him as 'Dr Coffey'. There was mutual respect; it was a community. The local Bohemia gathered in the Express Dairy café on a Saturday morning. This was sited at a strategic point on the top of the hill and next to the roundabout. You'd meet Damian Murphy, a pianist, Gerald Keon the painter, George Taylor the poet, all the local actors and intellectuals, over a cup of tea and a currant bun, discussing JellyRoll Morton, Barnet Newman or Proust, all very cosmopolitan and Left Bank.

Ray Davies, also at the art school, could be seen with his brother Dave in the corner shop (much later I was to appear on the same stage as part of a support band). Alan Jones, the pop artist lived thereabouts, as did Andy Hoogenboom and Keith Scott, members of the seminal Alexis Korner Band. I drove them to and from gigs in my Willies jeep. Later, through Charley Watts, I even ferried the Rolling Stones in the back. Mike Leigh lived there, as did Henry Lowther the trumpet player, the list is endless. It was a small world, and it seemed to revolve around the Broadway.

There were two watering holes, the John Baird, rather bland and modern, hosted the actors, the other, the Royal Oak, hosted the rest. Brian and I went many times to the Oak. It still had a strong flavour of the past, of the village pub, there was no actual bar, just barrels set up in a taproom, with an ale and roll-up atmosphere. Out the back an orchard with geese and chickens, was there even a goat? It was a fine setting for the *craic*, sitting under apple blossom on the hillside, overlooking the city. In due course it was pulled down and an ugly, brewery-driven carbuncle appeared. We stopped going.

There was also another place where one could get drink, this had a rare, almost Irish atmosphere. A short distance from Elms Avenue, in the grounds of Alexander Palace and on a separate hill, lay the Grove Bar. It was a typical, chalet-like London park building, but you could get a cup of tea and a cheesecake, or a glass of stout and crisps. Kids were allowed in, a rarity in those days. We would sit on the old bandstand with a pint out of the rain, or, with Brian and his children, grab a mad game of rounders. The site was extremely ancient, I believe Pepys drank there, also highwaymen who plied the infamous stretch of Great North Road at East Finchley. Eventually it closed down and became a 'One O'Clock Club' and a work opportunity for several of the women that I knew, including Mary Coffey and Mary Holman, later to become Mary Parsons.

In due course I moved to Muswell Hill. The flat, 88 Roseberry

Road, became known as the Two Fat Ladies Club, a rather loose hippie commune on the ground floor. It had been discovered by Brian of course, who was friendly with Henry Vidon, who lived upstairs. Henry, an ex-actor whose fame was to have once played St Francis in a black-and-white movie, lived with Arthur, described as his brother, though we had our own ideas. The flat smelled vaguely of creosote or varnish from the theatrical cardboard sets that he had constructed to ease his passage into obscurity.

They were extremely quiet. Unfortunately the flat downstairs was not. There was a drum kit in the front room and a number of regular and bizarre instruments, from saxophones and flutes to sitars, thumb pianos, harmonicas and bagpipe chanters. There were weekly avant-garde jazz sessions, in connection with The People Band, a notorious anarchistic jazz group with no leader and no limitations. Brian often visited to hear these goings on. The cacophony could be fairly extreme – the band had a reputation for driving their audiences away – and, for a time, I think his name became mud amongst the Vidons. Drugs were taken, films made, a parrot appeared, there were secret speakers in the front hedge to harangue passers-by, and parties shook 'The Fat Ladies' from top to bottom.

The changing occupants of the flat were disposed to communal activities, which ranged from making geodesic domes, soapbox carts and movies, to dowsing as well as kite and musical instrument making. We bought a range of ancient typewriters from jumble sales and all composed concrete poetry to go with the music. Sandra, who I was living with at the time, took it on as her thesis. Brian, not averse to the company of attractive young ladies, then took her on, they dined out, visited exhibitions and bookshops, discussed the work. Eventually Brian himself took to writing it, possibly under the influence of Sandra, though in his own enigmatic style. I formed a relationship with Bob Cobbing, who never published the poems but used my drawings instead, as illustrations.

About the same time Brian started Advent Books, his small poetry press. I stepped in as designer, typographer, printer and liaison officer. The press itself was an antiquated glorified Adana, in cast iron, it stood shoulder high in his hallway and was worked by a foot treadle, the paper being fed in by hand. One had to resonate in sympathy with its foibles, tune oneself into its springs and squeaks, oil it and caress it. Being nimble and more foolhardy, I was the main operator.

Paper floated over the hall, ink was mixed on the hall table, type was set in the dining-room and policy discussed in the kitchen, but from the chaos arrived a number of slim volumes. Work by Neil Mills, David Chapman, Brian, Gaston Bonheur, Augustus Young and myself. Brian's long prose poem *Monster* came out at that time, I had the idea that it should be a kind of uroboros swallowing its own tail. Brian liked this, a circular book, but it did give us binding problems, apart from the difficult design of the text. I never fully understood the poem, but we listened attentively down at the Fat Ladies to Brian's musical and entertaining readings, punctuated always by his irrepressible giggles.

The press was kept running by Brian's ongoing relationship with Bertram Rota, the rare bookshop, and his university sales in America. At that same time I started working in a similar but more professional capacity, with Asa Benveniste, who ran the Trigram Press. Trigram drew a lot of material from America, beat poets, artists and photographers. Its offices at King's Cross were a centre for experimental work, Asa having come originally from Greenwich Village. It had a distributor and its well-made books sold nationwide. I was actually waged.

Two acquaintances, Pete Brown and Roger Cross, resurrected the old Electric Cinema as a club. Tim Wilson, a fellow artist, and myself had the job of designing and printing all the posters. For this we got a VW busload of friends in free. Every week we set out in a smoke-filled vehicle for Portobello Road, how we got there can only be due to a Volkswagen homing instinct. We took Brian on a number of occasions, to see Kenneth Anger films and other avant-garde stuff. Brian enjoyed himself thoroughly, innocently oblivious of the drug-filled smoke, sitting there in his Harris Tweed with that irrepressible smile.

He was always a man of ideas and he generously doled these out, whether asked for or not. One idea in which he continually attempted to interest me, was that of a latter-day *Bartholomew Fair*, based on the characters in and around Muswell Hill. He was tickled by Eric, an ex-art student who had clambered on to a railway bridge in Crouch End and painted a huge 'NO'. This was to feature in the proposed work, although how was never exactly clarified. Needless to say, I never completed this project with Brian, being busier with painting or constructing UFOs.

When my present wife, another Mary, became pregnant at number 88 and craved only lettuce sandwiches, Brian, always the kindest of men, regularly appeared with them, freshly pulled from his back garden, where he grew them to accompany his radishes.

Dermot Goulding, the photographer, and myself (we worked together at St Martins School of Art at the time), took Brian to a concert at the Queen Elizabeth Hall. Brian slept through the whole performance, snoring loudly. No discreet nudging could wake him; we chuckled behind our hands. At the end, we asked Brian what he thought and apparently he had thoroughly enjoyed it. Augustus Young has a similar story – it was obviously a good spot for a nap.

Much later, I was involved with a rock band called the Fabulous Poodles. I wrote the lyrics, designed promotional material, did the styling, drove the van and acted as the warm-up act, dressed as a poodle riding a unicycle. When gigging at Southampton University, I called in on my old friend, now living there to be near his family. He insisted on coming, I guess the students thought he was just another old don reliving his youth. He was open to anything, still in his tweed jacket, arms crossed, laughing at the jokes and the lyrics. Advent, with help from Augustus, produced a book of these, 'Songs For The Poodles', his master's choice.

I saw him very few times after this, although we regularly corresponded. He sent books of poems and etchings, a medium that he discovered later in life. Maybe it was the smell of the ink, the directness of dry-point or the immediacy of being able to write straight on to the metal. He loved it, if he had started much earlier I could have taught him all the techniques. Still, they came thick and fast, very black and with a mysterious literary content.

We were always the best of friends. There was a kind of mutual admiration, neither of us completely understanding what the other was quite on about. He was ever capable of showing respect for those he thought deserved it, and there were many that received it. He would deliver criticism gently and only when needed, I never saw him in low spirits. His work often left me bewildered, but seemed to make absolute sense when he read it aloud. Akin to music, it resonated with something deep within. The actual meaning, if there actually was a single meaning, only came with time, and it was never obvious. It was simply and honestly Brian. He was a great man and is deeply missed.

CHAPTER SIXTEEN

Homeric Spirituality: The Metaphor of the Heroic in *Death of Hektor*

WACŁAW GRZYBOWSKI

I THE METAPHOR

The philosopher Paul Ricoeur has noted that metaphor in the service of the poetic function 'is that strategy of discourse by which language divests itself of its function of direct description in order to reach the mythic level where its function of discovery is set free.'[1] The free, song-line flow of sounds and images we find in Brian Coffey's 1979 long poem *Death of Hektor* might be said to confirm this, as the poem brings with it 'mythic' meanings, allowing its persona and the reader along with him to enter a world of poetic imagination, and through that, a realm of mythic archetypes. Ricoeur claims that metaphor has the capacity to shift between poetry and metaphysics by facilitating a move away from simple description of reality towards a mythic level.[2] This metaphysical dimension draws on an interrelationship between poetry, philosophy and theology. It is metaphysics that 'verticalizes metaphor', making it a mode of transcendence, while poetry visualizes 'speculative analogy' (metaphysical metaphor) through its imagery.[3] Commenting on Martin Heidegger's famous saying 'The metaphorical exists only within the metaphysical', Ricoeur argues that 'the metaphorical "raising" is also the metaphysical "raising"; true metaphor is vertical, ascending, transcendent metaphor.'[4] One finds a complementary thesis in the theory of symbol formulated by Thomas Merton, an American Trappist monk, poet and religious writer. Merton writes, 'the true symbol ... contains in itself a structure which in some way makes us aware of the inner meaning of life and reality itself ... A true symbol points to the very

heart of all being, not to an incident in the flow of becoming.'⁵ If
poetic metaphor has a structure similar to symbol, as Merton's literary
essays suggest, then it can be said to perform the same function.⁶
Coffey's remarks on the poetic 'trade', in 'A Note on Rat Island' (a
short article on Yeats' 'The Lake Isle of Innisfree') are not far from
Ricoeur's and Merton's intuitions, for Coffey defines poetic knowledge as 'the outwardly turned integration of the poet towards poem-
making and the inwardly turned gaze of the poet considering himself
in his place in the universe'.⁷

In Coffey's poem there is movement between the Homeric, mytho-
poetic mode and the metaphysical, first indicated through the image of
the 'unwitnessed unwitnessable start / void naming a "nothing exists"'
(*PV*, p.151). This alludes to *creatio ex nihilo*, the calling into being
of the multiple universe out of the 'void' of nothingness. The image
introduces a theological significance that compliments the mythic
dimension of the poem's initial vision of the garden. The presence
of biblical undertones, in the 'void naming a "nothing exists"', are
already implicit in the earlier mytho-poetic images of the opening lines
of *Death of Hektor*. The images of the garden and the void together
form a Creationist allusion. Indeed, between the two poles, the mythic
and the metaphysical, we encounter spiritual and moral realities,
described by Thomas Merton as 'the inner meaning of life'.⁸ In the line
'Back to first fault forward to last hope' (*PV*, p.151), Coffey achieves
a convergence of the allusion to the repenting Odysseus with the
biblical image of Adam's regret. The images of 'jasmin soft wind /
friend in grove hand gentle' are associated with the gentle wind of the
Lord God, *Philoanthropos*, the Friend of man, 'moving about in the
garden at the breezy time of the day' (Genesis 3:8),⁹ the sound of
which makes the first people hide 'among the trees of the garden'
(Genesis 3:8),¹⁰ after they have yielded to the temptation of false
omnipotence through 'the fruit of knowledge' (Genesis 2:17).¹¹ The
image of 'the green occasion of regret' (*PV*, p.151) juxtaposes the
Edenic longing implicit in the natural beauty of the garden with the
consciousness of tragic guilt, both Odyssean and Adamic, and may also,
on a biographical level, allude to the beauty of Irish landscape and the
author's personal sense of loss through his exile. The original violation
of the human condition transforms Edenic plenitude into 'desert not
ended at skyline' (*PV*, p.151). The original violation turns 'each …
heart void thought cloud', into 'ash' (*PV*, p.151), and yields to the destructive image of the 'habit ravening to prey on / giving unrestricted
to blood's last drop / in disregard of failure' (*PV*, p.151).

What is an heroic virtue in Eliot's interpretation of 'What the thunder said' – '*Datta*' (meaning 'to give')[12] – seems here to become the unleashing of destructiveness in Coffey's poem. Eliot's vision of valiance – 'The awful daring of a moment's surrender'[13] – by sole strength of which 'we have existed',[14] seems at first sight questioned by Coffey's discovery that the individual heroic adventure is 'a pawn of games man play / in disregard of failure' (*PV*, p.151), foreshadowing canto 8, which discloses the political manipulations behind the exploits of the warrior. In fact, on a deeper level there is agreement between Eliot's and Coffey's visions. However, this will not become clear until further metaphysical insights, in cantos 2 and 4 of *Death of Hektor*, bring out the latent meanings of these initial auguries. For the time being, canto 1 leans towards the Odyssean passion for adventure and the ensuing alienation.

Blinded by restless desire, the will turns the medium of time and space, in which it exists, into a stage for destructiveness. Thus 'slowly-swiftly' (*PV*, p.151) moving away from the 'unwitnessed' (*PV*, p.151) metaphysical beginning, time becomes the vehicle of fatal passion and unawareness. What is implied here is a veiled and perhaps personal confession of temptation from the voyager, represented by the author, by Odysseus and even perhaps by the exiled Adam moving further and further away from the source of life. The voyager 'turns back' (*PV*, p.151) and distances himself from the essential content of life, unaware of the destructiveness of time. Paradoxically, it is time that allows both 'turning back' and the 'scant return' (*PV*, p.151), both the escape from the essentials of human life through passion and the undoing of this estrangement through the contrite pilgrimage back home.

What the poetic voice was turning back from is suggested in the second canto of *Death of Hektor*. The cycles of nature, 'Rise and fall earth and water / to and fro waves of sea' (*PV*, p.152), point to the very metaphysical source of the universe – 'all is benignity / swan-down for cygnets' (*PV*, p.152). The word 'all' encompasses an expansive sublimation of sensual data raising 'benignity' to the level of universal metaphysical meaning. 'Benignity' signifies, therefore, the mysterious source to which the persona returns. To put it in more Thomistic language, the form of nature, its gentle dynamism, reveals the logic of mercy, the dynamism of *Purum Esse*, the essence of which is the pure act of existence, thus by necessity the act of the giving of life. Coffey's inquiry into Thomism as the core of Latin Catholicism is surprisingly close to the core of Celtic Christianity, to what the Fathers of the Church described as *theoria physica*, the knowing of God through the beauty of nature. This is not far from the ancient pre-Christian consciousness, which extracts the first metaphysical notion of the mystery of being, the *apeiron*, limitlessness, from the vastness of natural elements, 'earth air water fire' (*PV*, p.152). The image of 'swan-down for cygnets' provides a visual rhyme with the symbol of a cormorant feeding its nestlings with the blood from its heart, standing for Christ and His sacrifice, the shedding of His blood that gives new life to those who accept it. In these symbolic associations there appears a distant echo of the 'giving unrestricted to blood's last drop' (*PV*, p.151). It brings back its positive meaning as creative and regenerative sacrifice. The Pure Act of Being means mercy in giving oneself 'unrestricted'. Therefore what seems to imply the negative meaning of Eliot's interpretation of '*Datta*', restores itself as an essential virtue of being, *arete*, the courage to be, and therefore to give oneself. An impatient reader has to go back to the first canto and realize that destructiveness lies not in 'unrestricted giving' (Coffey), nor in 'the awful daring of a moment's surrender' (Eliot), but in the 'habit ravening to prey' (*PV*, p.151) on them, in the habit of lapsing into the passion of violence, of distancing oneself from the all-embracing 'benignity' and from oneness with Being.

II TIME

Coffey writes in the second canto 'yet in the unhushed quiet it moves' (*PV*, p.152). This is a reference to time and its thrust outward from the source to 'wear away wear away' (*PV*, p.152). But it is also the 'benignity' of Being that moves through time and permeates nature. In the line 'time like Camber sand blown a prairie fire below the dunes' (*PV*, p.152), the untamed flow of time spreads like a prairie fire and consumes its bonds with the world and with the past. There are, of course, legendary associations between the Trojan motifs and the matter of Britain. Wales takes its first Latin name, Cambria, from Camber, its first conqueror, the second son of the legendary Brute, a Trojan refugee. Therefore 'Camber sand' is a concise allusive image suggesting continuity of conquest and exodus through time, the corrosive influence of which represents the mainstream of history, a fragmentary record of strife and refuge. It is the consuming flame of time and history that erases ancestral knowledge. 'We cannot hold time fast in our sights' (*PV*, p.152), the persona says. 'We were not present to discover / how' (*PV*, p.152) potency became an act. Strangely enough, 'the vantage point in unrecorded past' (*PV*, p.151) of canto 1,

and of the 'hill-top watcher taking the Battle in at a glance' (*PV*, p.152)
of canto 2, is the gap of darkness, the fragmented memory and absence
of knowledge which can only be filled by the poetic imagination
investigating, inductively and intuitively, the truth about 'Hektor seen
from ages off' (*PV*, p.151). However, the shift of focus from the mythic
and the metaphysical to the historic necessitates the shift from suggestive images and symbols to a discursive tone. As in Eliot's *Four Quartets*,
where insight into metaphysical darkness brings forth argumentative
diction, the obscurity of the speaker's knowledge about the past
in *Death of Hektor* invites meditation, which is formulated in the
rhetorical uncertainty concerning the factual, and therefore historical,
transition of the past into the present, of the possible into the actual,
of prophecy or providence into freedom:

> We were not present to discover
> how what it was became what it is
> Nor see how one performs freely the long foreseen   (*PV*, p.152)

This meditation continues in canto 3 in a more condensed form. It starts
with the demythologized vision of the search for historical truth alluding
to the archeological search for Troy, 'For us it is point to point with pick
and spade' (*PV*, p.153). But, unexpectedly, the condensation of images
and allusions turns from the prosaic to the poetic. Already the expression
of the arduous collecting of 'night rubble earthquake residues' (*PV*,
p.153) is endowed with songlike alliterative spontaneity, which transcends our sense of the ordinary. What seems prosaic turns out to be
most unusual, 'the all too often often the all too much' (*PV*, p.153), and
heralds the appearance of the heroic 'black white' silhouette of 'whom
a moment's spotlight deifies / to tease appearances' (*PV*, p.153):

> white black dissolves bird in wind sky in dragons
> himher into what is of tribal tale the maze
>
> May be   Maybe   Dream it
> We do not steer the stars   (*PV*, p.153)

All of a sudden the burdensome search turns into a dream about
the past, about Troy, a vision of an actual figure that sets itself against
the falsity of 'appearances' highlighting their superficiality. The hidden
content of the textured maze of 'tribal tale' becomes a part of the
cosmic dance of the stars. We see, then, that not all of the past is lost. For,
like star constellations, myth partakes of revolving and illuminating
configurations, from which the truth of the past 'May be' extracted. The

dream vision of the tale offers the cognitive space for induction. Coffey's poetic argument thus repeats the thesis of Aristotle's *Poetics* that the poetic vision of man in tragedy is 'more philosophical and more elevated than history'.[15]

However, in canto 4 the initial reference to the mythical tale of Daedalus only occasions the return to a cosmic vision of creation:

> The Day One of peak tip peeping
> from waters not yet dyed in fablement
> predating our blind horizons   the place of 'not yet'
> where 'what will be' showed not at all   (*PV*, p.154)

The narrative voice re-evokes the Aristotelian opposition (and conjunction) of potency and act in being, making it the central ontological principle of the cosmic beginning. The space between 'not yet' and 'what will be' reveals the metaphysics of time and action. At first there is the creative action of nature triggered by the First Cause, the absolute 'benignity', which sets in motion the chain of changes and fertility. However, somewhere on the horizon looms the era of human creativity – 'Time ere poems' – and of free human acts – 'time ere plighted troth' (*PV*, p.154). They are absent now but later become the necessary completion of the virgin beginnings of the cosmos. The cosmic stage is thus prepared for the appearance of human potency and act so spectacularly unveiled in the Homeric epics.

Canto 5 situates Troy, and its history, in the context of this virgin beginning and the metaphysics of time.

> No one present to mark when the Isles appeared
> in a space of enduring stable tides
> shores that show no change of feature through five millennia
> (*PV*, p.155)

Forming 'so long so long', rising 'like a million year whale from squid-filled deep' (*PV*, p.155), the stage of nature blends into 'a stage for stories' and becomes the historical stage of 'the landmarks Hektor saw / Scamander's ancient course twin-peaked Samothrace / most distant Athos beacon-platform in clear light' (*PV*, p.155), whose names indirectly confirm the ancient authenticity of the Trojan episode. The Trojan landmarks have their 'name-givers' (*PV*, p.155) who have already turned the order of nature into *poiesis*, the work of human spirit, by adorning the natural surroundings with the words of human language. Landscape thus enters the realm of symbolic meanings. The scene is now set for the emergence of the hero as the epitome of free will. The shift from natural process to history finds its parallel in the juxtaposition, closing canto 5, of the 'slow accretion of snowdrift', standing for nature's time, with the dramatic pace of human subjective time, 'racing in stop-watch thousandths to the hour / for doomed Hektor to stand alone at the Skaean Gates' (*PV*, p.155).

The potency of free act and its actualization, radically different from natural cycles, intensifies human experience of being. This vision still encompasses metaphysical allusion, for the imperceptible drift of natural time seems to be a sign of eternal 'benignity' (*PV*, p.152), while the human dramatic act, materialized in time, seems to reflect the absolute Pure Act of Being standing at the birth of the world and still sustaining its existence. The contrast between natural and human time raises a question: which is closer to the Absolute Being? The metaphorical extraction of 'benignity' as the premise of all, in canto 2, suggests an affinity between nature and the mystery of the Creator. However, deeper meanings also conveyed indicate the free act of giving oneself as being implicit in the 'benignity' of the Absolute Being. Therefore, despite its transience, it is the human act that seems to evince the deeper reflection of eternity which, in fact, is not of infinite duration but a negation of time, beyond human comprehension, being the Pure Act of the one eternal 'now' (*PV*, p.151).

III THE HEROIC

For there to be a hero, there must first be a witness. Canto 6 makes Homer, the legendary blind bard of antiquity, one of the silent protagonists of the Trojan story: 'His work / abides witness to unfaltering sad gaze constrained' (*PV*, p.156). The sadness of Homer's vision comes from the contrast between light, which once must have 'entered eyes to brand memory / with noon's exact flame of sun mirrored in wind-stirred sea' (*PV*, p.156), and the darkness of the world he lived in, overshadowed by death. 'Black night for death' is set against 'colours of morning evening for life' (*PV*, p.156). A shadow falls on Homer's world with the 'maimed anatomy black white red of man at war', with the lament of 'women keening', with 'emptied hearts' (*PV*, p.156). As in earlier descriptive passages, metaphoric meanings rise from a density of details, penetrated by light and darkness, liveliness and lifelessness. In *The Rule of Metaphor*, Ricoeur emphasizes the universal and metaphysical character of the heliotrope, the solar metaphor.[16] Thus the 'noon's exact flame of sun' (*PV*, p.156) is not only the arresting image of the Mediterranean sunset, but also the symbol of mythic *arche*, of the

Heraclitean principle of fire, of Plato's *agathon*, the idea of Good, and of Aristotle's *Nous* or Reason, and it thus symbolizes the absolute measure of things and virtues towards which the human spirit aspires. The more vivid the vision of the ideal, the darker and more painful is the sense of loss brought by vice. Closing canto 6, the persona ponders upon Homer's prudence, which supposedly made him 'keep unsaid wordly in innermost anguished heart / what would not have pleased his client banqueters' (*PV*, p.156). In other words, the ancient poet does not endorse the gloom of destructive quasi-heroism represented by the 'self-approving lords' of canto 6.

However, Homer's innermost anguish is not entirely hidden in the *Iliad*, for the initial verses announce its main aim to be the presentation of the anger of Achilles (named also Pelid, meaning the son of Peleus), anger which deviates from the ideal of virtue, *arete*, which encompasses the virtues of courage, wisdom and restraint. Indeed, on the surface Achilles' vice consists in the quarrel with Agamemnon, his proud breach of solidarity with the Achaeans and the ensuing slaughter of them (including his friend, Patrokles) by Hektor and the Trojans. But even though his anger evaporates through reconciliation with his allies, it bursts out again when, out of revenge for Patrokles' death, he denies decent burial to dying Hektor, ill-treats his body and thus trespasses against divine laws. Therefore he is to bear punishment, as Hektor foretells in his last breath, namely his death at the hands of Hektor's brother, Paris. Homer makes Pelid compensate for defiling Hektor by honouring his father, Priam, and allowing him to take his son's body. This is what reinstates Achilles as the man of honour. However, his bouts of anger remain undeniable. Although they are overshadowed by the courage and splendour of his martial skills, the anger suggests that Peleus' son is not a spotless hero. In fact, his vice is typical of a warrior, pride and quick temper. Thus Homer sustains a difficult balance between respect for the memory of the hero and sincere fascination with his virtue and dexterity, alongside the higher aim of expressing a demonstrable and contrastive moral reminder about the essence of *arete*, which could not pass unnoticed by the more sober of the Greek bard's 'client banqueters' (*PV*, p.156).

However, Coffey's purpose does not entirely coincide with Homer's. The Irish poet presents a twentieth-century reinterpretation of the Homeric story. The *Iliad* says nothing of the slaughter of the Trojans and Hektor's child, which for Coffey, rich in epic and historical knowledge, is an obvious fact. Homer's vision of Pelid's glory seems as convincing as the splendour of Hektor or Paris. Compared to Cuchulain, the Celtic

hero, Achilles, in Coffey's vision, becomes the epitome of destructiveness:

> spher'd round with battle glory
> luminous like Cuchullain figure of War Itself
> belly-ripper head-splitter neck-lopper
> skewering fighters commoners heroes alike   (*PV*, p.157)

It is not clear whether this allusion to the Celtic epic refers to modern
Irish nationalism, but it most certainly brings out the inherent ambiguities of heroic legend. The fighter-hero of Muirthemne may be the
'comeliest of the men of Ireland',[17] but there are significant insertions in
Lady Gregory's Irish Mythology, speaking of him as a mad, berserk, merciless killer, dangerous even to his own clan.[18] The luminosity of the
hero figure, in Homer and in Irish mythology, entails both admiration
for his stamina and reputation as well as fear of his destructiveness.
However, the latter seems veiled in Greek epic, implied rather than
stated. Coffey, writing with the hindsight of the Second World War,
chooses to foreground this ambiguity.

Canto 8 refers directly to the Second World War through the final
powerful evocation of 'Doom über alles' (*PV*, p.158). However, it
concentrates on the broader political dimensions of war, prepared by
'ungodly' demigods of power, 'at creep from out their airy veils',
manipulating the sea of mass humanity whose 'ease-soft brains' hasten
their doom (*PV*, p.158). The counterpointed symbol of the river Xanthus 'rebelling at pollution' (*PV*, p.158) – in the *Iliad* used by Apollo
to stop Achilles from his final attack on the Trojans – now signifies the
rebellion of nature against the abuse of humanity, becoming also a sign
of protest against the passivity of human society in the face of evil.
Paradoxically, the deities of the political world are 'mastered / by Fate
they must accept nor comprehend' (*PV*, p.158). They succumb to the
unforeseen consequences of their trespass against the natural world and
human life, the consequences of which are unexpected but inevitable.

Canto 9, the shortest of the entire sequence, sets Xanthus, the 'voice
of nature in travail', against the full horror of war, the 'spectacle of
untrammelled strength obscene' (*PV*, p.159). Nature has 'its fill of
limbs of little souls sent shrieking / unworthied to vacuous dark all
sighs foreclosed' (*PV*, p.159). The ancient religious vision of the shad-
owy meaninglessness of souls in the afterlife is mixed here with the
absurdity of modern genocide, of Auschwitz and the Gulag, turning
'little souls' into trash, foreclosing 'all sighs' behind the barbed wire of
Soviet camps or the lead door of gas chambers.

With this tragic, historical context in the background, canto 10 returns to the Trojan stage to retell the final duel between the two main protagonists of the *Iliad*, 'on this fixed day of the tenth year of Troy besieged' (*PV*, p.160). Going beyond Hesiod's respectful criticism of Homer, the central point of which is the questioning of the revenge for kidnapping Helen as the real cause for the war, Coffey's poetic narrator seems to suggest that other motives, apart from sheer conquest, are incorporated into Homer's literary themes, which mollify and soften the real image of war. Achilles' anger and revenge for his friend's death is not countenanced as a valid motive. Rather, Coffey's Achilles is a sheer conqueror, similar in his pride and contempt for the defeated to a Nazi victor or any other ideological war victor. Thus the 'Glory for Greeks' (*PV*, p.160) actually means here the dishonouring of Hektor and his kinsmen. The similarity of the warrior's instinct, both ancient and modern, is apparent. The realistic account of the fight at the Skaean Gates and the profanation of Hektor's body culminates in the concluding metaphor: 'And / Doom now in the air like a cloudy mushroom swags / above Troy' (*PV*, p.160). The allusion to the nuclear threat is a swift metaphoric transfer from the misty misgivings of the heroic myth to the historical context of modernity, and post-modernity, summed up by William Carlos Williams' statement: 'The Bomb has entered our lives' (*Pictures from Breughel*).[19]

In canto 11, the vision of the 'doom' of Troy, as it becomes 'a dusty hill swept by cold winds', is used as a symbol of the 'past or future ravishment of any city' (*PV*, p.161). In fact, the image of the real destruction serves as a point of departure for more figurative and variegated meanings in the next stanza, relating to communal blindness in the face of catastrophe – 'Doom's rank perfect days the false assumption of security' (*PV*, p.161) – and to mean-spirited profits drawn from it by 'partner's treachery' and by conquerors themselves – 'coinage falsified   Niagara's of fairy cash corpses candles / chalices gold teeth spendthrift scrip to jack up naked power' (*PV*, p.161).

The leap from the concrete image of Troy's fall to the collage of condensed allusive details of conquest is graphically marked by a blank space between the initial part of the canto and the following one. Condensation allows the narrator to achieve a more universal perspective as well as quasi-metaphorical effects. Each separate image is more or less realistic, but, when put together with others, it presents a surreal, Breughelian landscape of moral debris. Apart from expressing the intensity of emotions, as Moriarty suggests (*ABC*, p.101), the spaces between the stanzas serve as a transition from one level of vision to

another, as in the two closing parts of canto 11, which again shift to
the 'Doom for Troy', signalled by the feigned retreat of the Achaeans
('ships a thousand dressed on the sea / feigning a clutching hand
stretching in from the west') and to the final attack on Troy 'foreshadowing fire sword fall like leftwards sloping script' (*PV*, p.161).

Thus they lead back to Hektor's death, re-evoked in canto 12,
envisioned as 'nothing nothing but eyeless dark', which falls as a
curtain of oblivion on the scene of atrocity, where his infant son,
Astyanax, is 'dashed by Achaean hand to earth from the walls / prudent
victor forestalling future revenge', and Trojan maidens are 'ripped rent'
(*PV*, p.162). The image of inhuman cruelty provides the background
for a spiritual perspective on Hektor's hope and despair. Hektor knows
only Fate as the supreme ruler of life and death. Therefore his prayer
'"What will be will be"' means acceptance of 'Doom':

> He had known no mothering saver of forlorn hearts
> no soft wings to shelter his wife Andromache
> He'd known no prayer pray cry-mercy-hoped-for prayers
> what we have forgotten and mock at   (*PV*, p.162)

Within these lines there is a comparison of pagan consciousness with
Christian spirituality, which offers a deeper and inwardly active hope
for the more direct intervention of God into human affairs, an assertion
of values that are ignored by modern secularism. However, Hektor's
ancient code of honour is sufficient for an awareness of human dignity,
thus for the demand of 'equal treatment from equal foe' (*PV*, p.163).

The vision of Hektor as the avatar of real heroism is brought to
light fully in canto 13. In its second stanza the narrator addresses him
directly and personally in a powerful vision:

> Hektor across three thousand years your gasped plea
> for befittingness has filled my ears since boyhood
> In pictures then I saw you stand beautiful against the sky
> facing Achilles facing the inescapable spear
> so strangely pictured by sentimental art
> one could hear the aesthete dame breathe 'How effective'   (*PV*,
> p.163)

As in the refrain of Eliot's 'Love Song of J. Alfred Prufrock' – 'In the
room women come and go / Talking of Michelangelo' – the aestheticism of superficial impressions serves as a counterpoint for the real
drama. The closing cantos of *Death of Hektor* reflect Coffey's modern
version of chivalric humanism. The initial verses of canto 13 make

clear that Hektor's heroism differs from Achilles', through the former's emotional and ethical bond with those he was closest to, and in a faint yet vivid bond with the spiritual, through his 'reverence for degree' and 'prayed prayer' (*PV*, p.163). Although the latter miscarry and are therefore 'unavailing', in contrast to the Achaean masculine individualism, Hektor's attitude is, in the final analysis, fully human. As canto 14 suggests, Homer's sympathy for him can be inferred:

> ... from how he shows
> Hektor's home wife child frightening helmet crest
> and how he shows Greek self-styled heroes
> at slaughter and jealous play   (*PV*, p.164)

The foregrounding of the chivalric-humanistic vision of Hektor serves to emphasize the fact that Agamemnon's fighters destroy the bonds with the human and spiritual world through acts of violence, *contra naturam*.

IV VERBUM BONUM

Canto 15, the last in the *Death of Hektor* sequence, shifts the focus from the undoubted courage of a man fighting for basic human values to the silent heroism of a woman:

> And he gave us his Andromache lamenting
> like any woman victim of any war robbed of her world
> her husband her child her friends her linen her pots and pans
> the years it took to put a home together living against the grain
> of great deeds   her woman's life   in her heart
> much held fast   word hidden for all   (*PV*, p.165)

Hektor is a foil for Achaean aggression. However, Andromache's feminine courage serves to foreground both the true and false bravery of men. Her heroism consists in carrying the burden of absolute loss. A migrant philosopher and lecturer, with a large family, Coffey himself knew the toil of 'putting a home together' and 'living against' the currents of the times. Moreover, behind this image there is obviously the theme of *pieta*, the vision of Christ's Mother mourning her son's dead body brought down from the cross. Andromache loses all that constitutes her life. What is left to her is the deep pain of irremediable tragedy, which makes her similar to the Gospel vision of the Holy Mary, who not only is violently and cruelly deprived of the one most dear to her – 'the most excellent of sons of man' (Psalm 45)[20] – but also is put to the margin of society with the death of her only son, the last man of her family able to take legal protection of her, according to Hebrew law. Obviously, dying Jesus gives her a new son, John, which is a legal act, proving she has no other children. Thus there is the community of Christ's pupils, who become her new family. Andromache seems more tragic, as she is deprived of any hope. However, there remains the secret life of her heart in which there is 'much held fast   word hidden for all'. With this, Coffey's allusions to Mary become even clearer, referring most directly to St Luke's description of the Holy Virgin keeping 'all these things [the significant events connected with Jesus] in her heart' (Luke 2:51).[21] The vision of the 'word hidden for all' resonates with Eliot's words from 'Gerontion', where 'The word within a word, unable to speak a word, / Swaddled with darkness' introduces the image of 'Christ the tiger' coming 'in the juvenescence of the year'.[22] Another Christological passage from 'Ash Wednesday', 'Against the Word the unstilled world still whirled / About the centre of the silent Word',[23] also echoes in Coffey's poem. Andromache's good word 'hidden for all' cannot be literally taken as Christ the Word; however, in the poetry of Coffey, a Catholic writing in the shadow of Eliot, Christological allusions are at the very least implicit. If spiritually overcome, Andromache's painful fate can still bring with it the message of true heroism and peace, as Coffey sees it. Her tragic, silent witness is the powerful protest against alienated individualism and egoistic warfare and conquest. The inward word of her heart seems intended by Coffey to express the need for a humane world, anticipating the hope of the Saviour, the one who is to reveal the power of perfect love, merciful justice and fortitude. As the ancient augury of Lao Tsy has it:

> Each may see how weakness
> Overcomes power, and delicacy conquers
> Inexorable obstacles in man.[24]

Coffey's poem therefore raises the question of chivalry or 'befitting-ness' (*PV*, p.163). Is it a pretence which veils hubris, primitive instincts, *libido dominandi* and the *Eros* of violence, or is it a natural virtue of human uprightness? The answer to this question has already been sketched earlier in relation to the theology of 'benignity', which is implicit in the primordial *bios theoretikos* or thinking life, and is developed in the Christian vision of *Purrum Esse* as the source and model for natural order and, beyond that, for human existence. Distant as it is, the Christological perspective in Andromache's 'word hidden for all' also adds a new dimension to Hektor's heroism. His 'reverence for degree' (*PV*, p.163) carries implicit nobility of heart. His 'prayed prayer' potentially reaches beyond the darkness of *fatum* and becomes the contemplation of eternal truth reflected in the life of mortals. So-called pagan spirituality, expressed in mythical allegories, pre-intuits one important value of Christo-centrism, the presence of eternal truth in human life, with the difference that the former often identifies it with fate, while the latter experiences the ultimate truth not as anonymous and blind, but as a personal 'giving [of] oneself unrestricted' (*PV*, p.151). Therefore, the natural stamina of bravery, as the basis of chivalry, can be instantiated by humanity, if it overcomes the instinct of alienation and violence, and uses the impulse of fortitude coming from the spiritual source of Being.

V THE METAPHOR OF THE HEROIC

In the third chapter of book 10 of *Lady Gregory's Irish Mythology*, entitled 'Arguments', one finds an interesting dialogue between St Patrick and Oisin, the last survivor of the so-called Fianna, the élite of fighting men under legendary Finn, his father.[25] An ancient author puts admonitions directed to Oisin into the mouth of the Apostle of Ireland, or the mouth of a Gaelic Christian representing the so-called Patrician legacy, who intends to convert the old and sick warrior from the way of adventure to pious life. However, Oisin's thoughts are entirely submerged in the nostalgic memory of the past glory of Finn and the Fianna:

> OISIN: ... I have a little story to tell about Finn; we were but fifteen men; we took the King of Saxons of the feats, and we won the battle against the King of Greece ... There is a greater story of Finn than of us, or of any that have lived in our time; all that are gone and that are living, Finn was better to give out gold than any of themselves.[26]

To this 'Patrick of the bells' answers: 'All the gold you and Finn used to be giving out, it is little it does for you now; he is in Hell in bonds because he did treachery and oppression.'[27] What is glorious to Finn's heir is seen as dishonourable by the Christian monk. The bravery and generosity of Finn is stained with violence and vice in the eyes of one contemplating 'the Son of God'.[28] With its direct charge against the myth of Achilles, and the legend of Cuchulain 'figure of War Itself' (*PV*, p.157), Coffey's *Death of Hektor* apparently takes St Patrick's side in this ancient dispute. Coffey juxtaposes Achilles' aggressive heroism, alluding to the horrors of modern war, with Hektor's dignity as the defender of human bonds. This contrast forms the initial, Homeric vision of the poem. However, alongside these historical images we encounter the deeper sphere of the poem, which is occupied by metaphysical and spiritual meanings. In fact, the vision of cosmic 'benignity', alluding to the revelation of God as the Pure Being, is extracted from the images of natural prehistory; the history of human strife foreshadows the prospect of redemptive messianic hope for the victims of violence. The last canto of the sequence, showing the heroism of Hektor's wife, Andromache, gathers together all these essential meanings in its final vision of the 'word hidden for all' (*PV*, p.165), which becomes the ultimate metaphor of the heroic. For the work of metaphor is based not only on a single comparison or combination of words, but on a series of tensions which accumulate in the poetic text. Here, the metaphor of the 'word' yokes together meanings distributed at crucial junctures in this poetic story, which seem, when viewed in isolation, to be contradictory or at least distant from each other. The 'word' unites in one vision Divine 'benignity', chivalric fortitude, lament over vain slaughter and martial ruthlessness with the poignant longing for loved ones, upright knighthood, messianic salvation and peace.

As such, Coffey's metaphor transfers the reader beyond the ancient Celtic 'Arguments' to find a ground of reconciliation between seemingly opposite attitudes. The Fianna's 'treachery and oppression'[29] are inexcusable; however, they exist side by side with what is good and true in Gaelic chivalry: the defense of community, generosity, the bond of solidarity, the bond with nature and contemplation of beauty. In fact, similar values, albeit more consistent and refined, are present and raised to the supernatural level in the Patrician fascination with the Son of God. The contemplation of nature's beauty and the moral beauty of the warrior's integrity are replaced here by the contemplation of 'the most excellent of all men', as Psalm 45 calls the biblical Messiah.[30] In fact, Psalm 45 starts where *Death of Hektor* finds its conclusion: 'My heart hath uttered a good Word.'[31] It foregrounds chivalric virtues – 'Gird your sword upon your side, O mighty one; / … In your majesty ride forth victoriously in behalf of truth, humility and righteousness'[32] – in order to defend law and justice and resist oppression.[33] St John's Gospel also starts with the vision of 'the Word', which in fact presents the theology of the Son of God, the second person of the Holy Trinity, incarnate into human condition: 'In the beginning was the Word … ' (John 1:1).[34] All four Gospels make clear that what is prophetically expressed through the ancient Near East images of warrior's prowess, in Jesus becomes radically inward and spiritual without losing the truth of fortitude. Thus, in Christian tradition, Christ's sword is His word, mercy and cross. His victorious ride in defense of truth and humanity is His dramatic confrontation with hypocrisy and doubt of his contemporaries. It valorizes His insistence on His identity as the Son of God, at the risk of humiliation, torture and death. In the Gospel vision, it is His mission to sacrifice himself for the sins of the world and to be its shield against spiritual darkness. It is also His inner struggle with darkness, in His desert fast, agony in Gethsemane and loneliness on the cross. The beauty of His courage is inseparable from His 'benignity', merciful wisdom and solidarity with humankind. Such allusions to Christ are intrinsic to the poetic metaphor of the heroic created by Brian Coffey. The image and likeness of God in man implies that the natural heroisms of Hektor and Andromache, and of Finn, find their source in the 'unrestricted giving of oneself' (*PV*, p.151) inscribed in Divine 'benignity'. Thus the metaphor of Andromache's 'word' in *Death of Hektor* points towards a fulfilment and embodiment of its various heroic dimensions by Christ in the New Testament.

NOTES

1. Paul Ricoeur, *The Rule of Metaphor* (London: Routledge, 1994), p.247.
2. Ibid., p.270.
3. Ibid., p.279.
4. Ibid., pp.287–88.
5. Thomas Merton, *Love and Living* (New York: Harcourt Brace, 1985), pp.54–55. This quotation is taken from Merton's essay 'Symbolism: Communion or Communication', which is one of the most crucial for his theory of art and literature.
6. This thesis can be found in Merton's 'Poetry, Symbolism and Typology' originally published as a chapter of *Bread in the Wilderness* (Collegeville: Liturgical Press, 1986) and later republished in *The Literary Essays of Thomas Merton* (New York: New Directions, 1985).
7. Brian Coffey, 'A Note on Rat Island', *University Review*, vol. 3, no. 8 (1966), p.26.
8. Ibid.
9. *The New American Bible* (Nashville, TN: Catholic Bible Press, 1987), p.4.
10. Ibid.
11. Ibid.
12. T.S. Eliot, *Wybór Poezji* (Wrocław: Ossolineum, 1990), p.93. Eliot's interpretation of the mythical word of thunder, from the Vedic fable (the Sanskrit 'DA' of Prajapati's teaching, directed to gods), sets the background for the first canto in *Death of Hektor*: 'DA/*Datta*: what have we given? / My friend, blood shaking heart / The awful daring of a moment's surrender ... '
13. Ibid., p.93.
14. Ibid., p.93.
15. Aristotle, *Poetics*, trans. Stephen Halliwell (Cambridge, MA: Harvard University Press, 1995), p.59.
16. Ricoeur, *Rule of Metaphor*, pp.277–78.
17. Lady Augusta Gregory, *Lady Gregory's Irish Mythology* (London: Bounty Books, 2000), p.359.

18. *Lady Gregory's Irish Mythology* contains a passage, in the description of young Cuchulain's fights, which very briefly but vividly speaks of his trance-like cruelty. After conquering Nechtan's sons, Cuchulain and his tutor, Jubair, 'went into the house and destroyed what was in it, and they set fire to it, and left it burning, and turned towards Slieve Fuad' with 'the heads of three sons of Nechtan' (*Irish Mythology*, p.349). There is no mention of the slaughter of men and women, but one guesses that the heroes did not spare those whom they found inside. Cuchulain returns to Emain still 'in anger' which makes Conchubar, the king of Ulster conclude that 'the young men of Emain will be in danger from him'. Therefore, 'three fifties of the women of Emain ... having their breast uncovered' (*Irish Mythology*, p.350) have to be sent to evoke his shame and soothe his battle trance.

19. Quoted by Brian McHale in *Constructing Postmodernism* (London: Routledge, 1994), pp.161–62, where Brian McHale explains the literary postmodernist apocalyptic obsessions.

20. *The NIV Study Bible* (Grand Rapids, MI: Zondervan Bible Publishers, 1985), p.831.

21. *New American Bible*, p.1148.

22. Eliot, *Wybór Poezji*, p.58.

23. Ibid., p.168.

24. Lao Tsy, *Droga*, trans. Michał Fostowicz-Zahorski (Wrocław: Arhat, 1992), p.78.

25. *Lady Gregory's Irish Mythology*, pp.298–305.

26. Ibid., p.299.

27. Ibid., p.300.

28. Ibid., p.299.

29. Ibid., p.300.

30. *NIV Study Bible*, p.831.

31. Thomas Merton, *The Literary Essays of Thomas Merton* (New York: New Directions, 1985), p.111. This is Merton's translation of the Latin version of Psalm 45: 'Eructavit cor meum verbum bonum'. Polish translation speaks of 'a beautiful word' that 'springs from the heart' of the Psalmist (*Biblia Tysiąclecia*, p.609).

32. *NIV Study Bible*, p.831.

33. *Biblia Tysiąclecia*, p.609.

34. *The New American Bible*, p.1189.

CHAPTER SEVENTEEN

'Hektor across three thousand years': Antiquity and the Modern Moment

ANDREW GOODSPEED

Brian Coffey's poem sequence *Death of Hektor* is not primarily about Hektor, nor indeed about his death; it is, instead, an extended meditation upon the intricate chronological difficulties of establishing a relationship between the modern reader and a major figure of classical Greek literature. Coffey makes this theme of connection across time explicit in the first lines of the first canto: 'Of what we are to Hektor Nothing to say / Of Hektor to us' (*PV*, p.151). Of this opening the critic Dónal Moriarty has expressed perplexity: 'Why, we might ask, does Coffey not open simply with the single question "[Of] what is Hektor to us [?]." This is, after all, the essential question that the poem addresses' (*ABC*, p.101). Yet to speak of Hektor to us (indeed, to all post-Homeric readers) has already been done, and in terms that the sequence shows to have continuing relevance. Indeed, *Death of Hektor* depicts a generally static title character, one whose circumstances and actions are present as choices to him but which are to us – as we observe him from a later age – his already enacted fate. Throughout the sequence, Coffey reminds his readers that they inhabit an era vastly removed from Hektor's own. It is this shifting perspective enforced by intervening time that is the true 'essential question the poem addresses', for in *Death of Hektor* it is by establishing how we relate to Hektor ('what we are to Hektor') that we come to define what 'Hektor [is] to us'. It is important here to note, however, that neither modernity nor classicism as discrete topics are of primary concern in the sequence. Instead, Coffey's poetical focus is upon the troubling and ambiguous interrelation between antiquity and modernity, and on the dissonance that disturbs apparent analogies between the ancient and the new.

Coffey presumes that his reader will understand, in the most basic civilizational sense, what Hektor is to us. He does not belabour his reader with a needless recitation of Hektorian accomplishments, nor does he establish the self-evident importance of Hektor and his story to Western cultural heritage. Hektor appears in the first line, named but otherwise unintroduced, a figure of instant familiarity. Coffey's treatment of him would, therefore, seem surprisingly scant if one believes that this poem is, in some dominant sense, about Hektor himself. In fact, after being named in the introductory section, Hektor does not appear as a major figure until the tenth of the fifteen individual cantos that comprise the *Death of Hektor* sequence (although, as we will note later, he reappears, named, in an important appearance at the end of canto 5). Coffey even records the death of the title as though Hektor were himself an object, as opposed to an active participant in one of literature's most famous duels:

> And we are forced to see godlike Achilles with aiding gods
> induce Hektor to the test he is doomed to fail
> *and* Achilles sent his pierced foe to darkness with jeering words
> promising his corpse would be food for dogs and fowl
> promising absence of due burial unremittable disgrace
> *and* Hektor dead the pallid Greeks drew near
> to stab a once feared foe   (*PV*, p.160)

Here it is Achilles who acts. Achilles induces Hektor to the test, sends his pierced foe to darkness, and issues the promise that the Trojan's dishonoured corpse will be left to the dogs – a promise that is contemptuously ironized when the 'pallid Greeks' creep forward to stab the dead body from which they once fled. Coffey does not elaborate upon 'the test [Hektor] is doomed to fail', and his ineluctable failure is presumed, so that Coffey jumps from the induction to the test to its inevitable result, Hektor lying dead, a pierced foe. Were this a poem primarily about Hektor, or specifically about the death of Hektor, it would be remarkably discontinuous and vague – for, based upon the information provided by this poem alone, there is little to suggest that a modern reader has any reason for establishing a relation to this person who appears, is doomed to be killed, dies, and is gone.

Coffey's concern, instead, is to examine how a modern reader (and, as we shall see, a modern poet) establishes an understanding of Hektor and, thereby, to examine why such a connection between antiquity and modernity has value. It is for this reason that the first section of the poem swiftly leaves the titular hero, and addresses matters not clearly associable with

Hektor. Having presented him and the difficulties of relating to his era, Coffey turns to a consideration of memory, and of the apparent void of time from which personal and cultural memory seem to originate:

> What scant return from turning back
> even a twenty year   to jasmin soft wind
> friend in grove hand gentle
> in the green occasion of regret   (*PV*, p.151)

It is difficult to establish of whom, and by whom, this passage is related; yet the purport is clear – memory, even in a twenty-year span, can both hold and lose matters of enormous importance. And if memory proves so feeble ('what scant return') that 'even a twenty year' can obscure friends and experiences, it would seem impossible to establish a connection across the millennia to the time of Homer, or to span the even greater chronological distance between a modern reader and the supposed time of Hektor. Yet something accomplishes precisely that connection as, in Coffey's expression, 'A vantage point in unrecorded past / supposes Hektor seen from ages off' (*PV*, p.151). Although it is uncertain that this vantage point is specifically Homer's, it is certainly not our vantage point; we are not 'in unrecorded past', as we are certainly in 'ages off'. Here is one of the crucial paradoxes with which Coffey grapples in *Death of Hektor* for, although Homer described Hektor in terms that later generations have found meaningful, we, in those 'ages off', cannot avoid acknowledging the intervening years that separate us from the figure of Hektor himself.

This concern with time intervening between an observer and that which he observes is central to Coffey's poem. To appreciate Hektor a modern reader may not merely read of him, but must also acknowledge the extraordinary differences between his own time and that of Homer, and that of the earlier era of Hektor. Coffey initially describes the passing of time in natural terms, making the movement from past to present seem almost entirely erosive – a brokenness that is echoed in the abrupt phrasing and discontinuities of the language itself:

> Rise and fall   earth and water
> to and fro   waves of sea ...
> yet in the unhushed quiet it moves
> it moves   it flows
> wear away wear away   earth air water fire
> time like Camber sand blown a prairie fire below the dunes   (*PV*,
> p.152)

Here the reader's cognizance of intervening time is problematic. Although Coffey's description of natural cyclicity and erosion leads to a somewhat bleak image of wearing away, he articulates this vision in terms immediately associable with ancient thought – the movement and flowing recalling Thales' assertion that 'all flows', and the erosive elements themselves grouping into the four Aristotelian elements: earth, air, water and fire. By expressing the processes of erosion in the language of antiquity, Coffey suggests the unstable perceptual position in which modernity expresses itself; one speaks of the unrecapturable past in the terms inherited from antiquity. Coffey 'borrows' from antiquity throughout the sequence, and his use of inherited forms for a new poem about past events creates a tremendously dynamic interplay between ancient inheritance and modern creativity – an interplay that is a formal enactment of his thematic concern with the applicability of the past to the present.

Having suggested this wearing away – of time and by time – in natural terms, Coffey then associates the past with human perceptions. In section five he revisits the image of natural erosion, repeating with near exactitude the 'wear away' line from section two (omitting the spacing break between 'wear away' and 'earth air water fire'), yet he proceeds to note that not all things are worn away, and that one can es-tablish some basic connection to the past. The perdurability of certain natural features connects modern perceptions with ancient observations of landmarks and land formations, so that the modern percipient need not feel wholly separated from the events of the siege of Troy:

> wear away wear away earth air water fire
>
>
> We can see the landmarks Hektor saw
> Scamander's ancient course twin-peaked Samothrace
> most distant Athos beacon-platform in clear light
>
> Of all marks named and old in memory before Troy was
> there were name-givers   Who then dare deny existence
> to those whose names are linked forever with Troy   (*PV*, p.155)

This section marks a significant turning point in the poem. In the first four cantos of the sequence Coffey observes time as a relentless process of obliteration that is beyond the bounds of human comprehension. For example, in the second section he observes that

> We can not hold time fast in our sights

> as if judging events in a moment unique
> like hill-top watcher taking Battle in at a glance
>
> We were not present to discover
> how what it was became what it is
> nor see how one performs freely the long foreseen   (*PV*, p.152)

The first four sections of the poem emphasize the modern percipient's essential powerlessness before time's changes ('One would have had to watch out ten thousand years / to notice change between the nodal crests'), yet in canto 5 his attention shifts to those things that have endured, and were observed, and of which the names and features are familiar to a modern audience. Here nature assumes a less antagonistic, less obliterative aspect. These are not mere random landmarks or notable mountains, but are natural formations associated – both by Coffey and in the cultural memory – with the action of Troy. We do not just see landmarks, but see 'the landmarks Hektor saw', and the Scamander is a minor river that has assumed major cultural proportions because of the Homeric bequest.

It is appropriate to ask, then, how this significant alteration, from time being imagined as erosive to a conception of time as resistible, is brought about. Coffey answers that it is the interest of stories to be embedded in time – 'Talk we do of years in ten times ten to the power nine / so long so long is making a stage for stories' (*PV*, p.155). Although the time intervening between modernity and an ancient past may be disjunctive, we are still fascinated by a character isolated by a deed so that the distance in time does not diminish our fascination with that person or his predicament.

> Time Time   There is the slow accretion of snowdrift time
> and there is time racing in stop-watch thousandths to the hour
> for doomed Hektor to stand alone at the Skaean Gates   (*PV*, p.155)

After being introduced in the first canto of the sequence, Hektor does not appear by name until this reappearance at the end of canto 5. Coffey does not allow his reader to escape the distancing implications of this 'slow accretion of snowdrift time', as the difference between Hektor's world and our own intrudes immediately with the modern reference to 'stop-watch' seconds. Throughout the sequence he insists upon this intrusiveness of modernity into his attempts to describe the heroic past of Hektor (a technique that resembles, but reverses, his borrowings of phrases or concepts from antiquity to create a sense of distance from modern readers). Even Hektor's death unleashes the quintessentially modern vision of destruction, 'Doom now in the air like a cloudy mushroom swags above Troy' (*PV*, p.160). A less careful poet might employ this technique of juxtaposition – the modern describing the ancient – merely to startle or to distract with inapposite analogies. But for Coffey this temporally doubled presentation of Hektor's story has a larger intention. With this technique Coffey reposes the apparently settled question of the connectedness of modernity and antiquity. By writing of ancient events in modern images, Coffey emphasizes modernity's difficulties in comprehending a classical world that is inevitably coloured by contemporary analogies and experiences. Although Homer's poetical accomplishments establish compelling characters on the 'stage for stories', Coffey's continued use of modern references insistently reminds the reader of the vast chronological distances being transcended. It is to Coffey's purpose to insist on this distance for, by the end of the sequence, he will argue that the intervening time is not something merely obliterative, nor is it an obscuring factor to be transcended by the modern poet. Rather, the whole of the *Death of Hektor* sequence will suggest that the intervention of time between ourselves and antiquity ultimately contributes to a more complete understanding of Hektor, and establishes a significant connection between Hektor and ourselves that antiquity itself was denied by its proximity to Hektor, and to Homer.

It is pertinent to pause here to observe that in grappling with the relevance of classical precedent to modern life and modern creativity, Coffey was engaging in an artistic experiment that tied him directly to the most advanced literary experiments of his own lifetime, that is, to the work of the Modernists. One of the more self-conscious proclamations of the Modernist movement was its repeated insistence upon remaking modernity with blocks of previous cultures, often classical. The appeal of reusing ancient material was widespread in Modernism, but the resulting attempts to forge a modernity out of classical examples often appear grafted upon determinedly contemporary writings. Eliot's Tireseas has little relation to, or integration into, the modern London on which he comments; Pound's Confucius fits uneasily into transatlantic modernity, and in *The Cantos* occupies instead the role of a rather gnomic model of proper conduct with which to reprove contemporary society; and Joyce's *Ulysses* largely appropriates the Odyssean structure of events without seriously integrating true classicism into its modernity. That Coffey had the Joycean example in mind while composing *Death of Hektor* seems incontestable, as he makes an indisputably Joycean reference to Homeric compositional techniques in the line 'He pared no fingernails not indifferent' (PV, p.156), which echoes a passage from Joyce's *A Portrait of the Artist as a Young Man*.[1] Yet where Joyce borrows the journey narrative and sequence of events of the *Odyssey* as a scaffolding for his parodic masterpiece, Coffey adopts the less architectural approach of examining the encounter of a modern reader with an ineluctably distinct antiquity. By emphasizing the difficulties of memory, time and cultural difference, Coffey demonstrates that the ancient and the modern are not conveniently interchangeable epochs. The difficulty that most occupies his attention, and which forms much of the matter of *Death of Hektor*, is the relentlessly intruding difference of perspective that passing time has forced upon a modern reader. We cannot now see Hektor from the classical perspective without that perspective being inevitably influenced by a perspective antiquity was denied – that is, the perspective of chronological distance. We cannot shed the years in between ourselves and Homer, or Hektor, and are frequently distracted by them.

In the poetical present of *Death of Hektor* – whenever it is that the 'we' of the poem are reading it – the classical world exists besides a modern sense of distance from that world. Although he notes that 'We can see the landmarks that Hektor saw' (*PV*, p.155), Coffey later observes that 'Hektor's Troy became a dusty hill swept by cold winds / image of past or future ravishment of any city / ready like trash junk rubble for earthmover caput out' (*PV*, p.161). Both statements are verifiable, but difficult to cohere. The immediate temptation is to see the landmarks Hektor saw, and to deduce from that evidence a sense of continuity between his world and our own. We see what Hektor saw. Yet the true continuity Coffey addresses is that of the image of Troy destroyed – something Hektor never lived to see – that a poet bequeathed to later generations. If Troy's destruction becomes, in Coffey's assertion, the 'image of past or future ravishment of any city' (*PV*, p.161), one is still left with the difficult task of establishing what precisely links the destruction of a noble ancient citadel to 'past or future' destructions of cities.

That link is Homer. Throughout the sequence, Coffey meditates not only upon the figure of Hektor, but also upon the poet who gave that figure his enduring expression. In the terms established by *Death of Hektor*, Homer is the linking figure who provides modern readers with the story that makes the past engaging and pertinent. In an elegant verbal parallel, Coffey observes in the second section that 'We were not present to discover / how what it was became what it is' (*PV*, p.152), yet by the sequence's end he can proclaim (in section fourteen) that 'Homer has shown us how indeed it was' (*PV*, p.164). In an irony of chronological distance, Homer himself has become obscure to modern readers, so that we know little of the poet himself: 'Homer where born where buried of whom the son / what journeys undertaken not known His work / abides' (*PV*, p.156). Homer truly does belong to the 'unrecorded past', at least in the factual details of his life. His work, however, remains, and that is what gives continuing importance to his life; and in this fact one perceives an encouraging analogous linkage between the hopelessly unreachable antiquity of Hektor and the relevance of his actions to a modern sensibility.

But although Homer's work doubtlessly abides there remains the question of how it has been changed by time. Scholars, for one, have intervened: 'Scholars   Establishment   Well-filled heads / how in vain hope of the definitive critic supreme ... / They say   let them say What poems have They made' (*PV*, p.157). Despite this academic obstructionism, Coffey suggests that a modern reader has, in fact, gained a certain perspective that may have been unattainable to those for whom Homer first composed the *Iliad* – 'what would not have pleased his client banqueters ... / yet at last might reach our raddled selves' (*PV*, p.156). His argument here is not merely the commonplace observation that modern readers will respond differently to Homer's Hektor than did pre-Christian Greek audiences in Homer's time. Instead, Coffey suggests, the distance between our world and Hektor's has made his story no less applicable to us than it was to the first audiences, for although we have lost the cultural similarities of ancient Greeks to Hektor's world, we have the added verifications offered by the intervening history between Hektor and modernity. What initially seems to present an unbridgeable distance between Hektor's circumstances and the present provides, in fact, ample verification of the ongoing human relevance of Hektor's fate and example.

The authorial persona Coffey adopts explicitly attests to the continuing pertinence of Hektor to his own experience of life, despite the irritating encrustations of aesthetic pretension he finds himself obliged to efface. In one of the (apparently) more personal sections of *Death of Hektor*, Coffey addresses his hero directly, subtly questioning the notion that there is 'nothing to say' of what we are to Hektor:

> Hektor across three thousand years your gasped plea
> for befittingness has filled my ears since boyhood
> In pictures then I saw you stand beautiful against the sky

facing Achilles facing the inescapable spear
so strangely pictured by sentimental art
one could hear the aesthete dame breathe 'How effective'   (*PV*,
p.163)

This satirical presentation of 'the aesthete dame' humorously leavens the more pressing point that it is Hektor's nobility, his urge towards the befitting, that still resonates across three thousand years. Those years have given Coffey the perspective of one who cannot look at so horrible a death (and the infamous damaging of the soul effected by Achilles' desecration of his corpse) and see only aesthetic effectiveness. Here, too, Coffey emphasizes the continuing relevance of Hektor's predicament and example. Although chronological distance has brought with it the sentimentality that can look at bloody death and regard it as merely an opportunity for aesthetic depiction, it has also sharpened the example of Hektor for those willing to interact imaginatively with his predicament. The three thousand years that separate Hektor from modernity have demonstrated only too horribly the need for the befittingness he seeks. Because we have three thousand years of evidence of the ongoing tendency of humanity to glorify the outrageous when it triumphs in battle, the sheer futility of his 'plea for befittingness' also gains in human resonance over time. We know that Hektor's plea will fail, even as he utters it, just as we know that he will fail the test to which Achilles induces him before Achilles issues the challenge. For a poet at the end of the twentieth century, the unanswered plea for befittingness of a man about to be slaughtered in battle possesses a terrible modernity.

It is this sense of the need for befittingness that the modern reader appreciates better than might Homer's first audience. For Coffey, the years between Homer and the present provide too much evidence of cruelty and barbarism to make Achilles anything but questionable, and likely detestable. Coffey's Achilles is relentless and without dignity or compassion:

belly-ripper head-splitter neck-lopper
skewering fighters commoners heroes alike
with ash-tree spear gift of his father weapon unique ...
tossing from it corpses to river Xanthus choking it
cursing the dying mocking the dead   action man galore
of slaughter   mindless glory   embodied hatred's stench of blood
cool malice   merciless   Achaean paramount
true professional   (*PV*, p.157)

This is not precisely the Achilles of Homer, who, amidst his slaughters, is tender with Patroclos, shares a leader's camaraderie with his soldiers and displays a meaningful compassion in releasing to Priam the corpse of his son. Coffey's Achilles is a more modern figure, a soldier of the age of the 'true professional' in war, whose 'cool malice' and 'merciless' activities render him a figure of ghastly recognizability to modern readers. To emphasize this modernity of Achilles as a 'professional' warrior, Coffey moderates the significant role played by the gods in Homer's depiction of Hektor's death. Where Homer presents Athena actively confusing Hektor by assuming the guise of Paris, Coffey presents almost in passing the 'aiding gods' who assist Achilles; Coffey's interest is less in adhering strictly to his Homeric precedent than in presenting those elements of Hektor's plight that still resonate in human experience three thousand years later. We do not recognize, in modern experience, the influence of the Greek gods, yet the figure of a calmly professional assailant without mercy is one that retains contemporary resonance.

By suggesting that Hektor's true value to modernity lies in his 'plea for befittingness' Coffey also undercuts some of the assumptions his readers may bring to *Death of Hektor*. As we observed, he presents his titular figure with no introduction, Hektor appears, unintroduced, and we are challenged to consider 'what we are to Hektor' and 'what Hektor is to us'. The immediate response is, of course, to revert to Homer. Yet Coffey does not permit his readers to take refuge in notions of heroism and glory that may suggest themselves in an imprecise or incomplete reading of the *Iliad*; what he omits is as important as what he includes. Coffey's Hektor is not the warrior Homer shows repeatedly killing Achaeans, but is instead the man who meets his ineluctable death with a dignified plea for befittingness. That Hektor killed others is in fact less important here than is the integrity of his concerns as he dies. Thus Coffey disrupts potential readings of Hektor as a hero. His death is not important because he was an heroic figure in warfare, but because he meets his death with an honourable concern for befittingness. It is in the dignity of the dying Hektor that Coffey finds the most meaningful answer to 'what Hektor is to us'; we are not to be misled by the excitement of his activities in warfare, but are to be moved instead by his dying plea for befittingness.

In the final two cantos of the sequence Coffey asserts that we can see, through our experience of the intervening time, 'how indeed it was', that is, to see in Hektor and Achilles the subtle shades of value with which Homer embues them. In canto fourteen, Coffey writes with uncommon emphasis of what modern readers can learn of Hektor and Achilles in Homer's presentation:

> His liking Hektor we infer from how he shows
> Hektor's home wife child frightening helmet crest
> and how he shows Greek self-styled heroes
> at slaughter and jealous play
>
> False picture false childhood standards war not human not good
> Conflict it is struggle dismembering steel unmanning bolt
> unworthying by unworthy grinning for who'd eat one raw   (*PV*, p.164)

Here there are no longer any ambiguities lost in time. In Hektor's age, as in Coffey's, there is the implacable fact, 'war not human not good'. Yet the means by which we infer that Homer liked Hektor are extremely important, as they are not martial, being instead the virtues of a home life, quietly lived outside of battle with a wife and child. It is this emphasis upon Hektor's domestic life that reveals his true relevance to modernity. After his plea for befittingness, he is killed and his body dishonoured, but his story does not end in this death; he leaves behind the cherished remnants of his life. For this reason Coffey does not end *Death of Hektor* with the death of Hektor, but follows instead the Odyssean – and, for that matter, Joycean – structure of concluding his work with the domestic aspect of his hero, and the most important figure in that life, his wife. *Death of Hektor* therefore ends not with Hektor, but with Andromache:

> And he gave us his Andromache lamenting
> like any woman victim of any war robbed of her world
> her husband her child her friends her linen her pots and pans
> the years it took to put a home together living against the grain
> of great deeds   her woman's life   in her heart
> much held fast   word hidden for all   (*PV*, p.165)

Here, alas, is the true continuity between antiquity and modernity that *Death of Hektor* explores. The connection is exact and explicit; the wife left behind by a death in combat laments 'like any woman victim of any war'. Here, at the end of the sequence, there is no time, or rather, there is no difference in time. Although readers may struggle to establish a sense of continuity between modernity and the ancient circumstances of Hektor's death, finding them in his still relevant plea for befittingness, there is no difficulty whatever in spanning the years between Andromache's plight and that of any woman 'robbed of her world / her husband her child her friends ... her woman's life'.

The true disaster of Hektor's death is not the loss of one life alone, but the concomitant destruction of the lives he shared with his family. Andromache is left alone at the sequence's end, just as she is left alone by the death of Hektor. Her pain is not attributable to the fact that the man she has lost is a hero, or would become a central figure of Western literature, but simply to the fact that he was her husband and she loved him. If Hektor is still meaningful to modernity in the decency for which he pleads at his death, his wife is equally resonant in her desolation after her family life is destroyed.

Coffey's presentation of time in *Death of Hektor* has thus come full circle. Where he once began by questioning 'what we are to Hektor' and 'what Hektor is to us', he eventually reveals the answer – they are predecessors whose pain and dignity are no less applicable today than they were in ancient Troy. Across three thousand years the extremities of human suffering do not differ, although the circumstances alter. After so much time it is apparent that Hektor's plight before a merciless enemy, and Andromache's familial calamity, befall women and men in many locations, and in many circumstances, in every era. Present loss is made no more excusable, or less poignant, by the precedents of antiquity. Yet those agonies may be slightly more bearable by the assurance of human experiential continuity to which Homer, and Coffey, contribute by their poetry. Although one may be faced with an implacable enemy, or stripped of husband and family, there remains the Homeric example of the past with which one can still feel a sense of community, and to which one may still establish a relationship, however distant and however despairing in its parallels. In establishing such a connection, Coffey's poem offers perhaps some little consolation through its persuasive engagement with Homeric antiquity.

NOTES

1. Coffey's line 'He pared no fingernails not indifferent' echoes the following passage from Joyce's *A Portrait of the Artist as a Young Man*: 'The artist, like the God of the creation, remains within or behind or beyond or above his handiwork, invisible, refined out of existence, indifferent, paring his fingernails.' James Joyce, *A Portrait of the Artist as a Young Man*, ed. Seamus Deane (Harmondsworth: Penguin, 1992), p.233.

CHAPTER EIGHTEEN

Coffey with TV:
A Personal Memoir

MICHAEL SMITH

I had been on the Arts Council for some time and had got to know Seán Ó Mórdha, the distinguished and award-winning television documentary maker. Seán was very interested in the Thirties Generation of Irish poets whose work I had vigorously promoted through New Writers' Press, and one day I raised the possibility of Seán making some kind of documentary on Brian Coffey, who was alive and reasonably well and living in Southampton. Seán showed immediate enthusiasm and asked me to find out if Brian would be interested in such a project. I said I would, and I set about contacting Brian right away. The response was positive. Always interested in new things, Brian thought the documentary would be fun to do.

Over a few weeks and a fair deal of correspondence Brian came up with the maddest notions about what should be covered by the documentary. He suggested the idea of renting a helicopter to shoot some footage over Newgrange! Seán's response was one of amusement. Other mad ideas were broached by Brian. Finally Seán decided that the best plan of action was simply to get Brian over and to play the whole thing by ear. That seemed to me also the best way forward. There was no script and no plan. The only format was Brian talking to me about more or less whatever would come into his head as we found ourselves in various places, which Seán would decide.

Brian came over with his wife Bridget and they stayed with Brian's brother, Don, in Terenure. I think they came on a Saturday. I managed to get some time off from my teaching job, and in my old Beetle I would ferry Brian around to the various locations. He looked frailer than the last time I had seen him, and the cold weather at the time wasn't exactly suitable for outdoor film-making. But Brian was his usual chirpy self and had himself well tucked up in a jacket and scarf. Initially we talked about all sorts of things except the documentary. That didn't help my anxiety, knowing that we were to start work on the following Monday. So I decided that we had better form some idea of what we were going to talk about, whatever about locations. Brian thought that he would like to focus on the 'making' of poetry, though he would not exclude he said, with a mischievous smile, his right to be digressive when he felt like it.

I put this idea forward to Seán, who readily agreed with it. He knew that so long as he had canned a week's footage, he could edit the material into a half-hour programme. I think Brian, however, was rather naïve about film-making and thought he could get away with all sorts of little tricks he had up his sleeve (in fact, he did try a few of these tricks, such as putting Terry Wogan forward as Ireland's greatest export to Britain, which Seán had to edit out).

Our first location was the National Library of Ireland in Kildare Street. Brian and I would emerge from the revolving door chatting and continue chatting in the portico outside, made famous by Joyce in *Ulysses*. Seán gave instructions about the pace of our walk and when and where we were to stop and talk. The big gate in front of the library entrance was opened so that the camera could get a good cinematic perspective. The film crew was small: Seán, his wife Kitty, a camera-man and a sound-man. Brian began talking before we made our exit. No doubt prompted by the library ambience, he started talking about the Celtic Twilight and its flickering ghosts. I simply listened, appreciative of Brian's sly jokes at the Celtic Twilighters. As we emerged from the revolving door I heard Seán shout 'Roll' and then, suddenly I froze. My mind went completely blank and I felt disoriented. My panicked response was to shout 'Cut!' to the amazement of everyone involved except Brian, who was quite nonchalant. Recovering, I said to Seán that I must have a cigarette or I would be totally useless. He acquiesced but couldn't help remarking that my cigarette was probably the single most expensive cigarette that was ever smoked in Ireland. That was really my one and only camera fright throughout the following week. Brian found the whole business rather amusing. 'There, there,' he said in his customary way, 'no need to worry'.

Our next location was on the other side of Leinster House, the National Museum of Ireland. Seán had got permission to keep a section of it clear of visitors. I had no idea what we were doing there except that it provided Seán with some visually interesting background. I can't recall whether it was Seán or Brian who spotted a three-faced head on a plinth. The multiple faces of the poet, his personae. That was enough to get Brian started. Always wonderfully and fluently articulate, Brian chatted on about poetry. As for myself, I was more preoccupied with Seán's instructions about the direction and speed of my walking. But it was Brian's show and I knew that anything he would say would be of interest. My role was to be talked at.

Where did we go after that? I think we went to Merrion Park, an appropriate enough setting since Brian's father and family had lived on Merrion Square for some years. Brian could recall seeing Yeats and George Russell. He also remembered how cold and uncomfortable was the Georgian house where he had once lived. In the Park, Brian talked about poetry as propaganda, political and otherwise. He was vehemently opposed to this; a deeply religious man, Brian considered poetry, or, more precisely, the poem, as a gift of the Holy Spirit, a gift that enabled a vision of something beyond the merely empirical. This did not, of course, exclude the comic: how could it when human life is seen *sub specie aeternitatis*? My most vivid memory of our stint in Merrion Park was Brian giving his own peculiar rendition of a Beatles song as well as a moving reading of some of Denis Devlin's poetry.

Later in the week there was a trip to the suburbs. During this, Brian read a section of his 'Missouri Sequence' and also a poem by Mallarmé. He read unpretentiously but with due regard to the cadence of the poetry. It is a part of the documentary that I treasure and I am delighted it is on film.

Our last trip was on a Friday, I think. We went to the Malahide estuary where Seán was convinced he could get some nice background footage. The plan was for Brian and myself to stroll along a narrow strip of beach, finally disappearing into the distance. Initially, things couldn't have been better. There was a fine strip of beach, the light was good and even a few splendid swans showed up. Seán was delighted with this. The camera began rolling and then, horror of horrors, a jet flew overhead drowning out all speech. We had to start again. But within a couple of minutes a group of local schoolchildren on a nature walk came along, shouting their heads off. Cut! A third effort was made. But the light was growing poor for filming, and to make matters seriously worse, the tide was coming in and the strip of beach was now quite flooded. However, there was no starting up again. It was Seán's last chance. Time and everything else was running out on him. We had to go for it.

Above the water-edge were extremely irregular dunes. We would have to make do with these. This last scene is quite comic on film.

Brian and myself moved off, Brian chatting away to his heart's content, totally unperturbed. But as we walked away from the camera into the distance, it was impossible for Brian and myself to stay on the same level. So what we ended up with was a scenario of these two figures finding it impossible to stay on the same level: an up-and-down stroll, two Beckettian figures fading with their talk into the distance. We had to tread carefully and, given Brian's frailty, I was all the time anxious that there might be a mishap. But Brian coped superbly, completely unfazed.

It had been a demanding week for all concerned, yet I think we all comported ourselves admirably and even enjoyably in the circumstances. That evening we adjourned to a pub where we had a few drinks to celebrate the mission accomplished.

On the Saturday, next day, I drove Brian out to Montrose where Seán taped Brian's conversation that ranged over a lot of subjects, including his memories of Beckett. I have never heard these tapes, but I hope they are safely stored in the RTÉ archives.

Brian had a profound admiration and affection for Beckett. He was always insistent that despite Beckett's professed atheism, he had a deeply rooted spiritual longing. This, I know, is debatable, and it has certainly been denied by many Beckett scholars. But I have always thought there was something in what Brian thought. Why should anyone be horrified by the absurdity of human life unless one felt that it ought not to be so? Swift had that *saeva indignatio*; and although it may be explained in terms of psychology or psychopathology, it raises the challenge of a Manichaeism that posits not only the forces of evil (the Devil) but also a god of some sort. Apart from his deep appreciation of Beckett's writing (and Brian had read everything by Beckett), it was Beckett's compassion for the human condition that I think most impressed him. He thought that too often the vaudeville dimension of Beckett's writings was overplayed by theatre directors, emphasizing the comic at the expense of the tragic vision that lay behind it. I think that is summed up in the following quotation from a piece Brian wrote on Beckett many years ago (and reproduced in this volume).[1] It was in fact during the 1970s in London, and Brian had not seen Beckett for some time:

> We were on a bridge, lake waters on each side. A mother was placing bread crumbs on her about five-year-old daughter's head, above which the birds, gulls and pigeons planed and hovered. The child was awaiting the alighting of airborne feet, webbed or

scratching, the small face of expectation and concern. I heard Sam exclaim: 'Look, Brian, look!' And I looked to see the scarred, wrecked and still beautiful features declaring his delight, his happiness at another like human sharing the feelings that had been his own much more than fifty years ago. *Ever the same anew.* The real Beckett ... who has discovered compassion and loving in the night of agony, in the man-made midden of malice.

Brian himself, as a believing Catholic, did not suffer the spiritual anguish of his friend Beckett. He was lucky, I suppose, in that respect. It gave equanimity to his personality that had nothing to do with smugness and everything to do with what we often mean by 'wisdom'. It was a wisdom from which I was fortunate to benefit over the many years of our relationship. Our week's filming with Seán Ó Mórdha was one more display of Brian's 'wisdom', his mischievous wit and broad tolerance.

NOTES

1. See Brian Coffey's memoir 'More and/or Less than Fifty Years Ago' about his friendship with Beckett, which appears in this volume as chapter 9.

CHAPTER NINETEEN

'Must not attempt escape / from here and now': Maurice Scully Reading Brian Coffey

KIT FRYATT

I 'HUMMING [THE WORDS]': SCULLY READING COFFEY

Maurice Scully reads rapidly. His tone is light without quirkiness, expressive without melodrama. As befits a poet whose unit of composition is, as he has often claimed, 'the book',[1] he doesn't allow his listeners time to brood over individual passages, lines or verbal effects. He describes this as an inclusive manoeuvre:

> Including the reader in another sense I'm rather keen on at this stage, in the sense of live reading, so the readers can get over the chimera of supposed 'difficulty' and just quite literally go with the flow and enjoy the experience and sense the form of the thing in the air, right there.[2]

At the Continuings symposium in October 2005, Scully read the seventh section of Brian Coffey's poem *Advent* (1975). He made Coffey's poem his own to the extent that its 'form … in the air' resembled closely a reading from his 'trilogy' *Things That Happen*,[3] or more recent work, such as that published in the sampler *Doing The Same in English* (2008).[4] Scully transferred to his reading of Coffey the same speed, the quizzical tone, the concern that the reader should experience the work 'right there' rather than be stalled by 'difficulty' that are hallmarks of his own performances.

Coffey himself was concerned with issues of performance and annotated poems for his own readings and recordings. Unfortunately, recordings of Coffey reading his own poems are not readily available, though the University of Delaware holds a cassette recording of selections from *Advent*, amongst other audio material. Some annotations

for a reading of *Advent* also survive, and were published by hardPressed
Poetry in the first issue of the magazine *The Journal* in 1999.[5] Scully's
poetry appears in the same issue, so it is reasonable to conjecture that
he was familiar with Coffey's annotations, but hard to say to what
extent they may have influenced his own performance, since the notes
are for the most part not discursive, simply a series of oblique slashes
to indicate pauses and breaks.

Scully's poetry sometimes resembles Coffey's on the page, too. 'The
Pillar & the Vine' describes insect or spider eggs in free-fall:

    tiny

                eggs

    fell
                    lightly

    moving
                    in the

    wind

                    around the

    edge of the

                base of the

            stopped

    stone pillar[6]

This resembles the opening of section 7 of *Advent* not just in its shape
but in its concern to complicate distinctions between organic and non-
organic matter:

    White   fir

                palm   salt

    cry   chill

	soil	sand	
glass			sea
	gorse	bee	
	shell	maid	
health		white	(*PV*, p.140)

These aural and visual resemblances suggest the interest of an exploration of Coffey's influence on Scully.

Coffey and his contemporaries Denis Devlin and Thomas Mac-Greevy have often been claimed as precursors of the neo-modernist poets who started to publish in the late 1960s, 1970s and 1980s: writers such as Trevor Joyce, Randolph Healy, Geoffrey Squires and Catherine Walsh. This assertion, initially voiced by Michael Smith of New Writers' Press, has become something of a critical commonplace, repeated a number of times by John Goodby in his book *Irish Poetry Since 1950* (2000) and endorsed by the structure of Alex Davis' essay on poetic modernism for the *Cambridge Companion to Contemporary Irish Poetry* (2003). Renewed critical attention to Coffey, Devlin and MacGreevy has begun to challenge their status as founding trinity. The original, rather *ad hoc* constitution of them as a group, in Samuel Beckett's 1934 survey 'Recent Irish Poetry', is being examined and re-read.[7] Coffey arguably presents a more interesting case with regard to Irish poets of Scully's generation than either Devlin or MacGreevy. He continued to publish late enough in his long life to be their contemporary as well as a precursor; his characteristic idiom seems closest to that of the younger poets. He shares with Scully, in particular, an observant, engaged, but non-interventionist *persona*.

The genealogical lines of descent often traced in Irish literary criticism, whereby, for example, Irish poets are seen as 'heirs of Joyce' by critics with backgrounds and approaches as different as Neil Corcoran and Andrew Duncan,[8] are less than helpful in exploring Coffey's relationship to younger poets, given the near contemporaneity of his later work with theirs, and their quizzical, challenging attitude towards hierarchy and authority. Rather than attempt the problematic task of identifying 'influence', I want to read back through Scully's 'trilogy' to find points of contact with Coffey's later poems, particularly *Advent*. Two such points of contact seem of particular interest: the first thematic, the second structural and attitudinal.

Both Coffey and Scully write extensively about domestic life, an emphasis that may at first seem odd, given Modernist reservations about identitarianism, expressed with exasperated brio by Scully in the *Metre* interview:

> As a prentice poet in the '70s the 'I' was very big in Irish poetry. It still is? Me, my, I. I love you. You love me. And Mumsy and Popsy down on the farm show my Roots are Real & deck me out with Colourful Relatives I can't wait to write about. A really strange hand-me-down Identikit.[9]

Scully attacks poetry that uses family history to make claims of autochthony and authenticity, but there is also an implication that in its preoccupation with 'Mumsy and Popsy ... Colourful Relatives', Irish poetry has evaded its responsibilities. Irish poets cast themselves as children, recipients of a 'hand-me-down Identikit'. Their subject matter and formal approach to it are inherited, precluding both formal experiment and the concern for futurity expressed in *Advent*. In Coffey and Scully's work alike, however, the poetic voice is adult, often parental. Though both poets also write about parents from the perspective of a son, the speaking voice is still adult, responsible, preoccupied by care. As such, it must negotiate power and authority, a process which draws attention to the two poets' similarities of structure and outlook. Both document the destructive effects of human imposition of order upon the world, and seek to derive pattern from their poetic material, rather than impressing preordained form upon it. At the same time – as the excerpts from *Advent* and *Livelihood* above illustrate – both poets explore and complicate notions of the organic and the artificial, nature and culture.

II 'OUR DEBTS & OUR SPIRITED / BABY DAUGHTER': FAMILIAR PERSPECTIVES

'Missouri Sequence', a work often considered to mark Coffey's return to poetry after a long 'silent' period – though its compositional history is more complex than this suggests – resonates with the sound and movement of the poet's children: 'one each minute / past my desk they go' (*PV*, p.69). Though merry, the children persistently remind the poet of his duty of care. Their play is equally a manifestation of genius and of unease: 'Tonight the poetry is in the children's game: / I am distracted by comparisons' (*PV*, p.69). The comparisons he proceeds to draw situate the poet between Ireland and America, living 'far from where / my mother grows very old', but near Byrnesville, a community that has received many Irish immigrants. The poet's children 'know nothing of Ireland / they grow American', but it is his reflection on their adopted national identity that reminds him: 'we must leave America / bitter necessity no monopoly / on Irish soil' (*PV*, pp.70–71). This speaker's situation is displaced, but it is not one that lends itself to facile celebration or theorization of 'liminal' spaces. As father and son, he has specific responsibilities that lie on both sides of the Atlantic, and he is forced to make a choice which he resents. The choice, as it turns out, has nothing to do with essentialism, or with its rejection and the assumption of a displaced persona, it is simply the result of being 'charged with care of others' (*PV*, p.72). The poet's resentment of it, however, flings him back into identitarianism: 'rejecting prudence to make of conflict / a monument to celtic self-importance' (*PV*, p.71).

'Missouri Sequence' deals self-reflexively with the recovery of poetic facility – we observe the poet 'writing verses at [his] desk' (*PV*, p.82), 'making poetry' (*PV*, p.83). In this process his children play an ambiguous role. Much as their game of Follow-My-Leader, which begins the sequence, is both poetic in itself and a distraction for the poet, so they are themselves both stimulating and ensnaring:

> The room is filled with children's lives
> that fill my cares who turn again
> to sudden starting words
> like birds in cages.   (*PV*, p.73)

In the third poem of 'Missouri Sequence', the speaker, among children recently released from school for the summer, resolves to 'show the poet as hunter, / one who would not let me be / among the children' (*PV*, p.78). The delicate phrasing aligns the poet with the muse figure he goes on to describe, and both with a 'hunter'. Depending on how we read the line-break, the muse is both one who persistently assails him ('would not let me be') even in the distracting company of his family, and one who removes him from that familiar context ('would not let me be among the children'). Towards the close of this poem, the speaker reflects on the intimate connection of poet and 'true muse fleshed': 'is a torment of oneself / cannot be done without' (*PV*, p.80), and here the children become, decisively, a distraction, a scattering of concentration:

> Her I would have stayed with
> but the children shouting
> in their scrambling play
> rushed on me scattering
> me everyway.   (*PV*, p.80)

None the less, the speaker's future depends on his discovery of equilibrium, a painful integration of the 'true muse' into the familial self, a process tracked in the final poem of the sequence:

> This much is certain
> he will not forget her beauty,
> he must not attempt escape
> from here and now.   (*PV*, p.81)

The more scattered references to family and children in Scully's *Things That Happen* display a similar ambiguity. In *Zulu Dynamite*, the second book of *Livelihood*, we find a portrait of the speaker which gives us an idea of how personal, familial and social identities might be subject to erasure: '*a charcoal sketch* / unemployed, passable education / late thirties, father, husband, poet *erase erase erase*'.[10] As in 'Missouri Sequence', with its critique of 'celtic self-importance', this is not an apolitical process, for all it might also be domestic:

> everything run through this tensely amalgamated
> shadow-corps so that so many young practitioners
> don't even know how much's been filtered out or that
> anything has been *erase* / *erase* in the first place[11]

Where Coffey's critique of 'celtic' identitarianism rests with the self, Scully suggests his speaker's entanglement in wider social processes that have become naturalized, so that 'younger practitioners' don't see them as constructed at all (the tongue-in-cheek paranoiac tone, incidentally, is typical of *Livelihood* and *Things That Happen* as a whole).

Scully's attitude to the familial as poetic material is set even before the beginning of the text of *Livelihood*. The book has as one of its frontispiece illustrations a drawing of birds by Leda Scully, the poet's daughter, done when she was 8 years old. Any sense of sentimentality generated by the inclusion of this drawing is mitigated by its quality: though naïve in style and treatment of anatomy, it demonstrates a precocious ability in handling visual space. The artistic accomplishments of the poet's children are a minor, but distinct theme in *Things That*

Happen, and as in 'Missouri Sequence', the poet finds himself awkwardly positioned between seeing them as genii of art and hindrances to his own artistic expression.

Children in Scully's poems often have a better eye for colour and visual space than adults: 'Talking colours with my son – he's five, I'm / thirty-nine / he's right, I'm an idiot'.[12] In interview, Scully pays tribute to the 'childlike intelligent directness' of Paul Klee, adding, 'My children have taught me a lot'.[13] None the less, children have to be excluded from the poet's workspace: early in the first volume of *Things That Happen*, *5 Freedoms of Movement*, we find the poet wedging a 'brick or two against the broken door to keep my little daughter out'.[14] The poem goes on to form, however, out of surrounding noises, what Scully calls the 'penetrating signature of ... everywhere I've lived',[15] including 'a baby's babbling'.[16] As in Coffey's poetry, children function, Romantically, as possessors of purer and less inhibited vision than adults, as obstacles to the poet's composition, and as the very material of poetry itself: 'children's lives / ... turn again / the sudden starting words' (*PV*, p.73).

Much of *Things That Happen* takes place in a domestic space, and readers frequently find themselves with the poet in his workroom, among his 'shaky' shelving and other 'lumber', from which inquisitive children have been perforce, but imperfectly, banished.[17] The domestic does not provide Scully with a retreat from political concerns; indeed, even the presence and energy of the poet's children become politicized. In *Zulu Dynamite*, the poet, living in an African country (Scully lived and taught in Lesotho during the 1980s) reflects on his rich neighbours:

> & the new occupants of
> the refurbished house are entertaining guests
> for the first time under the somewhat soulless
> glitter of its new chandeliers. every morning
> for the past two months now their workmen woke
> us a little too early for neighbourly good cheer,
> while the owners slept elsewhere.[18]

A place's 'penetrating signature' is not always matter for celebration, nor can it always find its way directly into poetry. Much of the material of *Livelihood* is sonic – there are repeated motifs of rain on a corrugated iron roof and a writing implement upon various surfaces – but the sound of these refurbishments, carried out while the house's owners were 'elsewhere', needs social and political context in order to become meaningful.

The poet notes the hierarchical, allegorical significance of the neighbours' display: 'their daughter is animated. she is wearing an / elaborate dress. expense as a category, neither / beautiful nor ugly, an exclusionary placard', and contrasts it with his own situation:

> my wife & I worry about our debts & our spirited
> baby daughter. & the difficulty of getting out of
> this mess & learning the language & dodging the main
> streets at rush-hour so as not to run into anybody
> we might owe money to.[19]

'Spirited' and 'animated' are synonyms, yet the poet's daughter, set within the ampersand-riddled framework of her parents' 'debts' and 'dodging', seems alive where the neighbours' daughter is blandly galvanised, animated only in the sense that a drawing or a clay model might be. This effect is magnified in the next stanza, in which the same adjective is used to describe the dinner guests:

> their guests are animated, courses served on silver
> platters, father at the head of the table, he
> seems not very much older than myself (but don't
> let's confuse fascination for envy), there is talk
> & movement &/but, from here it is utterly silent –
> listen – & sad. Ghosts ... [20]

This is at least potentially sententious – implying that the poet's precarious life is preferable to bourgeois comfort, which leaves those who enjoy it psychically dead as either 'animated' zombies or 'sad. Ghosts' – but something else is at work in the speaker's defensive tone. Denying that he is envious, he raises the possibility of envy; acknowledging that in age at least he is similar to the complacent *paterfamilias* across the road, he implicitly questions the extent to which his assumption of the duty of care for his 'spirited baby daughter' also places him in a position of patriarchal authority. This concern is mirrored in the structure of the poem, which is framed by two claims. At the beginning of the poem the speaker states, 'sometimes the facts almost *are* the emotions', and concludes, 'sometimes the facts and the emotions blur'. With the first claim, the poet asserts that the political facts of class and inequality coincide with his feelings about them; with the final, far blander claim, he seems to have assumed some of the authority he began by questioning.

III RESISTING 'AW. DAH.'

The characteristic speaker of both Scully's and Coffey's poems must confront his own negotiations with and assumptions of structures of authority. The dominant mood of both poets' work, however, is one of resistance to hierarchy and unease with the propensity of humans to interfere with and restructure their surroundings for their own convenience. Coffey and Scully use material that is immediately to hand – often domestic material, as we saw above – as the subject matter and structuring principle of their poetry, and their shared attitude to this material is one of non-intervention, non-manipulation, a 'Waiting Posture', as Scully terms it in the last poem of *Steps* in *Livelihood*.[21]

Advent is necessarily a poem which assumes a 'Waiting Posture': its voice, which is elegiac but also makes elegy problematic, observes and describes, but rarely intervenes in the poem's action. The poem's basic metre is a loose hexameter, minimally punctuated. Inverted commas are used to indicate direct speech and quotation, otherwise Coffey uses space and line breaks to indicate pauses. His syntax is fluid and can bear multiple, ambiguous interpretations. For example, this passage from the seventh section, describing a birth that encompasses the certainty of death, can be read in numerous ways:

> Look When parents raise an infant girl or boy
> to whom or what they pray as god what will be
> already they share hearts soaring mourning hearts
>
> Eden it kills us a promise no state here but of dust   (*PV*, p.141)

'Raise' in the first line might be literal, an act of lifting up the child to a sky-god, in which case the lines convey a ritualistic image. It might also mean 'to bring up', suggesting a much more attenuated and mundane temporal process: parents rearing children in their religious traditions. This ambiguity illustrates in microcosm *Advent*'s treatment of time, which subverts linear and realist assumptions about its nature. The moment of waking might be prolonged, as it is at the beginning of the poem, whereas historical eras and even geological time may pass rapidly: 'Tyrannic roaring   wrenched roots   gulped screams / millions of days and nights and unrecorded' (*PV*, p.113). How we read 'raise' affects our sense of what it means for parents' hearts to 'soar' and 'mourn': is it stark ambivalence, felt at a moment of ritual charge, or a pattern of changes occurring over a longer period of time? It also might affect how we perceive the passage's sense of reciprocity and futurity. Is the future present in the moment or act of raising a child ('what will be / already')? Do we understand parents and children to 'share hearts soaring mourning hearts', perhaps foreshadowing the deathbed scenes of the sixth section?

Coffey's reading notes give us a clue of how one performance might have sounded:

> Look When parents raise an infant girl or boy
> to whom or what they pray as god / <u>what will be</u>
> <u>already they share</u> / hearts soaring mourning hearts
>
> Eden / it kills us / a promise / no state here but of dust[22]

That 'Look ... god' is presented as a single sense or breath unit provides some tentative support, I think, for my intuitions about temporality above, while the emphasis on '<u>what will be / already they</u> <u>share</u>' suggests that Coffey wanted to convey both a sense of futurity residing in the present and a certain reciprocity between parents and child. The breaks in the last line, meanwhile, suggest an outworn, breathless reading, meditating on the nature of death and the fall of man. The unpunctuated original, however, might bear a more politicized reading, which we might annotate as follows: 'Eden: it kills us / a promise: no state here / but of dust'. The myth of Eden 'kills us' because it presupposes (or 'promises') the Fall and death. Moreover, the notion of a paradise and its promise of idyllic life without the need for social organization ('state'), are politically dangerous because they promote fantasies of indigeneity and nostalgic return like those exploited by the tyrant 'Kilroy' in the poem's third section:

> So spun so coiled his reasons round them
> Fed them spell of *Selves Alone*
> *No sun sets on us   This world our home*
> *Our country right or wrong*   and correctly
> Led them though crashing gods into eyeless night   (*PV*, p.124)

This explicit attack on demagoguery is the more effective because Coffey acknowledges the appeal of essentialism and nostalgia in the previous section. At the beginning of the poem's second section, the speaker's contemplation of a scene that is poised between the natural and the made prompts him to interrogate humanity's compulsion to personify its surroundings and its capacity to create nostalgic Golden Ages:

Willow   raincloak
fountain   poplar
jet water   wind arching
     rooted   dance

Why is it when we venture far in among ancient beeches
'Hush' we say   what greets a sudden presence

As if we had been waited for   expected

...

But how it was far back when first fires glowed
ere ever aisling bode unfeared in ruined time

Sleeper stirred summoned in dream and swift to wake
heart cold hair like quills white in mist white with dawn
and present She stood shook mist from ash white curls
eyes green and turquoise   bare smile
with what would he waking match her call but blood   (*PV*, p.117)

Variations in typography in *Advent* usually imply an exploration of boundaries between nature and culture, and the lines that begin this section are no exception, juxtaposing the names of trees with natural materials manipulated to human use ('raincloak', 'fountain'), giving examples of the ways we make metaphors of natural movement ('arching', 'dance'). Among 'ancient beeches' the speaker confronts the otherness of nature, discovering that human beings are not the world's primary presence, but expected guests. This manoeuvre, while it encourages a becoming humility on the part of mankind, inevitably personifies nature, forcing something aniconic into the iconic shape of a 'presence'. Trying to imagine prehistory, the speaker collides with a much more recent 'presence', the allegorized Ireland of eighteenth-century *aisling* poetry. Although he wishes to evoke a time 'ere ever aisling bode', the sky-woman interposes herself and her demand for blood-sacrifice, 'with what would he waking match her call but blood'. The personified image comes to dominate our thinking about nature while 'bright earth lay hushed' (*PV*, p.117). Sentimentally, we celebrate the earth as queen and mother, 'Alma Bountiful ... Alma Mother of all', while wreaking ecological ruin. The image of a maternal earth eventually declines into the love object of a sonnet sequence or the heroine of a fairy-tale, the opportunity to recognize the otherness of our surroundings definitively lost, because we have become enthralled by allegorical images or 'idols':

Laura false advent idol in quiet sufferance of gaze
herwards distracted while earth went on yielding fruit
by rules straitwaistcoated natural bounty in decline
See where thorns thicken grow through what sad centuries
while in idol grip beauty sleeping awaits unopened rose
Laura disclosed no better than wood or stone
yields a joy futureless that points to void beyond   (*PV* p.119)

Scully's approach to the allegorization of nature is more self-reflexive and ironic, but he shares many of Coffey's reservations about making nature meaningful in personified human terms. A 'sonnet' (Scully's sonnets are never fourteen lines of pentameter: perhaps another point of contact with Coffey's distrust of an idolised Petrarchan Laura) from *The Basic Colours*, the first book of *Livelihood*, rewrites 'Among School Children' to suggest the nature of some of these reservations.

The speaker, a teacher, takes a group of students outside to look at a tree. He names and anatomizes its parts, suggesting an eccentric conception of the way things – and perhaps by implication nature and human culture – relate to one another: 'underneath you know / is where the Roots go / to live & hold the Ground together'.[23] He employs a Yeatsian vocabulary of bole and leaves, and with his remark 'look at the Top / How compliant it is to the weather', parodies a complaisant Ledean body. Yeats' Leda epitomizes the natural body imposed upon and given political significance by culture; similarly, the chestnut tree at the close of 'Among School Children' leaves the radical otherness of nature behind to become assimilated to meaning. Scully's persona is scathing about the human capacity to impose significance on natural forms, and yet he finds an anthropocentric position impossible to abandon: the breezes move the leaves 'for literate / old Yahoos like us to note / & have sophisticated doubts about'.[24]

Scully's pupils, rather like those in the school which Yeats visited, are learning 'everything / In the best modern way'[25] – this education, the complacent speaker implies, is their ticket out of poverty and labour: 'this will cover your cracked earth in clover / this will keep you out of the mines / believe me, forever'.[26] Their bodies, however, seem to stage a revolt against their conversion to imprintable Ledean matter: 'hands, arms, eyes / organize & activate'.[27] This prompts a breakdown in their teacher's certainty:

it breaks up
into pieces the
truth

did you
know that
) the yellow castle   ) the terrace of life
) the germinal vesicle
) the
I see nodded each student in the dance
intent, pretending, chipping at the fact
to teach me something, something quite different
I see   I think).[28]

Terms associated with esoteric Buddhism ('yellow castle', 'terrace of life') now jostle with anatomical terminology – the 'germinal vesicle' is the nucleus of an ovum, the Ledean and Yeatsian 'yolk and white' in a primitive state. (The 'yellow castle' may also, incidentally, be a mischievous reference to *The Wizard of Oz* [1900], in which it is the home of the Wicked Witch of the West, who is dissolved, if not quite broken 'into pieces'.[29]) The speaker, at the beginning of the poem, confident that he could resolve the parts of the tree into a coherent and organic whole, has become incoherent. Tutorial authority now seems to rest with the students, 'chipping at the fact / to teach me something'. Like 'Among School Children', whose closing questions are often read rhetorically, but may in fact be genuine queries, this 'sonnet' engages with urgent issues of discrimination. What is the difference between intensity and pretence or between seeing and thinking? What is the different thing the students wish to teach their teacher? How can the grammatical structure 'I see' contain these possibilities?

Scully's poetry works to resist and subvert forms of authority that seek to impose meaning upon the human body and upon the otherness of nature. One of the most striking and explicit articulations of his anti-authoritarian position is the 'ballad' 'The Sirens', which forms the larger part of *Interlude, Livelihood*'s second interstice. 'The Sirens' begins with a pedantic speaker, again, 'facing' a symbolic tree 'in bloom', and noting 'Everything *correct*'.[30] The landscape it describes, however, is one of disintegration and terror. The sirens of the title are furies or fates as well as being literal klaxons: 'thread the streets / ferry the / dead'.[31] The speaker's attempts to mitigate this horror by emphasizing civility, wit and urbanity give rise to an allegorical figure:

Whereupon there
rose up a thing
called

Order – the giant
spinning in his
skin –

AW. DAH.[32]

Scully glosses this image as follows: 'The giant turning in his skin is the warrior's spasm, Cúchulainn [*sic*]. Awe-inspiring and a bit ridiculous. The AW. DAH. As command or as things in their place, can't be welcomed in without wiping its feet on the mat.'[33] Cúchulain's unruly body is aligned, ultimately, with a repressive force, but the 'spasm' can also perhaps been seen as the last stand of the Ledean body against authoritarian containment and order.

I want to conclude this reflection by comparing Scully's 'awe-inspiring ... ridiculous' Cúchulain with Coffey's much more mannerly and mannered version in *Advent*. Coffey chooses to show Cúchulain in death – a Christianized sacrifice, rather than 'pagan' Warped Man:

> Recall for us Cuchulain [*sic*] turning with perfect manners from fight
> when battle glory its fierce light faded in torn frame
> bound himself to upright stone so fairly to greet
> equal foe man to man and gently decline to earth
> But behind mere untimeliness in tossed pretence of real order
> design mere sketch act half-willed blurred effect
> veiled by record petrified in grey stone   (*PV*, p.143)

Despite the differences in presentation, there are numerous points of contact between Coffey's Cúchulain and Scully's. Both are bodies strained to breaking point by the weight of signification placed upon them: in Scully's poem the strain emerges as absurdity, in Coffey's as tragedy. What Scully calls 'AW. DAH.' might have its equivalent in Coffey's 'tossed pretence of real order', both signify imposed authority rather than genuine structure. Finally, if Scully's Cúchulain might be seen as a Ledean body 'spinning' in its rejection of authority's imprint, then we might also see the 'gentle decline' and 'half-willed blurred effect' of Coffey's hero as symptoms of resistance before his petrifaction into signification. Both poets confuse authority itself with its action upon its victims' bodies, because, in truth, that is how authority works to arrogate agency to itself. Both poets mount resistance – sometimes furious resistance – to authoritarian action upon nature and on human beings, and the results are two bodies of work that feel remarkably similar in spite of their difference in approach. It is perhaps this political sympathy, rather than formal resemblances, that makes Scully and Coffey contemporaries, and makes Scully's readings of Coffey unforced, natural and inclusive.

NOTES

1. Maurice Scully, 'Interview', *Metre*, 17 (spring 2005), pp.134–43 at p.141.
2. Ibid., p.141.
3. *Things That Happen* comprises four volumes: *Five Freedoms of Movement* (Buckfastleigh: Etruscan Books, 1987, 2002); *Livelihood* (Bray, Co. Wicklow: Wild Honey Press, 2004); *Sonata* (Hastings: Reality Street Editions, 2006); and a coda, *Tig* (Exeter: Shearsman Books, 2006). *Livelihood* is by far the largest of these, being made up of five books and three interstices.
4. Maurice Scully, *Doing the Same Thing in English: A Sampler of Work 1987–2008* (Dublin: Dedalus Press, 2008).
5. Brian Coffey, 'Reading *Advent*', *The Journal*, vol. 1 (1999), pp.36–40.
6. Maurice Scully, 'The Pillar & the Vine', *Livelihood*, pp.5–8 at p.6.
7. See Sinead Mooney, 'Kicking Against the Thermolaters', *Samuel Beckett Today/ Aujourd-hui*, vol. 15 (2005), pp.29–42; Seán Kennedy, 'Beckett Reviewing MacGreevy: A Reconsideration', *Irish University Review*, vol. 35, no. 2 (autumn/winter 2005), pp.273–88.
8. The phrase 'heirs of Joyce' is used to describe Irish neo-modernist poets on the jacket copy of a special issue of *Angel Exhaust* edited by John Goodby and Maurice Scully. *Angel Exhaust/Súitéar na n-Aingeal*, vol. 17, ed. Maurice Scully and John Goodby (spring 1999), back cover. However, the idiosyncratic style of the blurb suggests that it was written by one of *Angel Exhaust*'s regular editors, Andrew Duncan, rather than Scully or Goodby. See also Neil Corcoran, *After Yeats and Joyce: Reading Modern Irish Literature* (Oxford: Oxford University Press, 1997), p.vii.
9. 'Interview', *Metre*, p.141.
10. Scully, *Livelihood*, p.107.
11. Ibid.
12. Ibid., p.236.
13. 'Interview', *Metre*, p.140.
14. Scully, *Five Freedoms of Movement*, p.15.
15. 'Interview', *Metre*, p.142.
16. Scully, *Five Movements of Freedom*, p.15.
17. Ibid., p.72.
18. Scully, *Livelihood*, p.97.
19. Ibid.
20. Ibid.
21. Ibid., p.241.
22. Brian Coffey, 'Reading *Advent*', *The Journal*, vol. 1 (1999), p.40.
23. Scully, *Livelihood*, p.28.
24. Ibid.
25. W.B. Yeats, 'Among School Children', *The Poems*, ed. Richard J. Finneran (Basingstoke and London: Macmillan, 1991).
26. Scully, *Livelihood*, p.28.
27. Ibid.
28. Ibid.
29. L. Frank Baum, *The Wizard of Oz* in *The Wonderful World of Oz* (Harmondsworth: Penguin, 1998), pp.66–68.
30. Scully, *Livelihood*, p.137.
31. Ibid., p.140.
32. Ibid., pp.140–41.
33. 'Interview', *Metre*, p.138.

CHAPTER TWENTY

Brian Coffey:
A Child's Memories

JOHN COFFEY

It feels very strange to be thinking about a poet, Brian Coffey, who I knew as Dada. The truth is that his children, me included, knew little about his poetry and normally took little, if any, interest. What this felt like for him we will never know. He never told us.

In this personal note, as the eldest of his nine children, I record some of my memories of him as a parent, a record given without any of the trappings or balance of an academic paper. I also include some memories my brothers and sisters gave me about their own experiences of childhood. For most of us most of the time it was a happy childhood, despite the very real financial and other difficulties that our parents suffered while raising us.

As far as I can tell I was conceived in France and, had Hitler not chosen to by-pass the Maginot Line, would have been French rather than Irish. As it was, Dada and Mama left France in a great hurry in 1939 leaving most of their possessions behind them. Fortunately my grandparents in Dublin were able to house them temporarily until I arrived. Soon after my birth my mother moved to Dun Laoghaire and Dada to England as teacher in a school near Sheffield. I saw almost nothing of him until mid-1942 when I was nearly 3 years old.

He was then working very hard teaching maths during the day and teaching Radio Officers for the RAF at night. I remember going with him to Sheffield while he was measured for his very smart, light blue RAF uniform. That day he bought me a toy Spitfire that I treasured.

By now my sister, Mary, had also been born and I remember him spending time with the two of us telling stories that he invented. Bright pastel colours at the ready he drew vibrant cartoon pictures of animals and other heroes of his stories on our bedroom wall as he spoke. We would go to sleep in a room filled with crocodiles, sharks, dinosaurs, lions, tigers … all creatures that would, if not handled right, eat us whole while we slept. None the less, I don't remember ever being at all frightened by these stories.

He liked making things for us. For a birthday I think, he made me a wonderful set of wooden bricks. He had persuaded the school wood-work teacher to make him twenty-six 2-inch wooden cubes. Dada painted all of them, one for each letter of the alphabet, the six faces showing a capital letter, a lower-case letter, pictures of an animal, a plant and an object, and the final face set out a mathematical or chemical formula or a Euclidian diagram. Sadly, he used paint that flaked so that, in time, all the bricks became illegible.

He would take me for walks to see bomb sites, railway trains and beautiful parks pointing out plants, animals, trees and much else as we walked. I am sure it was him who woke my lifelong love of nature.

I think I had the best of his attention in these war years 1942–45, my other siblings still being too young to talk much with him. Once the war ended we had several years where he would be working far away and we would only see him during holidays.

In 1947 Dada and Mama with their then four children moved to St Louis in the USA. My parents were idealists. Both came from comfort-able backgrounds and were used to having plenty of money and servants to look after their needs. Perhaps influenced by Eric Gill and other social experimenters, they wanted their children to have a freer up-bringing with plenty of opportunity to experience nature at first hand.

The place they chose to live fitted their ideals perfectly. Bought and rented to them by St Louis University, it was a run-down fifteen-acre smallholding on a slope below the new Highway 30 in Webber Hill (Missouri, USA) with a former bootlegger's log cabin as the main house. There were also two old barns plus one newer barn and a clear water spring at the bottom of the hill. About half the property was woodland. There was some derelict and rusting farm machinery scattered about.

In February 1948, when we moved into our new home, there was no running water, no flush toilet and no bath. This, in one of the worst winters ever, was for us children a most exciting adventure. For Dada and Mama it must have been quite a shock since they had none of the practical skills needed to face the rigours of this winter. Fortunately, through our local parish church of St Anthony, they befriended our neighbours and soon were receiving excellent advice about building and plumbing.

Dada, helped by our farmer neighbours who knew him as 'Doc', designed and built our bathroom and toilet annexe ... I helped, of course (at least that's what I thought I was doing). We were all astonished when it actually worked and very pleased with his efforts.

Most of the time, though, Dada worked on his philosophy. It seemed to us that he was always at work on his papers, marking student essays and writing his lectures in a barely legible fine scrawl. You can still see these if you wish in the University of Delaware collection of his papers. His office (we were never supposed to enter without his permission) was in the hay loft of one of the barns. You had to climb a ladder to get into it. He would work there until late at night. In retrospect it was amazing that the barn never burned down as Dada was a very heavy smoker, at times having two cigarettes on the go at once and at times falling asleep with a cigarette attached to his lips. I remember him always having a book close by, sometimes a thick learned work but more often some science fiction work that I too enjoyed reading.

Another five children arrived while we were in the USA and at first these were happy times for the whole family. Unfortunately, in 1952, Dad had a row with his masters at the university that ended with him resigning his job. From then on, unable to get another university post, there was not enough money to go round, but Dada did have more time to spend with us. My sister, Mary, remembers that wherever we were playing in the woods, we would run out as soon as we heard the car start.

> Dada was going out! 'Dada can I come! Dada can I come! Dada can I come!' we would all shout. On the way home there was a steep hill and we would scream for him to go fast, and he did; and we screeched with ecstasy all the way down. We were so proud of him. It was fearless and like flying together.

He loved us all, but we were a handful: wild, inquisitive and bursting with energy. He had been brought up to believe that children should be 'seen and not heard'. Unfortunately for him, we did not conform to this model so he had to be stricter than his nature really allowed him. I escaped most of this period as I had been sent to a Junior Seminary, only returning for holidays, so I did not see the real suffering that the family went through at this time. We children never went hungry, but I know now that Dada and Mama both did. Dada was painfully thin.

They never lost hope. They tried growing strawberries and, with our help manning the stall, tried selling them by the roadside. They tried growing potatoes only to find the whole crop destroyed by Colorado beetle. They raised chickens. Capitalizing on Mama's considerable talent as a fabric designer, they tried to set up a silk-screen business. But none of their ventures earned enough to keep the family.

In 1954 the university wanted its property back as Dada and Mama could no longer afford the rent. Fortunately the university agreed to pay the family's passage back to England, where Dada had been offered a job as a mathematics teacher. Mama in particular was broken-hearted to be leaving this ideal life that they had set up together, but he too must have felt it. When we arrived back in UK the family was spread out among relatives until a house could be found, in the end paid for by other generous relatives.

It was during this period, between him losing the university post and coming back to the UK, that Dada's poetry writing resumed. 'Missouri Sequence' began in Webber Hill and was finished in Muswell Hill. I think I have the only copy of the only extant poem written by him between his marriage and 'Missouri Sequence'. It is an ode to my first tooth and even I, no critic of poetry, call tell that it is not one of his finest works. The truth is that family life, the war, philosophical research, essay marking and teaching for a living made his writing of poetry impossible.

Once his writing spirit reawakened he kept it up for the rest of his life, most of his poems being written in his last twenty years.

Back in the UK we children became more aware that he wrote poetry. The family would spend summer holidays under canvas at a farm in the country. He meanwhile would stay at home in Muswell Hill 'to look after the cat'. In reality he used these periods of relative peace to write. He sent us daily postcards with pictures of the cat and tales of its progress. He would also read more to us. My sister Ann remembers:

> At 13 Elms Avenue after dinner in the evenings of winter with the fire going and the comings and goings of us children Dada would be reading by the fire. He would recite some poetry occasionally but more often than not he would be quiet amidst all the sounds of family.

Advent began on one of our summer breaks, but was at least ten years in the making. I remember him showing me lines that had come to him and telling me that somehow the other lines had to be as good. It was not until the death of my brother, Dominic, on a motorbike in 1973, that *Advent* was properly born. The pain of this death seemed to release him and the poem was completed very quickly thereafter.

In that year, their children now grown and independent, Dada and Mama moved to Southampton to the house in Alma Road that they were to live in for the rest of their lives. Dada wrote more than ever and his work was becoming better known. They had many visitors and friends coming to stay. Our own children were able to call on them easily and enjoy their wit and company. Our son, Gaius, remembers that Dada would tell him tales. If these were untrue, Dada would wink at him as a signal. For quite a while we did not know why Gaius winked so much.

In the early 1980s my brother Joe took his family off to live in the French Alps. Dada and Mama used to visit them every summer. Joe tells us:

> As Dada moved into his eighties he became very frail, but his mind was as sharp as ever and his sense of fun – especially when cooking up some mischievous conspiracy with the kids – undiminished. Once we were playing Trivial Pursuits and he was on my team. To all the world he was fast asleep. That did not stop him coming up with most of the answers – for both sides! From the look on his face I am sure his eyes were twinkling behind the closed lids. He used to sneak off with my wife Lilian to go to the market in Thônes, where he loved to sit outside at a bar and watch events unfold – perhaps reliving a little his memories as a student in Paris. Mama was not allowed to go on these jaunts and would be deposited somewhere to paint. Her favourite spot was the little churchyard at the St Germain chapel overlooking Lake Annecy. The hermit, St Germain, had been visited there centuries earlier by St Francois de Sales, who occupied a special place in the hearts of both Mama and Dada.
>
> I remember we all decided to walk there once – a trip of about two miles through the woods and fields on the side of the mountain. Dada lost control of his legs on a (not very steep) slope and began to accelerate – Lilian bravely put herself between him and oblivion, so saving the day, and him.
>
> Another time we had taken them by cable car to a restaurant perched on a rock about 2000 metres up looking out over Mont Blanc. Dada insisted on walking around outside to take it all in. By this time of his life his stance had become so upright that occasionally he lost his balance backwards. He chose this moment to do this, leaving me to grapple him to the ground before he went over the edge. His response to these moments of the danger was amusement rather than fear.

The children loved him – his games, his storytelling, his sense of fun, his lack of respect for unnecessary rules. His solution for how to deal with authority – 'I'd machine-gun the lot of them' – lives on in them. My sister Kathy and her family stayed with Dada and Mama for a year. She writes:

> As the years went by Dada mellowed and became gentler with young ones. My own daughter, Terra Rose, the last of the eighteen grandchildren, has a lovely story to tell of him. Dada was 86 and Terra 4 years old. They played a game together where Dada pretended to be *Tyrannosaurus Rex*, towering over Terra and making scary roaring noises. As soon as he got too scary for her she could point two fingers straight at him and he would immediately start to crumble slowly to the floor saying 'I'm shrinking, I'm shrinking', like the Wicked Witch of the West in *The Wizard of Oz*. He would shrink all the way to the floor giving Terra a tremendous feeling of power.
>
> I learnt a lot watching him as an older man. I observed him in nature watching a bird or just noticing the wind blow through the branches of the trees. He didn't say anything but was so obviously present in the moment. There was a particular little bird that he liked to watch in a tree at the end of his road. On walks with Terra, holding her hand, they would stop at the tree and watch the bird together.
>
> My wild son Jacob, who was 6 at the time, got slightly different treatment. I think Jacob reminded Dada of himself and he tended to treat Jacob in a manner that put him down rather than encouraged him. Jacob needed to be put in his place. More of the Dada that I remembered from growing up came out when he was dealing with Jacob. On the day that we left England, after a year's stay with my parents, we were all saying our goodbyes and giving each other hugs. At the last minute Jacob ran back up the path to Dada, who was standing in the doorway, and gave him a big Jacob hug. Dada hugged him back and all was forgiven. It was a truly special moment for Jacob. He could leave loving Dada and knowing he was loved.

Silence was important for Dada. I remember him telling me that he was sure that the Holy Family spent much time in silence. Kathy again:

> The last time I visited while Dada was alive, I was saying good-bye to him and we just looked at each other without a word. We were totally present for each other just sharing our love. I could

leave knowing that I was loved.

And Mary:

> I remember in the last year of his life walking out in summer evenings to the pond on the common. We walked almost in silence and would sit in complete silence watching the birds wheeling, calling, landing … And it was great to *be* together *seeing* the same scene, listening, smelling. And there was peace between us and love and dignity and strange nobility in it.

His and Mama's Catholic faith was always there in the background. In our growing up I am sure that we never missed a single Sunday mass or holy day of obligation. He was habitually reticent about what he regarded as personal matters, so he told me little about his own faith journey. For me, his message was his example.

On his deathbed, his face behind an oxygen mask, he stretched his arms out giving each of us there a final hug. We were important to him and him to us.

CHAPTER TWENTY-ONE

Descriptive Checklist of Books and Pamphlets by Brian Coffey

THOMAS DILLON REDSHAW

This checklist of works by Brian Coffey (1905–95) provides exten-sive descriptions of each of Coffey's separately published works in an effort to suggest their *sui generis* character and to indicate a little of the publishing and literary history that Coffey's writings span. All the items listed here were examined in their original state or in full-size, colour Xerographic copies loaned and sent by Coffey's friends and publishers, chiefly: James Hogan, Anthony Rudolf of the Menard Press, London, John F. Deane of Dedalus Press, Dublin, and particu-larly Harry Gilonis of Form Books, London. Without their prompt and encouraging help this checklist would not have been possible.

Each entry here follows this format: transcription of title page or equivalent; colophon or its equivalent; description. Where a formal colophon did not prove present, publication information has been re-constructed as a colophon. Owing to that necessity, the texts of the extant colophons have been copied and edited rather than transcribed bibliographically. That said, the errors and omissions here are, of course, the doing of this bibliographer and not of his kind informants.

1.   1930

[Celtic decoration in single rule box] | POEMS | BY | BRIAN COFFEY AND DENIS DEVLIN | PRINTED FOR THE AUTHORS | BY | ALEX THOM & CO., LTD. CROW STREET | DUBLIN | *September 1930*

Poems. Chapbook, 14.5 x 11 cm, pp.[1–4] 5–23 [24–32], linen-sewn. Gray card cover with French flaps printed in dark blue, title in mod-ern display face inside double rule box, back blank.

2.   1933

BRIAN COFFEY | THREE POEMS | On sale at | LIBRAIRIE JEAN-
NETTE MONNIER | *17, Rue Bréa, 17* | PARIS (Vie) | *1933*

Colophon, on pp. [2, 16]: Two hundred and fifty copies printed for
the author February 1933. Printed by Imprimerie F. Paillart, Paris-
Abbeville, February 1933.

    Poems. Paper edition, 19. 5 x 14.3 cm, [i–ii], 5–15 [16] [xvii–xviii]
pp., linen-sewn. Limp card wrap covered in grey-blue, wove printed in
black.

3.

TO WISH YOU A BLESSING | on | CHRISTMAS DAY 1933

Poem: 'Yuki-Hira, *to my Father and Mother*'. Broadside folded in half,
18.3 x 11.9 cm, [4] pp. Cover and interior text printed in blue each inside a double-ruled box. Text of poem set in small capitals.

4.   1938

THIRD PERSON | BY | BRIAN COFFEY |LONDON | GEORGE
REAVEY THE EUROPA PRESS | 7 GREAT ORMOND STREET, WC1

Colophon, on verso of title page: Europa Poets VII. This, the first edition of *Third Person* printed on toned hand-made rag antique wove
deckle edge paper, is limited to 300 numbered copies. Copies number
I to XXV are illustrated with an original engraving by S.W. Hayter and
are signed by Author and Artist. Copies A and B are not for sale and
are reserved for Author and Publisher. Copies 28 to 300 constitute the
ordinary edition. Printed in Guernsey, CI, British Isles, by the Star and
Gazette Ltd for The Europa Press.

    Poems. Cloth trade edition, 22.5 x 15 cm, [i–xii] 13–28 [ixx–xxx]
pp., thread-sewn. Red linen boards, spine stamped in black. Blue wrap
printed by The Temple Press, Letchworth, Herts, with titling and back
matter in red giving the Europa Poets list. The original, tipped-in engraving by S.W. Hayter constitutes pp. [v–vi] in the signed copies.

5.   1965

DICE THROWN | NEVER WILL | ANNUL CHANCE | *a transla-
tion by* | BRIAN COFFEY | *of* | UN COUP DE DÉS | JAMAIS

N'ABOLIRA LE HASARD | *a poem by* | STEPHANE MALLARMÉ |
THE DOLMEN PRESS

Colophon, on verso of title page: Printed and published in the Repub-
lic Ireland by the Dolmen Press Limited, 23 Upper Mount Street,
Dublin 2. This translation first published in 1965.
    Poem. Cloth trade edition, 22.7 x 15.5 cm, [1–30] pp. linen-sewn.
Black paper boards, black end papers, faux vélin spine stamped in red.
Tan wrap printed in monochorme and red. Text note on front flap.

6.   1966

MONSTER | A CONCRETE POEM | by BRIAN COFFEY | DECO-
RATED by | JOHN PARSONS | DEDICATED TO | [copyright 1966]
| DEAR EARHOLES | Advent Books | 13 Elms Ave, | London N10

Colophon, at foot of title page: This edition of 500 copies consists of
474 copies numbered 1 to 474 and 26 copies marked A to Z and
signed by the authors.
    Prose poem. Accordion book, 21 x 32.2 cm, [1–14] pp., seamed
with adhesive tape on the long edge. Polychrome card cover shows sea
serpent devouring its own tail and serves as first and last page. Polychrome water image at either side of text in blank silhouette of swim-
ming sea serpent oriented vertically across the pages' seams.

7.   1969

THE TIME THE PLACE | BRIAN COFFEY | ADVENT BOOKS 1969

Colophon, on p. [6]: Advent Poems, 4. Printed by hand and published
by Advent Books, 13 Elms Ave, [London] N10. This edition consists of
26 copies in Ingres paper, signed by the author and the artist, and 250
numbered copies. The jacket was designed by Sandra Hill. Lithography
by Sandra Hill. Screen-printed by The Trigram Press Ltd, 148 Kings
Cross Road, WC1.
    Poem. Chapbook, 23 x 15 cm, [1–8] pp., linen-sewn into card
cover. Gray wrap. Cover gives lithograph in blue and pink.

8.   1970

THE VILLAGE IN THE MOUNTAIN | BY | GASTON BONHEUR
| WITH A TRANSLATION BY BRIAN COFFEY | ADVENT BOOKS
1970

Colophon, on p.15: Cover design by Hazel MacKinley. Type set in 11 pt Baskerville italic and printed by The Crescent Press, 32 Crescent Rd, [London] N22, for Advent Books, 13 Elms Avenue, [London] N10. This edition consists of 26 copies marked A–Z, signed by author and translator, and 250 numbered copies.

Poem. Chapbook, 22.75 x 16.5 cm, 16 pp., linen-sewn into card cover. Laid wrap giving McKinley's polychrome silkscreen on the front.

9.   1971

BRIAN COFFEY | SELECTED POEMS | [pressmark] | NEW WRIT-ERS' PRESS

Colophon, on verso of title page: Published in an edition limited to 250 copies, by New Writers' Press, 19 Warrenmount Place, S.C.R., Dublin 8, Ireland, 1971. Printed by the Dorset Press, Limited, 39 Hill Street, Dublin 1, Ireland. Design by Michael Smith.

Poems. Cloth trade edition, 23.4 x 15.9 cm, [A–B + 1–6] 7–68 pp., linen-sewn. Cased in red-blue linen grain boards. Spine stamped in gold. Gray laid endpapers. Series title on [B]; half-title on [1].

Paper wrap printed in light brown giving a portrait photograph of the poet by John Parsons on the front cover, author's note, Zozimus Books note on the flaps, noting the type arrangement by Liam Miller.

9a.

Paper trade edition, 15.4 x 22.4 cm, [1–6] 7–68 pp., 1,000 copies. Coated card cover printed in monochrome and blue. Front gives the Parsons photograph of Coffey; back repeats the author's note and the Zozimus Books note.

9b.

BRIAN COFFEY | SELECTED | POEMS | [pasted over pressmark] THE BELACQUA SERIES | (RAVEN ARTS PRESS / NEW WRITERS' PRESS)

Colophon, pasted over original on verso of title page: This book is published as part of The Belacqua Series by the Raven Arts Press, 31 North Frederick Street, Dublin 1, The Republic of Ireland, in associa-tion with The New Writers' Press, Dublin. First Published by the New

Writers' Press in 1971. Design by Michael Smith. Half-title page pasted over original text: The Belacqua Series (Raven Arts Press / New Writers' Press).

Same as 9. New monochrome paper wrap giving new, uncredited photograph of Coffey on front and amended note on the author on the back.

9c.

Same as 9a. New monochrome paper wrap pasted to the inside of the of the card cover of the original issue.

10.

VERSHEET 1 | [expanded rule] | *Edited by* Trevor Joyce | Brian Coffey | [man-in-the-moon pressmark] | NEW WRITERS' PRESS | DUBLIN 1971

Colophon, on verso of wrap: Versheet is printed by The Dorset Press, Hill St, Dublin, and published, in an edition of 500 copies, by New Writers' Press, 19 Warrenmount Place, S.C.R., Dublin 8, Ireland.

Poems. Chapbook, 23.3 x 13.4 cm, [1] + 6 pp. Printed on a single sheet, 45.6 x 25.3 cm, folded twice, pasted into wrap. Red card wrap. Front summarizes titled page; back gives Versheet statement, author's note, forthcoming authors and colophon.

11.   1972

BRIGID ANN | BRIAN COFFEY | ADVENT BOOKS 1972

Colophon, on p. [11]: Advent Poems, 9. Printed by hand and published by Advent Books, 13 Elms Avenue, London, N10. This edition consists of 10 copies (A–Z) signed by the author and 50 copies numbered 1–50. The jacket was designed by Bridget Rosalind Coffey.

Poem. Chapbook, 23 x 16 cm, [1–13] pp., linen-sewn into card. Sage green laid wrap printed in black front to back giving floral design by Bridget Coffey. Some examples have the same wrap printed on white stock.

12.   1974

ADVENT | by | Brian Coffey | ADVENT BOOKS | 1974

Colophon, on p. [2]: <u>Advent</u> by Brian Coffey is published by Advent

Books June 20th 1974 in an edition of 25 copies numbered 1–25 and is issued for presentation only. NOT FOR SALE. © Brian Coffey.

Poem. Typescript, 33 x 20.2 cm, [1–28] pp., unbound. Pages bear author's corrections in his hand and lines numbered at right-hand margin. Title page lists recipients, including: [Anthony] Rudolf, Lorna [Reynolds], [J.C.C.] Mays, and Oxford University Press.

13.

ABECEDARIAN | Words by Brian Coffey | Drawings by Sandra Hill, | Nick Marsh, Derek Norman | John Parsons and Diane Radford. | ADVENT BOOKS 1974

Colophon, on p. [32]: ABECEDARIAN is published by Advent Books, 48 Alma Road, Southampton in an edition of 250 copies numbered 1–250 and 26 copies A–Z signed by the author and the artists.

Alphabestiary. Chapbook, 21 x 16.75 cm, [32] pp. Text with illustrations linen-sewn into card cover. Wrap on coated card stock with monochrome illustration.

14.

IRISH UNIVERSITY REVIEW | [drawing of flying bird] | BRIAN COFFEY SPECIAL ISSUE
IRISH | UNIVERSITY | REVIEW | A JOURNAL OF IRISH STUDIES | Editor Maurice Harmon | Volume 5 Number 1 Spring 1975

Colophon, on verso of title page: The cover is from an original design by Bridget Ann Beckett. Printed by Richview Press Limited, Dublin.

Poems. Special issue, 23.2 x 15.1 cm, [1–8] 9–207 [208–14] pp., perfect bound. Monochrome cover on coated card giving bird image by Beckett on the front and Coffey's monogram on the back.

15.   1976

ADVENT III | THE TIME THE PLACE | and other poems | BRIAN COFFEY | ADVENT BOOKS | 1976

Colophon, on p. [18]: Advent III. The Time the Place and other poems. This edition of 300 copies is published by Advent Books, 48 Alma Road, Southampton. A few of the poems in this collection have already appeared in *Lace Curtain*, Dublin.

Poems. Chapbook, 21 x 14.7 cm, [a–d] 1–17 [18] pp., saddle-stapled. Pale ivory card cover reiterating title page.

16.

THE | BIG | LAUGH | Brian Coffey | Sugar Loaf | Dublin

Colophon, on p. [28]: Published in a limited edition of 500 copies of which this is number […]. Sugar Loaf, Highbury, Sandycove Road, Glenageary, County Dublin Ireland. Set in 9 pt Plantin by Koningsveld & Zoon (I), Ltd, printed in the Republic of Ireland by Task Print (Dublin) Ltd. On back cover: Drawings by Brian Coffey. Calligraphy by John Coffey.

Prose. Chapbook. 24.3–15.6 cm, [1–6] 7–29 pp., 1976. Text on cream laid stock. Frontispiece and twelve illustrations or 'concrete drawings' in polychrome and monochrome. Cover on textured pumpkin card printed in brown giving the title and author making a 'goalpost' design of the word 'HA'; back gives textual note and photograph of the author.

17.   1979

Death of Hektor | Poem by Brian Coffey | Engravings by Stanley William Hayter | CIRCLE PRESS 1979

Colophon, on p. [5]: This book is number […] of a limited edition of 300, 35 Artist proofs, with 10 copies for presentation, et 5 Hors Commerce.

Continued on p. [6]: Intaglio Printing: Printed on 285 gsm Crisbook J. Green hand-made paper with watermark SWH 1976. 5 plates printed by SWH 1976. 4 plates printed by Jack Shirteff, 107 Workshop, Wiltshire, produced on copperplates with a mixture of Burin engraving and etching techniques. Letterpress: Set in 18pt Garamond by Charles Mitchell, Woking, Surrey, Printed by Abbey Press, Abindon, on Velin Cove Rives Blanc 270 gsm. Text designed by Brian Coffey. Preliminary pages designed and printed by Michael Gray. Bookbinding: Origination design by Jack Shirteff. Design and production by Paul Haskell and Dieter Schulke, Dorset Bookbinding Co. Ltd, Wimborne, Dorset. Production: Produced during March to December 1979 by Jack Shirteff, 107 Workshop. Published by Circle Press Publications, Guildford, Surrey. Copyright Brian Coffey and S.W. Hayter 1979.

Poem. Artist's Book, 41.3 x 31.75 x 3.75 cm, pp. [1–8] 9–23 [24].

Text on six folio pages folded in half, followed by plates I–IX by Hayter, each with tissue cover. Contained in half-folio with three-quarter envelope opening, bound in black buckram. Interior faced with grey marbled paper. Slip-case covered in oatmeal linen with title stamped in black on the front.

18.   1981

[linocut in slate blue giving title in 'Greek' script over image of reclining woman] TOPOS | AND OTHER POEMS BY | BRIAN COFFEY

Colophon, on verso of title page: Published by Mammon Press, 12 Dartmouth Avenue, Bath. Copyright: Brian Coffey 1981. Thanks to Michael Smith of New Writers' Press, Dublin, for permission to reprint various pieces. Cover picture by Maurice Lovell.

Poems. Chapbook, 14.4 x 21.4 cm, [1–32] pp., sewn. Cover of mid-blue card repeating the title page in dark blue; mid-blue laid endpapers. Half-title page in 'Greek' script in blue; text in blue on vanilla paper.

19.   1982

DEATH OF HEKTOR | A POEM | BY | BRIAN COFFEY | The Menard Press | 1982

Colophon, on verso of title page: This is the first trade edition of *Death of Hektor*. It was originally published in 1979 in a limited edition by Circle Press with engravings by Stanley William Hayter. A photograph of the hill of Troy as it now appears was kindly supplied by the Turkish Embassy, London. Printed by Derek Maggs, 36 Sherard Road, London SE9 6EP.

Poem. Chapbook, 205. x 14.5 cm, [1–4] 1–15 [16] pp. Saddle-stapled. Cover in textured brown card printed in dark red. Back gives note on the poem. Title and author in ornamental type.

20.   1984

[in script] *poéms | d'amour | Paul Eluard*
[in script] *poèmes love | d'amour poems* | Illustrations by S.W. Hayter Versions by Brian Coffey

Colophon, on p. [5]: This book is number […] of a limited edition of 100, with 15 artists proofs, 6 presentation and 4 Hors Commerce copies.

Colophon, continued on p. [8]: The text is designed by Colin Brecken-ridge, set in 14/16 Imprint medium by Bath Typesetting Limited and printed letter press by The Blackett Press Bath on BFK Rives 210 gsm paper; the engravings on J. Green Crisbook NOT, and the lithographs on BFK Rives 250 gsm, printed by Jack Shirteff, Paul Kirkup and Sarah James at 107 Workshop, Wiltshire; the binding by Dorset Bookbinding Co. Ltd, Wimborne, Dorset. Published by 107 Workshop 1984.

Poems. Collector's edition, 33 x 23.5 cm, [1–92] in 4 signatures tied with white ribbon into card cover riveted together at the spine. Card cover wrapped in green and white Japanese paper stamped with author's name in red script. Monochrome lithographed drawings fac-ing two colophon pages. Three polychrome lithographs laid in be-tween signatures 2, 3 and 4. Nine monochrome, signed, numbered engravings laid in.

Contained in 35.7 x 25 x 4.3 cm black cloth box opening in two vo-lets at the front stamped with author's name in red on the exterior and with the title stamped in red on the interior.

21.   1985

BRIAN COFFEY | CHANTERELLES | Short Poems, 1971–1983 | [Press mark of a caped figure standing between M and P] | The Mel-moth Press

Colophon, on verso of title page: Published by the Melmoth Press, 42 Westbury, Wilton, Cork, Ireland, 1985. Designed and printed by the Elo Press Ltd, 49 Reuben Ave, Rialto, Dublin 8, Ireland. On back cover: Cover illustration by Brian Coffey.

Poems. Paper trade edition, 21.5 x 15 cm, [1–6] 7–61 [62], linen-sewn perfect bound. Laid card cover in tan. Front gives author, press in red above and below the title and mushroom cloud drawing in brown, all set off by a single rule box in red; back gives author's pho-tograph and note in brown and ISBN numbers in red.

21a.

Poems. Cloth trade edition.

22.   1986

ADVENT | *by* | BRIAN COFFEY | THE MENARD PRESS | 1986

Colophon, on verso of title page: The Menard Press, 8 The Oaks, Woodside Avenue, London N 12 8 AR. Printed by Derek Maggs, 36 Sherard Road, London SE9 6EP.

    Poem. Trade paper edition. 21 x 14.75 cm, [1–4] 5–42 [43–44] pp., perfect bound. Cover in buff card printed in brown. Front gives title in display type between two swelled rules; back gives note on the poem.

23.   1987

SLIGHT SONG | [text of poem] | *S. Mallarmé* | *trs B. Coffey* | *Men-Card* | *published by The Menard Press in London* | *Brian Coffey (8 June 1905)*

Poem. Postcard, 10 x 15 cm, [1987?]. Salmon card stock. Verso blank.

24.   1988

SALUT | [small capitals] VERSIONS OF SOME SONNETS OF MAL-LARMÉ | BRIAN COFFEY

Colophon, on p. [16]: Published in an edition of 120 copies by hard-Pressed Poetry, 1 New Ireland Rd, Rialto, Dublin 8, Ireland. Cover from a page of Mallarmé's mss supplied by the translator.

    Poems. Chapbook, 21 x 14.7 cm, [1–16] pp., single saddle staple. Cover in pale vanilla card bearing xerographic reproduction of a Mallarmé ms page; apricot fly leaves.

25.   1990

POEMS OF MALLARMÉ | Bilingual Edition | Versions in English | Introduction and Illustration | by BRIAN COFFEY

Colophon, on verso of title page: The Menard Press, 8 the Oaks, Woodside Avenue, London N12 8AR (Tel. 081-446 5571); New Writers' Press, 61 Clarence Mangan Road, Dublin 8. Printed by Icon Impressions Ltd, Yorkshire Street Mill, Bacup, Lancs. OL13 9AF.

    Poems. Chapbook, 21 x 29.5 cm, [1–4] 5–34 [35–36] pp. Printed in brown on oblong text saddle-stapled into pebble-textured vanilla card cover. Front repeats the title page, but gives the title and author in red letter.

26.

BRIAN COFFEY | Mort d'Hektor | *et autres poèmes Traduction par Denis Rigal* | EDITIONS FOLLE AVOINE

Colophon, on p. [117]: Achevé d'imprimer le 22 juillet sur les presses des éditions Folle Avoine.

Poems. Trade edition, 22.5 x 14.5 cm, [1–6] 7–113 [114–21] pp. Linen-sewn text in textured cover with French flaps. Front cover repeats the title page with the addition of the Éditions Folle Avoine pressmark; back cover gives note on author.

27.   1991

POEMS AND VERSIONS 1929–1900 | BRIAN COFFEY | [pressmark] DEDALUS

Colophon, on verso of title page: The Dedalus Press, 24 The Heath, Cypress Downs, Dublin 6W, Ireland. Published in Dublin on 15th November 1991. Cover design: The Graphiconies. Clóchur: Peanntrónaic Teo. Half-title page: the Dedalus Press, editor John F. Deane.

Poems. Paper trade edition, 22.7 x 15.7 cm, [1–4] 5–243 [244–48] pp., perfect bound.

Coated card cover printed in azure and monochrome. Front flap gives information about the book; back flap gives a note on the author.

27a.

Poems. Trade edition, 23.5 x 15 cm, [1–4] 5–243 [244–48] pp., linen-sewn. Dark blue imitation calf boards. Spine stamped in gold. Coated paper wrap repeats covers of the paper trade edition.

27b.

Poems. Presentation binding. Boards covered in blue textured calf. Spine and interior edges stamped in gold. Blue and gold bands. Three copies exist in this special binding. One was presented to Mary Robinson, Uachtarán na hÉireann, November 18, 1991.

28.   1993

form and existence | gave also | punished penalty | ask Lucifer | Brian Coffey | – a riposte to Harry Gilonis' FormCard no. 1 | formCard | no. 2 *Spring 1993* **| published by Form Books   42 A Lowden Road Herne Hill London SE24 0BH**

    Poem. Postcard, 14.7 x 10.4 cm, on orange card. Verso blank. The text of the poem is the text above given in bold.

29.   1994

salute/verse/circumstance | Salute/verse/circumstance is published | on 29 March 1994 | as a keepsake | to commemorate | Brian Coffey's reading | at Sub Voicive in London | on that day | [hare press mark] | Brian Coffey | form books, london 1994

Colophon, on verso of title page: salute/verse/circumstance | is published on 19 March 1994 as a keepsake to commemorate Brian Coffey's reading at Sub Voicive at the Three Cups, Holborn, London, on that day. The front cover is taken from a pencil drawing by Brian Coffey, 'against snares and wiles …' The hieroglyph of a hare represents the Egyptian verb 'to be', in the sense of being, existing, and persisting. Designed and typeset by Form Books. Published by Harry Gilonis at Form Books, 42 A Lowden Road, Herne Hill, London, SE24 0BH.

    Poems. Chapbook, 21 x 15 cm, [1–8] pp., saddle-stapled. Orange card cover bearing Coffey's drawing on the front and the poet's monogram on the back.

29a.

Same. Blue card cover.

Colophon, on verso of title page: salute/verse/circumstance was first published as a keepsake to commemorate Brian Coffey's reading for the SubVoicive reading series in London on 29 March 1994. It is reprinted to accompany the centenary conference 'Continuings' in Dublin , 21–22 October 2005. Designed and typeset by Form Books. The hieroglyph of the hare represents the Egyptian verb 'to be', in the senses of being, existing, and persisting. Published by Harry Gilonis at Form Books, 86 Orbel Street, London SW11 3NY, UK.

30.

OTHER FAN | of Miss Mallarmé | [text of poem] | version by Brian
Coffey | reprint from *Peacock Blue*, Heron Press, Newcastle-under-
Lyme, 1994. | this card done to commemorate Brian Coffey's invita-
tion as a guest | of honour at a party to honour 25 years of The
Menard Press. |formCard no. 50 | *for 3 April 1995* | this card pub-
lished by Form Books 42 A Lowden Road Herne Hill London SE24
0BH

Poem. Postcard, 14.7 x 10.4 cm, on light yellow card. Verso blank.

31.

Glendalough | [text of poem] | Brian Coffey (18 June 1905 – 14 April
1995) | reprinted from *Lace Curtain* no. 5 (spring 1974), Dublin |
[published by Michael Smith, to whom thanks] | formCard no. 53 for
25 April 1995 | this card published by Form Books 42 A Lowden Road
Home Hill London SE24 0BH

Poem. Postcard, 14.7 x 4 cm, on mid-green card. Verso blank.

32.   1997

BRIAN COFFEY IN SIGHT OF ALL | [text of poem] | *reprinted from*
Lace Curtain *no 5 (Dublin, spring 1974)* | *– thanks to Michael Smith.*
FormCard | *Irish Modernism Series* no. 1 April 1997

Poem. Postcard, 14.5 x 10.5 cm, red card stock. Verso blank. Printed
by Harry Gilonis, Form Books, 86 Orbel Street, London SW11 3NY,
UK.

Brian Coffey: A Bibliography

AENGUS WOODS

Comprehensiveness is the dream of the bibliographer. It is rarely achieved however, and in many cases the very volume in which the bibliography appears can serve to undermine any claim to completeness. In addition many authors have work that escapes cataloguing due to the obscurity of the publications or the passage of time. The present case is no different. Brian Coffey's earliest poems were published under the pseudonym Coeuvre in *The National Student*, University College Dublin's student newspaper. These include 'The Eternal Thought', 'Wednesday Night' and 'Sada' (a prose work), all published before the appearance in 1930 of Coffey's first book *Poems,* a shared publication with Denis Devlin (in which 'The Eternal Thought' reappears). However, copies of *The National Student* from this period have proved difficult to find and in the absence of precise references I have omitted them from the present work.

I have chosen to refer to the work listed in the second and third subsections as 'translations'. This is perhaps controversial, given that Coffey himself was prone to calling such works 'versions'. However he occasionally used the term 'renderings', while in one publication he merely stated that the poems were 'after' their original author. In the spirit of compromise I have decided to revert to the most commonly used term for these practices. The author's own variations are duly noted at the individual entries.

In 1966 Brian Coffey established Advent Books, a small imprint that remained in operation until 1986 and published twenty-one volumes of poetry by Coffey and other writers. While all Advent publications authored or edited by Coffey are included below, the complete list of all Advent Books is to be found in chronological order as an appendix.

Thanks are due to Harry Gilonis for his assistance and keen eye. I would also like to acknowledge the groundbreaking work done by

Parkman Howe in the bibliography included in his 1981 Ph.D thesis 'Time and Place: The Poetry and Prose of Brian Coffey', held at University College Dublin. Notwithstanding, errors in that work have here been amended, while it should be stated that any occurring in the present work are solely the responsibility of the present author.

WORKS BY BRIAN COFFEY

Books and pamphlets

ABECEDARIAN (Southampton: Advent Books, 1974), with drawings by Sandra Hill, Nick Marsh, Derek Norman, John Parsons and Diane Radford.

Advent (Southampton: Advent Books, 1974); republished in trade edition (London: Menard Press, 1982).

Brigid Ann (Southampton: Advent Books, 1972).

Chanterelles: Short Poems 1971–83 (Cork: Melmoth Press, 1985). CONTENTS: Poem – Poem – For What For Whom Unwanted – The Time The Place – Call The Darkness Home – All Out – In Sight Of All – Leader – Cold – No Fault – The Gaugeless State – A Word With A Homing Book – 'It Was Fun Was It' – Poem – Poem – So – Fidelities (Liminal – Answering Mindful – Eleison I – Eleison II) – The Two Old Poets – Toolin Replies – Scrub – Hidden – Dream-West – Window in the Sky – Painterly – Short Circuit – Cave – ABECEDARIAN – The Prayers (An Extract).

Death of Hektor (Surrey: Circle Press, 1979), with illustrations by S.W. Hayter; reprinted in trade edition (London: Menard Press, 1982).

Monster: A Concrete Poem (London: Advent Books, 1966), decorated by John Parsons.

Poems (Dublin: Printed for the Authors by Alex Thom & Co.,1930), a shared publication between Brian Coffey (B.C.) and Denis Devlin (D.D.). CONTENTS: 11th September 1930 (B.C.) – O Paltry Melancholy (D.D.) – ...To A Romantic... (B.C.) – Before Lepanto: The Turkish Admiral Speaks To His Fleet (D.D.) – The Eternal Thought (B.C.) – Adam's house (D.D.) – Prologue To 'Morven' (B.C.) – Now (D.D.) – The Love Song From 'Morven' (B.C.).

Poems and Versions 1929–1990 (Dublin: Dedalus Press, 1991). CONTENTS: Preface by J.C.C. Mays – Yuki-Hira (pre-1933) – 'THREE POEMS' (1933) – Exile – Dead Season – Quay – 'THIRD PERSON' (1938) – Dedication – White – Amaranth – I Can Not See With My Eyes – All We Have – Content – A Drop of Fire – Spurred – Thirst – The Enemy – Patience No Memory – Gentle – Third

Person – One Way – Bridget Ann (1972) – Xenia (1978) – 'SELECTED POEMS' (1971) *Observations Poems Experiments 1931–1971* – Odalisque – Davy Byrne's of a Saturday Night – On the Rooftops – Of Su Tungpo – Bridie – Syllables For Accents – The Friendly Silence – You – Latin Lover – Dreams What Returns – 'The Nicest Phantasies are Shared' – Whose Who – Headrock – *Nine A Musing 1960* – A musing – *Missouri Sequence 1962* – Nightfall, Midwinter, Missouri – March, Missouri – Muse, June, Related – Missouri, Midsummer, Closure – The Monument 1964 – Mindful of You 1965 – How Far from Daybreak – Moicel et Soim (1980) – ADVENT 1975 – DEATH OF HEKTOR 1979 – 'CHANTERELLES' 1985 – Poem *I am where I have been* – Poem *What Might be Said* – For What For Whom Unwanted – The Time The Place – Call The Darkness Home – All Out – In Sight of All – Leader – Cold – No Fault – The Gaugeless State – A Word with a Homing Book – 'It Was Fun Was It' – Poem *To Sleep Sometimes I Dream* – Poem *He Dreams her when Sun Rising* – So – Fidelities – Two Old Poets – Toolin Replies – Scrub – Hidden – Dream-West – Window in the Sky – Painterly – Short Circuit – Cave – Abecedarian – The Prayers – *PABLO NERUDA* Twenty Love Poems and The Unhoping Song.

salute/verse/circumstance (London: Form Books, 1994, 2005); published as a keepsake to commemorate Brian Coffey's reading at SubVoicive in London on 29 March 1994; reprinted to accompany 'Continuings', the Brian Coffey centenary conference, Dublin, 21–22 October 2005. CONTENTS: *Mallarmé toasts the young poets at the dinner of 9.ii.1893.* – SALUT – Madame Mallarmé her fan – Eventail *de Madame Mallarmé* – 'form and existence...' – 'content fitting...' (by Harry Gilonis).

Selected Poems (Dublin: Zozimus Books, New Writers' Press, 1972); reissued in new wrappers as part of the Belaqua Series (Dublin: Raven Arts Press, 1983). CONTENTS: I: HOW FAR FROM DAYBREAK – II: MINDFUL OF YOU (1965) – III: From FOUR POEMS (1964) – The Monument – IV: MISSOURI SEQUENCE (1962) – Nightfall, Midwinter, Missouri – March, Missouri – Muse, June, Related – Missouri, Midwinter, Closure – V: From NINE A MUSING (1960) – A Musing – VI: From THIRD PERSON (1938) – White – Gentle – Third Person – One Way – VII: OBSERVATIONS POEMS EXPERIMENTS (1931–71) – Odalisque – Davy Byrne's of a Saturday Night – On The Rooftops – Of Su Tungpo – Bridie – Syllables For Accents – The Friendly Silence –

You – Latin Lover – Dreams What Returns – 'The Nicest Phantasies Are Shared' – Whose Who – Headrock.

The Big Laugh (Glenageary, Co. Dublin: Sugar Loaf Press, 1976), with drawings by Brian Coffey and calligraphy by John Coffey.

The Time The Place (London: Advent Books, 1969).

The Time The Place and Other Poems (Southampton: Advent Books, 1976). CONTENTS: The Time The Place – Call the Darkness Home – All Out – In Sight Of All – Leader – Cold – No Fault – The Gaugeless State – A Word With A Homing Book – 'It Was Fun Was It'.

Third Person (London: Europa Press, 1938). CONTENTS: Dedication – White – Amaranth – I Can Not See With My Eyes – All We Have – Content – A Drop of Fire – Spurred – Thirst – The Enemy – Patience No Memory – Gentle – Third Person – One Way.

Three Poems (Paris: Jeanette Monnier, 1933), printed for the author. CONTENTS: Exile – Dead Season – Quay.

Topos and Other Poems (Bath: Mammon Press, 1981). CONTENTS: Topos – Two Old Poets – Toolin Replies – Scrub – Hidden – Dream-West – Window in the Sky – Painterly – Short Circuit – Cave – Mindful of You.

Versheet 1 (Dublin: New Writers' Press, 1971); edited by Trevor Joyce. CONTENTS: White – What All Is Grace – Though Promise None – Poems from Daybreak (1969–70) – 35 – 44 – 45 – 46.

Poems Published in Journals, Periodicals or Individually

'24 from Daybreak', *Lace Curtain*, no. 3 (summer 1970), p.20.

'Advent', *Irish University Review: Brian Coffey Special Issue*, vol. 5 no. 1 (spring 1975), pp.31–70.

'All Out', *Lace Curtain*, no. 5 (spring 1974), p.36.

'Answering Mindful', from a set of two poems collectively titled 'Fidelities', *Poetry Ireland*, no. 1 (autumn 1962), pp.22–24.

'Answering Mindful', *Poetry Ireland*, no.1 (autumn 1962), p.23.

'Antiochus got an ague ...', *Ireland To-day*, vol. 2, no. 9 (September 1937), p.32.

'Bella', *Dedalus Irish Poets: An Anthology*, edited by John F. Deane (Dublin: Dedalus Press, 1992), p.254.

'Connexus', *Lace Curtain*, no. 5 (spring 1974), p.37.

'Dead Season', *Lace Curtain*, no. 4 (spring 1971), pp.11–12.

'Eleison I', *Lace Curtain*, no. 3 (summer 1970), p.18.

'Eleison II', *Lace Curtain*, no. 3 (summer 1970), pp.18–19.

'form and existence', *FormCard no. 2*, Form Books (spring 1993).

'For What For Whom Unwanted', *Niagara Magazine*, no. 7 (winter 1977), pp.5–15.

'from Missouri Sequence [:] III Muse, June, Related', *Niagara Magazine*, no. 3 (1975), pp.21–23.

'Glendalough', *Lace Curtain*, no. 5 (spring 1974), p.35; reprinted as *FormCard no. 53*, published by Form Books, London (25 April 1995) to commemorate the death of Brian Coffey; reprinted in *Etruscan Reader VII* (with Alice Notley and Wendy Mulford), edited by Nicholas Johnson (Newcastle under Lyme: Etruscan Books, 1997).

'Image as a Young Lady', *Ireland To-day*, vol. 1, no. 7 (December 1936), p.18.

'In Sight Of All', *Lace Curtain*, no. 5 (spring 1974), p.35; also published as *FormCard Irish Modernism Series* no. 1, London: Form Books (April 1997).

'Kallikles', *Ireland To-day*, vol. 2, no. 2 (February 1937), p.10.

'Latin Love', *Horace whom I hated so*, edited by Harry Gilonis (London: Five Eyes of Wiwaxia, 1992), unpaginated.

'LEO' [a satirical prose poem], *Irish University Review: Brian Coffey Special Issue*, vol. 5, no. 1 (spring 1975), pp.111–85, with accompanying drawings by Geoffrey Prowse.

'Liminal', from a set of two poems collectively titled 'Fidelities', *Poetry Ireland*, no. 1 (autumn 1962), pp.22–24.

'Mindful of You', *University Review*, vol. 3, no. 7 (1962), pp.17–24.

'Missouri Sequence', *University Review*, vol. 2, no. 12 (1961), pp.29–46.

'Moicel et Soim', *Cyphers*, vol. 12 (1978), p.9.

'Morning Offering', *Ireland To-day*, vol. 2, no. 11 (November 1937), pp.33–34.

'Nine – A Musing', *University Review*, vol. 2, no. 10 (1961), pp.30–35.

'North Wind', *Ireland To-day*, vol. 2, no. 8 (August 1937), p.48.

'Odalisque', *Ireland To-day*, vol. 1, no. 7 (December 1936), p.18.

'Ones' from a set of 'Four Poems', *University Review*, vol. 3, no. 3 (1963), pp.10–16.

'Plain Speech for Two', *The Criterion*, edited by T.S. Eliot, vol. 17, no. 70 (October 1938); *The Collected Edition* (London: Faber & Faber, 1967), pp.37–38.

'Poem' ['He dreams her when sun rising'], *Niagara Magazine*, no. 3 (1975), p.24; republished in *Irish Examiner*, 20 October 2005.

'Poem' ['To sleep sometimes I dream'], *Granta: Irish Issue* (December 1976), p.5.

'Reading Advent', *The Journal*, edited by Catherine Walsh and Billy Mills (Dublin: hardPressed Poetry, 1998); reprints a short selection from 'Advent' (pages 27–28 and 33–34 of the Menard Press edition) with Coffey's reading notation included.

'Recourse to Fiction' from a set of 'Four Poems', *University Review*, vol. 3, no. 3 (1963), pp.10–16.

'The Inside Story' from a set of 'Four Poems', *University Review*, vol. 3, no. 3 (1963), pp.10–16.

'The Monument' from a set of 'Four Poems', *University Review*, vol. 3, no. 3 (1963), pp.10–16.

'The Navigator', *Ireland To-day*, vol. 2, no. 1 (January 1937), p.49.

'Three Poems From Daybreak' ['28', '33', '43'], *Lace Curtain*, no. 4 (summer 1971), pp.8–10.

'Topos', *Lace Curtain*, no. 6 (autumn 1978), pp.38–43.

'With My Love', *Lace Curtain*, no. 5 (spring 1974), p.36.

'Xenia', *Irish University Review*, vol. 8, no. 1 (spring 1978), pp.38–39, with accompanying drawing by Brian Coffey.

'Yuki-Hira' published as Christmas Card by the author (1933); reprinted with an introductory note by the author in *Choice: An anthology of Irish poetry selected by the poets themselves*, edited by Desmond Egan and Michael Hartnett (Newbridge: Goldsmith Press, 1973, 1979), pp.28–29.

Translations Published as Volumes

(i) Gaston Bonheur

The Village in the Mountain (London: Advent Books, 1970).

(ii) Paul Éluard

Poémes d'amour (Southampton: 107 Workshop, 1984). Limited edition of 100 with 15 artists proofs, 6 presentation and 4 *hors commerce* copies; original etchings, engravings and lithographs by S.W. Hayter. CONTENTS: SECTION I: Le fou parle/The unhinged man speaks – Poèmes/Poems – Poèmes pour la paix/Poems for peace – Poisson/Fish – Pour vivre ici (1918)/To live here (1918) – A Fernand Fontaine/To Fernand Fontaine – Fidèle/Faithful – Vache/Cow – Mouille/Soaked – SECTION II: L'Egalite des sexes/Equisex – Les Gertrude Hoffman Girls/The Gertrude Hoffman Girls – Denise disait aux mervielles/Denise was telling me marvels – Celle de toujours, toute/She of all days, all – Poème/Poem – De 'Comme deux gouttes d'eau'/From 'As two drops of water' – November 1936/November 1936 – D'un seul poèm entre la vie et la mort/From one poem between life and death – Tuer/To kill – SECTION III:

Blason des arbres/Blason of trees – Les 7 poèmes d'amour en guerre/The 7 Songs of Love in War – SECTION IV: Avis/Notice – Comprenne qui voudra/Dig it who will – l'Extase/Ecstasy – En vertu de l'amour/In persuance of love – Certitude/Sure – Marine/Seascape – Le Phénix/Phoenix – Chanson/Song – Matins/Matins.

(iii) Stéphane Mallarmé

Dice Thrown Never Will Annul Chance (Dublin: Dolmen Press, 1965), a translation of *Un Coup de dés n'abolira jamais le hasard,* including an introduction by Brian Coffey and a translation of Mallarmé's 'Preface' to the poem.

Poems of Mallarmé, bilingual edition (London and Dublin: Menard Press and New Writers' Press, 1990), versions in English, introduction and illustration by Brian Coffey. CONTENTS: Introduction: 'The fascination of what's difficult ...' – Foreword – Short Bibliography – Sonnet ('Oh si chère ...')/Sonnet ('O so dear ...') – Brise marine/Salt Sea Breath – Don du poème/Gift of the poem – Petit air I/Slight song I – Petit air II/Slight song II – Petit air (guerrier)/Slight song (Warrior) – 'Toute l'âme résumé'/'How it is with art' – Le tombeau d'Edgar Poe/The tomb of Edgar Poe – Tombeau (Anniversaire janvier 1897)/Tomb (Anniversary January 1897) – 'Quelle soie ...'/'What silk ...' – 'M'introduire ...'/'Me to bring forward ...' – 'A la nue ...'/'By the swagging heap ...' – 'Mes bouquins ...'/'My Own Books Closed ...' – Sonnet ('Pour votre chère morte, son ami. 2 novembre 1877')/Sonnet ('For your dear dead one, her friend. 2 November 1877') – THE ISLAND [an illustration by Brian Coffey] – Prose pour des Esseintes/Prose for des Esseintes – Brian Coffey: select bio-bibliographical note.

Salut: *versions of some sonnets of Mallarmé* (Dublin: hardPressed Poetry, 1988); limited edition of 120 copies, translations facing originals. CONTENTS: Mallarmé toasts the young poets at the dinner of 12:11:1893/Salut – Triptyque ['Smoke the pride full ...'/ 'Tout orgueil ...' – Spring up from the croup ...'/'Surgi de la croupe ...' – 'A work of lace ...' /'Une dentelle s'abolit ...' – How it is with art/Toute l'âme résumée.

(iv) Various

Etruscan Reader VII (with Alice Notley and Wendy Mulford), edited by Nicholas Johnson (Newcastle under Lyme: Etruscan Books, 1997). CONTENTS: Painted Dreams (after Reverdy) – The Village in the Mountain (after Gaston Bonheur) – The Joy-Mad Ship (after

Rimbaud) – The Wasted Wine (after Paul Valéry) – My Familiar Song (after Paul Verlaine) – 4 No-Necks (after Robert Desnos) – The Brain-Scoop Song (after Alfred Jarry) – Topos – The Song of the Ill-Loved (after Apollinaire) – The Chimeras (after de Nerval) – The Seven Songs of Love in War (after Éluard) – La Dernière Nuit (after Éluard) – Salut (after Mallarmé) – Triptyque (after Mallarmé) – How it is with art (after Mallarmé) – Madame Mallarmé her fan (after Mallarmé) – Other fan of Miss Mallarmé (after Mallarmé) – Six Poems (after Éluard) – Glendalough [not a translation].

Other Published Translations

(i) Guillaume Apollinaire

'The Song of the Ill-Loved' [selections from the poem, comprising of 'The Song of the Ill-Loved' – 'Aubade Sung on Laetare Sunday a Year Ago' – 'Reply of the Zaporogian Cossacks to the Sultan of Constantinople' – 'The Seven Swords'], *Irish University Review: Brian Coffey Special Issue*, vol. 5, no. 1 (spring 1975), pp.85–94.

(ii) Gaston Bonheur

'The Village in the Mountain', *Irish University Review: Brian Coffey Special Issue*, vol. 5, no. 1 (spring 1975), pp.104–08.

(iii) Yves Bonnefoy

'The Heart, The Water Untroubled', *Irish University Review: Brian Coffey Special Issue*, vol. 5, no. 1 (spring 1975), p.109.

(iv) Paul Claudel

'Saint Peter', *Irish University Review: Brian Coffey Special Issue*, vol. 5, no. 1 (spring 1975), pp.81–82.

(v) Robert Desnos

'The 4 No-Necks', *Irish University Review: Brian Coffey Special Issue*, vol. 5, no. 1 (spring 1975), pp.95–96.

(vi) Paul Éluard

'(A version of) La dernière nuit', *The Beau*, no. 1 (1981), pp.30–32.
'(A version of) The Seven Poems of Love in War', *The Beau*, no. 1 (1981), pp.26–30.
'Every happy woman has …', *Irish University Review: Brian Coffey Special Issue*, vol. 5, no. 1 (spring 1975), p.101.

'From One Poem Between Life And Death', *Irish University Review: Brian Coffey Special Issue*, vol. 5, no. 1 (spring 1975), pp.102–03.

'Heart on the tree you had but to take ...', *Irish University Review: Brian Coffey Special Issue*, vol. 5, no. 1 (spring 1975), p.99.

'In Order To Live Here', *Irish University Review: Brian Coffey Special Issue*, vol. 5, no. 1 (spring 1975), p.100.

'Soaked', *Irish University Review: Brian Coffey Special Issue*, vol. 5, no. 1 (spring 1975), p.102.

'There are so many things ...', *Irish University Review: Brian Coffey Special Issue*, vol. 5, no. 1 (spring 1975), pp.99–100.

(vii) Alfred Jarry

'The Brain-Scoop Song', *Irish University Review: Brian Coffey Special Issue*, vol. 5, no. 1 (spring 1975), pp.83–84.

(viii) Stéphane Mallarmé

'Dice Thrown Never Will Annul Chance', *Stéphane Mallarmé Selected Poetry and Prose*, edited by Mary Ann Caws (New York: New Directions, 1982), pp.107–27.

'Madame Mallarmé her fan', *eonta magazine,* London, vol. 1, no. 2 (1991), p.24.

'Other Fan, of miss Mallarmé', *Peacock Blue* (Newcastle under Lyme: Heron Press, 1994), p.35; reprinted as *FormCard no. 50*, Form Books, London (3 April, 1995), 'This card done to commemorate Brian Coffey's invitation as a guest of honour at a party to honour 25 years of the Menard Press'.

'Salutations', *The Iron Flute: a magazine for poetry* (London, 1964), unpaginated; republished as 'Salut', *Irish University Review: Brian Coffey Special Issue*, vol. 5, no. 1 (spring 1975), p.79.

'Slight Song', *MenCard* (London: Menard Press, 1987, 1990).

'The Faun An Afternoon', *Towards Harmony: A Celebration for Tony O'Malley on the occasion of his 80th birthday September 25th 1993* (Dublin: Dedalus Press, 1993), pp.31–33.

(ix) Pablo Neruda

'Twenty Love Poems and The Unhoping Song (a rendering not a translation)', *Irish University Review*, vol. 3, no. 1 (spring 1974), pp.51–65.

(x) Gérard de Nerval

'El Desdichado', *Irish University Review: Brian Coffey Special Issue*, vol. 5, no. 1 (spring 1975), p.73.

'The Chimeras', *The Poet's Voice*, vol. 3, no. 3 (1987), pp.31–35.

(xi) Pierre Reverdy

'Heart on the Wheel', *Irish University Review: Brian Coffey Special Issue*, vol. 5, no. 1 (spring 1975), pp.97–98.

'Painted Dreams', *The Poet's Voice*, 2nd series, no.1 (1994), p. 29.

(xii) Arthur Rimbaud

'The Joy Mad Ship', *Irish University Review: Brian Coffey Special Issue*, vol. 5, no. 1 (spring 1975), pp.75–78; reprinted in *Soleil + Chair*, edited by Harry Gilonis (London: Writers Forum, 1991), unpaginated.

(xiii) Paul Valéry

'The Wasted Vine', *Irish University Review: Brian Coffey Special Issue*, vol. 5, no. 1 (spring 1975), p.80.

(xiv) Paul Verlaine

'My Familiar Dream', *Irish University Review: Brian Coffey Special Issue*, vol. 5, no. 1 (spring 1975), p.74.

(xv) W.B. Yeats

'L'attrait de ce qui est difficile' [a version in French of 'The fascination of what's difficult'], *Poems of Mallarmé*, bilingual edition (London and Dublin: Menard Press and New Writers' Press, 1990), p.6 [part of the author's introduction].

Essays and Articles

(i) Literary

'About Poetry', *Dedalus Irish Poets: An Anthology*, edited by John F. Deane (Dublin: Dedalus Press 1992), pp.253–54.

'About the Poetry of Denis Devlin', *Poetry Ireland*, no. 2 (spring 1963), pp.76–86.

'A Cold Eye Cast on the Abbey Theatre', *Arts in Ireland*, 2/4 (1974), pp.18–27.

'A Note on Rat Island', *University Review: Special Yeats Edition*, vol. 3, no. 8 (1966), pp.25–28.

'Denis Devlin: Poet of Distance', *Place, Personality and the Irish Writer*, edited by Andrew Carpenter (Gerrards Cross: Colin Smythe, 1977), pp.137–57.

'Extracts from "Concerning Making"', *Lace Curtain*, no. 6 (August 1978), pp.31–37.

'For the Record' *Advent VI: Denis Devlin Special Number* (Southampton: Advent Press, 1976), p.21.

'Geoffrey Prowse 1941–72', *Irish University Review: Brian Coffey Special Issue*, vol. 5, no. 1 (spring 1975), p.29.

'In Dublin', *Commonweal* 46 (3 October 1947), pp.597–98.

'Introduction', *Dice Thrown Never Will Annul Chance* (Dublin: Dolmen Press, 1965), a translation of *Un Coup de dés n'abolira jamais le hasard* by Stéphane Mallarmé, unpaginated.

'Introduction', *The Heavenly Foreigner* by Denis Devlin, edited by Brian Coffey (Dublin: Dolmen Press, 1967), pp.7–13.

'Joyce! What Now?' *Irish University Review*, vol. 12, no. 1 (spring 1982), pp.28–31.

'Memory's Murphy Maker: Some Notes on Samuel Beckett', *Threshold*, no. 17 (1962), pp.28–36. Reprinted in *Eonta*, vol. 1, no. 1 (1991), pp.3–8.

'Of Denis Devlin – Vestiges, Sentences, Presages', *University Review*, vol. 2, no. 11 (1961), pp.3–18. Reprinted in *Poetry Ireland 75* (winter 2002/03), pp.82–100.

'The Painter Geer van Velde', *London Bulletin*, vol. 2 (May 1938).

'Thomas MacGreevy: In Tribute to Thomas MacGreevy Poet and Connoisseur of the Arts: Tributes by Six Learned Irish Friends', *Capuchin Annual* (1968), pp.277–302.

'Tributes to George Reavey', *Journal of Beckett Studies*, vol. 2 (summer 1977), p.8.

(ii) Philosophical

'Notes on Modern Cosmological Speculation', *Modern Schoolman: A Quarterly Journal of Philosophy*, vol. 29 (March 1952), pp.183–96.

'Remarks on Maximilian Beck's *Existential Aesthetics*', *Modern Schoolman: A Quarterly Journal of Philosophy*, vol. 25, no. 4 (May 1948), pp.266–69.

'The Common Good and the Principle of Finality', *Proceedings of the American Catholic Philosophical Association*, vol. 23 (1949), pp.97–107.

'The Notion of Order according to St Thomas Aquinas', *Modern Schoolman: A Quarterly Journal of Philosophy*, vol. 27, no. 1 (November 1949), pp.1–18.

'The Philosophy of Science and the Scientific Attitude: I', *Modern Schoolman: A Quarterly Journal of Philosophy*, vol. 26, no. 1

(November 1948), pp.23–35.

'The Philosophy of Science and the Scientific Attitude: II', *Modern Schoolman: A Quarterly Journal of Philosophy*, vol. 26, no. 4 (May 1949), pp.331–36.

(iii) Scientific

'On the Constitution of Certain Compounds Formed by the Action of Alcoholic Hydrochloric Acid on Unsaturated Ketones', co-authored with Hugh Ryan, *Royal Irish Academy Proceedings*, 39, Section B (September 1930), pp.434–39.

'The Action of Alcoholic Hydrochloric Acid on Certain Unsaturated Ketones', co-authored with Hugh Ryan, *Royal Irish Academy Proceedings*, 39, section B (November 1929), pp.107–13.

Reviews

(i) Literary

Review of *A Short Survey of Surrealism*, by David Gascogne; *Criterion*, vol. XV, no. 60 (April 1936), collected edition (London: Faber & Faber, 1967), pp.506–11.

Review of *Les Meilleurs Textes* by Sainte-Beuve; *Criterion*, vol. XVI, no. 65 (July 1937), collected edition (London: Faber & Faber, 1967), pp.716–21.

Review of *Mission de Léon Bloy* by Stanislaus Fumet; *Criterion*, vol. XV, no. 59 (January 1936), collected edition (London: Faber & Faber, 1967), pp.335–40.

Review of *Position Politique du Surréalisme* by André Breton; *Criterion*, vol. XV, no. 60 (April 1936), collected edition (London: Faber & Faber, 1967), pp.506–11.

Review of *Salavin* by Georges Duhamel; *Ireland To-day*, vol. 2, no. 1 (January 1937), pp.86–87.

Review of *Sense and Poetry* by John Sparrow; *Criterion*, vol. XIII, no. 52 (April 1934), collected edition (London: Faber & Faber, 1967), pp.515–18.

'Thomas MacGreevy: A Singularly Perfect Poet' (review of *Collected Poems* by Thomas MacGreevy); *Hibernia Review of Books* (4 February 1972), p.10.

(ii) Philosophical and Scientific

Review of *Albert Einstein* by Leopold Infeld; *Modern Schoolman*, vol. 28, no. 4 (May 1951), pp.312–14.

Review of *Albert Einstein: Philosopher-Scientist* edited by Paul Arthur Schilp; *Modern Schoolman*, vol. 28, no. 4 (May 1951), pp.312–14.

Review of *A New Theory of Gravitation* by Jacob Mandelker; *Modern Schoolman*, vol. 29, no. 2 (January 1952), pp.155–56.

Review of *A Philosophy of Mathematics* by Louis O. Kattsoff; *Modern Schoolman*, vol. 26, no. 2 (January 1949), pp.190–91.

Review of *Aristotle's Physics* by W.D. Ross; *Criterion*, vol. XVII, no. 67 (January 1938), collected edition (London: Faber & Faber, 1967), pp.351–52.

Review of *Art and the Social Order* by D.W. Gotschalk; *Modern Schoolman*, vol. 26, no. 4 (May 1949), pp.371–72.

Review of *A Source Book in Greek Science* by Morris R. Cohen and I.E. Drabkin; *Modern Schoolman*, vol. 26, no. 4 (May 1949), p.372.

Review of *Elements of Analytic Philosophy* by Arthur Pap; *Modern Schoolman*, vol. 27, no. 3 (March 1950), pp.229–32.

Review of *Elements of Symbolic Logic* by Hans Reichenbach; *Modern Schoolman*, vol. 25, no. 3 (1948), pp.198–202.

Review of *Hasidism* by Martin Buber; *Modern Schoolman*, vol. 26, no. 4 (May 1949), p.372.

Review of *Heredity East and West* by Julian Huxley; *Modern Schoolman*, vol. 29, no. 4 (May 1952), pp.350–51.

Review of *L'Origine des Mondes* by Paul Labérenne; *Criterion*, vol. XVI, no. 62 (October 1936), collected edition (London: Faber & Faber, 1967), pp.151–53.

Review of *Methods of Enquiry* by C. West Churchman and Russell L. Ackhoff; in *Modern Schoolman*, vol. 29, no. 2 (January 1952), pp.157–59.

Review of *Out of My Later Years* by Albert Einstein; *Modern Schoolman*, vol. 28, no. 4 (May 1951), pp.312–14.

Review of *Philosophical Physics* by Vincent Edward Smith; *Modern Schoolman*, vol. 28, no. 4 (May 1951), pp.310–12.

Review of *Philosophy and Politics* by Bertrand Russell; *Modern Schoolman*, vol. 27, no. 3 (March 1950), pp.226–29.

Review of *Philosophy of Mathematics and Natural Science* by Hermann Weyl; *Modern Schoolman*, vol. 27, no. 3 (March 1950), pp.232–33.

Review of *Physical Science and Human Values: A Symposium with a foreword by E.P. Wigner* by E.P. Wigner and other authors, *Modern Schoolman*, vol. 26, no. 3 (March 1949), pp.263–65.

Review of *Studies in St Thomas* by A.G. Hebert; *Criterion*, vol. XVI, no. 64 (April 1937), collected edition (London: Faber & Faber, 1967), pp.564–66.

Review of *The Atmospheres of the Earth and Planets* edited by G.P. Kuiper; *Modern Schoolman*, vol. 27, no. 4 (May 1950), pp.332–33.

Review of *The Development of Logical Empiricism* by Joergen Joergensen; *Modern Schoolman*, vol. 29, no. 2 (January 1952), p.155.

Review of *The Face of the Moon* by Ralph B. Baldwin; *Modern Schoolman*, vol. 27, no. 4 (May 1950), pp.332–33.

Review of *The Foundations of Arithmetic* by Gottlob Frege; *Modern Schoolman*, vol. 29, no. 2 (January 1952), p.157.

Review of *The New Physics* by C.V. Ramon; *Modern Schoolman*, vol. 29, no. 2 (January 1952), pp.152–55.

Review of *The Next Development in Man* by Lancelot Law Whyte; *Modern Schoolman*, vol. 26, no. 4 (May 1949), pp.372–73.

Review of *The Philosophical Frontiers of Physics* by Vincent Edward Smith; *Modern Schoolman*, vol. 25, no. 3 (March 1948), pp.202–04.

Review of *The Primeval Atom* by Georges Lemaitre; *Modern Schoolman*, vol. 29, no. 4 (May 1952), pp.326–29.

Review of *The Sphere of Sacrobosco and Its Commentators* by Lynn Thorndike; *Modern Schoolman*, vol. 27, no. 4 (May 1950), pp.332–33.

Review of *Whitehead's Philosophy of Time* by William H. Hammerschmidt; *Modern Schoolman*, vol. 26, no. 3 (March 1949), pp.269–70.

Review of *Worlds in Collision* by Immanuel Velikovsky; *Modern Schoolman*, vol. 28, no. 2 (January 1951), pp.162–64.

Works Edited by Coffey

Advent VI: Denis Devlin Special Issue (Southampton: Advent Books, 1976).

The Complete Poems of Denis Devlin, University Review (special issue), vol. 3, no. 5 (1963); reissued as *Collected Poems* (Dublin and Oxford: Dolmen Press, Oxford University Press, 1964).

The Heavenly Foreigner by Denis Devlin (Dublin: Dolmen Press, 1967).

The Lace Curtain, A Magazine of Poetry and Criticism, no. 4 (spring 1971), assistant editor to Michael Smith.

Translations of Coffey

Mort d'Hektor et autre poèmes, translated by Denis Rigal (Le Housset, Bédée: Editions Folle Avoine, 1990).

WORKS ON BRIAN COFFEY

Books

Moriarty, Dónal, *The Art of Brian Coffey* (Dublin: University College Dublin Press, 2000).

Special Issues of Periodicals

Irish University Review: Brian Coffey Special Issue, edited by Maurice Harmon, vol. 5, no. 1 (spring 1975).

Selected Essays, Articles and Interviews

Beake, Fred, 'Brian Coffey 1905–1995: A Personal Appreciation', in *Ink Feathers: An Anthology of the 4th Six Towns Poetry Festival* (Newcastle under Lyme: Heron Press, 1995), pp.41-42.
'The Poetry of Brian Coffey', *The Poet's Voice*, 2nd series, vol. 3, no.1 (summer 1996), pp.79–82.

Davis, Alex, '"Poetry is Ontology": Brian Coffey's Poetics', in *Modernism and Ireland: The Poetry of the 1930s* edited by Patricia Coughlan and Alex Davis (Cork: Cork University Press, 1995), pp.150–72.
'The Irish Modernists and their Legacy', in *The Cambridge Companion to Irish Poetry* edited by Matthew Campbell (Cambridge: Cambridge University Press, 2003), pp.73–93.

Dawe, Gerald, 'An Absence of Influence: Three Modernist Poets', in *Tradition and Influence in Anglo-Irish Poetry* edited by Terence Brown and Nicholas Grene (London: Macmillan, 1989), pp.119–42; reprinted in *The Proper Word: Collected Criticism – Ireland, Poetry, Politics* by Gerald Dawe, edited by Nicholas Allen (Omaha: Creighton University Press, 2007), pp.142–58.
'The European Modernists: MacGreevy, Devlin and Coffey', in *Irish Poetry Since Kavanagh* edited by Theo Dorgan (Dublin: Four Courts Press, 1996), pp.32–41.

Gillis, Alan A.,'Denis Devlin, Brian Coffey and Samuel Beckett: Across the Tempest of Emblems', in *Irish Poetry of the 1930s* by Alan Gillis (Oxford: Oxford University Press, 2005), pp.96–140.

Green, David D., 'A Return to *Advent*', *The Beau*, no. 1 (1984), pp.73–78.

Howe, Parkman, 'Brian Coffey: An Interview', *Eire Ireland: A Journal of Irish Studies*, vol. 13, no. 1 (1978), pp.113–23.
'Interview with Brian Coffey', *Irish Times*, 11 June 1975.

Johnson, Nicholas, 'Brian Coffey: a poet had once fallen silent', *Angel Exhaust: Colonies of Belief – Ireland's Modernists* edited by Maurice Scully and John Goodby, 17 (April 1999), pp.69–75.

Kersnowski, Frank, 'Brian Coffey', in *The Outsiders: Poets of Contemporary Ireland* (Fort Worth, Texas: Texas Christian University Press, 1975), pp.155–56.

Mays, J.C.C., 'Brian Coffey (1905–1995)', in *The UCD Aesthetic: Celebrating 150 Years of UCD Writers* edited by Anthony Roche (Dublin: New Island Press, 2005), pp.87–98.

'Brian Coffey's Review of Beckett's *Murphy*: "Take the Warning While you Praise"', in *The Recorder*, vol. 18, nos. 1 and 2 (Fall, 2005), pp.95–114.

'Brian Coffey's Work in Progress', *Krino*, no. 4 (autumn 1987), pp.62–72; reprinted in *Krino 1986–1996: An Anthology of Modern Irish Writing* edited by Gerald Dawe and Jonathan Williams (Dublin: Gill & Macmillan, 1996), pp.332–41.

'Introductory Essay', *Irish University Review: Brian Coffey Special Issue*, vol. 5, no. 1 (spring 1975), pp.11–29.

N11 A Musing (Dublin: Coelacanth Press , 2003); republished as *Little Critic No. 18* (Clonmel: Coracle Press, 2006).

'Passivity and Openness in Two Long Poems by Brian Coffey', *Irish University Review Special Issue: The Long Poem*, vol. 13, no. 1 (1983), pp.67–82.

Mills, Billy, 'Behind all Archetypes: on Brian Coffey' (London: Form Books, 1995).

Mills, Billy and Walsh, Catherine, 'Brian Coffey: A Tribute' in *Ink Feathers: An Anthology of the 4th Six Towns Poetry Festival*, (Newcastle under Lyme: Heron Press, 1995), p.40.

Morgan, Jack, 'A Modern Revenge Poem – Brian Coffey's *Topos*', *Notes on Modern Irish Literature*, no.5 (1993), pp.14–18.

'"Missouri Sequence": Brian Coffey's St Louis Years, 1947–1952', *Éire-Ireland: A Journal of Irish Studies*, vol. 28, no. 4 (1993), pp.100–13.

'Yeats and Brian Coffey: Poems for their Daughters', *Studies: An Irish Quarterly Review*, vol. 88, no. 351 (autumn 1999), pp.270–77.

Obituary, 'Brian Coffey, 89, a poet from Ireland who taught Science', *New York Times*, 2 May 1995, section B, p.7.

Obituary, 'Death of the scientist and poet Brian Coffey, *Irish Times*, 18 April 1995, p.7.

Obituary, *Washington Post*, 4 May 1995, p.C7.

Rudolf, Anthony, 'Obituary: Brian Coffey', *Independent* (London), 18 April 1995, Gazette, p.12.

Sharkey, John, 'Brian's Brain', *Lace Curtain*, no. 5 (spring 1974), pp.33–34.

Smith, Michael, 'A poet of seriousness and rigour', *Irish Times*, 20 April 1995.

'Irish Poetry Since Yeats: Notes Towards a Corrected History', *Denver Quarterly*, no. 5 (winter 1971), pp.1–26.

'Obituary: Brian Coffey', *Independent* (London), 17 April 1995, Gazette, p.10.

'Passing on the gift of poetry', *Irish Times*, 4 June 2005.

Smith, Stan, 'Against the Grain: Women and War in Brian Coffey's *Death of Hektor*', *Études Irlandaises*, no. 8 (December 1983), pp.165–73.

'On Other Grounds: The Poetry of Brian Coffey', *Lace Curtain*, no. 5 (spring 1974), pp.16–32; reprinted in *Two Decades of Irish Writing: A Critical Survey* edited by Douglas Dunn (Manchester: Carcanet, 1975), pp.59–80; also revised and reprinted in *Irish Poetry and the Construction of Modern Identity* by Stan Smith (Dublin: Irish Academic Press, 2005), pp.49–56.

Suberchicot, Alain, 'Poésie anti-nucléaire et myth prolongé chez Brian Coffey et Jonathan Griffin', *Études Anglaises*, vol. 40, no. 22 (1987), pp.154–66.

Tucker, Bernard, 'What is the Colour of Pi?: Conversations with Brian Coffey', in *Reviewing Ireland: Essays and Interviews from the Irish Studies Review* edited by Sarah Briggs, Paul Hyland and Neil Sammells (Bath: Sullis Press, 1998), pp.299–304.

Young, Augustus, 'Music and Mantras', *Guardian*, 21 April 1995, p.T21.

Selected Reviews

Anon., review of *Third Person*, in *Times Literary Supplement*, 3 September 1938.

Alexander, Joy, review of *The Big Laugh*, in *Fortnight*, 14 January 1977.

Boland, Eavan, 'Two Poets', review of *The Big Laugh*, in *Irish Times*, 11 September 1976.

B.[urke], P. [addy], review of *Poems*, in *The National Student* (December 1930), pp.141–42.

Carew, Rivers, review of *Dice Thrown Never Will Annul Chance*, in *Dublin Magazine* (autumn/winter 1965), p.102.

Cronin, Anthony, 'The poetry of Brian Coffey', *Irish Times*, 20 February 1976.

Dawe, Gerald, review of *Death of Hektor*, in *Sunday Independent*, 9 October 1983.

Review of *Death of Hektor*, in *Poetry Ireland Review*, no. 15 (winter 1985/86), pp.36–38.

Denman, Peter, review of *Poems and Versions 1925–1990*, in *Irish University Review*, vol. 22, no. 1 (spring/summer 1992), pp.190–91.

Durcan, Paul, 'Brian Coffey: A Neglected Voice', *Cork Examiner*, 28 August 1978.

Fear Na gNoc, review of *Poems*, in *Sunday Independent*, 28 September 1930.

Friedman, Barton R., review of *Irish University Review: Brian Coffey Special Issue*, in *American Committee for Irish Studies Newsletter*, vol. 6 (December 1976), pp.5–6.

Halsey, Alan, 'Of Hektor To Us', review of *Death of Hektor*, in *PN Review 35*, vol. 10, no. 3 (1983), pp.73–74.

Harmon, Maurice, 'Difficult Adventures', Review of *Poems and Versions 1929–1990*, in *Poetry Ireland Review*, no. 35 (summer 1992), pp.93–97.
Review of *The Big Laugh*, in *Irish University Review*, vol. 7, no. 1 (spring 1977), pp.136–37.

Howe, Parkman, review of *Irish University Review: Brian Coffey Special Issue*, in *Christian Science Monitor*, 22 October 1975, p.18.
Review of *Irish University Review: Brian Coffey Special Issue*, in *Éire-Ireland*, vol. 12, no. 2 (summer 1977), pp.151–55.
Review of *Irish University Review: Brian Coffey Special Issue*, in *Hibernia Fortnightly Review*, 26 March 1976, p.29.
Review of *Topos and Other Poems*, in *Irish University Review*, vol. 12, no. 1 (spring 1981), pp.111–13.

Lloyd, David, review of *Selected Poems* and *Irish University Review:Brian Coffey Special Issue*, in *Granta* (November 1976), pp. 23–25.

Ní Chuilleanain, Eilean, 'Danger, Poets at Work', review of *Versheet 1, in Irish Times*, 8 May 1971, p.10.
Review of *Advent*, in *Cyphers*, no. 26 (winter/spring 1986/87), pp.52–54.

Pilling, John, review of *Poems of Mallarmé*, in *PN Review*, vol. 17, no. 3 (Janaury/February 1991), p.64.

Suberchicot, Alain, review of *Death of Hektor*, in *Irish University Review*, vol. 13, no. 2 (autumn 1983), pp.260–61.

Sullivan, Daniel, review of *Irish University Review: Brian Coffey Special Edition*, in *Education Times*, 14 August 1975, p.13.

Turner, Bill, review of *Topos and Other Poems* and *Death of Hektor*, in *Iron Magazine*, no. 42 (February 1984), pp.56–57.

Other Media

BBC Radio programme on Brian Coffey, Augustus Young (director),

1983.

Brian Coffey: A Visual Record, Seán O Mórdha (director), RTÉ television broadcast (28 April 1986).

APPENDIX: ADVENT PRESS PUBLICATIONS

Series I

The Commodious Dragon by David Chapman, Advent Poems 1 (London, 1968), edition of 250 signed and numbered. In wraps designed by the author.

Dedication by Neil Mills, Advent Poems 2 (London, 1968), edition of 276 with 26 lettered. Printed by Trigram press. Cover designed by the author.

In Memoriam, Titanic Anniversary, April Fifteenth, 1969 by Hazel G. McKinley, Advent Poems 3 (London, 1969), broadside.

The Time The Place by Brian Coffey, Advent Poems 4 (London, 1969), edition consists of 250 numbered and 26 lettered. Jacket designed by Sandra Hill.

Poems by John Parsons, Advent Poems 5 (London, 1970), 250 numbered copies. Jacket and frontispiece designed by the author.

Poems by Michael Smith, Advent Poems 6 (London, 1971), edition of 150.

Seven Seas by George Reavey, Advent Poems 7 (London, 1971), edition of 226 with 26 lettered and signed.

Village in the Mountain by Gaston Bonheur, translated by Brian Coffey [Advent Poems 8] (London, 1970), edition of 250 with 26 lettered and signed by author and translator. Jacket designed by Hazel McKinley.

Brigid Ann by Brian Coffey, Advent Poems 9 (London, 1991), edition of 50 with 10 lettered and signed by the author. Jacket designed by Bridget Rosalind Coffey.

Intruder by Robert Driscoll, Advent Poems 10 (London, 1972) edition of 190 with 26 lettered and signed.

Series II

Rosemaries: A verse sequence by Augustus Young, Advent I (Southampton, 1976), edition of 300.

Jamaica Days by Robert Boswell Gibb, Advent II (Southampton, 1976), edition of 300.

The Time The Place and other poems by Brian Coffey, Advent III (Southampton, 1976), edition of 300.

Songs For The Poodles by John Parsons, Advent IV (Southampton, 1976), edition of 300.

Pilgrimage by Michael Smith, Advent V (Southampton, 1975), edition of 300.

Advent VI Denis Devlin Special Issue edited by Brian Coffey, Advent VI (Southampton, 1976), edition of 300.

Out of Series

Monster: A concrete poem by Brian Coffey (London, 1966), edition of 500, decorated by John Parsons.

Abecedarian by Brian Coffey (Southampton, 1974), edition of 250 and 26 lettered and signed by author and artists. Drawings by Sandra Hill, Nick Marsh, Derek Norman, John Parsons and Diane Radford.

Advent by Brian Coffey (Southampton, 1974), edition of 25 for presentation only.

Dánta Gráda/Love Poems by Augustus Young, published by Menard Press and Advent Books in conjunction (London and Southampton, 1975), edition of 500. Jacket designed by Brigid Ann Beckett with calligraphy by Dennis Hadfield. Second edition 1980, expanded and revised.

The Credit: Book II/Book III by Augustus Young, published by Menard Press and Advent Books in conjunction (London and Southampton, 1986), cover designed by John Parsons.

Index